MEN AT WAR

CHRISTOPHER COKER

Men at War

What Fiction Tells Us About Conflict, from The Iliad to Catch-22

OXFORD
UNIVERSITY PRESS

OXFORD
UNIVERSITY PRESS

Oxford University Press, Inc., publishes works that further
Oxford University's objective of excellence
in research, scholarship, and education.

Oxford New York

Auckland   Cape Town   Dar es Salaam   Hong Kong   Karachi
Kuala Lumpur   Madrid   Melbourne   Mexico City   Nairobi
New Delhi   Shanghai   Taipei   Toronto

With offices in

Argentina   Austria   Brazil   Chile   Czech Republic   France   Greece
Guatemala   Hungary   Italy   Japan   Poland   Portugal   Singapore
South Korea   Switzerland   Thailand   Turkey   Ukraine   Vietnam

Oxford is a registered trade mark of Oxford University Press in the UK
and certain other countries.

Published by Oxford University Press, Inc
198 Madison Avenue, New York, New York 10016

Published in the United Kingdom in 2014 by C. Hurst & Co. (Publishers) Ltd.

www.oup.com

Oxford is a registered trademark of Oxford University Press

Library of Congress Cataloging-in-Publication Data is available for this title
Coker, Christopher
Men at War
ISBN 978-0-19938-297-2 (hardback)

1 3 5 7 9 8 6 4 2

Printed in India
on Acid-Free Paper

CONTENTS

CONTENTS

Human nature—does it develop except by its power of observing itself?

E. M. Forster, *Aspects of the Novel*, 1927

Like many animals characters seem to be threatened with extinction. But in reality the world is swarming with them, one has only to invent them in order to see them. Whether they are malicious or comical, it is better if they don't vanish from the face of the earth.

Elias Canetti, *The Secret Heart of the Clock*, 1989

I expect [the novelist] to show me Man as he always is in the man of today, my contemporary—and vice versa, to show me my contemporary in Man as he always is. …. [He] should have no plans for educating me, but should leave me to reflect (or not) on the basis of the portrait with which I am presented.

Karl Barth

A NOTE ON REFERENCES

The books in which each character appears are referenced by title and page number only. Full mention of the editions used can be found in the bibliography.

1

AN ABSOLUTE TRUTH

'A writer's job is to tell the truth. His standard of fidelity to the truth should be so high that his invention, out of his experience, should produce a truer account than anything factual can be. For facts can be observed badly; but when a good writer is creating something, he has time and scope to make of it an absolute truth.' (Hemingway, *Men at War*, 1979, xiv).

The way we think about war is always changing. It is still the theme of countless films, a good many novels (though only a few are really inspiring) and occasionally some poetry. No aspect of life is untouched by war. It is deeply contaminating and no life which comes into close contact with it remains unaltered for long. It claims more than the lives of those who do battle; non-combatants have always been its principal victims. It leaves women widows and children orphans. It leaves death and destruction in its wake, but it does far more. It affects not only how life afterwards is lived, but how it is understood. What could be more fundamental to our sense of meaning than the belief that human beings have been at their most inventive and ingenious when warring against each other? As Odysseus puts it, 'we are men to whom Zeus has given the fate of wearying down our lives in painful wars.' And the wearying will doubtless continue for some time yet.

'War is part of the intercourse of human beings', wrote Clausewitz, the greatest philosopher of war we have, and Ernest Hemingway (one of the greatest writers on war) recycled the quote as the first chapter division of his war anthology, *Men at War*. Hemingway admired

1

Clausewitz; he called him 'the Einstein of battles.' Tolstoy did not and guyed him mercilessly in a passage in *War and Peace*. We don't tend to think of the great Prussian writer in the context of fiction but Hemingway used his work to divide his stories into sections which he believed defined the salient elements of war as a human experience: danger, courage, suffering, uncertainty, resolution, and fortitude among others. To Clausewitz's observation he added his own: 'war is fought by human beings', a fact frequently overlooked by many military historians in the past who used to think that faceless soldiers moved across the countryside to the dictates of their generals, who alone were deemed worthy of human interest. Today most recognise that the existential demands that war makes of those who fight it are as important as its existential appeal—on the one hand the sound and the fury and the extraordinary sacrifices it demands; on the other the excitement and the comradeship, and yes, even the aesthetics. This is why fiction is so important—it renders fact back to itself in sharper and shapelier tones.

Only a great writer can do this. In *The Thin Red Line*, the author James Jones depicts a soldier called Bell who finds himself in the middle of a vicious firefight in the Pacific theatre. 'In a film or a novel they would dramatise and build to the climax of the attack ... It would have a semblance of meaning and a semblance of emotion ...[but] here, there was no semblance of meaning, and the emotions were so many and so mixed up they were indecipherable. They could not be untangled. Nothing had been decided; nobody had learned anything ... Art, Bell decided, creative art, is shit ....' (Jones, 1998). But great art can make the real more real. Harold Bloom insists that a great writer can show us aspects of reality that otherwise we would not see unless we were shown them (Bloom, 2002, 647). The case for art is not that it offers us an escape from reality; on the contrary, it animates it. Bloom goes on to add, and it is a vital insight, that our fictional heroes are not larger than life. They are life's largeness which is why we admire them and seek them out (Bloom, 2002, 4).

Whenever I am asked to define war, I go back to the Greeks I read at school. For Thucydides it was 'the human thing'; for the poet Pindar, it was 'the thing of fear'. One, a historian, offers us the most compelling definition; the other, a poet, (second only to Homer himself in the eyes of the ancients) gives us an insight into the experience for the individual soldier and society at large. Both definitions are interesting

enough, but in themselves do little to help us pin war down. To understand war you have to grasp the tension between history and fiction,
between Thucydides' and Pindar's definitions, which have both been at
the centre of the struggle to come to terms with war as a human
experience.

Since the arrival of the novel in the eighteenth century the tension
between historical and fictive accounts of war has become more apparent. Pindar, who wrote Odes to the heroes and the Olympic athletes,
and Thucydides, the first military historian, at least lived in the same
community of ideas. Both ancient literature and history dealt with epic
themes. Once the novel came into being in the eighteenth century with
its emphasis on the interior life, and later the psyche, of its main characters, the two camps came into conflict and have continued to square
off ever since. For the historian, war continued to be epic; for many
novelists it became tragic.

'All this happened more or less', writes Kurt Vonnegut at the beginning of his novel *Slaughterhouse-Five*, 'the war parts, anyway, are
pretty much true', which challenges the reader to decipher the 'more
or less', and to deconstruct the 'pretty much' (Vonnegut, 2000, 1).
What in the novel is 'true'? What is memoir, and what do we have to
take on trust? Vonnegut wrote his novel nearly fifty years ago. Fast forward to Tim O'Brien's *The Things They Carried* (1991) which marks
a radical departure from every other fictional treatment of war. Like
Vonnegut, O'Brien has experienced war at first hand and sought to
relay the experience through a particular kind of fiction. He draws a
distinction between 'story truth' and 'happy truth', an allusion to Daniel Defoe's famous description of the novel as 'lying like truth'. O'Brien
is arguing that telling a story which is technically inaccurate yet truthful about the sensation of war is one of the most honest ways to convey its experience. And O'Brien does this through the characters we
meet. In relaying their stories he questions the role that imagination
plays in helping to form our memories and our own version of the
truth. In the process he offers a dramatic re-definition of literature, re-
fashioning its power to move the reader.

He gives the reader a shockingly visceral sense of what it feels like to
tramp through a booby-trapped land carrying 20lb of supplies and
14lb of ammunition along with radios, assault rifles and grenades.
These were the things the men of Alpha Company would carry with
them. But there was much else besides. One of the characters of the

book carries 7oz of premium dope, another a packet of condoms. A third, a devout Baptist, bears an illustrated New Testament that had been presented by his father who taught Sunday School in Oklahoma City. They had with them all they could, including 'a silent awe for the terrible power of the things they carried.' (O'Brien, 2009, 7).

But there were other burdens, including the weight of their memories. Often they carried each other, the wounded or the weak; friendship is one of the minor keys of grace in O'Brien's work, part of the emotional wiring of his characters. And they bore those memories all their lives. For the most part they conduct themselves with dignity; but they are human, prone to fear and sometimes panic. Others display a sort of wistful resignation; they might be afraid, but they are even more afraid to show it. But apart from the haunting poetry of it all, O'Brien is insistent that what he is recounting isn't 'the truth', and the last thing he can do as a writer is to draw a moral from the tale he tells. In many cases a true war story cannot be believed. Often the crazy stuff is true and the normal stuff is not. Because the normal stuff is invented to make the reader believe the craziness is credible. O'Brien insists that you cannot tell a true story because it is beyond telling (O'Brien, 2007, 68). Which is why he thinks literature is more instructive than history in the same way that the late philosopher Richard Rorty believed only literature, not philosophy, could teach the importance of compassion.

You can only extract a meaning by unravelling the deeper significance behind it. Historians can do the first, but not the second, and even then it is difficult to find a moral through 'the fog of war'. Clausewitz meant by the term that no general can see the whole picture. O'Brien means that no soldier can generalise and therefore tell a moral:

War is hell, but not the half of it, because war is also mystery and terror and adventure and courage and discovery and holiness and pity, and despair and lying and love. (O'Brien, 2009, 76)

War can make a man, but it can also unmake him; it can make a soldier feel more alive, but also take his life. And in the end, writes O'Brien, a true war story is not about war at all: it is only about memory. Whatever you recount to the people back home, they will never listen anyway, which is why, even if there is a moral to tell, it will never be understood (O'Brien, 2009, 81). But at least if there is no truth, there is still a story. Stories are for eternity when memory is erased, when there is nothing to remember except the story. What O'Brien achieved in *The Things They Carried* was to create an entirely new kind of war literature. The novel's title page carries a sub-title, 'a work of fiction'. It is also a work of fact, amplified through fiction, which unlike non-fiction allows the reader to see with his own eyes and thus take part in the redemptive power of story-telling.

But much more is at stake in the battle between history and fiction than 'imagined memories' and 'poetic reconstructions' of fact. In a speech in 1937, Hemingway told an audience that the 'truth' in war is dangerous to come by. When a man goes in search of it, he may not come back. But if twelve men go out and only two come back, 'the truth they bring will be the truth and not the garbled hearsay that we pass as history.' (Hemingway, 2003, 279).

At heart, historians have a different interest which Hemingway somewhat disingenuously ignored—they want to relay to us 'the why' of war more than the experience for the individual soldier. At the Battle of the White Mountain (1620) which triggered the Thirty Years' War the soldiers on the Catholic side shouted '*Sancta Maria*'. Fifteen years later at the battle of Nordlingen (1634), the last great Catholic victory, the Spanish soldiers went into battle shouting '*Viva Espana*. Anyone privileged (or unlucky) enough to have witnessed both battles would almost certainly not have appreciated the significance of the contrasting battle-cries. For the significance lay in the contrast between them, in the contrapuntal key that only a historian—looking back—can grasp (or invent) (Danto, 1965, 241–2).

Fiction writers rarely concern themselves with these larger historical movements or the rationale of specific wars. Their focus is narrower, and more penetrating: what did the death of a Spanish soldier mean to others, or his possible death mean to him? How did he imagine it before it happened? Was Hemingway right in claiming that cowardice is almost always simply an inability to suspend the functioning of the imagination; that courage is the ability to live completely in the present moment with no before and after, and as such is the greatest gift a soldier can acquire?

It is a clash, in essence, on two levels: between instrumentalists and existentialists. The novelist is not interested in the higher realities of war—the strategies and stratagems of generals, the policy, the meaning for those at the time off the battlefield, on the outside looking in. The

5

novelist's truth is an existential reality, or what Hemingway once called 'the ultimate loneliness of contact with the enemy.... where each man knows there is only himself and five other men, and before him all the great unknown.' (Hemingway, 2003, 89). This is not to say that historians never try to capture the existential reality of war. John Keegan's classic book *The Face of Battle* (1976) is a case in point. But any historian of worth must also insist that the micro-view is not necessarily the truth of war, it is only the truth of a particular experience, and they are right to suspect that even good novelists tend to mistake the existential truth for the wider meaning. In doing so, novelists run the risk of denying that a war can have ideological meaning for those who fought in it; that, decades later, soldiers can still be proud that they fought for something they believed worth fighting for. In the end, both parties entertain different conceptions of meaning. The historian judges a soldier's death allegorically, as the expression of patriotism, perhaps, or belief in a cause. The novelist will judge it in existential terms, as something unique to the character concerned. His task is not necessarily to make sense of the event, but to make sense of the experience, including for some, its apparent 'senselessness'.

Let us take by way of example a moving passage from Stephen Crane's novel, *The Red Badge of Courage*, which deals with the death of a soldier called Jim Cochrin:

> The youth had watched, spellbound ... His face had been twisted into an expression of every agony he had imagined for his friend.
> He now sprang to his feet, and getting closer, gazed upon the paste-like face. The mouth was open and the teeth showed in a laugh.
> As the flap of the blue jacket fell away from the body, he could see that the side looked as if it had been chewed by wolves.
> The youth turned with sudden, livid rage, towards the battlefield. He shook his fist. He seemed about to deliver a Philippic.
> Hell—
> The red sun was pasted in the sky like a wafer. (*The Red Badge of Courage*, 43–44).

The Philippic is associated with Demosthenes, who was always denouncing Philip of Macedon in his speeches and ultimately paid for his temerity with his life. In the novel the whole point is that the Philippic is never delivered. Instead his unbearable scream is a protest all the more eloquent for being unarticulated. What Crane gives us instead is an expression of rage—there is no condemnation of war itself or its human waste, or its futility, or the cost of battle. It is because the character cannot find any meaning in war, or because if there is one it has been blown away like his fellow soldiers, that the young man's Philippic breaks off with one word—'Hell' (which may bring to mind, of course, 'War is Hell!'—the most famous observation about the American Civil War by the Union commander General Sherman).

The novel, as Crane said in the sub-title to his own, is an 'episode' not only of the war but also in the life of one young man, the hero of Crane's tale who joins up to fight for a cause and dreams of writing himself into the history books, and who becomes in time a more mature soldier who is willing to fight not for fame but for the friends he has made. The novelist, Crane insists, deals with war's 'tragedies—hidden, mysterious, solemn.' (*The Red Badge of Courage*, 18). A novel initiates us into its mysteries and allows us to see war for what it is, 'the red animal—the blood-swollen god.' (*The Red Badge of Courage*, 19).

Novelists are now even more central to our understanding of war than they were in the nineteenth century—just think of the thriving industry around historical reconstructions of the First World War which has produced such prize-wining works as Pat Barker's *Regeneration* and Sebastian Faulk's *Birdsong*—because we are much more given then we were to thinking of war as 'the human thing'. In stripping away many of its abstractions we have reduced it to its human core. As Michael Herr adds in *Dispatches* 'war stories are nothing more than stories about people.' Glory vanished from war in 1915 (it did not survive the industrialised killing grounds of the Western Front); and much of its glamour went in Vietnam, a war in which, to judge from many writers, nothing in particular happened, except individual human pain. 'You can tell a true war story', insists O'Brien 'if you just keep on telling it.'

Historians, of course, often fault writers for this reason—they accuse them of conveying the reality of war only through surfaces; they fault them for rendering a primary emotion in such vivid colours that it is impossible to stand outside an individual life and generalise about the war being portrayed. The fact is that novelists have political opinions like everyone else, and philosophies of life, which occasionally intrude into their work, sometimes unhappily. Even so, they are embodied in a narrative structure, in the plot, character and attitudes, and in the imagery. What novelists attempt to capture, more or less, successfully, is not the surface at all, but the essence of war, the *experience*.

Of all the major writers to have discussed the remarkable power of fiction to illuminate reality, the most important for this study is Milan Kundera's *The Art of the Novel*, especially for what he has to say about the most important aspect of literary as opposed to popular fiction: not the plot (the action) or the writing (most war fiction is indifferently written) but the characters with whom many readers may identify. As soon as you create an imaginary being, you are confronted by the question 'what is the self?' (Kundera, 1988, 23). No doubt that question has taken on peculiar urgency since the invention of psychology, he adds; Dostoevsky's characters are far more complex than Homer's. Literary figures from the nineteenth century such as Henry Fleming or Hadji Murat are more recognisably 'human' than Homer's for that reason—they are more like us. But Kundera's point is that even in stories where there is little characterisation, little light or shade, or little emotional or psychological depth, once a character acts, he has to believe in himself as a person, and reveal to himself and others what makes him different from everyone else in the story.

We find in literature, then, characters who experience self-discovery while never really pinning themselves down. For the self is an endless quest of self-discovery that has no resolution. The quest itself is a person's life, and war is an unforgiving environment which finds men out very quickly. Some discover that they are cowards, others that they are much braver than they imagined; some fail the test, others come through. And literature even reveals the hollow men who are dead to the world, as they are in real life, men like the American driver of a jeep in a death camp in Nazi Germany which had just been liberated, who left his radio blaring on with its jazz music in the midst of indescribable horror, his soul (wrote Erich Heller) 'clearly disassembled in the presence of God.' So, if in life the self will always remain elusive, we must not expect literature to provide characters that know themselves. Literature cannot transcend its own limitations, any more than we can the limits of our own physiology. What we have is an existential quest and each of the characters in the book illustrates, in varied and often paradoxical ways, what Kundera might call war's 'existential code' (Kundera, 1988, 29).

The characters of Kundera's own novels, he explains, are defined by that code which reveals itself progressively in particular situations or through concrete actions. In *The Unbearable Lightness of Being* (1979), the novel that fully established his name, there is a section, 'a

Word Misunderstood' in which he examines the existential codes of his two main characters, Franz and Sabina by analysing a number of words that are important to them both: 'woman', 'fidelity', 'betrayal', 'music', 'darkness', 'light', 'paradox', 'beauty', 'country', 'cemetery', 'strength. Each, however, has a different meaning for the characters concerned. For Kundera this approach is not psychological (as it was for Dostoevsky) or aesthetic (as it was for Proust), it is phenomenological, a word Kundera defines as the investigation of the essence of the human condition.

And that is precisely the purpose of this book. I hope to grasp the essence of war as a cultural phenomenon through its existential codes, as those codes are instantiated in twenty-five different fictional characters and the key concepts illustrated by the stories in which they appear: betrayal in the case of Norman Mailer's General Cummings; courage in the case of Stephen Crane's Henry Fleming; the warrior ideal in Homer's incomparable Achilles; the traumatised victim in Sophocles tragedy, *Philoctetes;* the dutiful soldier in Virgil's *Aeneid;* the common soldier's good humoured defiance of authority in Hašek's stories, *The Good Soldier Švejk*, and so the list continues.

Which brings me to the question Kundera asks, one that brings us back to the age old battle between literature and history: what can literature say about any historical phenomenon like war, which has in turn a historical dimension? War changes the world and the world changes war. Honour for Achilles is not what it is for Fabrice in Stendhal's *Charterhouse of Parma*, not only because the characters are different. What would Achilles have made of a young *poète maudit*, a dandy but also a true soldier, like Fabrice? Honour now meant different things in the light of different honour codes. The courage displayed by Achilles is not the courage of standing firm under fire. What Kundera insists is that history itself is merely a reflection of the human situation; it is not a stage upon which the human situation unfolds. War is shaped by human impulses, dreams, weaknesses, and often peoples' surprising strength; it is not some impersonal Leviathan, but an all too human tale in which contingency, chance and accident unfold inexorably. It is a little bit like the story of *Jacques the Fatalist*, Diderot's grim little tale in which at one point the hero joins up to fight simply because he has been disappointed in love. He gets a bullet in the knee for his pains in his first and only battle, and limps along for the rest of his life: end of story (Kundera, 1988, 38).

We can take history to be a grotesque parody, or an endless set of possibilities which we—as characters in our own drama—cannot always anticipate or necessarily determine. Fiction, through its characters and the stories which shape their lives, is merely a set of possibilities that are open to all of us. And this is the essence of war, too. I have written this book because some of its possibilities still remain to be realised.

'War is the father of all good things; war is also the father of good prose', declares Nietzsche in *The Gay Science* (Section 92, 2001). It is not one of the philosopher's most famous aphorisms, and there is perhaps a reason for that. More often than not, war tends to father some very bad writing indeed. Popular novels far outsell the good ones, and that is unfortunate, for they rarely find a language adequate to the intensity of their theme. Popular war novels are inhabited by a familiar cast of characters, instantly recognisable: the cowardly officer disguising his cowardice; the young recruit who discovers himself in battle; the tough but compassionate non-commissioned officer. None of this is necessarily untrue to life, but it does not add any extra insight into reality. These characters live on the page, but very few live off it; they are not necessarily one-dimensional, but they inhabit only one dimension: the book in which they appear. It is only in great fiction that we encounter all too fallible human beings in whom we can sometimes see something of ourselves.

There is another problem with popular writers—many of them have a way of claiming that battles encapsulate historical turning points. 'Can the foot soldier teach anything important about war, merely for having been there?' asks O'Brien (O'Brien, 2003, 22–23). He thinks not; all he can tell are war stories. It takes a great novelist like Stendhal to show us a young Fabrice totally bewildered at Waterloo, in every sense 'unhorsed', or out of his depth. Tolstoy always said that everything he knew about war came not from his own experience on the battlefield, but from Stendahl's description of Waterloo. Hemingway insisted that once you had read Stendahl you would *be* at Waterloo. Lawrence Durrell claimed that one of the significant forces that a novel on war brings out, is that for most soldiers on the battlefield nothing appears to be happening. 'The action is always over a hedge somewhere in another corner ... and then they ask if you were there. Well, you weren't.'

And there is something else to consider, writes Michael Herr:

In war, more than any other life, you don't really know what you're doing most of the time. You're just behaving, and afterwards you can make up any kind of bullshit you want to about it, say you feel good or bad, loved it, and hated it, did this or that, the right thing or the wrong thing, still what happened, happened. (Herr, 1979, 25).

What Tolstoy can never be accused of doing, even at his most preachy, is slotting characters into their appointed roles as an example of 'cowardice', or 'courage', 'heroism' or 'selflessness'. In war, real people are not so easily slotted into symbolic frameworks; in great literature the characters we remember are so complex that they do not always know themselves. In real life, anyway, few soldiers aspire to become emblems of anything in particular. Most just wish just to survive the experience. Some may want to make a difference, but the difference is not always intended; it is demanded of the hour, or the circumstance in which they find themselves.

And whenever a writer tries to recapture the experience of war he is also entering into a contract with his readers. The enduring life of a novel lies not only in the author's ability to draw us into a story, but the freedom he gives the reader to see what we wish to see. No author owns the story he is telling; ownership is shared. The reader is in some ways a co-author because he often lives through fictional characters, and willingly enters their world and participates in their lives, and he lives his own life more intensely for it. Fictional characters—at least the ones we are likely to remember long after we have finished reading the book, become so real on the page that they often take on a life off it.

The silliest argument is that great writers have been opposed to war, though many have been pressed into service as 'pacifists' including Homer and Virgil, and even Shakespeare. The sensible attitude to adopt, writes Harold Bloom, for those great writers he considers 'canonical', is to expect a multiplicity of viewpoints. The greatest writers, he reminds us in *The Western Canon* are subversive of all values, both ours and their own (Bloom, 1996, 29). Homer may have loathed war. 'Atrocious; the scourge of man; lying and two-faced' are the terms he uses to describe it, but in Achilles he created the greatest warrior in literature. We have been encouraged to conspire with Achilles in the mystique Homer wove around him—this ungodly, god-like man whom we have disavowed from time to time but always returned to and endlessly transfigured. If Achilles himself is horrified by the thought of his own death we aren't; we are constantly transported by it.

We should not read any work of literature to find a moral. The true use is to develop and nurture one's inner self, and this is best achieved by throwing oneself into the inner world of the characters the great writers portray, many of whom are as real, and often more vital, intelligent and captivating, than the great majority of people we will meet in real life. It is we, ultimately, who must determine whether war can be justified in any or all circumstances, and we are much more likely to arrive at some intelligent judgement than if we just follow the news, or adopt a quasi-ideological position.

There is another point Bloom makes when he writes that Shakespeare will not make us better, or worse, but he may teach us how to overhear ourselves when we talk to others (Bloom, 1996, 31). I doubt whether anyone whose understanding of war is derived from graphic novels or video games or Hollywood movies that tend to glamorise it will find this book very comforting. Nor will many servicemen or women if they are not given to reflecting on their own profession, or have not yet shared in the trials and travails of Henry Fleming.

The best war novels do not take a stand against war; they leave it to the reader to puzzle out its moral, if there is one. What they celebrate is the small acts of friendship, the struggle of individuals faced with extraordinary circumstances to keep faith with their friends, as well as themselves. Their message reinforces our faith in humanity, which is why professional soldiers still read Homer. What they learn is that no defeat is ever final, not even the fall of Troy, because art allows us to remember, and what we remember often inspires us to struggle on.

The late philosopher Richard Rorty wrote that you cannot create a memorable character without thereby making the suggestion about how the reader herself might act, for the concreteness of a character is a matter of being embedded in a situation in which the reader can, out of her own life, imagine analogies. 'There but for the grace of God go I'; 'what would I do for the people I count among my friends?' (Rorty, 1999, 167). Fiction in that sense conditions the way we look at the world, a point made recently by Keith Oatley, a cognitive psychologist, in his book *The Passionate Muse*. Reading really does make us different people. We view life differently, usually more positively. A person who inhabits the fictional world of the novel is likely to hold onto the idea of human goodness more than a person whose knowledge of the world is derived solely from newspapers or from watching TV. The imaginative world is where individuality triumphs, and so too belief in human goodness. One can only be heroic in life, as in war, by being true to oneself, and often this can best be done by imaging what our favourite fictional characters would have done in similar circumstances. The importance of fiction is that in revealing us to ourselves, often for the first time, it allows us, in Nietzsche's words, to aspire to 'become' what we are.

The works I have chosen are those that for me best illustrate the phenomenon of war. Some I have re-read again, only now grasping the central message (Manning, *Her Privates We*); others I have read for the first time—Balzac's *Colonel Chabert*, and, more surprisingly perhaps, Remarque's *All Quiet on the Western Front*. Some of the characters appear in just a few brief pages (Colonel Moredock in Melville's *The Confidence Man*); one, Dr Strangelove, is the product of a screenplay in which he has fewer than fifty-eight lines of speech. But they have all taken on a life of their own, and they all make war come alive on the page or screen when they are depicted. War needs its writers, however critical, and will continue to do so. The best will continue to illuminate war's still unending story.

As for the choice of characters in this book, it is restricted to those works of literature which have never been out of print and which as a result have become in many cases household names. Some readers will be disappointed to find that their favourite characters do not appear such as Prince Andrei looking up at Napoleon at Austerlitz, or George Osbourne meeting his death at Waterloo. But there is a reason for this. This book is not intended to be a work of literary criticism; it is intended to illustrate the 'existential criteria' that make war the phenomenon it is. Which is why I have grouped the characters into five character types which the great writers have returned to time and again: villains and victims, heroes and warriors, and of course survivors. It has been a challenging and interesting task to revisit books of my youth (such as the first *Flashman* novel) and those that were central to my classical education like the *Iliad* and the *Aeneid*, though I am no longer able to read them in their original language. Above all re-reading many of them has been instructive because I am not exactly the same person I was when I first read the works; and I am a different person, in part, because of what the books have made me.

2

WARRIORS

At an early stage of my life I developed some fixed ideas of what a good war novel should look like. We should judge it by its extraordinary, larger than life characters, and they do not come larger than Achilles chasing Hector around the walls of Troy, or Aeneas carrying his destiny on his shoulders. On the page of course, we do not find the Marvel comic heroes that we do in Hollywood. Our Marvel Comic superheroes are, of course, a great deal darker than they used to be; some of them are almost as bad as the villains that dog their lives. But fictional heroes, beginning with Achilles, have a complexity which other fictional superheroes significantly lack.

For warriors both reflect their times and transcend them. As war has become increasingly instrumentalised and the data flows continue to flood in (now through the video streams of drones) so the existential dimension continues to be hollowed out, as does the belief in the very idea of 'character'. Yet the challenges—the realities soldiers still face— have not changed much since Homer. Technology may have transformed the battlefield into a battlespace, but as long as war remains what the Greeks called it, 'the human thing'—warriors will continue to have a better grasp than the rest of us of what war actually means.

The warriors discussed in this book are fascinating and complex creations. And they are all remarkable in their own way. Of the five character types I shall discuss the warrior is the most rewarding to discuss but the most difficult to pin down. And for fiction writers it has been the greatest challenge—to make a true larger-than-life character believable on the page.

The warrior is much more than a brave man, and he is much more than a man who loves his profession, though he will be born with what we call a vocation; he will answer the call. To be a warrior is much more than a philosophy of life, it is often something akin to a religious calling, and it involves killing, and killing others with skill. Whenever we try to explain an experience we create metaphors. But then we find a paradox in the metaphor, and forgetting that the map is not the territory we proclaim that the paradox exists in nature or life. We think of war as a duel and duels have strict rules and protocols. You can be cashiered for fighting a duel, and shamed for not. You can be imprisoned for killing your opponent, and shamed if you kill your opponent inappropriately. Unlike a duel, war is all about killing, and once the killing starts it is easy to lose control and forget the 'rules' which is why, above all, we expect warriors to be men of integrity.

Warriors inhabit two dimensions of war: the instrumental and existential. Most soldiers (though not all) inhabit only one. They serve (usually) a state, either because they choose to (for them war is a profession, as before the modern era it was largely a trade) or because they have no choice—they are conscripted, and many conscripts serve it very well. Some even discover themselves to be warriors in the heat of battle. Of necessity, modern warriors serve others, not only their unbounded will. But they also derive much of their self-esteem from the extent to which they are esteemed by others. We admire them, in turn, not only for their professionalism (another 'modern' attribute) but for their sense of duty or service. But in the end they are defined by the fact that they derive their humanity from war. They have a vocation; they hear the call. When going into battle they reaffirm themselves. To use the language of existentialism, they become authentic human beings.

The *Iliad* is a poem of loss—of friends, family, cities. But there is also a celebration of excellence which could only be displayed once, but if it burned brightly it might be remembered 'with advantages'. Death for a Greek was far more terrible than for a Christian. Without a belief in 'heaven'—an afterlife worth dying for—what counted was this life. At one point in the epic, Ajax, Odysseus and Phoenix (Achilles' old tutor) visit him in an attempt to persuade him to return to the fight. In an extraordinary scene Achilles claims that glory is not worth winning if a man has to die. Death is the great leveller. It spares no-one. We are all equal, in that respect, Achilles claims. Homer allows us—if only very briefly—to be party to Achilles' own struggle with his mortality, but in the end he goes willingly to his death. The poem ends with the funeral games—a ritual of loss—in Book 23, along with the Trojans' mourning for Hector in the book that follows it. The last line of all, 'such was the burial of Hector, breaker of horses' is, as Achilles himself knows all too well, merely a prelude to his own death, that of the greatest warrior in western literature.

Achilles' voice is strangely absent for much of the poem. In the passages in which he does appear, Homer explores what drives him on. It is a fine portrait of obsession, and Achilles wins every time, perhaps because he fears he will not (there is always something to prove, if only to himself). Is this one of the distinguishing marks of our humanity—our tragi-comic tendency to love the worst people and devalue the best? The heroes on the Greek side, at least, are a pretty rum lot, but Achilles is by far the most terrifying. Homer's genius is to build an entire story around a person who is seriously dysfunctional, but still magnificent at the same time, a man so many soldiers over the ages have wished to be, but also feared they might become.

The warrior has remained the lodestone of war fiction ever since Achilles and perhaps the poets tended to take them too much at their own estimation of themselves. After all, they are only human, even if the critics of war think of them as plying an inhumane trade. But not all of them ply it inhumanely. The warrior ethos is what a writer usually celebrates and by the time Virgil was writing—six hundred years after Homer—a different kind of ethos had come to the fore, one with which we ourselves are much more familiar. Virgil tells us that fame makes the small seem great and the great seem greater, and few warriors in history have been more famous or more celebrated than Aeneas. Even if few of us read Virgil today in the original (as my generation did at school), and even though Virgil no longer remains what he once was, the centrepiece of the western canon, Aeneas' story is still worth telling. In his *Life of Virgil* (1697) Dryden recounts that Aeneas is always falling into 'ill-timed Deliberation'. Achilles is extroverted; Aeneas is not especially introspective (as we understand the term), but he is much more cerebral. The problem is that it is difficult to *identify* with him. Whatever his merits as a patriot of a country not yet forged, a proto-patriot, perhaps, and whatever his undoubted skill as a soldier, he is pretty colourless as a man. He is like a photographic negative of Achilles. Yet if we can't identify with him, we can at least admire his determination. If Achilles is a mythical figure who has a primal integrity to be himself, Aeneas is the first literary character who has to be himself within the bounds of duty.

And what makes him so vivid is that he is a conflicted warrior—his fame is not what he have asked for or wanted. He is always reproaching the Gods for choosing for him a destiny which he has not chosen for himself. He would have preferred to have remained in Troy, dying by the side of his brothers. But patriotism seeks him out and puts his piety to the test. Aeneas is, from the beginning, the foot soldier of a cause larger than himself. We see him escaping from Troy carrying Anchises, his father, on his back; later leaving Dido, his only real love, both for duty, braving all to found Rome. Cautious, sometimes resentful, burdened by cares, resolute but reluctant; he is, at heart, a lonely figure (perhaps all warriors are) who finds no joy in the mission, or fulfilment at its end. In that lies his true heroism. Every time Aeneas feels he would rather be somewhere else, he is being tested, of course. What makes us warm to him (separated as we are by history and culture—by *mores* that are not our own and attitudes which we can no longer recognise in ourselves) is his piety. Not in the religious sense of duty that we owe the gods, or the responsibilities that the citizen owes the state, but the understanding that others are counting on him (the men he has brought from Troy; the ancestors to whom he owes a debt too). Aeneas' piety is not a crude '*pro patria mori*', he has not been brainwashed. To be impious in these circumstances would be to be unjust. The *Aeneid* shows us what patriotism was before it degenerated into nationalism.

There are many different kinds of warrior not represented in this book: they include some who are even more frightening than Achilles, like Beowulf, the hero of the greatest classic of Old English literature, who not only spears but crushes his enemies to death.

The thief
Fell in battle, but not to my blade
He was brave and strong but I swept him in my arms
Ground him against me till his bones broke
Till his blood ran out. (Glover/Silkin, 1989, 9).

Beowulf was a bezerker inspired in combat with divine fury that marked him out from his peers and made them respect him all the more. How different are the chivalrous knights celebrated by the medieval *chansons de geste* whose archetype was Roland and his friend Olivier, and Amadis (the knight after whom all other knights tried to model themselves, including the greatest fictional knight of all, Don Quixote). Defending himself against a priest who tells him to 'get real'—'Go home—stop this wandering!' the Don proclaims his achievements: 'I have set injuries and insults straight, righted wrongs, punished arrogance, conquered giants and trampled on monsters.' (Bloom, 2002, 40). And he has done all of this in emulation of Amadis. The importance of imitation is that it has enormous potential to shape not only behaviour but the way we perceive the world. When the Don ventures out into the world in search of glory, the banal objects of the Spanish countryside are metamorphosed by his obsessive attachment to the Amadis story—peasant women become damsels in distress; windmills become imposing giants; even a flock of sheep are transformed into maleficent enemy warriors. Mimetic desire may seem absurd to those who don't buy into the myth but for those who do it transfigures everyday objects and enriches life (Fleming, 2004, 16). And just because today we only know of Amadis from reading the greatest comic novel in the western canon, should not make us dismiss it out of hand. Amadis was as well known as Achilles at one time in European history. He appeared for the first time in Garci Rodriguez de Montalvo's *Amadis de Gaula*, one of the many *romances fronterizos* which told the story of the valiant deeds undertaken by a fictional warrior against the Moors in the 're-conquest' of Spain. The greatest fans of all were the conquistadors who set out to conquer the New World. In our eyes, Amadis may be a cartoon figure in a way that Achilles simply is not but he had a much greater influence on the impressionable minds of the young men who set off across the Atlantic, like Achilles en route to Troy, in search of wealth and adventure, and even reputation.

It is because of the power of Homer's language that Achilles still evokes a response from the young men we send to do battle today. He is not completely 'other'; they can still recognise themselves in him (he would find it much more challenging, of course, to recognise himself in them). Of non-western warriors the most famous, perhaps, but also most enigmatic are the Japanese Samurai who achieved a spiritual depth perhaps unequalled in any other culture, as well as a taste for poetry (the haiku) which is rare in a warrior, and a taste for *sepukku* (the ritual suicide that expiated failure) which, fortunately, is rarer still. Both the medieval knight and the samurai warrior could not be more distant from us. Culture matters. The only non-western warrior to appear in these pages, Hadji Murat, is an orientalised western version of a Chechen warlord, but the critic Harold Bloom thinks him if not the greatest of Tolstoy's characters, by far the most sublime. And it is telling that Tolstoy himself, who had long since turned against war and embraced a militant form of Christian pacifism, created Hadji so late in life, and left the novella unpublished at his death (he seemed to be keeping faith not with war, but with that religious element—the votary, the warrior, an anachronistic figure, or so Tolstoy now thought, at a time when war was becoming mechanically destructive).

Georg Lukacs, the Marxist critic, advised us to locate the invisible army of serfs that made his world go round. And we are finally shown one in the novella, *Hadji Murat*. But the story is not his, but that of the man who gives the tale its title. Has anyone bettered Hadji Murat wounded, dying but still defiant, 'limping heavily ... dagger in hand straight at the foe.' 'Circumstances have compelled Hadji Murat to become an outcast, albeit a dignified and even honoured figure', writes Bloom. 'Though superbly suited to his context he is aware that the context is dissolving for him, leaving him alone except for his handful of men.' (Bloom, 1996, 344). But there is a problem with the context, or rather there are several. The context vindicates the warrior as more heroic than the rest of us, but more of a victim when the context dissolves. Tolstoy made Hadji Murat as magnificent a figure as he could. But when you take the historical context out of the story what you are left with is merely the glamour, and he does tend to glamorise him, setting a precedent for bad books and bad movies that now abound, in which everyone from Billy the Kid to Carlos the Jackal see themselves and are seen by others as 'warriors' too. Tolstoy was not to know that warriors would reappear a century later in the many and variegated forms that we know today—including, in their own eyes at least, suicide bombers from Chechnya.

For many the warrior as traditionally conceived lives on, not in real life so much as the imagined lives of others. Patrick O'Brian's great sea captain Jack Aubrey has his own roots in the great sea narratives of Forster and before him Marryat, but he breaks free of both. Aubrey lives off the page in a way that Forster's Hornblower really doesn't. In the thousands of pages that make up the series (twenty completed novels in all), we see that war does not consume Aubrey. He may be a warrior but he is also a person with a marked humanity which is revealed most when playing music with his friend Dr Maturin, or engaging in wordplay or philosophising about war and about life. He is perhaps a little too 'modern' in his sensibilities against flogging and hanging, the severities which kept Nelson's navy together but then no generation can pass judgment on another without reference to its own concerns which is why each gets the fictional heroes it thinks it deserves. But in the moral uplift of O'Brian's tales, the novels strike at a truth about war that warriors are not made, they are born, a truth that in these egalitarian times we are not always willing to acknowledge. Part of the attraction of the novels derives from the ease with which Aubrey lives his role as a warrior, and the unquestioning acceptance of that role by the men he leads into battle. Here is a true professional who can only be himself by moulding his crew into a team and inspiring them to follow his lead.

Aubrey lives off the page as well as on it because he represents a much simpler age that took war on trust; sailors these days are expected to be like oncologists whose professional speciality is studying cancer but whose professional *vocation* is fighting it. His vocation—so some believe—should be to combat war, not glory in it which makes one feel guilty reading the O'Brian oeuvre. But we read fiction to better understand ourselves. To say that war is madness is like saying sex is madness: true enough from the standpoint of a stateless eunuch but merely a provocative epigram to those who must make their arrangements in the world as a given. To be a citizen, argued the novelist John Updike, is to participate in the passions and emotions of a community that will continue to wage war. But we should continue to say that war is madness if only to urge reflection on the warrior—to keep him from loving war too much (Temes, 2003, 140).

It may be difficult, but it is not impossible to suspend disbelief enough to conjure up a world without war (Aldous Huxley did it in *Brave New World* and Isaac Asimov in his stories of robots, like *The Caves of Steel*), but it is very challenging indeed to imagine war without warriors. Without them, its popular appeal would be much diminished. They are the supreme characters in the military canon. They are, for many of us, and not only young male adolescents (for men form 99 per cent of combat soldiers) the figures with whom we identify most, more for their faults perhaps than their virtues. War, like religion, has its saints and sinners.

The moral danger in the future lies in failing to ask ourselves clearly enough whether our moral actions are real or simulated. Warriors by tradition get in close for the kill: Achilles in the face to face encounters which punctuate the text of the *Iliad*; Aeneas closing in on the savage but noble Turnus; Hadji Murat dying in a magnificent last stand; Aubrey boarding the enemy ships. Vollmer, a character in a short story by Don DeLillo, safe in his space station orbiting the earth, is a strikingly different and lesser figure. He is largely disengaged from the action down below; he is even in danger of becoming dissociated from war itself. He has no emotions to speak of. He is largely disengaged from the situation, and what is more striking is that he has difficulty recognising what is real, or making out its shape. For him, war has become as virtual as a computer game. Is Vollmer even a warrior? Is it not a provocation to include him in this section? It is, but it is an informed one, I hope. For the US Military is intent on calling computer hackers 'cyber warriors', and drone pilots 'cubicle warriors'; it seems determined to recycle the concept, even at the risk of devaluing the currency.

But even today's drone pilots may soon become superannuated. For we are about to enter a new world in which robots will range across the battlespace. There is a robot, *JAKE-1* (Jungle Automatic Killer—Experimental Model No. 1) which appeared for the first time in *Weird Tales* (1981), deployed on a Pacific island alongside Marines placed under the control of my namesake, Sgt Coker. In *A Boy and His Tank*, Leo Frankowski presents us with a super computer which needs a human crew member to operate it because 'associative human thinking' is better at devising battle tactics than logical machines. But Frankowski's book veers on science fantasy rather than science fiction, and *Weird Tales* is—something else altogether! An intelligently imagined realisation of what an autonomous fighting machine might look like remains to be written. Whether a robot would be the 'hero' of its own story is another matter entirely. Whether it would be the main 'character' of the story depends on whether it could be deemed to have a 'character' at all. Whether it would be regarded by its designers as a 'warrior' is a moot point. Perhaps, by then even the idea of the warrior may only survive in the imagination thanks to computer games, or comic books like *Weird Tales*.

Achilles: The Consummate Killer

The Iliad, Homer

If Homer did indeed dislike war, then he has much to answer for, for in Achilles he created the greatest warrior in literature who has inspired non-fictional warriors ever since. He is the warrior who outfights every other, and we tend to overlook his faults; his petulance, his emotional mood swings, and his killing sprees—for he is a consummate butcher. Butchery is what combat often meant in Homer's world—*ergon* (work) the Greeks called it, and it often went on hour after hour. The combat zone was a killing ground and no one kills as relentlessly or skilfully as Achilles. Of the *Iliad*'s 15,000 lines, battle takes up a third, made up of 300 individual encounters. Achilles appears in very few, but it is his appearances we remember long after we have forgotten the deeds of other heroes, including Ajax, who was considered by Homer to be second only to Achilles himself.

Homer may well have disliked war, but he is much more ambivalent about warrior values. Achilles displays all the characteristics the Greeks celebrated most: he is physically perfect; undoubtedly fearless; undaunted by lesser warriors (i.e. other warriors); and he is capable of acts of chivalry, especially to women, and of showing compassion to old men. He is also eloquent, and when the Greeks are not fighting they are always debating amongst themselves. He is also capable of flashes of rare insight into the evils of war and the folly of the young men risking all for so little. But we should not forget what he is: a consummate one-man killing machine, as heartless at times as Arnold Schwarzenegger's Terminator.

Achilles really is an unappealing figure, a type we will not find in any professional military today. Plato found him dangerous because he lacked emotional intelligence; Vico thought him barbaric and often childish in his emotional range. Shakespeare tackled him twice—once when the traumatised Lucrece looking at a painting of the Trojan war sees Achilles' figure suggested only by his hand and spear ('a hand, a foot, a face, a leg, a head/stood for the whole to be imagined'—the bodily focus makes Achilles an object of masculine aggression, as much to be feared as admired). The other time, in *Troilus and Cressida*, he guyed him mercilessly as an effete poltroon. But even Shakespeare could not diminish the man in our collective imagination, and no author has ever managed to produce a warrior like him since. It is his ambivalent nature that makes him so fascinating; brutal one moment, generous-hearted the next—and always on a hair-trigger response to avenge any slight or questioning of his status, imagined or real.

Even Homer is at times in awe of his creation—at other times, he clearly finds him frightening. He too could not rein Achilles in, but he also could not bring himself to describe his death. He prefers to end with Hector's, the warrior with whom we most identify today. Not even Homer could distort history (or in this case mythology). Achilles' death is more ignominious than Hector's; it is not a true theme for epic poetry. And Hector at least dies gloriously, at Achilles' hand, and in full view. War claims the lives of the noblest and best, and it is not quite fitting that Achilles, too, will be brought down by the man who started it all, Paris, an archer by trade (a man who prefers to fight his battles from a distance, rather than hand-to-hand).

The conflicting pictures we have of Achilles is the product of history. He is on the cusp of an age, between the Bronze Age and the Iron Age to come, and the Bronze Age was by far the most frightening period in ancient history. If we understand the historical context we can better grasp Homer's dilemma.

In writing the *Iliad*, Homer was tapping into a set of stories that were in wide circulation between 1200 and 800BC. His striking innovation was the introduction of Achilles: half-man, half-god. Achilles is perhaps the first celebrity warrior, if we take frequency (*celebriter* in Latin) to be at the heart of celebrity. No warrior has been quoted as much; a search for 'Achilles' returns over 20 million Google hits at the time of writing. The difference is, of course, that he is famous not for being famous, but for his actions, and he is at the top of the triple A-list of warriors because he established the benchmark against which everyone else on the list has been judged, whether fictional or real. Not bad for a purely fictional character.

The *Iliad* opens in the ninth year of a seemingly endless conflict in which the Greeks, led by Agamemnon, go to war against Troy to revenge a humiliating act: the 'abduction' of Helen by Priam's son,

Paris. Abduction is what our Victorian forefathers used to call it, but Helen of course goes willingly enough. In those nine years the Greeks loot the Trojan countryside and sack the cities of Troy's allies, but they can make no headway against the city itself. Homer shows us only one pitched battle on the Trojan plain and he concentrates on only two months of fighting. Like a Hollywood screenplay, the action begins almost immediately with a rift within the Greek camp which introduces us to two of the principal characters, the commander Agamemnon and the greatest warrior, Achilles, two poles of the Greek warrior ideal. Because it is not a work of history, we do not get a tedious prologue explaining the first nine years of the war (this is fed to us during the course of the action in flashbacks which we now associate with the movies); and the battle scenes which begin with Book IV and give the poem its forward propulsion do not get more graphic. They are the most vivid ever conceived before computer enhanced special effects enabled Steven Spielberg to replicate the D-Day landing scenes in *Saving Private Ryan*.

The real theme of the story is what historians nowadays call the collapse of primary group cohesion when Achilles refuses to go on fighting and retires himself and his followers from the field. The cause is once again a woman, the beautiful Briseis, a prize of war who Achilles had earmarked for himself but who Agamemnon, as his superior officer, claims for his own. It all begins with an infection that seizes the Greek camp on the tenth day of the outbreak. The prophet Calchas reveals that the epidemic has been sent by no less than Apollo himself to punish the Greeks for dishonouring one of his priests, Chryses. Chryses has come to the Greek camp to beg for the return of his daughter Chryseis, who had been taken by Agamemnon as a trophy, a prize he had refused to give up. Under pressure from his own men, he is forced to do just that, but not before demanding compensation in the form of Achilles' own trophy, Briseis. After Briseis leaves him, Achilles sits on the beach and cries like a child: tears of rage, to be sure, but perhaps, Barry Strauss speculates, tears of loss as well (Strauss, 2007, 106).

Much has been made of the slight Achilles experiences at Agamemnon's hands. Commentators have puzzled ever since about what we should conclude from this, but there is an unhappiness in Achilles that explains his petulance and occasional adolescent rage. The sulking in his tent, his refusal to return to battle even at the imprecation of

Phoenix, his old tutor. It is an act of supreme solipsism and at one point Achilles even entertains an appalling thought: what, he asks Patroclus, if only the two of them survive the war and everyone else did not? What is striking is not just the extent of his self-regard, but also the extent of his self-centredness. When Achilles finally relents and allows his friend to go into battle wearing his own armour Patroclus becomes an avatar, an extension of Achilles himself. What he is dreaming of is the ultimate vengeance, living in a world in which only he is left.

All he asks of Patroclus is that he should not be reckless, he should not over-extend himself. But hubris breeds nemesis, as the Greeks never tired of telling us, and Patroclus ignores his friend's advice. Hector rides out to challenge him. He is aided by the god Apollo, who knocks Patroclus down, stunning him temporarily and splintering his shield. Euphorbos spears him in the back with a javelin. Hector finishes him off by driving his spear into his belly. The ultimate affront of history is that it rarely takes sides. 'There is', as Esmond Romilly wrote in 1937, thinking of his friends killed in defence of Madrid, 'something frightening, something shocking, about the way the world does not stop because these men are dead.' (Cunningham, 1986, 376). Or as Auden put it more lyrically, and pointedly, in his poem *Spain* which appeared some years later, 'we are left along with our day and the time is short, and/history to the defeated/may say, alas, but cannot help nor pardon.'

In the aftermath of Patroclus' death there is an unseemly debate as to who can claim his armour. Euphorbos insists that it is owed to him (he struck the first blow, after all), but before he can press home his claim he is killed by Menelaus. Hector eventually secures the armour, but Homer cannot resist telling us that the gods think the whole debate unseemly. The *Iliad* is a much more complex tale than it is often taken to be. Debates are at the centre of the action just as much as the actual killing. Heroism is a contested concept and there is everything to contest, for with heroism goes *kudos*—or reputation; the argument over Patroclus' armour is one in which reputation and glory are of primary concern. There are many ways in which both can be won or lost, and, once lost, they are rarely won back.

Achilles himself now steams into battle to avenge the death of his only friend, and in the fighting that follows Hector is killed. His posthumous fate is to be dragged in the dust around the walls of the city by an unappeased Achilles. The Achilles who rejoins the war is still the man of the earlier books, but he has undergone a transformation; he has been brutalised in the course of the fighting. We know he was gentler in the earlier days, more pragmatic, less emotional, less brooding. War has changed him and not for the better. It may even have traumatised him in subtle and distinct ways, of which he is unaware. We may look for signs of trauma, although Homer himself did not, but just because they are not mentioned does not mean they are not there. In the end, only a night-time visit by Priam himself persuades the greatest warrior in history to return the body for cremation. The poem ends with Hector's funeral, which as Achilles well knows, will be followed by his own death.

Such are the bones of a story which have been picked clean by scholars ever since. Even in the ancient world they tried to tease out some of the darker meanings, the things that Homer implied but left unsaid. One of them, in our sex-obsessed age, is the homo-erotic friendship of Achilles and Patroclus, which inevitably begs the question of whether the greatest warrior in history is gay. The Greeks themselves could not agree. Plato argued that Aeschylus was talking nonsense—Patroclus was too old. Aeschines, refreshingly modern, said that the relationship was implicit, even though Homer never mentioned it. But Homer leaves us guessing. Achilles' sexuality is not really of interest to anyone but pedants or antiquarians. That he loves Patroclus is never in question, nor the fact that the love is unconditional, but 'love' means many things. It can mean no more, and certainly no less, than the intense friendships which are forged between men in battle. What impresses us most about Achilles is surely his simple single-mindedness. He loves Patroclus, but he loves war more, and he loves his reputation most of all. He loves the glory and the fighting and the status he achieves. He constantly fashions his own celebrity.

The *Iliad* spans only seven weeks of a ten year long war. And only a third of its lines mention Achilles. Nevertheless, the poem is largely his tale. It is about his anger, his rage at being robbed of his spoils, a woman captured in battle with whom he has fallen in love; and later his rage against the Trojans for the death of his only friend. What makes the poem work is its level of analysis. We see Achilles in three different lights.

First, he is the petulant young man who withdraws from the fight and hands the Trojans a series of victories which brings the Greeks to the verge of defeat, at the cost of hundreds, perhaps thousands of lives.

27

He is a solipsistic, self-preoccupied fighter, with little regard for anything but his own honour. The Greeks try everything to reconcile him to the common endeavour, employing flattering words and gifts, and arguments, plenty of them, nearly all of them compelling and all in vain. Achilles eventually rejoins the fight after Patroclus is killed in battle, at which point the war becomes a personal vendetta.

If anger is the theme of the first few books, revenge is the theme of the next—this is the second light thrown on Achilles' character, and it casts a more menacing shadow. Vengeance takes a terrible turn when Hector falls. Achilles drags his body round the walls of Troy for eleven days. So vengeful is he that the gods themselves turn against him. Apollo calls him, 'murderous Achilles', a man who knows no decency, who is implacable and barbarous in his ways, like a wild lion (Meir, 2011, 88). And we are equally shocked because Homer has ensured that we really can root for both sides. In many respects Hector is the greater man, although Achilles is the greater warrior. He has a humanity we admire in our heroes, and the Greeks did even then. His patriotism is never in question, or his special reverence for his father, or the love of his wife and son, the young Astynax whose fate is already sealed (later he will be thrown from the walls of Troy).

And then, in the last books, we see Achilles in a completely new light. Hector's father, Priam, enters the Greek camp secretly by night and prevails upon Achilles to return his son's body so that his spirit can be laid to rest. It is one of the greatest reconciliation scenes in world literature. Achilles comes through. Both men lament old age and death. 'We'll probe our wounds no more, but let them rest, though grief lies heavy on us … this is the way the gods ordained the destiny of men to bear such burdens in our lives while they feel no affliction.' (Ibid., 89).

Carl Reinhardt writes that Achilles comes up against his own limits, he fights to the edge of his strength and expends his energy, but these limits do not point directly or indirectly to anything beyond themselves; 'the limit lacks any double sense; it remains one-sided in the here and now.' (Meir, 2011, 91). But Achilles' limit is still amazing. It is not limiting, it is an expression of human greatness, albeit on a heroic and slightly superhuman scale. In the world of the *Iliad*, ordinary Greeks found a heroically enlarged reflection of their own wish to push the limits, to test themselves.

'Mythic' is a rather overused term. Like epic and iconic, we apply the term to anything that is larger than life. It may be that only a poet, and only one like Homer, can make a character mythic. He certainly satisfies all the requirements of myth.

First, like any myth, the story of the *Iliad* is rooted in death and the fear of being forgotten, which translates into a craving for immortality. Only we humans are aware of death, and only we can overcome it through memory. We can be said to have two heredities, a biological and cultural one. All other species only have a biological. Myth of course is a purely cultural construction, and in the form of social legacy can be transmitted to generations far removed from us in time and even sensibility. We still live by myths; our myths just happen to be different. They still help soldiers establish a transcendent value that challenges selfishness, but the myths we promote seek to help us identify with the rest of the human race. We tell ourselves stories quite foreign to Homer's age. We tell ourselves a story that Achilles did not; that we are human only to the extent that others recognise their humanity in us.

Certainly one feature of myth is that it is usually inseparable from ritual. As Karen Armstrong writes, its characters are incomprehensible in a profane setting (Armstrong, 2005, 3). The *Iliad* ends with Patroclus' funeral and the sacrifice of the Trojan prisoners of war to appease his vengeful spirit. And she quotes George Steiner's remark that all art provides us with access to the meaning of myth, 'it breaks into the small house of our cautionary being', so that 'it is no longer habitable in quite the same way as it was before.' (Ibid., 148). Imagine war without myth, imagine war without art. The artist and the mythmaker are the same. Our art, however, is no longer poetic. The epic poem died its death on the Western Front in 1915. Today the war poets no longer resonate as they did. It is the novel that allows us to enter another world, even that of soldiers fighting against us, so much so that you can even empathise with the enemy if a novelist is accomplished enough. You can transcend your own tribe, class or nation. Homer gets us to admire the Trojans as well as the Greeks, but only because they worship the same gods, and both speak the same language.

And as a myth, the *Iliad* takes us, as all myths do, to the extremes of life, well beyond our ordinary experience (Ibid., 3–4). Soldiers who read Homer will look into their experience largely beyond anything they will themselves encounter. Achilles is a larger than life figure, but he also is life lived at the extreme, at the edge. His world is inexpressible even in Homer's poetry. It takes us into the mystery of our own humanity.

And as Armstrong reminds us, myth is not really about storytelling at all. The narrative may be compelling but its purpose has always been to teach a moral, or a lesson in human behaviour. The Greeks read the *Iliad* to understand how to behave, to discover the rules or protocols of human existence without which co-existence with each other would have been difficult indeed. Achilles' excessive grief, his passion for war and excessive rage, in no way diminish the hero, although they may the man. For what is heroic about him is the final reconciliation with Priam which allows him to salvage his reputation. He abides by the code of the gods who are disgusted by his single-minded urge to destroy Hector (in a sense to 'airbrush him' out of history). As a result of their intervention the corpse that Priam takes away is undefiled, as perfect in death as in life.

It is the gods who provide the last element of the story. In Homer's day they walked amongst men, and their earthiness is important. The gods are forever darting in and out of the ranks, trying to live vicariously through the mortals they aid, as well as destroy. They highlight the fact that life without mortality is essentially empty. The fate of Achilles is for us lastingly significant in the way the life of Apollo or Zeus is not. For we too, are mortal, and confront the same challenges. The gods are the politicians who send men out to fight in their name. They have power, but no real moral authority. They are not revered by any of the heroes who clearly despise them. At one point Achilles even challenges Apollo himself to fight. And when they do go into combat, they make a hash of it (Book 21) and become rather absurd and ridiculous figures (the wish fulfilment of every soldier who wishes to see the politicians do the fighting they have to endure).

But if the heroes are mortal and therefore lesser figures than the gods, the war allows its actors to experience divinity themselves; not to become gods or god-like, but to find the divine in themselves, and in the process to discover what it means to be a human being. Myth, after all, is all about reaching a higher plane of self-knowledge. Soldiers have returned to the *Iliad* to live more fully, to understand themselves, and it is not surprising that when Freud and Jung 150 years ago began the very modern search for the soul, they returned to myth, to the archetypes, to the stories of Oedipus, and others, to help them in their quest.

In the history of myth there is only one possible contender to Achilles, and that is Arjuna in the *Bhagavad Gita*, which in the form we know it today appeared centuries after the *Iliad*, but which drew on myths that were as old as Homer's. Much of it takes the form of dialogue between Arjuna and Krishna, a god who has taken the human form of the warrior's charioteer. The discussion is about the ethics of war. For when Arjuna sees the battlefield on which he must fight the next day he sees everyone who has ever been dear to him—how can he kill those whom he loves, or respects, including the teachers from whom he has learned so much? Krishna is a resourceful god, and employs every argument he can to persuade Arjuna to fight.

He tells Arjuna that reason dictates that he should fight; after all, men must kill for a higher purpose. When this fails to convince him, he tells Arjuna that he owes it to himself, and invokes his manhood; does he wish to be shamed in front of so many? When this too fails to motivate Arjuna, he falls back on metaphysics; while you may kill another man, you will never kill his soul. Realising this is also not working, he invokes the true argument for war; he has left his best argument to the last. In life, more often than not, one has to take sides; to make a choice; to stand and be counted. What intrigues so many warriors today about Achilles is that he makes his own choices, they are not made for him by a superior officer, or by politicians behind the lines. Achilles is not even above challenging Apollo to a fight; he is not in awe of the Gods. It is this ability to choose; to make a stand and pick a fight, that Krishna tells Arjuna is the only release there is from karma. It inheres not in desisting from action but acting regardless of risks and regardless of consequences.

Krishna later reveals himself to Arjuna and tells him that the Age of Heroes is coming to an end, just as the Trojan War brings the Greek Heroic Age to a close. He tells him that the outcome of the battle is already decided—just as the gods have decided the fate of Troy. The difference between the two greatest warriors in literature is that Arjuna is willing not only to die in battle, but to lay down his life and offer no resistance. Such a thought would never cross Achilles' mind; he would rather sail home and never fight again. But that is only one difference and it is not the most important. Krishna tries to put heart into Arjuna with a variety of arguments that all fail to move him. But one does. It is entirely alien to the western warrior tradition, and in the case of Achilles it would almost certainly have fallen on deaf ears. Arjuna must fight, but will achieve spiritual enlightenment by surrendering his ego. Fight he must, for this is his destiny, but he must give up all desire, including the desire for fame: 'Be intent on action, not on the fruits of action.' Take the 'me' and the 'mine' out of his deeds (Armstrong, 2006, 364).

Achilles and Arjuna have much in common. Warring is, for both of them, what they do; they are born warriors. But Achilles is locked into a different metaphysics of action. Violence is his moral essence, as it is Arjuna's, and neither are immoral: they employ violence justly. But unlike Achilles, Arjuna in the end is prepared to renounce fame and thus achieve a kind of happiness or contentment. It is disinterested participation that brings release from karma, or so the Hindu myths tell us. This attitude to war is not one that Achilles shares. In the Underworld, Achilles meets Odysseus once again and complains bitterly about his existence—he never quite gives up the fight, even once it is lost. That is why, in the end, he is diminished as a man for all his magnificence as a warrior.

What we do not know about Achilles is how he might have dealt with his grief over Patroclus' death, had he lived longer. Grief is the price we pay for love. Mourning is natural, and can go on for a long time; beyond the norm, it can turn into frozen depression after bereavement. But if grief does not get smaller, life often gets bigger. The problem, which Plato recognised (and he was nearer in time to Achilles than we are) is that his life was very restricted and cramped, and his grief was, even by the standards of his day, considered excessive. But perhaps there was a reason. Patroclus was his only true friend. He did not know the 'band of brothers.' We cannot begrudge him the intensity of friendship because there is nothing else he could claim except rage. Readers are often awed by it, but none can envy it. None of us would wish to be Achilles the man, as opposed to Achilles the warrior.

His violence, ultimately, must be seen perhaps as an objective correlative of an existential unhappiness. And what makes him unhappy—as Plato recognised—is that he does not like others enough to die for them, and he has so few friends that he cannot see death as meaningful for the others that are left behind. Death allows us to live life to the full. By acknowledging that our death can have meaning for others we can slacken our neurotic grip on life and thus come to relish it all the more. It is the knowledge of death, after all, that teaches us how to live (Eagleton, 2012, 210).

If the *Iliad* is grounded in myth it is also rooted in history. We must remember that Achilles is a Bronze Age warrior and the Bronze Age witnessed the most radical transformation of warfare before the widespread use of gunpowder (Watson, 2012, 280). One of those changes was the chariot, but Achilles is living at the end of the Bronze Age, when iron weapons were in use, and the chariot was already on the way out. In the *Iliad* they are used mostly to bring the heroes onto the field of battle (in a felicitous comparison, Edward Luttwak invites us to think of them as golf buggies, bringing golfers to play the next hole).

The main point about Bronze Age warfare is that it made male collective violence far deadlier than ever before. Quite probably, the scale of killing was not to be equalled until the twentieth century. And as warfare escalated, so social life became more masculinised and 'heroic'. The Alpha males come to the fore. More important still was the changing attitude to death. For the first time in history, death at human hands became more common than death through famine, or as a result of natural catastrophe. And as death became omnipresent, so it became final. Homer's after-life is really nothing of the kind. It is devoid of anything that we would consider animates life, of anything that makes life worth living. Hence Achilles' horror at the thought of his death; life is all there is. That is why for the warrior it had to be lived so intensely, manifest in a lust for killing and an unappeasable appetite for plunder. By the ninth year of the war he claims to have destroyed no fewer than twenty-three cities. He is a killer not just on the battlefield, but off it as well. He is a destroyer of other people's lives and livelihoods. He is akin to a pestilence, and long before Troy falls (he is fated to die first, of course), he has single-handedly destroyed the lives of its allies, including their economy, influence and above all prestige.

And what the Greeks esteemed most about him is what we esteem least: his skill in killing other people. Soldiers are much too squeamish to boast about it today, but Achilles is a consummate killer, as well as a relentless one. 'Death hath ten thousand several doors/For men to take their exits' says the Duchess of Malfi. Homer's battlefield doesn't have quite that many but it has more than any other in history, I would be willing to bet—far too many for our post-modern sensibilities. Today it really is difficult to wade through the description of how a man can kill another man in 148 different ways. The *Iliad* describes in gruesome detail the exit and entry points, the sharp points made— spear by spear, or sword or arrow, through flanks, crotches, navels, stomachs, chests, ears and chins. One of the most challenging difficulties for readers of Homer today, those who are serving in the field, is relating in a world of heavy-duty firepower to one in which the defining language of combat concerns 'strokes' and 'lunges' and 'parries' and 'heroically endured scars'. And this is just a sample of what is on offer, a *table d'hôte*, not the full *à la carte* menu of death that Homer describes.

In Homer's world the characters are quite implacable. The scene of a warrior begging for life occurs five times in the poem and every time the suppliant is slain. When the two sons of Antimachus offer ransom to Agamemnon if he will spare their lives, the king reminds them that their father had urged the Trojans to slay Menelaus when he came as an envoy. They will have to pay for their father's disgrace, and not only does Agamemnon kill them, he hews off the head and arms of one of them for good measure. But we are always reminded by the poet that Achilles does not slay in an ignoble way, even when moved by the death of Patroclus. Agamemnon is ruthless and unreflective; Achilles slays because this is what war demands. There is an equality between slayer and slain which is why he calls Lycaon a 'friend' when he despatches him to the Underworld. Lycaon is the son of Priam, but he is also half brother to Hector. Achilles rejects his pleas for clemency, but he does so in an impressive speech. We all risk death in battle, he tells him. Patroclus was a great man and paid with his life. Achilles is a greater man still, but even he will not be spared. 'There will be a morning or an evening, or a noonday, when my life shall be taken by some man in battle, whether it be with a blow of the spear or with an arrow from a bow.' (Griffin, 1979, 53) (Book 21).

Achilles perfectly understands the dynamic of killing. His speeches possess depth and truth which transform a mere narrative of killing into an insight into death itself. And death is constant in Homer's world. It is the one fixed point against which the hero measures himself and others. The rank and file, it is clear, have very little stomach for the fight. They rush to their ships and home the moment they see a chance; they have to be kept in the field through constant hectoring and rebuke. It is the heroes who are committed to battle even though their end is often gruesome in the extreme—warriors lying in the dust, wounded in the bladder, stretched out on the earth like worms, their guts spilling out, bellowing in pain or roaring like a roped bull; dragged behind chariots for the edification and entertainment of the enemy; chopped into pieces by the men in the ranks before their bodies are thrown into rivers or left to the dogs or the carrion birds, as their spirits descend into the Underworld where they will recall with bitterness the men they once were. No wonder that even heroes as great as Ajax and Hector occasionally run away. Not even Achilles himself is immune to fear. At one point the god Poseidon tells him not to tremble so much.

Every age, inevitably, reinterprets Achilles and gets the heroes it deserves, not only those it wants—with really great literature, fictional characters take on an imagined life beyond the page. What we have in Achilles is a character full of human frailties, with a humanity recognisably our own. He is a consummate killer, but he kills according to a code, and is revolted by the mean-mindedness of Agamemnon and the callousness of Odysseus. What we find in Achilles, wrote Thomas De Quincey, is the most intelligent of the heroes (Odysseus excluded), one who is given to the greatest reflection on the nature of war and the impossible demands it makes. As Jasper Griffin remarks, at times his speeches are the shortest in the book. At other times, Achilles reflects on distant times and places; these lines, their long epithets symmetrically placed, seem to bring the action to a halt for a timeless moment of contemplation. This is no mere ornament, but part of the character of the man. He is the only hero to question and criticise the heroic destiny of battle, and the heroic purpose of death. If, as De Quincey writes, his character is fixed, 'raised by a single flash of creative imagination', it is much more multi-dimensional than often thought.

Achilles has an integrity most of the other characters in the epic signally lack. As Heraclitus insisted, a man's character is his fate. And what I think soldiers can identify in him today is that character means everything, especially as they find themselves subordinating more and more of their own 'character' to the demands of their own military culture.

Homer's world is not our own, it is a personalised one. We learn where the butchered hail from—their home towns and their kin, and their patronymic names, and most meet with a unique death recorded in surgical detail. Homer even tells us who does the killing. We are much more sparing with the details today and we hardly ever get to hear who was responsible for taking the life of the soldier killed. Being blown up by an Improvised Explosive Device in Afghanistan is as soulless as it gets.

For Achilles, death was a brutal business. Even so, for a hero like Achilles (rather than the rank and file) it was met on equal terms—soldiers love the hand to hand contests that actually form a very brief part of the *Iliad*, and the necrologues, the long speeches when the heroes address each other by name, and often genealogy, and usually but not always empathise with the other's impending doom. Today in a country like Afghanistan death is just as brutal, but it is also faceless and sudden; it is all ambushes and fire fights and snipers with rifles, and improvised explosive devices; it is 'off stage', and 'in the wings' and frequently inglorious. Improvised Explosive Devices are not merely a feature of the battle zone; they are the battle that is being waged.

At the US Naval War Academy in Annapolis the students who study the *Iliad*, the first book on a course called 'the Code of the Warrior', confess that they would rather be 'a Hector who wins.' (Finch, 2005, 158). They clearly have much less admiration for Achilles, the man, as opposed to the warrior—but who are they actually cheering on? Hector seems to be the more humane of the two fighters, but that is actually quite deceptive. The point is that he has so much more to lose than Achilles, a wife and a baby son. But he is quite willing to part from them for fame. His tenderness to his wife *is* touching, but he tells her to her face that he prefers to die alone if that means winning glory and being remembered in the centuries to come. What our military find challenging is to identify with an all-male culture in which honour can only be won in the context of battle and bloody combat. Greek society was too much in love with death. To be in love with one's own death is to be out of love with other people. In Homer, death is treated as the most significant feature of our humanity. Humans are defined by their mortality. By the time of Plato the Greeks had changed—death was still important in defining a life but dying on a battlefield for others—for one's city, or for one's friends—took the sting out of death. A warrior was now defined by his sociability, his love of others, and that remains the heart of the warrior ethos today.

Towards the end of the *Iliad* we find Achilles in murderous pursuit of Hector. We know how the story will end. So do both protagonists. Hector is destined to die and be followed shortly by Achilles himself, and all they can console themselves with is the thought that they will never be forgotten. On they run, past the walls of Troy, and the springs of the River Scamander, whose god Achilles had once challenged to a fight. At this point Homer, as so often in the story, digresses to remind us of happier times.

> And here, close to the springs, lie washing pots
> scooped out in the hollow rocks, and broad and smooth

> where the wives of Troy and their lovely daughters
> would wash their glistening robes in the old days,
> the days of peace before the sons of Achaea came ...
> past these, they raced. (In Manguel, 2010, 250).

Past these they race still, with students from the Naval War Academy no doubt rooting for Hector, but hopefully recognising a 'loser' when they see one!

Aeneas: The Pious Man at Arms
The Aeneid, Virgil

It was Virgil's great genius to use an established literary form, the epic, and change its focus. His hero is the first to be recognisably one of us, unlike Achilles, who remains inextricably mythic in our imagination. Aeneas is a man of many contradictions who can be cruel to those who love him and merciless when crossed, but who is also demonstrably vulnerable. Virgil takes us into the life of a warrior who we will never meet in reality, then reveals his inner self. The more we learn about him, the more we can relate to him. The more conflicted Aeneas becomes, the more universal his appeal. It is his humanity we admire, the self-doubts and self-betrayals and the unspoken but all too evident psychological exhaustion. There are times when Aeneas would love to have been left alone by the gods and excused his mission. It is Virgil's genius as a writer to allow the reader to judge this fallible hero. In the end, more often than not, we forgive him—we even forgive his part in the death of Turnus, the only other finely-drawn character in the epic.

And so, we imagine, do the gods. After all, of all the heroes of Troy, the gods chose Aeneas to lead the exiles into the future because they knew what we only gradually find out in the course of the poem: Aeneas' importance is as a man, rather than a mere warrior. And the difference highlights the tonal contrast with the *Iliad*, that almost biblical text which no Roman aristocrat could escape reading. Centuries later, the playwright Bernard Shaw would pen a comedy, *Arms and the Man*, to illustrate the paradoxical ways in which war itself (arms) can mould the man (the warrior). Homer had taken war as a given, a necessary evil, a viewpoint that allows his characters only very limited scope to influence war itself. Virgil is much more 'modern' in showing

37

war as an evil but sometimes a necessary one (without it there would have been no founding of Rome). And by their own actions men can make war less wicked. Arms and the Man really are conjoined. The relationship is dialectical, and whereas Shaw explores the comic elements of that dialectic, Virgil explores the tragic. The great writers have explored war in both its manifestations which is why it is not Homer, but Virgil who is recognised as the real father of today's war fiction.

Virgil had the fortune—good or ill—to be writing in the shadow of Homer. As such, he sought to be true both to the greatest poet of the classical world, and also to his own times, which were as distant from the Homeric Age as we are from the heroes of the mediaeval romances, the *chansons de geste*. You can see why our Victorian forefathers loved Aeneas and why we are much more ambivalent about him; 'pious' seems to be the best word to describe his character. Readers are trapped in their own time as much as the authors they read; neither can escape history. And we look upon Aeneas far more sceptically than the generation that fought for Britain's imperial destiny. The Victorians found in *The Aeneid* a Victorian hero, a virtuous man who carries his father out of Troy even though he unaccountably loses sight of his wife; a warrior whose exploits have already impressed the Carthaginians and Dido, whose womanly wiles he will escape, just as he escaped Troy; the founder of a nation who battles against the Latins and finally defeats the greatest of them, Turnus, a man every bit as noble as Hector. It was fine by them that Aeneas should be a bit of a cad, overcoming his sexual desire as Englishmen were expected to do when confronted with the conflicting needs of desire and duty. It was fine by them that Aeneas was an Imperialist who was quite happy to expropriate the land of 'a lesser breed'. Our Victorian forefathers loved his self-denying nature, his absolute obedience to the gods, his single-minded vision of a future in which Rome would triumph over every adversity and every other people; his piety. Many must have thought Aeneas positively 'British' in his devotion to duty.

But 'pious' should not be conflated with 'patriotic' as it sometimes is. Aeneas is frequently portrayed as a patriotic prig, an ancient Rupert Brooke who is fated to die on foreign fields, or if not die, fight most of his professional life on them with undisguised pride of country. Robert Fagles tells a story of how Yeats on befriending a 'plain sailor man' helped him to read some of Virgil's poetry. When Yeats asked him what he thought of the hero, the sailor replied: 'what hero?' 'What hero?

Why, Aeneas', replied Yeats. Said the sailor: 'Ach, hero? Him a hero! Bigod, t'ought he waz a priest.' (Fagles, 396–397).

But the Latin word pietas had a variety of meanings: patriotic is one of them, to be sure. Another is pious in the way we now understand the term, faithful to the gods. And equally important, it means 'familial', fiercely loyal to family (especially his father, the *pater familias*). And it also meant loyal: loyal to those who fought with him, the 'band of brothers' who were also 'family' of a kind, and often in a soldier's eye, closer than those to whom he is bound by blood. It is precisely Aeneas' individuality as a faithful son, a proud patriot, an inspiring leader of men who invest their faith absolutely in him that allows him to speak to us in a way that Achilles never can.

The main importance of Aeneas is what his character tells us about duty. The very word etymologically comes from the Latin *debere* which means 'to owe', and one can distinguish at least three ideas of duty in Virgil's poem which define Aeneas the man, and distinguish him from his main protagonists. The characters are all individuals, even if many of them are under-developed as we would understand the term: they lack an inner psychic life. But duty is what unites them all, and Aeneas' very special sense of duty is what differentiates him from everyone else. Most of the warriors are dutiful in the sense of serving the community. They may be the purveyors of violence, on a hair-trigger response to any perceived threat to their status, but they also serve their communities—they have a moral character, even when engaged in amoral acts. On another level they acknowledge a debt they owe to their families. Sons respect their fathers, and feel intensely loyal to the ancestors. Because they feel themselves in debt to them the debt is central to their very identity. In the case of Aeneas, his ancestors are far away, dispossessed of their city, Troy, but not its name. He too is jealous of his status as a warrior, and mindful of his duty to his father, whom Gide memorably remarked was a burden he had to bear all his life, long after Anchises died. But it is his fierce sense of duty that makes Aeneas the man he is, as well as an archetypal warrior in the eyes of many soldiers, even today. Ultimately, however, his real duty is to himself. In honouring his nation, his family and his followers, he is proving that he is truly in possession of a great soul, and because he is judged by others by the purity of his soul, so he is required to disregard his own personal losses, and serve the interests of others. In order to be honoured by others, he must never dishonour himself. He becomes what others want him to be: the hero they need, but perhaps do not always deserve.

Aeneas has a strikingly modern understanding of duty. Today's officers are taught that duty can only be understood in relation to selfhood, and the different ways in which selfhood is constructed through the recognition of others. But it is also a difficult balancing act, because duty to the ideal, unquestioning obedience to the dictates of state, or in Aeneas' case the demands of Jupiter, also comes at a price. 'Every subject's duty is the King's, but every subject's soul is his own', the disguised King Henry tells a doubting soldier on the eve of Agincourt. Is Aeneas ever in danger of losing his soul? If Virgil thought so, he did not live long enough to tell us (he died before completing the poem). The Romans certainly did not think so. The *Aeneid* became propaganda almost at once and Aeneas a paragon of the dutiful soldier.

And a lot will depend, of course, on what a soldier thinks of war itself. Virgil's own attitude has long been debated. Was he a closet pacifist who sold out by writing an epic poem in which war (arms) shares equal billing with humanity (the man every Roman wished to become)? Some have argued that in creating a hero for the times in which he privately did not believe, he bequeathed the western world a defining stereotype: a divided warrior who is not entirely in love with his own profession, a character who is believable because he is conflicted.

I think this all misses the point. Montaigne, a former soldier, came to hate war (as many warriors often do). If war is a necessary evil, it is important that we never fall in love with it entirely. It is often the warrior's unhappy fate to fall out of love with war, to recognise it as an evil which they embrace only because others (less conflicted than themselves) often do. Virgil is not taking sides. No one before the late modern era—with its revolutionary dream of a world at peace thanks to democracy or commerce or the humanitarian impulse—could have imagined a world without war. But Virgil has the insight to tell a tale of arms and the man—for war is what a man makes of it. The key scene occurs in Book VI when Aeneas descends into the underworld to visit his father Anchises, first passing through a region defined by the Judgement of Minos as the place most fitting for those who have lived wretched lives. There he sees warriors famous in the ancient world.

> Here Tydeus come to meet him, Parthenopaeus
> shining in arms, and Adrastus' pallid phantom. Here
> mourned in the world above and fallen dead in battle,

> sons of Dardanus, chiefs arrayed in a long ranked line.
> Seeing them all he groaned—Glaucus, Medon, Thersilochus,
> Antenor's three sons, and the priest of Ceres, Polyboetes,
> Idaeus too, still with chariot, still with gear in hand.
> Their spirits crowding around Aeneas, left and right,
> beg him to linger longer .... (*Aeneid*, VI, 557–65).

These names have long since been forgotten, but they would have been well-known to any educated Roman reader: Parthenopaeus, one of the Seven against Thebes (the story we know from Aeschylus' play of the same name), and for Aeneas more familiar faces such as Adrastus, a Trojan warrior and Idaeus, a charioteer of Aeneas' father, Priam. But the figure who disconcerts Aeneas the most is Diopholus, another of Priam's sons, whose face has been hacked to pieces, his ears ripped from his head and his nostrils slashed, presenting a perfect figure of misery, not enhanced by what Virgil calls, 'a disgraceful wound' which forces him to lurk in the shadows to hide both his deformity and his shame. What is the cause of his disgrace? After Paris' death, Diopholus took Helen as his wife but was betrayed by her to Menelaus once Troy fell—Menelaus had taken the standard revenge of the cuckolded husband: cutting off the nose and ears, and no doubt the genitals as well (Homer, far less modest than Virgil, would have given us the full monty). Aeneas learns (and this is the message Virgil wishes to convey) that those who engage in war for the wrong reasons, out of desire for revenge or lust for loot, live a life without merit and will pay the ultimate price after their death. Diopholus is condemned to endure eternity in the Underworld, wearing useless armour and displaying his shameful wound. Aeneas looks in vain for Achilles and Hector, Patroclus and Ajax, men who have lived a meritorious life, a life which has enhanced that of their friends. They are absent because they are elsewhere, in a better place; they merit, quite clearly, a better fate.

Aeneas arrives in Italy to find an elderly king who is willing to let his only child, a daughter, marry him. All the auguries are favourable for a peaceful co-existence between the Trojans that Aeneas has led into exile and the Latins; intermarriage will help them both forge a new race. The problem is that the king's daughter already has a suitor, Turnus, who has the support of her mother, and Turnus is soon able to inflame passions and take advantage of local suspicions of the strangers in their midst. He exploits the most innocent of mistakes when Aeneas' son, Ascanius, out on a hunt, unknowingly shoots the pet deer of an Italian farmer, Tyrrhus. Ascanius can hardly be blamed for his ignorance, and the Trojans are quick to offer compensation. The Italians prefer instead to rush to arms, and yield the moral high ground. The reason for war is spurious, and the king, instead of standing by Aeneas as he is minded to, abdicates responsibility in turn by allowing Turnus to lead them into battle. *Furor impius*, irrational blood lust rather than piety, has unleashed a conflict that will only end in Turnus' own death.

Aeneas wins over a local king Evander to his cause (his village is the site of the future Rome) and recruits the king's son Pallas, a lucky break because Pallas is a brave warrior and noble man. The battle line of Latin heroes is strikingly different and could not be more brutally arraigned. First to the march is 'brutal Mezentius, scorner of gods', and Turnus, who Virgil sketches deftly in a hideous travesty of war:

> Triple plumed, his high helmet raises up a chimera
> With all the fires of Etna blasting from its throat
> And roaring all the more, its searing flames more deadly
> The more blood flows, and the battle grows more fierce.
> (*Aeneid*, Section 9, lines 11–14).

And finally a woman, 'the warrior girl, Camilla' ('a virgin seasoned to bear the rough work of battle'), one of course who has no business on a battlefield in the eyes of the ancient world, and who is fated to die fighting for a hopeless cause. All of these characters will meet their end (Mezentius in Book X, Camilla in Book XI). Turnus' 'shade', we are told in the very last line of the poem, will go 'with a groan of outrage' to the underworld to join Diaphobus, not Achilles, in the company of those who engage in unjust wars. For Virgil is also offering us not only the first pious warrior, but the first warrior to fight a 'just war'.

The battles that ensue merely reinforce the message: only Aeneas can deliver victory. Brave though they are, Trojans like Nisus or Euryalus cannot prevail, and it is only when in Book X Aeneas himself enters the field that the war's fortunes turn in their favour. It is too late to save Pallas who is killed by Turnus. Aeneas' mourning for Evander's son is clearly heartfelt. Aeneas knows that he has betrayed Evander by putting an end to his 'own empty hopes' of glory.

> Unlucky man you must
> behold the agonising burial of your son...
> is this how we return? Our longed-for triumph?
> (*Aeneid*, VII, Section 7, lines 21-23)

It is a question that raises, in the most direct way, some other questions about war and its human cost, and Aeneas has reason himself to question the loss of those he loves most: Creusa, his wife; Dido, his lover; and now Pallas, his friend. To make sense of these losses, he must view them all as 'collateral damage' in the fulfilment of his own destiny and that of Rome.

In the last three books of the epic we see Aeneas at his martial best, despatching his enemies with clinical ruthlessness, cutting down the mighty Theron, hurling his javelin through Pharus' mouth, and ripping out the breast and breast plate of Maeon, both at once. Later we see quite a different warrior. On learning of the death of Pallas at Turnus' hand, he goes berserk, as soldiers often do, showing no mercy to those who beg for it. When Magus does so, he grabs his neck and digs his sword blade deep down to the hilt, and when Tarquitus does the same, he smashes his head to the ground, abandoning him to the carrion birds. And when, after seeing his brother Lucheus killed, Liger begs for his life, Aeneas tells him ironically that no brother should desert a brother, reinforcing the 'moral' he wishes to impart by carving wide open Liger's chest with its 'hidden cache of life'. What makes these hundred lines so startling is that Aeneas' wrath is even more alarming than Achilles' after he learns of Patroclus' death. At least Achilles suffers from a deep feeling of guilt that he allowed Patroclus to wear his armour and be killed in place of himself. Aeneas has no reason to feel any responsibility for Pallas' fate: he died in a fair conflict. Here Virgil is showing us that *furor impius* can strike a pious man, too.

Virgil does not spare us the atrocities Aeneas commits in blind rage. He acts very badly, and he and we know it. We shouldn't judge a Roman warrior by our own standards, of course, but we can judge him by his own. There is a plurality of values and norms just as there is a plurality of cultures and temperaments; but a plurality is not an infinity. The number of values a human society may embrace and still retain a semblance of humanity is finite (though we may never agree on the exact number) which is why (argued Isaiah Berlin) we can understand why others pursue the actions they do, or what it would be like, in their circumstances, to pursue them ourselves. Even when he is dishonouring his good name, Aeneas is recognisably more human than Achilles. None of us, I suspect, can attempt to cast ourselves in the role of Achilles, but Aeneas is a recognisable type, and he is demonstrably human in his passions. We may never understand Achilles, but we can

Aeneas, and we are in a better position as a result to condemn him when he acts out of character, when he steps out of his allotted role and is in danger of losing touch with the humanity that makes it possible for both of us to recognise each other (Haidt, 2011, 317).

And Virgil also shows us Aeneas at his best. His recklessness does not last long. Eventually he is so sickened by the slaughter that he proposes the conflict be settled in a single hand-to-hand fight with Turnus. But Turnus prefers the war to continue as before. He lives for combat, in a way that Aeneas clearly does not. Aeneas throws his spear, piercing Turnus' armour and entering his leg. Turnus asks to be spared, and would have been but for Aeneas seeing the trophy he has taken from Pallas after his death. Oblivious to appeals for mercy, Aeneas thrusts his sword into Turnus' chest.

Turnus, claims Bloom, is the real hero of the second half of the *Aeneid*, as Dido is of the first. Virgil was not writing the *Turneid*, but we can suspect he might have been happier doing so. Certainly, Turnus is a more attractive figure than Aeneas in many respects, as Hector is in the *Iliad*. One presumes that the Naval Academy cadets would be rooting for Turnus, too. And Bloom also observes, quite correctly, that Turnus' death is more poignant than Hector's. 'Hector dies with a Hemingway-esque or Spanish grandeur', he writes; Turnus dies miserably. 'He stands defenceless, unable to speak, trapped grotesquely in a waking nightmare. Aeneas hurls a spear into a mere object, not a man, and the poem breaks off abruptly with gratuitous butchery.' (Bloom, 1987, 37).

But then it is very difficult to see what else he could have done. Ever the realist, Aeneas could not afford to let Turnus return home and begin the war anew, this time at a time of his own choosing. Well, this is what we would tell ourselves. Of course, we also tell ourselves that killing Turnus will not restore Pallas to life, either. Reasons of state and reasons of humanity should collude, not collide. But Aeneas is not a modern man with a twenty-first-century sensibility. The idea of the sensitive warrior, long a cliché of popular story-telling, is seldom one truthful to war itself.

What does Aeneas feel after Turnus' death? The classical world was not given to psychological introspection but human nature changes very little over the centuries, even if cultural instincts are always in flux. Aeneas is likely to have been no different from any other warrior over the ages. He is angry with Turnus because it is his friend, and not he, who has paid for the founding of Rome. The guilt of survival is very real, and it is natural to turn against others as a consequence. Aeneas is mourning because something 'sacred' has been stolen from him—friendship. Afterwards, Aeneas would have felt the same sadness that Achilles does after his murderous blood lust is satiated: sadness for Hector, the bravest of the Trojans, as well as for Priam, who has paid the ultimate price for the 'abduction' of Helen with the loss of his eldest and dearest son. And we must always remember that sadness, though real, is also a default mode. Aeneas will kill Turnus again if he must; to do otherwise would be to let the side down; his friends, his gods and of course ultimately Rome.

Virgil never really describes Aeneas. He is faceless, and faceless, too, to the reader, because he is impossible to 'read'. But although we are never told what he looks like, we are perpetually told what he is looking *at*—always beyond the horizon, to the destiny of Rome. Looking at Rome requires him to bear a burden on his shoulder that is always crushing him, stifling his individuality, robbing him of a personal life.

It is Virgil's genius to give the reader the gift of seeing the future that Aeneas cannot. For time and again in the poem Aeneas is blind to the milestones on the journey to Rome. Anchises tells his son that the purpose of Rome is empire—to teach the ways of peace to those they conquer, to tame the proud. Again, the reader would know by the Augustine Age that the empire was now 'eternal', and at least some would have grasped that it came at great cost. And perhaps a perceptive Roman reader, in tune with Virgil's own sensibilities, might have appreciated the bitter irony of the last scene in the poem, the fact that Rome's birth is marked by murder, an unworthy act of violence by a worthy man. Aeneas finds himself ensnared by the paradox that lies at the heart of the story—the vengeance that brought about the destruction of Troy marks the birth of the second Troy, Rome. There is no escaping vengeance; blood calls for blood, and violent death remains the story of history. Hector and Turnus both fall victim, one to the self-centredness of Paris, the other to the selflessness of Aeneas—but in both cases the outcome is the same.

Hadji Murat: Confrontation with the Self
Hadji Murat, Leo Tolstoy

The exploits of Aeneas speak for themselves. The *Aeneid* brings to life a whole human world of passion and courage with which we can still identify 2,000 years later. Most novelists are instinctively heroic themselves. Some, in thin and not so thinly disguised guises, are the characters they describe, such as Tolstoy himself in first of the *Sevastopol Sketches*. For Tolstoy was a soldier who in his youth fought both in Chechnya and the Crimea. No doubt this explains why he remains the supreme war writer and why *War and Peace* remains the supreme war tale, though his short novella *Hadji Murat* (1912) comes near to challenging its pre-eminence.

Aeneas himself is a lonely, divided soul all too aware of the terrible personal cost he will pay as an agent of destiny. Hadji Murat is different. He is fighting not against destiny but against the enemy within; his is a battle between his own divided loyalties, torn between desire for revenge and love of family. Tolstoy exposes these divisions in a ruthlessly economical way. Although this short novella is crowded with minor characters, from the Chechen leader Shamil, to the Russian Tsar, Nicholas I, it is almost entirely about the story's eponymous hero.

Tolstoy draws no moral and makes no bold claims about history or war or cultural misunderstanding. Sometimes he allows the historical record to speak for itself. He incorporates into the story actual historical documentation like Hadji Murat's account of his own life, and Vornotosv's letter to Chernyshev (chapters 11–13) We can infer his contempt for the Russian scorched-earth tactics in Chechnya, but we are largely left with our own thoughts on his hero, a man hopelessly torn by conflicting thoughts and loyalties.

Tolstoy wrote in his diary that he wished to draw a complex hero who was both devil and angel, sage and fool, strong man and weakling (in terms of moral courage) (*Hadji Murat*, xxiv). The weakness, fanaticism and savagery come from the conflict within him, and what Tolstoy shows us is that for the man of war, the only release from that conflict is combat. Combat is the ultimate form of catharsis for the true warrior; even if he does not survive, his memory will remain of his deeds. If he is lucky, writers will even remind others of his end as representative of the person he was. And when the end comes for Hadji, he really is ennobled. He is purged of anger and desire, and even his passion for revenge. He is spared the conflicting passions and emotions that have dogged him at the end of his life. He dies the brave man he always was and leaves the world finally, true to himself.

We first meet Hadji on a cold November night in 1851 riding into Makhket, a Chechen village hostile to the Russians. The Russians had fought a long war of attrition in their attempt to subdue what we now call the trans-Caucasus, with its patchwork of ethnic rivalries and murderous, never-ending tribal feuds: cut-throat rivalries within the same family, vendettas within the same tribe, hostilities between different tribes of the same ethnicity, hostility between tribes of different ethnicities, and the near-permanent stand-off between all these and whoever happens to rule—or, in this case, wishes to rule—Russia. Murat, one of the greatest of the Chechen warriors, and the former right hand man of their leader, Shamil, has come to submit himself to the Russians after breaking with his leader. He briefly finds shelter with one of the families in the village but has to flee. War produces divided loyalties. Shamil was a charismatic leader who in real life united most of the Circassian tribes in a *jihad* against the Russians until he was finally defeated and captured eight years after the date of Tolstoy's story. But he was as cruel and capricious as the man he was fighting, Nicholas I, and he only maintained his own position by dividing and ruling his own supporters. This is a society where scores are settled by death, and anyone and everyone can be betrayed. In the end, Hadji will be killed by a party of Cossacks who number among their ranks Akhmet Khan, whose father was one of his old enemies.

A day after arriving in the village, he crosses over to the Russian lines largely unhindered even by the Chechen horsemen who somewhat half-heartedly try to detain him. He has enemies aplenty, as he knows, but he is also a hero in the eyes of most Chechens. He is their most ferocious champion, and by far their most successful. He has survived so far partly by choosing his enemies well, and with the Russians as his new friends, he hopes to return, make Shamil his prisoner and eventually unite the Chechen nation under his own rule. Hadji cannot escape his times or his culture, of course, and we may be inclined to view both as rather disturbing. He dreams only of personal revenge, after all. 'He dreamt of descending on Shamil with his men to the sound of singing and cries of "Hadji Murat comes upon you!"'. He dreams of seizing

47

Shamil and his wives and hearing the wives weeping and sobbing (Ibid., 358). And he expects, in his naivety, that the Russians with whom he has been at war for years will allow him to unite their enemies.

Tolstoy wants us to see his lack of political calculation as redeeming. To dream such dreams can be a symptom of small-mindedness, but it can also be a manifestation of nobility. The Chechen way is a hard one; it is a warrior society, and each warrior is entitled to dream of revenge. It has an honour code, if for us a very primal one. And Tolstoy never ceases to remind us that the Russian dreams of military glory are equally empty. Russian soldiers too dream of hand-to-hand fighting with swords; they accept the fiction that the war they are fighting is a medieval exchange of blows between warriors, each keen to prove his mettle. The reality is more depressing. We can see the death of the young soldier Avdeev, a pathetic young conscript who dies, so his wife and mother are told in an official letter, 'defending the Tsar, Fatherland, and the Orthodox Faith' far from home. He is killed in a brief skirmish just at the point where Murat gives himself over into Russian hands.

By then the conquest of the trans-Caucasus entailed no daring raids or set piece battles but a relentless advance involving forest clearance and the destruction of food supplies. The Russian policy is to destroy the Chechens' homes and to harry them with raids; we witness one of those raids, recounted by Tolstoy in his usual didactic fashion. The village to which they lay waste is by chance the one in which Hadji has spent his last night before going over to the Russian side. The son of his host who had helped him is bayoneted in the back. The son's grand-father, who survives, contemplates the ruins of his life. He has even lost the cherry trees he had planted and the beehives he has cultivated, which were an essential part of his life. 'The wailing of women sounded in every house and in every square.... the young children wailed with their mothers... the hungry animals howled too ....' (*Hadji Murat*, 422). It is the same sound of wailing, of course, that Hadji had dreamed of in the night he spent in the village—the wailing of Shamil's wives after the death of their husband at his own hands.

The world from which this Chechen warrior emerges is not one with which it is easy for a western reader to identify today. Tolstoy never published the work in his lifetime, aware perhaps of how it might be received. Hadji is a man of his culture and his time—a bleak and unrelenting one—but his vitality allows him to be true to one, and rise above the other. Tolstoy wanted us to admire him and, in our sympathy for him, we are perhaps in danger of overlooking the world from which he emerges in the opening pages of the tale. It is not our world, any more than it is Tolstoy's, but if we find ourselves rooting for Hadji—as we must, indeed, as we *ought*—it is because of Tolstoy's portrait of him. His intelligence and charm are never in doubt. This is probably not true of the real life character on which Tolstoy based his hero, but it is certainly true of the man portrayed in the tale. He masters every situation, impressing everyone he meets with his nobility (a touch, certainly, of the nineteenth-century romanticisation of the noble savage). He is a man who commands the loyalty of his followers and wins the respect of his Russian hosts including the most sympathetic, Butler, who is able to appreciate Hadji's qualities and pay him the respect one soldier owes to another he admires. What distinguishes him from practically everyone else in the story is his essential good nature. Hadji may be ferocious in battle but by his own light, he is not a dishonourable man. The Russians had expected 'someone grim, cold and distant, yet here was a totally unaffected person, smiling so good-naturedly that he did not seem to be a stranger at all but an old familiar friend.' (*Hadji Murat*, 363).

Perhaps the exaggerated courtesy his new friends extend him is that of a people who are not entirely sure of their own authenticity as warriors. The young Colonel Voronsky, whose father is the Commanding Officer, asks a common soldier whether he has heard of their guest. 'That I have, sir. We have given him many a licking.' 'Yes, and he's given us as good as he's got.' (*Hadji Murat*, 365). It would not be too much of a stretch to say that Hadji is lionised, especially by the bored and sequestered wives of the senior officers on the frontier, who adopt him as a dinner guest. They too, are seduced by his manner and good humour—and of course, by his looks. He has the look of a warrior, which many of their husbands do not. Even Butler, the most sympathetic Russian soldier, is a bit of a phony. His sole consolation for the boredom of frontier life is to dress in a Circassian costume, and to ride his horse like a native. With his friend Bogdanovich, he has twice ridden out and laid in ambush, as Chechen tribesmen do, but they returned to camp without killing or capturing anyone. Even in play-acting, they fail to play the part successfully.

Given that Tolstoy stacks the cards against his own side, we have to ask whether we would actually like to meet Hadji in real life. He is after all a warrior, and we are now suspicious of the type even at home.

And some readers will not find him as admirable as the author. Indeed, the book is difficult because it asks us to take sides with a man who is historically off-side with his own sensibilities. Can you admire Hadji without colluding with him, or to put it differently, 'can you enjoy the book without being a closet warrior yourself?' (if only one who battles through books). At a dinner party that the Russian Captain holds in his honour, someone recounts an incident in which he ordered the killing of twenty-six captives. 'It can't be helped', is the general response, 'À la guerre comme à la guerre. War is war.' (*Hadji Murat*, 381).

In this world of treachery no-one trusts the other. Hadji may be politically naïve but he has a native cunning. He knows what to say. He has come, he reassures his Russian captors, to serve the Tsar to the last drop of his blood—he knows well enough that Vorontzov will not believe him. But while he may not be believed, he may still be needed—at least for now. In this world of deception and deceit, appearances and words count for much. Hadji has entered a world with which he is unfamiliar. He is always thinking of the past, of the slights and humiliations imposed on him by Shamil. He expects the Russians to recall that he had once been loyal to them, twelve years earlier, until his enemy Ahmed Khan denounced him. But Vorontsov, if he had ever known this, has forgotten. Russia's eyes are pinned entirely on the future, and in its world, there is no place for existential passions like revenge. It is brutally instrumental. Enemies can be captured, killed, turned or suborned. The pressing and only fear that occupies Hadji's mind is that he may shame himself as he once did when he ran away from a camp of an old enemy, Hamzad. For the Russians there is no shame in betraying friends or using them, or even running away to live to fight another day, and from the start they intend to use Hadji for their own purposes. The only shame they feel is in failure.

The distance between these two worlds can never be closed, as Voronztov's *aide de camp* discovers when he questions Hadji's faithful retainers. Each is different from the other, but all put loyalty to Hadji first, and it is their loyalty which allows them to desert Shamil, if not with a good conscience, at least with a certainty of what must be done. The Russians find Hadji and his followers difficult to read. One is a young man, always frivolous, always playing with life—his own and that of others. Coming over to the Russian side for him is a game, and another game will be played another day. For the others, loyalty to

Hadji trumps everything; they will follow him unquestioningly wherever he goes; loyalty to Hadji does not imply disloyalty to Shamil, whom they still regard as a holy man. They can live with two conflicting thoughts at the same time, but for how long? Only Hadji remains impossible to read, and he still is, even now. The extraordinary power of the book is the way in which Hadji deflects all attempts to analyse him, and so remains defiantly his own man to the end.

There are two other themes in Tolstoy's characterisation of his hero. The first is the great warrior's love of his family which Vorontzov mentions in his letter to the Minister of War, revealing Hadji's hope that the Russians will ransom his wife and children. The second is his devotion to Islam. Neither of these will he ever betray. And in the end it is Russia's failure to come through for him and his increasing concern for his family, especially his worthless son, that persuades him to desert and return to Shamil.

At this point the Russians are beginning to lose patience with him. They have placed him under house arrest at Nukha, a town on the southern slopes of the Caucasus, a hundred miles east of Tiflis. No longer trusting the Russians, he tries to rescue his family with the help of tribesmen who have remained loyal to him. But the plot never hatches. The tribesmen are too scared to come over to his side. In the end, Hadji resolves to return to the mountains, perhaps to fight on, perhaps to surrender, for he is ever mindful of the tale of the falcon which was caught and lived for a time among men before it returned to its home in the mountains. It returned wearing jesses on its legs, and the other falcons spurned it. When it failed to return to the world of men, they tore it to pieces. And in a sense this is to be Hadji's own fate. The skill of Tolstoy's characterisation is that he makes him simultaneously pathetic and magnificent. His death, like his life, invites us to see him in both manifestations.

His companions check their rifles, sharpen their swords and daggers and grease their blades with lard. They ride out with a Cossack escort that always accompanies them whenever they leave the town. Turning on the escort, they dispatch most of them, leaving the others to return with news of their escape. They are soon overtaken and find themselves surrounded, forced to make a final stand. A large troop of Cossacks catch up with them, and the end is almost certain. When it comes a few paragraphs later, Tolstoy gives us perhaps the most extraordinary death scene in literature:

...summoning the last remnants of his strength, he lifted himself above the rampart and fired his pistol at a man running towards him. He hit him and the man fell. Then he crawled completely out of the ditch and, with his dagger drawn and limping badly, went straight at the enemy. Several shots rang out. He staggered and fell. A number of militiamen rushed with a triumphal yell towards his fallen body. But what they supposed was a dead body suddenly stirred. First his blood-stained, shaven head, its papakha gone, then his body lifted; then, holding onto a tree, Hadji Murat pulled himself fully up. He looked so terrifying that the advancing men stopped dead. But suddenly he gave a shudder, staggered from the tree, and like a scythed thistle fell full length on his face and moved no more.

He did not move, but could still feel, and when Hadj-Hah, the first to reach him, struck him across the head with his great dagger, he felt he was being hit on the head on with a hammer and failed to understand who was doing this and why. This was the last conscious link with his body. He felt no more, and the object that was trampled and slashed by his enemies had no longer any connection with him. Hadj-Hah put a foot on the body's back, with two strokes hacked off its head and rolled it carefully away with his foot so as not to get blood on his boot. Blood gushed over the grass, scarlet from the neck arteries, black from the head. (*Hadji Murat*, 463)

The Cossacks ride back with Hadji's head in a saddlebag, its face still showing in the set of gnarled blue lips, despite many gashes and wounds, 'a childish, good-natured expression'. He died like a real man, the Russians are told. '"It can happen to anyone", said Butler, not knowing what to say. "That's war."' (*Hadji Murat*, 455)

Writers acknowledge no constraint other than that of language itself on their attempts to impose some kind of order on the world but it does not follow from the fact that language fails to describe reality that all attempts to do so fail equally. In this respect, writes Terry Eagleton, there is a unique kinship between fiction and morality. The author shapes the reader's moral vision by reorganising reality. The real world is held at arm's length so that certain moral truths about it may more effectively be brought to light. This is not a lie. You cannot lie in fiction because of the contract with the reader. The reader does not expect or assume you are interested in being truthful. Heroes never deceive us, though they may deceive themselves (Eagleton, 2012, 145–6). The whole point about fiction is to give us a moral truth which is quite different from the historical truth. Novelists may have given up trying to do even that (O'Brien—'if there is a moral, don't believe it') but the fact is that the reader, at least the intelligent or discerning one, will draw one whether the author likes it or not. This is part of the contract, too, which is why fiction can be truer than life. History got it right at Trafalgar, allowing Nelson to be dispatched by a French bullet (it is the exits, not entrances that count most). But it got it hopelessly wrong when Byron died of fever in Greece rather than on the battlefield, and when Rupert Brooke died in the field, but not the field of battle. Fiction can re-imagine the fate of its characters, the better to tell the moral it wants to convey. In that respect, of course, writers are often kinder to their characters than history might have been (Eagleton, 2012, 145–6).

In many novels, death in battle constitutes the nucleus of a life story. For Hadji it merely provides an epilogue and this perhaps is what distinguishes the warrior from other brave men. Tolstoy begins the story with an analogy, one of the most moving in literature. The narrator recalls a midsummer walk through a colourful field where he noticed a Tartar thistle in full bloom. In his attempt to pick it up he is pricked at every turn. It does not yield easily and by the time he has plucked the flower, the stalk is in shreds and the flower itself no longer seems as fresh and beautiful as before. How bravely had it defended itself, and how dearly had it sold its life. On his way home he comes across a Tartar thistle bush that has been crushed by a cartwheel but still stands defiantly, still unbowed. And so we arrive at the story that the narrator has to tell about one of the greatest warriors in the literary canon.

Hadji is always at war with whatever makes him weak. His love for his wife is touching, but we never see or know whether it is deserved; his love for his son certainly is not because the son loves Shamil more, and despises his own father. The divided loyalties without are reflections of the divided loyalties within, which may prevent any soldier from committing fully to friends, country or cause. War is a power game, and there is always someone in power, exercising it over others, or robbing them of the chance to live their own lives. Hadji is an authentic Chechen hero. He is not prone to the psychological interrogation in which Tolstoy's very modern Russian characters engage, but he is a man frightened of failing to be himself. And when he dies he is never more alive, precisely because he has been spared the pain of confronting himself.

Hadji has a quality which the novella's other characters lack—from Shamil, who is merely a murderous fanatic, to Nicholas I, who in

Tolstoy's portrait corresponds fairly closely to the man we know from history: mean-spirited and reactionary to the core. The admirable characteristics which Homer gives Achilles and Hector, writes Bloom, are brought together in Tolstoy's hero. Nevertheless, he manifests neither the murderous rage against mortality of Achilles, nor Hector's collapse into passive acceptance of his fate at the end. Hadji goes out fighting. Indeed his death is one of the more heroic and harrowing scenes in literature. Tolstoy gives us the apotheosis of the hero, not a lament for his defeat (Bloom, 1996, 338).

Every warrior lives a provisional life—not because he does not know whether he will make it back from the battlefield but because he does not know how he will act, or react, under pressure. He is perpetually a 'work in progress', like a book that is still being written. He is often unknown to himself. This is ironic, of course. The ultimate irony is that he does not entirely live his own life, for it is also lived by the reader. His life doesn't even end with his death. He lives on posthumously in the memory of other people. He is what the future makes of him, a bundle of clothes on the floor in the case of Tolstoy's young officer Vladimir at Sevastopol, or an inspiring sacrifice in the case of Hemingway's Robert Jordan. In both cases it is all a matter of luck—death really does undo some, and make others. Nothing illustrates our own contingency better than mortality—few deaths are freely chosen. Hadji's is.

And the real Hadji Murat, who would otherwise have been forgotten long ago, lives on because a Russian writer took up his pen. His death is the perfect ending to what comes as close as any to the perfect war story. It is sad and unyielding, and devoid of sentimentality. The experience allows us to see Hadji's defiance not as a vice but as a human quality that never leaves him, not even at the point of death. He is in every way specific to his culture, in his clothes, his attitudes and his attachment to his religion, but he is also recognisably a man. That is why all literature is universal, illuminating human nature at precisely the point at which it seems to be most parochial.

'Lucky Jack' Aubrey: The Warrior as a Leader of Men

Aubrey–Maturin Series, Patrick O'Brian

Jack Aubrey, of all the great naval heroes, is by far the most believable. There are not, to be frank, that many. Before O'Brian, C. S. Forester's Hornblower was the only major literary naval figure popular with many writers, including Hemingway. When the series begins, he is a junior Captain; by the end he is a full Admiral. But like many literary heroes he is somewhat flat, always himself, with a pre-set, unalterable nature. He is more unusual than most action heroes in being especially introspective, internally reserved, given to black moods and prone to (but never in danger of succumbing to) self-doubt. But that means we know he will never face a moment of internal reckoning. If Hornblower has a personality, it is not his own, but the one Forester gives him, in which he is very similar to another Napoleonic figure, Sharpe, in Bernard Cornwell's series of novels. Try as Hornblower or Sharpe do to know themselves, they and we know only as much as their authors will allow.

O'Brian's Aubrey is different. He helped to revivify a genre that had come to seem clichéd and tired. O'Brian re-invigorated the idea of what a traditional naval hero could be, in a world which is by turns romantic and brutal. Altogether he wrote twenty books featuring Aubrey as the hero (one was left uncompleted at his death). The very first, *Master and Commander* (1970), which introduced Aubrey to the world, is one of the best. The film of the same name which came out in 2003, starring Russell Crowe as Aubrey, took the storyline from several books, including *HMS Surprise* (1973), *The Fortune of War* (1979), and *The Letter of Marque* (1988). As the novels span a large part of O'Brian's writing career, and as Crowe's performance is considered to be definitive, it seems sensible to draw my portrait from these novels, including *The Far Side of the World*, which also appears in the film's title. This choice has one other advantage. O'Brian's books were published in the same chronological sequence as the events they describe. *Master and Commander* is set in 1800, *The Far Side of the World* after the conclusion of the Napoleonic wars.

Like Sherlock Holmes, Aubrey has his Watson, an Irish-Catalan doctor, Stephen Maturin, who is not only the ship's surgeon but also a

British spy. Like Watson he is a writer. But he is unlike him in one critical respect: he doesn't record Aubrey's exploits, so much as live them. He records his thoughts, which wander off at times into philosophical reflections. As Maturin notes, for a student of human nature, there is no better subject of study than a ship: its crew shut up together, unable to escape his gaze, their passions heightened not only by war but the everyday hazards they have to face. The captain and crew offer a perfect discordance of 'incompatible tempers, mewed up together in a box' (*Master and Commander*, 44); 'so full a ship, so close-packed a world, moving urgently along surrounded by its own vacuum.' (*HMS Surprise*, 172). And many of the impressions of life at sea as the ship beats on through dull seas, largely indifferent to human suffering, are not Aubrey's but his own.

It would be wrong, however, to think that the popularity of O'Brian's work owes much to Maturin's philosophising. Critics and readers do not read the same author. The former are much more interested in the authenticity of the novels and their narrative thrust; the latter in the action. Writers, too, often sympathise with the critics' position; as one of the characters in Anthony Powell's war novels remarks, 'action is, after all, exciting rather than interesting.' (Powell, 1973, 114). But action can be very interesting indeed when it reveals character (as Aristotle tells us, character is best revealed in action), and Aubrey has both in spades. Maturin too is an action hero of sorts whenever he is running down traitors in the service, or men who have sold out their country for gold. His exploits are no less exciting than Aubrey's. Both men have an enormous, if not uncritical affection for each other. Each can see the other's faults, but as they talk about war and life, and music, they enlarge the field of each other's thoughts. At some deeper level, they need each other to fully develop as characters. For what Maturin shares with Aubrey is something he cannot share with any other member of his crew, neither officers nor rankers: the intimacy of equality. If they cannot overhear themselves speak, they can at least overhear each other.

In their conversations they are consistently discovering something of themselves. It is the interaction between them, between commander and civilian (both men of their time) that works so well. Maturin can appreciate the man of action in a way Aubrey can't, especially when he succumbs to those darker moments of despair that follow the elation of battle. Maturin reinforces the commander's belief in himself in those long moments at sea, though in combat Aubrey is always self-possessed and entirely himself. Both men don't just occupy their roles, they live them. Any series of books is bound to be formulaic at times, and the Aubrey series is no exception, but the character grows in the telling of his tale, as the action slows down. His naval career is becalmed in six novels set in 1813, and it is during that phase of his life that the reader really gets to know him, almost as well as he knows himself—to probe his mind, his mood, his melancholy.

Aubrey is far from a perfect commander, but what he lacks in human perfection he makes up for as a commander of men. He is the archetypal 'born leader' who inspires respect for being 'lucky'—'Lucky Jack', the men call him, knowing well enough that luck has only a part to play in his success. The main explanation is what Aristotle called 'character' and we prefer to call 'professionalism'. It is the human imperfections that highlight the professional virtues, but there is enough of the man to make the Commander more interesting than he might otherwise be: he exhibits an intelligence which is constantly informed by an avid sense of inquiry—an attitude shared, in a less intellectual sense, by his friend Maturin. Had he been 'frozen' in his professional role, he would have been as fundamentally uninteresting as Hornblower. O'Brian's writing is better than Forester's, which is why the books have generated interest among literary critics who often dislike the plots but admire the characterisation. What both readerships, I think, find important about the series, is the dialogue, a crucial instrument of both action and characterisation.

Character aside, what are the other essential building blocks of an O'Brian novel? First, there is the setting: always, of course, the sea. O'Brian's novels have a lyrical thrust that gives them forward propulsion, even when there is nothing happening in the way of action. On the *HMS Surprise* we see a ship sailing over a thousand miles before the unvarying routine of the day obliterates both the beginning of the voyage and its end; even time ceases to exist, 'so that it seemed normal to all hands that they should travel endlessly over this infinite and wholly empty sea, watching the sun diminish and the moon increase.' (*HMS Surprise*, 154). And then there are the ships of which O'Brian writes lovingly. They are characters in their own right, and Aubrey has as much love for them as he does for the crews who sail in them. In the *Surprise* Aubrey sees a splendid sailing ship, but not without its faults:

'By the wind she left much to be desired; there was a slowness, a tendency to gripe, a want of ease that no fresh combination of sails would overcome.' (*HMS Surprise*, 249). Ships, like men, have to be mastered. When Maturin re-joins the *Surprise* he finds that Aubrey has transferred her 'personality' 'with a 36 gun frigate's main mast, her fore and mizzen raked strongly aft, and her sides repainted black and white— the Nelson checker.' (*HMS Surprise*, 148). The change, Aubrey tells his friend, will move her 'light airs' to go the extra knot: 'She is as stiff as—why, as stiff as you can imagine; and if we cannot get an extra knot, I shall be amazed.'

And finally, there is the endless discovery of life as the ship sails into seas charted but still full of surprises, and full of ever more resourceful French commanders out to sink British shipping. The action scenes are extremely well done, none better than the engagement with the *Berceur* and *Marengo* in Admiral Lenoir's Squadron in the Indian Ocean. Aubrey is determined to produce 'an elegant chaos', a wonderful description of a battle at sea, and so he does, in several vividly written pages. Sword in hand, feeling 'a wild and savage joy, a fullness of being like no other' (we are told in the opening pages of *The Thirteen Gun Salute*), Aubrey comes alive most when he is in action, whether he is fighting the French or the Spanish, or inspiring his men. His personality is defined almost entirely in relation to other people through action, whether it is his enemies, or the men he is called to lead into battle.

The sea, the ships and the action define Aubrey the man—but, in truth, Aubrey is defined by his nature; that of a seaman, who has been nominally at sea in his imagination since the age of nine, and in reality since the age of twelve. He is a consummate professional who can read a man's character in his 'rigging'. A ship's crew, he knows, comes to resemble its captain. When he joins his first ship, the *Sophie*, he sets himself the task of whipping a crew into an aggressive fighting force, after his own heart. Aubrey must master the crew in order to master the ship, making it both into an instrument of war and of his will. It is no easy task, as O'Brian is always at pains to remind us, since the men from whom crews were fashioned were usually drawn from unpromising stock; many have no self-esteem, or esteem for others; some are 'hard bargains from the gaols'. Some include 'quota men' from the inland counties, mostly furnished by the beadle, and middle-aged foreigners from as far afield as the Levant, pressed into service in circumstances that remain obscure. In *The Far Side of the World*, O'Brian describes the various gradations of men, painting a positive periodic table of naval life in the eighteenth century, some 'striped Guernsey-frocked tarpaulin-hatted, kinky-faced, red-throated, long-swinging, pig-tailed men', many resentful of being pressed out of the Merchant Navy, others landsmen from bricklayers' clerks (a naval term for men who had a rudimentary education and had seen better days), to those who had not, who were strangers to duty and discipline in any walk of life. Many are middle-aged, some quite elderly: 'Seamen salted to the bone', 'Such a mass of sea-going knowledge'. The gunmen, honest enough, but lazy, have to be whipped into shape whenever Aubrey takes command of a new ship; he makes their lives a misery until they have 'learnt to serve their pieces as they ought to serve their God.' (*HMS Surprise*, 103). And most important of all, perhaps, are the officers, who hold the ship together. Many of them are absurdly young and all are dedicated to performing their duty, many believing, as Aubrey does not, in loyalty to the King: the aged, mad George III sequestered away in Windsor.

How, then, is Aubrey to master such a disparate, unpromising collection of men? We catch a glimpse of him in *The Far Side of the World* moulding his men into a crew, anxious for the northern winds early in the voyage, first because of the simple-minded love of running the wind, the ship racing through the monstrous seas with only a scrap of close-reefed storm-canvas, but mostly because with topmasts struck down and lifelines rigged fore and aft, this was exactly the kind of animation that forced a crew to work together (*The Far Side of the World*, 94). His philosophy is set out in the very first book: 'There is no forcing a willing mind', or in this case, an unwilling crew (*Master and Commander*, 78). Nelson's navy was a harsh world governed by Articles of War and Court Martials, often ending in sentence of death, or summary punishment by the lash, administered unsparingly by weak and strong captains alike; cowardice was punished severely, as was negligence and disaffection. 'Death ran through and through the Articles, and even where the words were utterly incomprehensible, death had a fine comminatory, Leviticus ring.' (*Master and Commander*, 86). But the Articles cannot make a ship sail faster, or a crew more committed. What makes a great commander of men, Aubrey's example suggests, is to observe the law in spirit, not letter—particularly whenever, as often happens, the two collide. A sailor, remarks a character in *HMS Surprise*, knows nothing of the law, 'but there is no body of men more tenacious in custom, nor more alive to equity and natural justice.' (*HMS Surprise*, 2) Aubrey is, as such, perfectly in tune with his men. This can be observed, for instance, in his attitude towards prize money. In this period, until it was abolished in 1917, the crew from the captain downwards kept a percentage of any booty from the capture of a ship. Prize money was an incentive to battle and, among the series' characters and readers alike, there are those who suspect that Aubrey may like prize money too much. He is no better and no worse than his men, or the age.

This allows him to lead from the front and mould his crew into a team. Because he takes pride in them, they take pride in him. Aubrey wins their respect because he sets standards without which they will not survive at sea, or in battle, for long. He mixes with his men like young Harry on the eve of Agincourt. Because he inspires them, they come to believe in themselves. And always we are reminded he is driven by what made Nelson's navy the most formidable fighting force ever to set out to sea: its 'professionalism' (perhaps the first time the term could be used). We see the gunmen going from gun to gun, putting preventer-breechings to the guns, to hold them tight against the side; others securing the boats; all moving about with no orders given; 'and as they worked they glanced at the captain while he, just as often, put out his hand to test the strain on the rigging and turned his head to look at the sky, the sea, the upper sails.' (*HMS Surprise*, 158). Finally, Aubrey is successful in his quest to captain his ship, to bring it entirely under his command.

And command he does, for he is not given to discussing his strategy or tactics with his senior officers. Aubrey believes a captain is there to command rather than ask advice or preside over a committee. He has known of captains who are given to calling councils of war but invariably the outcome has been a prudent retreat, or absence of decisive action. Aubrey leads from the front. He mingles with the men, fights by their side and often trains with them. In preparation for the attack on the French ship *Diane*, anchored at St Martin-de-Roy, he organises and participates in night attacks, at some danger to himself. He is, remarks a sailor, a great man: 'I doubt they would do so much for anyone else. It's a quality only some men possess.' (*Letter of Marque*, 154).

It is his professionalism that makes Aubrey a successful warrior. Character may indeed be revealed in action but what O'Brian shows is not only the character of one man, the commander, but of the crew he forges and re-shapes to his own purposes. Do not despise action, as a character in *Master and Commander* remarks, 'It has a wonderful way of reconciling a man with himself, and with everybody else, sometimes.' (*Master and Commander*, 248). It is called team spirit, and in forging a team Aubrey is second to none. In battle with the Spanish frigate *Cacafuego*, the *Sophie*'s deck is described as 'a beautiful pattern of movement—the powder passing up from the magazine, the gun crews with their steady nerves, a wounded man carrying a dead man below, his place instantly taken without a word—no collisions, no jostlings, almost no orders at all.' (*Master and Commander*, 321).

O'Brian insisted that his readers would meet with no wholly virtuous, ever-victorious or necessarily immortal heroes in his work, but did he protest too much? (*The Far Side*, x) I am not convinced. At times he seems to have borrowed too much from the old sea yarns and not enough from history. A little less Forester, perhaps, might have helped. Aubrey is too much of a stock figure at times (though how could he not be, appearing as he does in over twenty books); not only that, he is something of a super-hero, a man who not only survives shipwrecks and the perils of storms but a man who fights in more great fleet battles, and in more single-ship actions than any real historical figure. Aware of this criticism, O'Brian always insisted that eighteenth-century warfare really did produce such men, and that service at sea was quite different from today's policing operations against Somali pirates and drug runners in the Caribbean. Even an unconsciously fertile imagination could scarcely produce the frail shape of Commodore Nelson leaping from his battered 74-gun *Captain* through the quarter-galley window of the 88 gun *San Nicolas*, and hurrying across her deck to board the towering *San Josef* with its 112 guns. The records and archives O'Brian consulted were full of actions that, if less spectacular than Aubrey's, were in no way less spirited.

But if at times Aubrey is a little too heroic to be true, Maturin saves him from himself—or from what he might have become in less assured narrative hands. It would be hard to think of two characters more dissimilar: the seaman of action, no more himself than when boarding a French or Spanish ship; the doctor never more alive than when exploring the atolls of the Indian Ocean, or adopting a pet sloth who Aubrey 'debauches' through alcohol. O'Brian knew what he was about. Aubrey gains a great deal from having Maturin as his closest friend. It roots him partly in a civilian world, the world of most of O'Brian's readers; it prevents him from glorifying war too much (the doctor, though a good swordsman, abhors violence). Maturin's scepticism may or may not rub off on Aubrey (we do not see it, if it does), but it is affecting, because such friendships between serviceman and civilian are rare, certainly in time of war. It anchors the hero to the world which will have to work out the peace when it comes, when old enemies are reconciled. Hopefully Aubrey will be able to be as just as alive in that world, too.

Vollmer: Spectator Sport War
Human Moments in World War III, Don DeLillo

In *Dispatches*, Michael Herr tells the story of a news photographer, Tim Page, who went to places other photographers would not and got wounded many times as a consequence. His friends tried to talk him into leaving Vietnam, saying: 'Hey, Page, there's an air strike looking for you'. His talk was endlessly self-referential. He spoke of himself in the third person and was interested in only two things: himself and the war. And then one day a London publisher asked him to write a book with the working title 'Through with War', the purpose of which would be to take the glamour out of war. Page could not get over it.

Take the glamour out of war? I mean how the bloody hell can you do that? Go and take the glamour out of the Huey, go take the glamour out of a Sheridan … it's like taking the glamour out of an M-79. (Herr, 1979, 198–199).

The glamour has become the technology—the Huey helicopter and the Sheridan tank, and today's drones.

Human Moments in World War III opens with a note about its main character, Vollmer, in which we learn that he is an 'engineering genius, a communications and weapons genius', a veritable post-modern warrior with degrees in science and technology. He has even run science projects and authored research papers. War by now has become high-tech, too. The point of DeLillo's tale lies in the sub-text rather than text of the story. War exists on the margins of Vollmer's consciousness. It has become merely a 'routine'. The presence of war in the tale is actually its absence. All the characters I have discussed so far have embodied courage, which includes fear, risk-taking and sacrifice: the existential code of war. Vollmer is the great exception, and the possible face of the future.

Of course, war is present at the beginning in remarks about strategy and weapons systems. It is there in Vollmer's belief that the world is nostalgic for the old wars, a nostalgia reflected in the fact that the ships and planes of the present are named after ancient battles, and the simpler weapons of the past. It is there in the story's portrait of his grandfather, an army vet, which he keeps on his console, but most of all it is there in the hope that his death might arouse some sentiment in a grateful nation's uncomplicated soul. But in DeLillo's vision of the future, war has become entirely instrumentalised. Vollmer cannot even express empathy for those he is instructed to take out, and because he cannot really act except through a weapons console, we cannot define his character from his actions. He is merely asked to react: to zap everything that moves on the planet below, anything which is considered 'hostile'. He is as much a mystery to himself at the end as he is to the reader at the beginning. Indeed, he slowly disappears in the course of the tale into the vast mystery of the Earth below.

Vollmer is a twenty-three year old serviceman with a longish head and close-cropped hair. He is a member of an orbital space capsule surveying a world in which nuclear weapons have been banned. Now safe for war—World War III is in its third week. For Vollmer, in this, his first mission, war has become a series of housekeeping arrangements. Pilots have all the home comforts: good food, video cassettes and piped music. For them, war is waged by checklist, checking the instructions, the codes and the simulated firing. There is no danger of boredom—'the only danger is conversation'. The orbiting space station is not one of those war stations which drone pilots—today's cubicle warriors—now man, but the parallels are interesting. Like a drone, the spacecraft is designed primarily to gather intelligence; like a drone, it can also take out anything that moves below. Like drone pilots today, war for Vollmer takes place at a firing panel where he can wear slippers and distinctive clothes—in his case a football jersey bearing the number 79, 'a prime of no particular distinction.'

But the space capsule most of all is a weapons platform from which he and his comrade can zap enemies with laser guns, 'a well behaved beam of photons', an engineered coherence. The system requires two men sitting back-to-back, synchronising their actions. It is activated by voice identity clearance—they need to produce a voice print that matches the print in the computer's memory bank before they are authorised to fire. In DeLillo's future, nuclear weapons have been banned but the world has moved on, and war with it—into a science fiction age of photons, mosons and charged particle beams.

Vollmer, apart from the anonymous narrator, is the only character in the story and the narrator has no personality that we can readily discern. Indeed, he is desperately anxious for the mission to be as 'characterless' as possible, which is why he is annoyed by Vollmer's attempts to discuss strategy and the new techniques of war. Vollmer is even willing to discuss politics, although he complains that World War III (unlike the other two) is proving to be acutely boring, offering no moments of intensity. In this war, Vollmer complains, people have become semi-detached. War no longer brings people together. Not only is he nostalgic for the past, he is also critical of the new language of war, with its debased locutions, and its new set of actors: 'high-dynamic officers', 'conceptual paradigm officers', and 'status consultants'. War, as we have traditionally known it, has largely vanished from view, as has the humanity that used to be central to it. Human beings are still in the picture, but they have become fragmented. War has its human moments still; never more so, says the narrator, than when they forget there is a war on.

Vollmer has become almost totally dissociated not only from war but from his own humanity, living as he does in an online, virtual world. Humanity is so fragmented that it really has become embodied in a series of 'moments'—photographs at a console or the clothing one wears (a particular football shirt) remind the pilots of what they 'are'. What irritates our anonymous narrator most is that Vollmer is himself a 'human moment' in an otherwise fully regulated and neutralised environment. When he sits at his firing panel he sees the photographs of Vollmer's grandfather when he was a young soldier in sagging khakis and shallow helmet, a rifle strapped to his shoulder. 'This (too) is a human moment, and it reminds me that war, among other things, is a form of longing.' What remains frightening to him are Vollmer's human insights, his non-scientific perceptions. He is especially annoyed when one day Vollmer confesses that he is happy. The narrator reproaches him: happiness is outside their frame of reference.

Attend to your tasks, do your testing, run through your checklists. I want to say 'forget the measure of our vision, the sweep of things, the war itself' ... I want to say, 'happiness is not a fact of the experience, at least to the extent that one is bold enough to speak of it'. (*Human Moments in World War III*, 36).

DeLillo was writing in 1983 when the Information Age was still in its infancy, and drones (such as those used in Vietnam) were relatively crude devices. All this has changed. The Information Age has arrived with a vengeance; drones have come into their own, and fully autonomous robots are probably not far behind. What the author captures is the changing face of war as it is reduced increasingly to information flows, and how it changes the personalities of those who are called upon to process them. The two pilots in the tale do not even bond personally; they are not part of a band of brothers. And they are so far removed from the people down below on the planet, those who are there either watching or targeting, that when they hear a human voice crackle though their transmission system, they are utterly confused. They retreat back into a silence that they cannot even share with each other.

This passage is at the core of DeLillo's story. What they are picking up is a remote signal, some 'selective noise', which the narrator imagines has the 'touching quality of some half-remembered and tender event, even through the static, the sonic mist.' Colorado Command thinks it must be a weather report from 22,000 miles away. Only later does Vollmer deduce that they are picking up signals from radio programmes of forty years ago. They recognise laughter, and commercial breaks, and theme music, all intensely affecting, even when the signals are at their weakest. This is a world very different from the one they inhabit, where the existential codes have been hollowed out and war itself has become largely one-dimensional. The conversation and laughter they pick up by chance on the radio transmission reflects a very different world of inner feelings. Laughter arises when we find life particularly ironic, or when we find it metaphorical (when we see life for what it really is by comparing one thing with another). It is the use of metaphor which separates us from among other things, our nearest relatives, chimpanzees.

Vollmer's world is not entirely devoid of metaphor, but he remains trapped in the present, even when eavesdropping on a barely remembered past. And what this translates into is a striking lack of interest in the mission, or empathy for his targets. He even actively abets the dissociation by trying to create 'a structure of the commonplace' on the spaceship as a psychological refuge from the war. The situation is actually inverted: it is war that has become commonplace and, one imagines, unending—a routine exercise in risk management which makes it all the easier to find oneself removed from the actual combat down below.

Space is as much a metaphor as a plot device; in space there is zero gravity. To be dissociated from one's actions is not the same as to be distanced or divorced; it is to be disembodied (it is to lack feeling, sensitivity). We learn only by seeing and we see 'feelingly'. To see feelingly is to allow reason to move us within the constraints of the suffering body which is why Wittgenstein concluded that the body in pain is the most graphic reflection of the human soul. The challenge of military technology is that it creates death but destroys the experience of it. It is much easier to become desensitised, distanced from the consequences of one's actions—it is another thing altogether to become utterly disconnected from what one's actions mean. Acting without meaning, we are in danger of being stripped of our moral core.

In the thirty years since DeLillo wrote his story, some neuroscientists like Susan Greenfield have come to suspect that the increasingly two-dimensional screen existence of many young people has begun to reduce their ability to empathise with others. US college students have shown an alarming decline in empathy with a particularly sharp drop in the past decade (Greenfield, 2011). Some of us spend up to eighty hours a week playing videogames, cut off from human contact in the 'real' as opposed to 'virtual' world. Normally, we learn to empathise through real conversations, or when we engage in eye-to-eye contact, and from very early infancy we interpret body language in order to nurture our emotional intelligence. But when our two pilots are at the firing consoles, targeting people below, they sit back to back. The system has been so designed so that they do not have to look each other in the eye. 'Colorado (Control) wants to be sure that weapons personnel in particular are not too influenced by each other's tics and perturbations.' For them, war has become rather like the video games we play today. Insight into other peoples' motivations and ways of looking at the world are no longer available. Video games also deny us this. They create worlds of outward movement rather than inner feeling.

DeLillo's story offers a bleak warning of what happens when people become dissociated from war. The point is that Vollmer still clings on to some aspects of the existential code. There is still something in him of the 'poet and primitive seer'. He still believes in the immanent, vital forces of life, and still remembers with nostalgia his youthful dream of flying. But such thoughts or reflections are no longer directed at anyone, even those he is asked to kill; they are directed, if at all, at the planet below, not its inhabitants. Occasionally, the Earth's orbit will put him in a philosophical temper; he has a privileged vista, after all, and in his attempts to be equal to the experience, he meditates occasionally on the human condition. But Vollmer knows such thoughts are surplus to requirement; it is not what twenty-first-century warfare demands of its practitioners.

Even then, Vollmer no longer sees the Earth as he once did, in a poetic idiom. 'He doesn't see it anymore as storm-spirited, sea-bright, breathing heat and haze and colour, as an occasion for picturesque language, for careful play or speculation.' (*Human Moments in World War III*, 25) He simply looks out the window, eating almond crunches, the wrappers floating away in zero gravity. Without empathy, of course, one cannot project—projection means the ability to put yourself in a position of another person, allowing you to adopt a different perspective (one can even visualise what the world might look like from another person's vantage point). From there you may be able to figure out what someone is thinking or feeling merely from their expression or their behaviour. But all of these are directed at other people, not other things. You cannot empathise with the planet, though you may well want to save it, and one suspects Vollmer would not even be capable of that. What he likes most about the Earth or rather, to use his own words, what he finds most 'interesting', are 'the colours and all'.

3

HEROES

The fact that all the great heroes of fiction—from Tolstoy's Prince Andrei to Hemingway's Robert Jordan—have never been out of print suggests that they have the same kind of timeless appeal off the page as on it. The minor heroes of literature quickly disappear; they are rooted in the time of their creation. What falls in and out of fashion tells us more about ourselves than about the characters that still inspire us. It tells us about the changing character of war, but little, if anything, about its unchanging nature. Great heroes, however, haunt the collective consciousness, occasionally rebooted through film and television, or re-imagined in graphic novels. Every war produces heroes, and every age gets the heroes it deserves. In epic poetry, heroes were the principal characters, both godless and semi-divine—as in the case of Achilles, a man so many soldiers wish to be but also dread they might become. In the modern novel, heroes are less grandiose, more passive and, consequently, more sympathetic; some are even reluctant heroes and these engage our sympathy even more. The modern novel, wrote Baudelaire, should have 'no heroes or monsters'.

Heroes are as heroic as warriors—so what is the difference? Warriors as a rule don't find war particularly ironic; heroes often do. Since the mid–nineteenth century, novelists have employed characters to bring out three objective ironies about modern war that are to be found in *The Sevastopol Sketches*, three short stories based on Tolstoy's eye-witness account of the siege of the city during the Crimean War

(1853–6). Whenever we read *The Sevastopol Sketches*, the twentieth century looms—just as when Napoleon invades Russia in *War and Peace*, we know how the story will end. Fiction and history are always interacting with each other in subtle and often hidden ways. Take Andrei Bolonsky at Austerlitz, or Fabrice Del Dongo at Waterloo— once you have read the novels, the historical accounts can never be the same, just as our knowledge of history inevitably colours the reading of novels.

The Sevastopol Sketches really did break new ground. They are a mixture of reportage and literature, mediated through an anonymous narrator (Tolstoy himself), and through a variety of characters (mostly officers) who live on the page through their emotional responses to largely visual and aural impressions. This is what makes the *Sketches* not only good reporting but great literature and ground-breaking fiction. The book is also unique in not having a single hero. Although it is full of episodes in which some of the characters display great personal heroism at risk to their own lives, they are heroic despite themselves. They are largely passive; events happen to them. As such, they are very 'modern'.

Take the ironic distance between the character and event. Much as the characters may wish to shape events, they find events shaping them. None of them are in control of their own destiny. In the first Sketch Tolstoy sets the scene by depicting life in a city under siege. Unlike the other two Sketches, there is only one hero in the first of the three: the Russian people. They find a stage on which to make themselves famous even though most of them remain anonymous, another irony of war that Tolstoy captures so well. The narrator is an impressionable young man whose patriotism runs away with him. He is full of patriotic zeal to throw himself into the fight, but notices at once that it is impossible to read on a single face signs of any particular enthusiasm, any special readiness to die, or any particular resolve. Life continues, even in a siege. Even among the defenders there are no extraordinary men, just ordinary people 'equally blameless and equally wicked', and who is to judge between them? This is why Tolstoy insists that the only true hero of his story is the Truth, and one of its central features is perhaps, the greatest irony of all: the gap between expectation and reality.

The main character in the second tale is the young Infantry Lieutenant Mikhailov, who overcomes his fear of death by subordinating everything to duty. Duty is the one thing that may allow a man to overcome the mismatch between character and situation. As a young man, he is weighed down by the anxiety that consumes all young people who have yet to discover themselves, and subject themselves to the tests of life. The greatest anxiety of all in war for any responsible, halfway committed soldier, is whether he will do his duty. Freud famously defined anxiety as 'Angst vor etwas' or 'anxious expectation'. We are anxious only because of what others expect of us.

And then there is the ironic distance between illusion and reality, illustrated most vividly by the death of the older Kosteltzoff's brother in the third and final story. Vladimir dies as he would have wished to, in the thick of battle. It is we, the readers, who see the irony of his death, reduced as he is to a bundle of clothes on the floor. We may recall earlier scenes when he daydreamed about charging into the enemy ranks, his brother with his sabre in hand, he with his musket (Tolstoy, 2006, 276). The irony is that he dies in one register, but lives in another. With two different registers there is always a chance of incoherence. But that is not the point Tolstoy is making. Vladimir's character is all of a piece. Just as there are no villains or heroes in Tolstoy's world, there are no fools or enlightened men. We live our lives according to the stories we tell ourselves and others. Our friends are a captive audience before whom we enact an idealised version of our own life— the life we would like to lead, in their eyes as well as our own. Living life always demands a sense of proportion, the balance between illusion and reality which cannot be resolved entirely in favour of either unless life becomes impossibly one-dimensional. And war is no different, except for the fact that it rarely allows us to hold to our illusions for long. It has a register of its own, which is often mock-heroic.

In his *A Treatise of Human Nature*, David Hume wrote 'when I enter most intimately into what I call myself I will always stumble on some particular perception or other of heat of cold, light or shade, love or hatred, pain or pleasure.' For Hume the key word is 'stumble'—we are at the mercy of unexpected sensations, unintended encounters with life. We are vulnerable to the contingent. We have character when we treat the stumble as an opportunity rather than a threat, an opportunity to win through, to master passions or emotions, to regain control and in the process discover more about 'oneself'. The characters in this book are 'heroic' because the reassert control. They do not lose it, and thus see 'self' dissolve before their eyes. But what makes many of them different from the rest of us, what makes them the heroes they are is that they go one step further. They put themselves in harm's way. They put themselves at risk quite self-consciously, sometimes to test themselves, usually because they have been ordered to do so.

This is certainly the case with the young Henry Fleming, the hero of Stephen Crane's *The Red Badge of Courage*—he has the distinction of being the first democratic hero in the literature of war. There is a famous passage in the book, 'At times he regarded the wounded soldiers in an envious way. He conceived persons with torn bodies to be peculiarly happy. He wished he too had a red badge of courage.' (*The Red Badge of Courage*, 41). The passage is read as a metaphor, but perhaps it has another meaning. At the battle of Antietam (1863), some soldiers noticed a queer phenomenon. Fearful at first of going into battle, like Henry, they soon lost their terror and were seized by a peculiar fearlessness, heralded by everything in sight taking on a crimson hue; quite literally they 'saw red' (Hillsman, 2004, 80).

And Henry Fleming is much more than just an individual; he is a common man in a struggle for the re-consecration of a nation committed to the democratic ideal. He does not live in a gilded cage, and for that reason in these democratic times, his fate resonates with us much more than does Prince Andrei's at Borodino. Both are nineteenth-century characters, but Henry is much more representative of today's soldiers. Henry just happens to be a common man who has read Homer. Homer's world is as distant from his as Henry's is from ours. But our world is one that both Andrei and Henry would recognise in themselves, in their own thoughts and actions.

Henry may fail his first baptism of fire, his first test, but he returns to the field to expiate his shame, and he wins through in the end. Henry wants glory without sacrifice or effort and finds he can only shine as a member of a team. He finds out the truth of Plato's admonition that one can fail at being a man, that when we are estranged from others, we are estranged from ourselves. Only with his identification with his friends does a simple youth become a complex man. The test that war throws up, though violent, vicious and often lethal, is not unrepresentative of life itself. We are all tested in different ways: we all find that we are not what we think we are; we often in danger of falling out of love with ourselves.

The heroic continued to survive in the story telling itself. In Brigadier Eugene Gerard, Conan Doyle (one of Crane's contemporaries) created a different kind of hero who is as old as war itself—the story-teller, a man who in his own words (and what we know of him we know entirely through the tales he himself relates) is a young brigadier of the Hussars of Conflans, 'gay, riding, plume-tossing, debonair, the darling of the ladies and of six Brigades of Light Cavalry.' Gerard is not quite a Jungian archetype, but he is typical of a breed of soldier who has now died out—the romantic, the storyteller, the entertainer who knows war for what it is, but will never allow that to get in the way of a good story. Gerard is a born raconteur, and his wit allows him to distance us from the reality of war, and see only what he wants us to see, not war, of course, but the brigadier himself. 'We were great travellers in those days (we French of the Grand Armée)', he tells us, but 'we went in larger parties than were convenient to those whom we visited, and we carried our passports in our limbers' (Doyle, 2010, 221). As he tells us, the French Army entered many cities as conquerors: the cavalry in front of the Grand Armée, the Hussars of Conflans in front of the cavalry and, of course, always Gerard at the head of the Hussars.

All this is a world away from war today and was so even in the 1940s when one of the natural born heroes Antoine de Saint-Exupéry, looking back to the era before the First World War wrote 'today when we are more dried out than any brick, we smile at …. the costumes, banners, songs, music, victories [of the past]—there are no victories nowadays, nothing that conveys the poetic impact of Austerlitz.' (Saint-Exupéry, 1986, 134). He might well have been writing from the combat zones of Afghanistan or Iraq but story-telling remains one of the central features of war as an existential experience, and no one told a story better than Conan Doyle.

The First World War really did change everything and there could be no hero more different than Frederic Manning's Bourne. As Bernard Bergonzi writes, Manning speaks of war with a Shakespearean inclusiveness, presenting the humour of war as well as the horror and pathos, and there is something Shakespearean too, in his mixture of the profound and mundane, the profane language of the soldiers and the probing, existential reflections in which Bourne engages at critical moments in the story (Bergonzi, 1996, 183). But we know all of Shakespeare's heroes personally; they are larger than life figures even when they are defeated by it. There could be no biography of Bourne, not because we do not know enough but because there is not enough to know (his war is largely devoid of dramatic content except for his death, and even this is described in only a few sentences—he dies as he lived his life, without fuss).

The modern hero is often an individual with a different set of attributes from those in the past—he may have self-deprecating humour, greater self-knowledge and a good-hearted response to those who are less (or less than) heroic themselves. Bourne is, for me, the most modern hero because of his stoicism rather than heroism. Indeed, it is his stoical attitude to life which is truly heroic. He is not acting egotistically, or out of a sense of duty, still less for love of country, though he may entertain these emotions or thoughts at different times. He is not acting because he feels duty-bound, or because he feels that the world will be a better place for his actions. He is acting entirely out of love, and it is a particular kind of love, one that lies outside oneself, one that it truly selfless. Bourne has two particular friends, Shem and Martlow, and the novel is about their comradeship, one of the major keys of grace in war. They have little and everything in common. Little in that they come from different social worlds, and everything in that they all belong to the trenches, to that famous band of brothers, the comradeship that war forges in the proximity of death and danger, in the vicissitudes shared in common at the Front. This is not the least of the remarkable aspects of the war for us today, looking back. Manning's belief in the rightness of the cause for which they were fighting never wavered, unlike Wilfred Owen's or Siegfried Sassoon's. But in both cases even when invalided out they went back to fight by the side of their comrades. In the military parlance of the time they 'answered the call'. They did their best and for the most part uncomplainingly; they took great pride in 'coming through' for each other, even if this much reduced the chances of coming back.

Most soldiers do not go to war expecting to rise to the occasion; many would rather not be asked to. Many have no personal vocation for heroism, and some not even for war. The heroic finds them out in ways that can be deeply moving. No one has captured this better than Ernest Hemingway in the best of his novels, *For Whom the Bell Tolls*. Set in the Sierra de Guadarrama mountain range between Madrid and Segovia, the action takes place over four days and three nights. The Spanish Civil War inspired one other major work of literature, André Malraux's *Man's Hope*—what distinguishes both is that the authors wrote their books whilst the war was still being fought.

The hero of Hemingway's tale is a young American volunteer, a demolitions expert, a sapper. Hemingway wrote sparingly and the battle scenes are few but vividly sketched. The whole work is structured around two vivid episodes: the bombing of the mountain stronghold of the guerrilla leader, El Sordo, and the account by Pilar, the wife of another guerrilla leader Pablo, of a notorious atrocity in her own village. But it is Jordan's tale, and the book and the best lines are his own grand soliloquies. He is a foreign interloper in someone else's war, but he is on the side of democracy against an enemy that he knows will be victorious. But it is his death at the end which is a sort of victory—a moral re-consecration of an immoral war. To ask why he sacrifices himself is a hopelessly naïve question. Why did Scott battle the Antarctic, or Luther nail his theses on the cathedral doors at Wittenberg? Actually, Luther told us: 'I can do no other'. Ask anyone why they raced back into a fire to save a child, or a soldier why he threw himself on a grenade to save a friend. These acts were impulsive, but not spontaneous. They were the actualisation of a life in which questions about the utility of 'throwing away' life in a senseless act of self-sacrifice are as much out of place as challenging the 'wisdom' of taking part in an Arctic expedition. We are what our actions make us, and it is his actions that confirm the authenticity of the actor, not the other way round.

Inspiring though Hemingway's story is, I confess myself, nevertheless, often defeated by his writing. There is so much that is wrong with *For Whom the Bell Tolls*. It is not just the style which grates, the use of the word 'fug' for 'fuck' and the attempt to render a local dialect with 'thees' and 'thous' which from today's vantage point is intensely irritating. The problem is that the novel is clumsy and inspiring by turns. There is much that rings false, but a lot that rings true. It has a raw, elemental power of its own. It is authentically 'Spanish' in scenery, and the human passions Spain evokes But if it deserves a place with the others in this book it is because of the characterisation of Robert Jordan, the first great American fictional soldier since Henry Fleming. Jordan's life has an emblematic, almost archetypal quality that makes his final struggle our own.

Finally, in the person of Curzio Malaparte we meet with a new kind of hero who witnesses all on our behalf. The Italians say that a good book is 'read in one breath', and *Kaputt* is just such a book. There is no plot so much as a series of chronologically fragmented episodes drawn (in part) from the author's own experiences—or what he tells us he experienced, though we have every reason to doubt him. We are complicit in his fabrications, his spinning of potentially bogus tales. But that, too, is a feature of war; it stimulates storytelling, but whose stories do we find believable, and whose stories do we instantly disbelieve?

Kaputt is a sprawling novel filled with people, but few fully realised characters apart from the author, who is the hero of his own story. And just as there are no characters with psychological depth, so we cannot be worried about the kind of person that he is. He is motivated by a wish to observe the war from the inside, and he is not judgemental of war itself. Indeed, he obviously enjoyed every minute. Malaparte was a great writer who was both empowered and limited by his political perspective. We do not have to like his fascism, or his self-serving attacks on it as the war drew to an end, to admire his technique. We have to take the novel on the terms the author sets out, and not judge either too harshly. The interest of the novel lies elsewhere—not in the moral or psychological lessons that it draws (for there are none) but in the author's acute observation and his extraordinary descriptive powers. And there is one primary property in the work: disgust. Although Kant's aesthetic theory allows no place for disgust as a response to a work of art, disgust—given sufficient distancing—can be seen as a violent instance of the Kantean sublime. We are complicit in what he shows us. He allows us to see a feature of war which is as old as war itself, but which has rarely been revealed in the literature—the presence of the dead. Their silence is deafening, though they are not so silent, of course, because we hear them speak inside our heads. Their un-vocalised speech is conveyed in what Penelope Fitzgerald calls 'non-realised tenses' and Malaparte allows them to protest eloquently against their own condition.

The realities soldiers still have to face when deployed in the field have not changed much since Homer. The technological challenges may have transformed the battlefield into a battle space but as long as war remains what Thucydides first called it, 'the human thing'—as long as it incorporates the human factor—heroes will still answer the call. For the hero is a man who finds that he makes a difference for others in a world in which making a difference can be a matter of life and death; sometimes he can even inspire the rest of us to fight on.

Our contemporary heroes may be reluctant and improbable, but they are real. We will have met them in real life (though we may not always recognise them at the time). If they appear to be smaller than the heroes of the past that is because we measure them against ourselves, and it is ourselves that we find most wanting. But there is a truth in all of this which is depressing. We still produce old-fashioned heroes; we will encounter them in books by former soldiers or embedded journalists. The best of the latter is Sebastian Junger's incomparable piece of reportage, *War*, a graphic account of a heroic unit that found itself facing the worst of the fighting in Afghanistan in the Korangor Valley in 2005. We still produce men who win medals for daring, and win them in fights that are still worth fighting. Heroes are still in demand because there are indeed monsters out there in a variety of manifestations, from fanatical terrorists and jihadists to ethnonationalists and murderous insurgents. But novels don't produce many heroes these days. It is not that the works produced are essentially anti-war; most are not. But it is true perhaps to say that as the western novel has grown smaller, so have its characters; they no longer illuminate 'the heroic' as they once did.

Henry Fleming: The Democratic Hero
The Red Badge of Courage, Stephen Crane

Good-natured is the word that comes most to mind when thinking of Henry Fleming, the hero of Stephen Crane's novel, *The Red Badge of Courage*. It is also the first word that comes to mind when thinking of the two brothers Vladimir and Mikhail Kozeltsov in Tolstoy's *Sevastopol Sketches*, which greatly influenced Crane in his writing. In later years, he tried to distance himself somewhat from *War and Peace*, which he read after completing his own novel, but he never lost belief in the *Sketches* or Tolstoy's commitment to telling the 'truth' about war and its challenges. Without Tolstoy, Crane might never have made his own breakthrough.

It is not necessarily kind to compare a writer to Tolstoy because no other writer is ever likely to surpass him in his understanding of war, but some have been inspired by him to write some insightful works, and Crane is one of the very few whose insights are strikingly original. Of all the novels in the book, *The Red Badge of Courage* is one that a soldier will probably identify with most; this is not unimportant for every great novelist wants us to see ourselves in the characters he portrays. It helps that the book is one of the shortest in the literature on war. Twenty-four short chapters remind us of the twenty-four books of the *Iliad*. Like the *Sevastopol Sketches*, *The Red Badge of Courage* shows young men struggling with fear. Crane took the study much further by allowing Henry Fleming the space to come to know himself.

Fleming also happens to be a young man born with none of the advantages of life that Vladimir and his brother enjoy. He is not even an officer, though not uneducated, and he is just as given to the pursuit of glory as Tolstoy's young men. The fact that he is not an aristocrat, as nearly all 'heroes' had been before, makes Crane's novel more modern; indeed, Henry is the first 'democratic' war hero to appear in literature. He is the kind of soldier we can imagine equally at home in Da Nang or Hué, or even in the streets of Fallujah, doing his own bit to make the world safe for democracy.

The Red Badge of Courage is also democratic in form. It is plainly written, as plain as Walt Whitman's poetry, a style so familiar to us today that it is difficult sometimes to remember that we are reading a nineteenth-century author. In Henry Fleming we have a young man who is believable because we could encounter him in everyday life. Crane judged the public mood perfectly; after the experience of the Civil War, the democratic mood required democratic heroes. The Civil War was truly appalling, more so for the South which called up 80 per cent of its young men who were eligible for military service. The South subscribed, of course, to a culture of honour. Bertram Wyatt-Brown illustrates this by quoting a letter which a young Confederate officer wrote to a female friend in which he compared his fellow soldiers to Homer's heroes 'who fought like brave men, long and well'. The real point of the war for him, as for many, was that it was a simple test of manhood (Gilligan, 2000, 231). And the South's young men paid a terrible price. By the Spring of 1864 half had been killed.

Crane's novel is different in another respect. The late nineteenth-century novel was psychological. Its authors were deeply interested in a man's inner thoughts and feelings. *The Red Badge of Courage* tells us about the psychology of men caught up in war, but Crane tells us very little about Henry as a man. His character is largely unformed, and that in a sense is the point. What we see how a boy full of youthful illusions about the glory of war, gleaned largely from books, becomes a man, but a man whose loyalty to the group makes him a soldier. It is one of the first books to look at the significance of primary group cohesion, the extent to which a battle is often determined by whether the men hold together, and retain their belief in each other.

The army makes Henry. It teaches him the survival skills needed in battle, including primary group loyalty, and we know he survives the war because he appears thirty years later in the short story *The Veteran* which Crane wrote towards the end of his life. By the end of the novel he has learned the need for discipline, and the importance of moral courage. He is much more self-aware and far more intuitive, though none of this is rationalised. He may be moderately well read, but Crane does not give him much of an intellectual life and he is not given to deep reflection. He has no real personal philosophy. None of this diminishes him as a character, though inevitably he is less interesting that he might have been if Tolstoy rather than Crane had conceived him.

Conrad called Crane *the* impressionist of his age and Crane's novel, adds Sergio Perosa, is a triumph of impressionistic technique; nearly every scene is filtered through his point of view, or seen through his eyes—everything is related to his vision, his sense perception of incidents and details (Perosa in Crane, 2005, xvii). On encountering his first dead Confederate soldier, Henry sees that the soles of his shoes have been worn thin; death conspired to expose to his enemies that poverty which in life he had perhaps concealed from his friends (18). He is an ideal witness because he has imagination, even if it runs away with him at times. As when he comes upon some of his dead comrades in the forest:

> 'His disordered mind interpreted the hall of the forest as a charnel place. He believed for an instant that he was in the house of the dead, and he did not dare to move lest those corpses start up, squalling and squawking.' (*The Red Badge of Courage*, 60).

His misanthropic eye is clearly that of a young man living on the edge. What makes Henry such a fine witness is his remarkable powers of sight—he sees what most others miss. But at this stage he is still denied the power of insight into his own character.

His journey of self-discovery is not a long one, but it is tortuous. It also could be read as a metaphor for America's own journey from adolescence to manhood, its own re-consecration to the ideals that gave it birth which encouraged many historians in the last century to see the Civil War as a second revolution, one that would introduce the world to industrial warfare. The features that were to become so common in the First World War, including trench warfare, were part of the Civil War landscape too. Inevitably, the first industrialised war of railways and telegraphs and armoured battleships and mass-produced, machine-made weapons, uniforms and shoes created a landscape of its own. The rival armies are seen as giant machines, and machines expend energy quickly and waste resources, both material and human. Torn and twisted bodies express 'the awful machinery in which the men had been entangled', and the battle itself is compared to 'the grinding of an immense and terrible machine.' (*The Red Badge of Courage*, 40–41).

Part of the fear of death in the modern era is its anonymity—it is now visited from afar, from an unseen enemy: random, impersonal and depersonalising. Wilfred Owen wrote home, 'My nerves are in perfect order.' Samuel Hynes makes much of this in *The Soldier's Tale*. 'Not nerve, but nerves, a one-letter vocabulary change that makes a fundamental change in soldierly values. *Nerve*, traditionally, is the inner source of brave actions; *nerves* ... "in perfect order" means only the control of fear.' The French historian Marc Bloch who served at the Front in the First World War, put it thus—bravery had become a 'sort of plodding fatalism, a determination, a cold-blooded effort of will.' (Hynes, 1998, 90). It is that which made the American Civil War so different from the wars the young Henry had read about in the Greek epics. 'He had dreamed of battles all his life—of vague and bloody conflicts that had thrilled him with their sweet fire ... but awake, he had regarded battles as crimson blotches on the pages of the past ... he had long despaired of witnessing a Greek-like struggle. Such would be no more, he said. Men were better or more timid.' (*The Red Badge of Courage*, 4–5). In the world of war that he enters on his enlistment in the Union cause, he finds to his dismay, like Tolstoy's Vladimir, that there is little hand-to-hand fighting. It is the soldier's lot to fall victim to the gun. Ulysses Grant, the most famous Union commander, called war 'pounding'; and no one did it better than he in the war of attrition that the Civil War became.

Traces of this depersonalising influence of war can perhaps be seen in the anonymity of Crane's characters. We do not learn of Henry Fleming's full name until the eleventh chapter. We never learn Wilson's. In the Darwinian environment, the fittest do not always have names—

to stick out is dangerous. What the machine rendered impossible was the old stories of war as told by Crane's forefathers. The battlefield had become disjointed and diffused; it lacked coherence. Crane's refusal to tell a story is part of the larger trend that runs through literature in the early industrial era—a refusal by writers to embed the battle in a political framework, even though the sub-title of the novel (one usually omitted from modern editions) is 'An Episode in the American Civil War.'

Stripped of all his illusions, condemned to finding himself on a killing ground where the enemy is frequently unseen, Henry soon discovers that as far as war is concerned he knows very little; and about himself even less.

We find Henry on the eve of the great battle, prey to all the usual thoughts about mortality. He concludes that the only way he can prove himself is to go into the blaze and then, 'figuratively to watch his legs to discover their merits and faults.' (*The Red Badge of Courage*, 11). He cannot make out whether his friends are all in the same position, or whether their courage is real but merely concealed. One of the first questions he asks a soldier, who we later learn is Jim Cochrin, is whether his friends will cut and run when they come under fire. Another soldier, the Loud Man (whose name we will never discover) tells him that he wont be running himself, not because he is the bravest man in the world, but because he intends to do his 'share of the fighting'. But Henry has sealed himself off from others in his fear. He is isolated and alienated; he finds himself trapped in what he calls a moving box with iron laws of tradition enclosed on four sides that will punish anyone who deserts his post or fails to come through for the others.

It is a fraternity that relies for its effectiveness on what historians call 'primary group cohesion', the chief factor in combat motivation. Loneliness and alienation breed fear, and Henry is never more fearful than when he is alone with himself and his thoughts. Up to this point he has marched along with the others, but considered himself separate from them. At night, even when the campfires dot the landscape like 'red peculiar blossoms', he remains 'a few paces in the gloom', 'a mental outcast', 'alone in space'. Even in the darkness of his tent he cannot escape reflecting on death, even as the light from the campfires penetrates the gloom. His inability to face fear in the light is his chief problem.

Then the moment arrives when Henry faces his first test of battle. Instead of charging at the enemy as he had hoped, he and his colleagues find themselves under fire when the soldiers in the front break and the 'Johnny Rebs' come charging after them. In one of the most famous passages of the novel, Henry loses his fear as adrenaline kicks in:

> He suddenly lost concern for himself ... He became a man, not a member. He felt that something of which he was a part—a regiment, an army, a cause or a country was in a crisis. He was welded into a common personality which was dominated by a single desire ...

> There was a consciousness always of the presence of his comrades about him. He felt the subtle battle-brotherhood more potent than ever than the cause for which they were fighting. It was a mysterious fraternity born of the smoke and danger of death. (*The Red Badge of Courage*, 26).

Henry's survival comes from finding himself a member of a group. It gives him the best chance of life. It is not yet a form of redemption because he finds immediately after the engagement that he still cannot live on equal terms with others, which is why he still experiences the feelings of self-disgust that will haunt him for many pages of the novel. What Crane intuited based entirely on his readings on war we now know to be scientifically true. Social psychology and neuroscientific research indicate that the process that drives us to separate into groups is a real one. Shared emotions really can give a unit a common sense of purpose by activating neural areas of the brain usually associated with fear. Scientists now believe that a neural network that includes the nucleus accumbens, more popularly known as 'the pleasure centre', is responsible for generating the desire to be part of a group. What is significant is that it is also part of the limbic system associated with generating feelings of fear. Using functional magnetic resonance imaging, we can see how bonding with the band of brothers actually works. But this is not how writers, or for that matter their readers, think that people respond to events—and it is how we think we do that is still important.

Henry's fear remains but it will take a different form as the novel progresses—fear that he will betray not only himself, but others. He is on the way to enlightenment but he has many more trials to face before he can become one of the brothers and thus finally come to be at ease with himself.

Briefly rallying to the flag, Henry's will collapses as his courage deserts him. As the men next to him cut and run, he runs too, and as he feels death will choose those nearest to it, he runs with the zeal of a sprinter to keep everyone in the rear. He literally outruns his friends. It is a race, fiercely competitive in the way that most races are. When he finds that the line has actually held because his friends have stood firm, his self-esteem takes a terrible knock and he directs his anger against them. Only blind ignorance and stupidity could explain their actions. He is clearly surrounded by fools who are incapable of rational thinking. Finally, he turns his thoughts to the absurdity of the entire situation. The battle was not even a battle but a 'perfunctory popping' of bullets. His friends were brave because they thought their actions would decide the war, and that they would carve the letters of their names into the history books. Some of them have paid for that illusion with their lives.

Henry returns to the field and joins up with the retreating column. He must now conceal his shame as his friends question him about the fight and his role in it. But his ordeal is soon cut short by the death of the only soldier whose name we know, and by implication the only one that Henry has truly befriended, Jim. Jim's death is the most poignant passage in the novel. He is every bit the brave soldier, though modest in his bravery as he was in life. 'Well, he was reg'lar jim-dandy for nerve, wa'n't he?' remarks the tattered man in a little awe-struck voice.

Jim's death does nothing to restore Henry's spirits or steel him for battle. He is relieved to see the army in retreat as a perverse form of vindication for his own cowardice. But the battle is far from over. Another unit marches to the sound of gunfire. Preoccupied with his wounds, he is horrified to think that the battle might now be won. How could he live with himself knowing that he had made no contribution to the final victory? The thought is even more shaming. When he finally manages to rejoin his unit he is relieved to find that the shame does not have to be shared. No one has actually seen him flee from the battlefield a few hours earlier. Henry is still inclined to see himself through the eyes of others. Philosophers have been especially interested in the human tendency to see ourselves from the outside. We often aspire to an objective view of ourselves that the philosopher Thomas Nagel describes as 'the view from nowhere', and we do this for a particular purpose: to be esteemed not only for what we do, but for who we are. We wish to be valued by other people.

And in no time at all, he gets back his old self-assurance, even his swagger. He is now able to think of himself as a man of experience. In his self-absorption he even begins to despise those who fled with him as being 'more fleet and more wild' than was absolutely necessary. They had fled the field of battle out of terror, he out of discretion. 'He could see himself in a room of warm tints, telling tales to listeners. He could exhibit laurels. They were insignificant; still in a district where laurels were infrequent, they might shine.' (*The Red Badge of Courage*, 66).

And no sooner does he entertain such thoughts than the unit gets orders to relieve a command that has been posted some time ago to the trenches. When they come under attack again, Henry rises to the occasion. He throws himself into the struggle with gusto, loading and reloading his gun until there is no one left to shoot at. For the first time his comrades see him not only as a soldier, but as a bit of a 'war-devil'. 'He had slept and awakened and found himself a knight.' And then they are ordered to undertake an assault themselves, going forward into a curtain of bullets, bodies exploding in 'crimson fury'. They burst into cheering, and find themselves tuned in strange keys. But the pace cannot be sustained for long, and the moment the regiment ceases to advance, the flutter of musketry becomes a roar. No amount of pleading by their commanding officer can rouse them to go forward again. They fall back into the woods in disarray.

This time the fight is different. When the Colour Sergeant is killed, Henry rescues the colours, and with this gesture their fortunes turn. They repel the enemy assault, though they get no thanks for their pains. The Colonel is furious that they have not sustained their own advance. They had 'stopped about a hundred feet this side of a very pretty success.' (*The Red Badge of Courage*, 86). He calls them 'mud diggers' and in time the insult strikes home. The only praise the Colonel will award is to Henry for rescuing the colours, and for the first time, the unit sees Henry as more equal than most.

And so to Henry's final encounter with himself. He is still ashamed, but this time not for himself, but for the regiment. He is ashamed that they have been called 'mud diggers', which is almost as bad as being accused of being slackers. And because his shame is all the deeper, he feels it can only be expiated by his dead body lying torn and bloody on the field. Even now he is still dreaming of his own glory. And it is at this point in the narrative that Crane brings home the horror of war, and Henry's circumstances as the battle rages around him, as bodies twist into impossible shapes and one man has his jaw blown away. This is as cruel as anything you will find in the literature of the First World War (the only contemporary echo is Tolstoy's *Sevastapol Sketches*).

The regiment bled extravagantly. Grunting bundles of blue began to drop. The Orderly Sergeant of the youth's company was shot through the cheeks. Its supports being injured, his jaw hung afar down, disclosing in the wide cavern of his mouth a pulsing mass of blood and teeth. And with it all, he made attempts to cry out. In his endeavour there was a dreadful earnestness as if he conceived that one great shriek would make him well. (*The Red Badge of Courage*, 91).

It is not sure of course whether this is Crane talking, or Henry thinking; Henry can also turn a vivid image, as when he sees the artillery shells arching in the sky as 'rows of cruel teeth that grinned at him.' (*The Red Badge of Courage*, 32).

The Colonel finally comes running along the line: '"We must charge 'em!", they shouted. "We must charge 'em!" they cried with resentful voices as if anticipating a rebellion against this plan by the men.' But there is no rebellion and the men rush forward, almost unthinkingly and certainly recklessly, with Henry to the fore carrying the colours. We leave Henry after the fighting has ceased, still mindful of that moment of betrayal, not entirely assuaged by his recent experiences but much more confident that the next time they face a crisis, he will not fail. Having received the primary sacrament of war, the baptism of fire, their boyhoods were behind them, writes Philip Caputo of his own time in Vietnam. 'Neither they nor I thought of it in those terms at the time. We didn't say to ourselves: we've been under fire, we've shed blood, now we are men. We were simply aware, in a way we could not explain, that something significant had happened to us.' (Caputo, 1978, 127). But, of course, even if a soldier survives a battle, it does not mean that his courage will hold, or that he will survive the war. We are left with an incomplete story.

Henry James, as he was coming to the end of one of his greatest novels, *The Portrait of a Lady*, confided in his notebook his worry that his readers would think the novel was not really finished, that it had 'not seen the heroine to the end of her situation.' James resolved that Isobel Archer will stay married to her husband, even though she has found out that he is a mercenary wretch, and even though she remains in touch with a former suitor to whom she could escape if she chose to. But he concluded that the novel finished on this note because it was the 'right' note on which to end. 'The *whole* of anything is never told; you can only take what groups together, what I have done has that unity— it groups together. It is complete in itself.' (Sontag, 2007, 22).

What makes a novel work is that a man's life never ends, even if he survives the fighting. He brings the fight back with him when he returns home. And the changes in his interior life that we are allowed to witness will not necessarily equip him to survive the next challenge down the line. His character is not fixed, which is why all great fiction is necessarily inconclusive. A novelist can only help us grasp 'what groups together', and which episode in a life is complete in itself before the hero confronts the next challenge. Only if a character dies can we have closure, because there is no possibility of change.

Crane's book ends with some of the most famous lines in the literature of war. Henry's nightmare fear of cowardice is now in the past. Crane adds, 'He was a man.' The phrase these days is not heard as often as it was, say, thirty years ago. It sounds dated. What does manliness mean these days? Today even soldiers find it embarrassing—and for a reason. We are more inclined that our forefathers to see that one can be man enough to be a soldier, only to find on returning home that war has not made one more of a man. What it means, I think, is that Henry has tested himself against the criteria that society employs. We now test ourselves by other criteria. To be a man today is to be what one wants to be in the eyes of others. It is now merely a shorthand for what Kafka called 'the indestructible self'. For many of us it will be defined in different terms and by different criteria. Manliness, even for a soldier, is not what it once was.

Each of us has to measure our indestructible self and define it in whatever ways we can and whatever way society permits. Some will measure their own manliness in terms of a weekend retreat into the mountains, hunting bears or paintballing friends. In war much more is expected. Those who throw themselves into battle have to ask more of themselves than most of us, and many may find that they are equally wanting in other more idiosyncratic ways. And that is what makes war so unkind. The feeling is evoked in us, wrote Arthur Miller in *Tragedy and the Common Man*, 'when we are in the presence of a character who is ready to lay down his life, if need be to secure one thing—his sense of personal dignity.' (Gilligan, 2000, 103). Not every reader thinks Henry has been changed by the end of the novel: many think that he still unformed, impressionable and still self-regarding. But for me Crane does affect a change in the young man that is visible, though it may not be long lasting. He now admits to his fears, not to confess but to conceal them. He understands courage but does not boast of his own. He understands war without rejecting it; he has fewer illusions but he now has hope.

Brigadier Gerard: The Hero of His Own Story
The Complete Brigadier Gerard, Arthur Conan Doyle

What a novel my life is, Napoleon once declared—and indeed, Napoleon dominated the imagination of the nineteenth century. The Napoleonic wars also gave us the greatest war novel, *War and Peace*, as well as a series of short stories by perhaps the greatest storyteller in English literature, Arthur Conan Doyle.

Conan Doyle is best remembered, of course, for the Sherlock Holmes stories. 'The world is sweeter for my presence', he tells his amanuensis, Dr Watson, and the life of literature is more colourful because Doyle gave him life. He also created in Brigadier Gerard, a young French cavalry officer at the time of the Napoleonic Wars, a hero who he loved more than he did Holmes, and whose exploits were captured in a series which first appeared in *The Strand*, the same magazine that carried the stories of Sherlock Holmes. The stories were later collected in two volumes, *The Exploits of Brigadier Gerard* (1896), and *The Adventures of Gerard* (1903), and they 'date' back to the 1840s when Gerard tells his tales, with the exception of one, 'The Road to Minsk', which he is moved to relate after seeing the despatch of another French army to Russia, thirty years after Napoleon's death on St Helena. These tales are entertaining, but they also illustrate a vital existential return of war: story-telling. Soldiers tell tales. 'We are here to live the stories, not compose them', the young Odysseus is told by his father in Zachary Mason's retelling of the *Odyssey*. But soldiers are as good at spinning a tale as any epic poet or novelist. They also inhabit the stories they tell. They are, after all, the principal characters in their own life.

The similarities between Gerard and Sherlock Holmes are perhaps worth a mention, as are the differences. Gerard shares with Holmes his French blood. In *The Greek Interpreter*, Holmes tells Watson that his grandmother was the sister of Vernet, the French artist. 'Art in the blood is likely to take the strangest forms', he remarks. In his case it is the art of detection: in Gerard's it is the art of war. There is also a dark side to Holmes. He lives in darkness, in a world peopled by villains, guttersnipes and worse. London, he declares, in the very first story in which he appeared, 'is a great cesspool into which all the loungers and idlers of the Empire are irresistibly drained.' For Gerard, Europe is a cesspool too, where rotten soldiers flourish in the chaos the rival armies leave in their wake. In Spain, Gerard encounters the worst of all, bandits, who embody atavistic values that enlightened Europeans thought they had seen the last of, and which can be seen in Goya's paintings, the *Disasters of War*. Battlefields, too, attract their fair share of idlers: young men on their uppers, or who want to rise in the social scale; adventurers who are not averse to helping themselves to the spoils of war ('to the victor belong the spoils'); and a fair share of villainous thugs, bandits, and adrenaline junkies, those who cannot make a go of peace, the brutal, the rapacious, the terminally bored.

Gerard's world is distressingly dark at times, especially for a set of short stories that were meant to entertain and amuse. Gerard has his run-ins with a variety of criminals, or ordinary men whose criminal tendencies war has brought out, characters like *El Cuchillo* ('The Knife'), and another called simply 'the Smiler'. He even has his Moriarty in the much more appealing figure of Captain Alexis Morgan, aka Marshall Millefleurs, an officer cashiered from the British Army for cheating at cards who now leads a polyglot collection of French stragglers, English deserters and Portuguese brigands. He is also a master of disguise who passes himself off as a Capuchin monk with no trouble. In his account of the retreat from Moscow we see the squalor of war; in his adventures in Spain we see that war produces monsters. *El Cuchillo* has a fondness for blank verse, and also a taste for cruelty (he buries alive a young officer named Subiron). He is a very different character from the bandit leader *El Sordo* in Hemingway's *For Whom the Bell Tolls*. All this is a sore trial for a man who has been brought up to think of war as a game played under fixed rules, and that when the rules are broken a forfeit has to be paid. What Gerard likes most about the English who take him prisoner in Spain is their 'sportsmanship', which is signally lacking in the Cossacks who act so barbarously in the retreat from Moscow, hanging back in the shadows until they can kill the stragglers or sell them into slavery; or the Poles who will kill a Russian officer on sight; or Spanish peasants fighting for the Catholic church in the first religious war since the mid-seventeenth century.

But we must not pursue the similarities with Holmes too far, for the differences are just as intriguing. Conan Doyle never drew a scene in the Holmes stories with the Tolstoyean eye he brings to the Gerard tales. In 'How the Brigadier Rode to Minsk', Gerard himself paints a picture as well as the Russian novelist, describing a long black line of soldiers in retreat, snaking across the white plain, trudging 100 miles, and then another 100, and always the same white plain and the same lines of men. 'Weary, ragged, starving ... the spirit frozen out of them.' (*The Complete Brigadier Gerard*, 267).

Furthermore, there is not a trace of Holmes' darker nature in Gerard—his cocaine habit, his melancholic moods, his dismal violin playing. Gerard loves life and life loves him back, and we love him all the more for it. He loves the things Holmes does not, especially honours and applause. He loves praise, especially from the Emperor. On bravery he refuses to say anything. He acknowledges that some say that Murat was the bravest of Napoleon's Marshalls, others say Ney. He himself believes that he is the bravest of them all but declines to acquaint others with this opinion. He has none of Holmes' modesty when it comes to public self-promotion, but he also does not lack courage (the soldier's stock in trade). It was acute of Conan Doyle to realise that Gerard needed that much vivacity to make his heroic deeds believable. As Michael Chabon writes, Gerard exceeds Holmes in one trait, in which the great detective, by his own admission, was always deficient: a rich and loveable humanity (Chabon, 2010, 27).

There are two things that he is slow to forget, Gerard tells us: the face of a pretty woman and the legs of a fine horse. (*The Complete Brigadier Gerard*, 139). Holmes has only one woman in his life, Irene Adler, and although one of his finest cases features a racehorse, Silver Blaze, we never see him on the back of a horse once in four novels and fifty-six stories. The Brigadier meets his own Irene Adler—actually, he is bested by two women in the course of his campaigns. The first, Sophie, lures him into a trap at Minsk, but also springs him from captivity. And then there is the Princess of Saxe-Felstein, with whom he plays a game with all of Germany as a stake. It is not the least of his endearing qualities, however, that when he fouls up, he admits it readily.

Holmes' aversion to women is not the mark of a misogynist. He merely has such a rational mind that there is simply no room for emotion, even love. Gerard has no intellectual resources at all. He has no philosophy of life, and certainly no philosophy of war. What war offers him is a life of adventure and occasionally the chance to enrich himself. He pillages two paintings from Venice: the *Nymph Surprised* and

St Barbara, the second of which he sends to his mother, the first of which he keeps for himself. It is striking how far Gerard does indeed lack depth. He is not a man of ideas. He is not given to introspection. He is not in the business of diagnosing himself. But then, unlike Holmes, who has his Watson, and Jack Aubrey who has another doctor, Maturin, he tells his own tales, and the stories inevitably suffer from the telling. There is no self-critique; no implicit questioning of some of his methods. But the stories also gain from the Brigadier's endearing self-regard which, in the words of Philip Pullman, make him the most 'preposterous and delightful of companions'.

Gerard is a Gascon, like D'Artagnan, but he is more like Porthos than any of the other Musketeers. He hails from a family of good repute, but one which has never prospered. He lacks funds to cut the figure he would like, especially among the ladies, and it is perhaps this insight into his inner life—the only one we are given—that explains his desire to succeed, to be the bravest and the best of Hussars. His self-regard is as monstrous as Holmes' self-absorption and both are rendered all the more real by their telling lines: 'It's true that I have to depict myself sometimes as brave, sometimes as full of resource, always as interesting, but then it really was so, and I had to take the facts as I found them.' (*The Complete Brigadier Gerard*, 181). Marshall Massena picks him for a mission because he knows a fine soldier when he sees one, at which point Gerard adds, 'that was the best of serving with those good old generals;' they instantly recognised a man of distinction when they saw one (*The Complete Brigadier Gerard*, 134). About Napoleon he never says a harsh word except to complain that instead of taking him to Moscow the Emperor had left him behind at Borodino to guard the lines of communication. It is a decision that is incomprehensible, and one that confirms him in his judgement that his master was no longer the man he once was. Gerard is almost felled at the battle of Eylau. Nevertheless, it would have been a glorious death, he remarks, perhaps meriting seven lines in *The Moniteur*, 'Pelaret had eight lines, and I'm sure that he had not so fine a career.' (*The Complete Brigadier Gerard*, 32).

We excuse him his vanity and his self-conceit (a stock trope for a Frenchman in English literature, particularly in the late nineteenth century) because he has wit, and often a wonderful turn of phrase. Of Massena, a notorious spendthrift, he writes, 'he clutched onto his position as he did to his strongbox and it took a very clever man to loosen him from either.' (*The Complete Brigadier Gerard*, 133). Of another, Marshall, Jomini, he complains that his pen was always sharper than his sword (*The Complete Brigadier Gerard*, 158). He has the authentic swagger of the old veteran even in writing. It is my habit, he says, to talk of what interests myself, and so he hopes that it may also interest his readers. What you see, he tells us, is a man who is 'a piece of history' who now lives among the shadows. And Gerard can tell a tale as well as anyone:

> For twenty years we were teaching Europe how to fight, and even when they had learned their lesson it was only the thermometer, and never the bayonet, which could break the Grand Army down. Berlin, Naples, Vienna, Madrid, Lisbon, Moscow—we stabled our horses in them all. Yes, my friends, I say again that you do well to send your children to me with flowers, for these ears have heard the trumpet calls of France, and these eyes have seen her standards in lands where they may never be seen again. (*The Complete Brigadier Gerard*, 110).

What he does not admit to, of course, is the human cost of the Napoleonic epic. But then he is almost entirely lacking in self-knowledge. He admits he has never made it higher than Chief of Brigade, but in the service of the Grand Army—a career open to all the talents, or so we are told—one has to serve with the Emperor on campaign to rise to the top. Napoleon, who has extinguished liberty by enslaving half of Europe, and fraternity by declaring war on the other half, seems to have only paid lip service to equality too, even in the army.

Many readers, writes Sebastian Faulks, believe that Conan Doyle was the supreme storyteller of British fiction. He would not dispute the claim himself, except in one particular: too much of the action in the Sherlock Holmes stories is given in speech. It is a convention to have a narrator 'frame' the narrative, but the danger is that it can put the action at arm's length (Faulkes, 2011, 59). This is not a failure of the Gerard stories. There is action both on the battlefield and off it. Like Conrad's Colonel Feraud, he is an excellent fencer, who is chosen by his Regiment to fight the champion of the Hussars of Chambarant. He insults six fencing masters for the sake of practice in the week before the duel, thus having the 'privilege' of being called out seven times in as many days. And he will hazard his life in a fair fight, especially for a lady. If he cannot win her, still at least he has a fair field in which to try. He is quite ready to despatch other suitors like Hippolyte Leseur, who 'if he lives still limps with a bullet lodged in his knee.' (*The Complete Brigadier Gerard*, 380). Like Othello wooing Desdemona, he tells tales to the woman he will eventually marry, relating the night he swum his horse across the Danube with a message for Marshall Davout: 'To be frank, it was not the Danube, nor was it so deep that I was compelled to swim, but when one is twenty and in love, one tells the story as best one can.' (*The Complete Brigadier Gerard*, 382).

These are the types of stories that soldiers tell each other, tales of bravado and risk taking, and of chivalry (towards both women and enemies deserving of it). These are the tales of men who though quick to anger if their honour is affronted, are unwilling to hold grudges for long. These are the tales in which soldiers like to imagine themselves, as great-hearted, and they are not, it must be said, entirely untrue. We must understand, he tells us, that a man who spends a lifetime on the battlefield will meet with many strange experiences, and take many risks. And there are stories aplenty of narrow escapes, including one from the German Dragoons on the road to Paris in 1814. With the grim humour of a soldier, he writes: 'well, I had Dragoons behind me and the Hussars in front ... but for the honour of the Brigade I had rather be cut down by a Light Cavalryman than a Heavy!' (*The Complete Brigadier Gerard*, 23).

And, above all, there is the old soldier's unequivocal devotion to the great commander; in this case, the Emperor. Unfortunately it is not a devotion which is entirely requited. When he first meets Napoleon in 1807 he is chosen for a mission because the Emperor wants an agent who will not penetrate too deeply into his plans. He is chosen precisely because 'he is all spurs and moustaches with never a thought beyond women and horses.' (*The Complete Brigadier Gerard*, 93). The Emperor tells him not to think and endeavouring to obey him in this as in everything else, Gerard tells us that he did just that. We can believe him, too (*The Complete Brigadier Gerard*, 99). He is good at thinking himself out of a tight spot (and he is especially good at escaping) but in the world of politics he is entirely at sea.

At the end of his life all he has left are his memories and a hundred francs a month of half pay. Like many soldiers, he cannot relinquish the past. He wears the ribbon of the Cross of Honour on his coat lapel, but we know him only as a civilian 'with an air and manner' of the Hussar he once was. We know that he is still alive at the time of the Crimean War when the Emperor's nephew took his country to war once again against Russia. He tells us how he cheered the soldiers as they left. 'Up threw my cane. *Chargez en avant, Vive l'Empereur!* It was the past calling to the present. But, Oh, what a thin piping voice!' (*The Complete Brigadier Gerard*, 266).

Conan Doyle was a fine historical novelist and the Gerard tales are all the better for their historical authenticity. The characters he drew were not untrue to history. Gen. George Napier, who spent years in the Peninsular, also managed to airbrush out Goya's atrocities of war in his own account of his career. He wrote that there was never any personal animosity between French and British officers, 'and I hope (this) will always be the case. I should hate to fight out of personal malice or revenge, but have no objection to fighting for "fun and glory"' (Haythornthwaite, 1996, 13). The sentiments could well be Gerard's.

One will not find the *Sevastopol Sketches* in these tales, but Conan Doyle was an even better storyteller than he was a novelist, and if Gerard will never outdo Andrei as a character, or even Lieutenant Kozeltsov, he comes pretty close. 'There is no greatness where simplicity, goodness and truth are absent', wrote Tolstoy in *War and Peace*. Owen Dudley-Edwards claims that there is a Tolstoyean totality about the Gerard stories, and especially in the use of irony. There are many ironies in the Brigadier's life (this time rendered as comedy); the irony of being something of a dunderhead but the wisest fool in the Grande Armée, and the luckiest man in the Hussars; the irony of faithfully serving an Emperor who has little respect for him; and the greatest irony of all in seeing war as a glorious game while showing us scenes of unspeakable cruelty in Spain and Russia, both of which seem to escape him (Conan Doyle, 2010, xii).

Conan Doyle was a master storyteller, but Gerard is a flat character. It would be interesting to know why he is so conceited. Does he have a Gascon chip on his shoulder like D'Artagnan? Is it his family's reduced circumstances or his failure to make it above the rank of Brigadier? We really do not know. He is not particularly interested in interrogating himself, let alone scanning his emotions. He is what he is because the author uses him as a vehicle for telling some wonderful tales—the tales that old soldiers used to tell. Gerard is an inspired comic invention. War brings him adventures and the love of the 'ladies' as he gallantly calls them, to whom he remains loyal even when they deceive him. There are darker moments, to be sure. But they are passed over quickly. We do not see the squalor or brutality of war; all we are allowed to see is the 'glamour'.

Conan Doyle's stories are glamorous because Gerard is such a good raconteur. He is incapable of feeling pity for himself even in his reduced circumstances, propping up a table at a café, doubtless while others buy him a drink. He is a born optimist with a touching if somewhat self-deceiving faith in the father-figure of Napoleon who treated him as a father would a not-too-bright son. Gerard is a conduit for action, and action often sounds like the *Just So Stories*. But he really is out of his depth, as are so many soldiers when dealing with calculating politicians, shocked by the behaviour of ambitious generals—especially the Marshalls who owe Napoleon everything but betray him in the end. And he is even let down by his own countrymen who reconcile themselves to the restoration of the Bourbons and settle for peace because of their fear of failure. Gerard has outlived both the man and his age; all he has are his memories.

And yet, it would be wrong to make him out as something of a victim. This is not Conan Doyle's purpose or point. We should not read too much into a man who is not given to reading other people, and certainly not himself. There is some pathos in his story, to be sure, but it is not rendered by the author. The novelist William Faulkner once wrote that 'the problems of the human heart in conflict with itself ... alone make good writing.' For Freud what makes a rounded person is one in whose 'soul' Eros and Thanatos struggle for dominance. In shaping a life, they make it impossible to be at peace with oneself for more than a short period. It is this struggle, wrote Bruno Bettelheim, that makes emotional richness possible, and explains the multifarious nature of a person's life (Bettelheim, 1982, 109). Holmes has this complexity; Gerard simply does not. In real life a soldier who threw himself into the fight as often as Gerard would be thought to have a death wish—but Gerard has no personal quarrel with the Emperor's enemies and derives no pleasure from killing them. He just loves living on the edge. He is neither morbidly attracted to death nor narcissistic. Gerard lives in the real world because of the stories that define him, not the other way round.

Goethe, whom Napoleon famously met, said that in seventy-five years he experienced only four weeks of being truly at ease. An inescapable sadness is part of life. Gerard either does not experience it, or he suppresses it in the telling of his tale. We can conclude what we like. The decision to include Gerard's stories in this book was a difficult one, but in the end I decided to do so because they illuminate what war is for so many readers—action-packed, and the action is not entirely untrue to the experience itself. It is one of the reasons why so many young men join up.

After all, Gerard has lived in the fast lane. And even if only half true, his life story would be extraordinary. We must not pity him, but warm to the old rogue. We do not have to believe all his stories to find the storyteller himself believable. This is the point about all storytelling, and every war gives rise to stories—bleak, uncompromising, grim, and frequently sordid. But it produces adventure stories, too, and Conan Doyle's was a more trusting age. Most of the stories appeared before 1903, before the glory of war was blown to pieces in the trenches, and the glamour wore off. So let us leave the Brigadier, drinking his favourite wine of Suresnes, and telling old tales in the café to anyone who will listen, or buy him a drink. Let us leave him with his salutation to us, the readers. 'Gentlemen, an old soldier salutes you and bids you farewell.' (*The Complete Brigadier Gerard*, 377).

Bourne: The Stoic Hero

Her Privates We, Frederic Manning

Many readers have viewed *Her Privates We* as the supreme story of the Great War experience and I would not dispute the claim. It is a short tale framed between two battle scenes, both set in the Somme with an interval behind the lines during the latter half of 1916. What makes it so authentic is its anonymity. In a prefatory note the author, Frederic Manning, tells us that he had drawn no portraits; his interest is in the anonymous ranks whose opinions, though often ill-informed and prejudiced, were real and true enough for them. Manning himself had served in the war, enlisting as a private in the Shropshire Light Infantry. After some weeks of basic training he was selected as an officer-cadet, but was returned to his unit for drunkenness and fought at the Somme as a private. Despite receiving a commission for a second time, he drank too much and was up before a Court Martial. In the last year of the conflict he offered to resign his commission and the offer was accepted. He wrote *Her Privates We* ten years into the peace, not under a pseudonym but a number—Private 19022. This is how he appeared on the cover of the first edition in 1930, and the book, originally titled *The Middle Parts of Fortune*, produced the most sympathetic hero of the trenches—Private Bourne. What makes him so authentic a figure is that he is not particularly heroic, but rather stoical. The heroism of war is to be found not only in its sung or unsung deeds, but also the stoicism in which it is endured.

Bourne is not only stoical but interesting which is why we take an interest in him. He observes life at the Front on our behalf. He is an interlocutor between the reader and another world, a soldier with unusual intellectual resources and a fine cast of mind. Above all, he is not the caricature figure that we might expect if we knew the First World War only from its poetry.

Poetry still defines the experience of the First World War for the English. Think of the poets who still haunt the English consciousness, especially the two most famous, Wilfred Owen and Siegfried Sassoon, and the images they convey. We recognise these without reading a single poem: the uncaring generals sending men to their deaths across a lunar landscape, to be blown apart, or trapped on the wire of No Man's Land.

The war lives through the poetry, which is particularly problematic, because the poetic 'memory' of the war is often wilfully misleading. What much of the poetry represents is not the total experience of the war, but a highly selective one—an edited, expurgated version of the poets' response to the challenge of modern warfare. The essential difference between the war they experienced and the war experienced by many in the rank and file, including Manning, was that its truth for each differed significantly. Truth for the soldier meant his own subjective experience, which was far from being entirely negative. The truth for the poets, claims Maurice Genevoix, was not 'their truth, but *the* truth' that would in time become part of modern memory (Panichas, 1985, 485).

Owen invoked Keats in a variety of ways to help him define his own response to the conflict but Keats' 'poetical character' was part of the dilemma. Keats argued that the poetic character is made up of light and shade, that it lives in 'gusto', that it exaggerates, indeed that it must do if it is to have any character at all. 'What shocks the virtuous philosopher delights the chameleon poet', Keats once observed. The poet is Pascal's 'poet but not an honest man'. Reading much of the poetry you would never guess that men such as Graham Greenwell could see the war as a 'great adventure' which, if for no other reason, invested the experience with meaning for him (Greenwell, 1935). Units such as the Second Battalion of the Royal Welsh Fusiliers earned a reputation for aggressive trench warfare; they often conducted raids into No Man's Land simply to combat the tedium of trench life. If Owen was a much better soldier than his poetry reveals, so too was one of the Royal Welsh's best, Siegfried Sassoon. Yet you would never know from his account of his own career at the Front that he volunteered for nocturnal missions crawling through the deep corn in No Man's Land with a couple of bombs in his pocket, and a knobkerrie in his hand (Simpson, 1985, 149).

The challenge of writing poetry in a time of war was more complex than simply the distortion of poetic character on the small canvas of the battlefield as opposed to the larger canvas of life. Since the war poets refused to give meaning to the suffering they described, they were unable to relate it to history. 'Of pity, grief and sorrow there is much in their poetry', writes one critic, 'but these emotions do not attain to the tragic.' The war poet, he argues:

> functions as conscience, as sensibility and as the voice of anger or pain, but he seldom rises above these functions and the aspects of ugliness or suffering upon which they are based. Enveloped in the tragedy of war he sees only magnified particulars and details—no event becomes 'luminous' in his mind. (Johnston, 1964, 134).

Instead, the war poets threatened to rob the dead of their dignity and death of its significance. Their poems often lack an objective sense of restraint, certainly of self-proportion. And they compounded these faults because what they witnessed, horrific as it was, inspired them to write in a mood of understandable anger. Manning's account of the war is very different; it describes the life of a soldier who not only survived it, but felt it to have been necessary, and who never departed from that belief—any more than did the great majority of soldiers with whom he served.

Both titles of Manning's novel come from *Hamlet* and a brief exchange between the young prince and his friends Rosencrantz and Guildenstern. When Hamlet enquires after their mood, Guildenstern says that they are neither too happy, nor too depressed—'on fortune's cap we are not the very bottom.'

HAMLET: Then you live above her waist, or in the middle of her favour.
GUILDENSTERN: Faith, her privates, we.
HAMLET: In the secret parts of fortune? O, most true she is a strumpet.

This is one of the central themes of the novel: the role that fortune or chance play in war, the most unpredictable of all activities. A soldier lives in a world of contingency—'the middle parts of fortune'. And the coarseness of Hamlet's exchange explains why Manning felt it so important to defy convention and use the language of the ordinary soldiers in the trenches. Humour and coarseness are attendant themes of war, striking affirmations of humanity in the presence of death.

It is perhaps worth mentioning, in parenthesis, that the usual absence of obscenity until the 1960s robbed the war novel and its characters of the tonal difference that is often part of a person's individuality. This is what Manning should be remembered for. In his novel he made it possible for authors to say exactly what they wanted to say in the coarsest language—the language of war. And he made it possible to say it directly. A soldier says of the officer who took the binoculars he had taken from a dead German soldier 'And now the bastard's wearin the bes' pair slung round his own bloody neck. Wouldn't you thought the cunt would 'a' give me vingt frong for em anyway.' When Bourne asks him ironically whether he has learned these choice phrases in the army the young man replies that all he has learned is drill. 'I knew all the fuckin' patter before I joined.' (*Her Privates We*, 37–38). Your language is deplorable, says Bourne in an ironical reproof, 'quite apart from the fact that you are speaking of your commanding officer.' Hidden in the exchange is the bond between that two that will blossom and end in tragedy when the young man dies—despite the gap in their age and what the generation would have called their 'station' in life they enjoy a strange equality forged in war.

Language is the key to conveying the truth of any experience. Henry Manning's novel, even today, is often still read in the expurgated version, blunting the insight and passions of the men he portrays on the page, denying them their true voice. But thanks to Manning we are now impervious to the coarse language on the page. What we still find distressing is not the coarseness of the language, but the coarseness of life, and especially the squalid actions that war tends to bring to light. Even Norman Mailer, who became famous for using the most famous of all four letter words, felt compelled to use the word 'fug' instead in *The Naked and the Dead*. 'So you are the young man who can't spell "fuck"' remarked Dorothy Parker when she was first introduced to him. But Mailer had the last word. As he once noted when someone complained about the overuse of obscenity in war fiction, authors have recourse to words like 'shit' so that occasionally they can use words like 'noble'.

If fortune is one theme of the novel, it is handled subtly. In the very first pages a young officer tells Bourne that 'you and I are two of the lucky ones ... and if our luck holds we'll keep moving out of one bloody misery into another, until we break.' (*Her Privates We*, 5). Later we learn that the officer has been killed by a shell while on trench duty. The Colour Sergeant speaks not for the officers but for many of the enlisted men, with the conscious indifference that allows the men to cope with the fortunes of war:

> You know, to my way o' thinkin', some of us'ns 'ave a dam' sight more reli-
> gion that some o' the parsons who preach at us. We're willin' to take a
> chance. 'uman nature's 'uman nature, and you may be right or you may be
> wrong, but if you bloody well think you're right, you may as well get on
> with it. What does it matter if y'are killed? You've got to die some day.
> You've got to chance your arm in this life, an' a dam' sight more'n your arm
> too sometimes. Some folk talk a lot about war bein' such a bloody waste;
> but I'm not so sure it's such a bloody waste after all. (*Her Privates We*, 76).

Bourne himself is sympathetic to this view because he understands the implications the words are intended to convey. 'Life was a hazard enveloped in mystery and war quickened the sense of both in men; the soldier also, as well as the saint, might write his *tractatate de contemptu mundi* and differ from him only in the angle and spirit from which he surveyed the same bleak reality.'

When everything is governed by chance, it is difficult to take the patriotic speeches seriously. Manning is at pains to tell us that Bourne may surrender to the mood of the moment, but he never succumbs to the patriotic bullshit. He dismisses sacrifice as a vicarious atonement for the failure of others. When a commanding officer tries to tell the men the plan of attack and the importance of winning, they all have to think of it from the point of view of their own concrete and individual experience. And when he insists that after the pounding the Germans will receive, they will offer no resistance. 'A still small voice from the back whispers, 'what ... 'opes 'ave we got then?'" (*Her Privates We*, 147).

There is an atmosphere of profound resignation in the way Manning tells the story. No false heroics, no empty phrases sustain us or the men. The prose is plain and spare. 'He neither hurried nor slackened his pace; he was light-headed, almost exalted, and driven only by the desire to find an end.' (*Her Privates We*, 1). This is our first description of Bourne when he finds the safety of a trench. He meets up with three Scotsmen who are almost as spent and broken as he is. They, too, are at a loss to know what to do. Under their bravado, it is easy enough to see the irresolution of weary men seeking in their difficulties some reasonable pretext for doing nothing. Manning never misses a moment to tell us how war can hollow out emotions and passions, which is why the dead seem to Bourne to have such empty and senseless expressions on their faces. When he rejoins the men he lost contact with on the first page, he is struck by how, under the brims of their helmets, he sees living eyes moving relentlessly on blank faces. The anonymity continues with the first roll call after the battle, as name after name is called, then for a moment the general sense of loss becomes focused on an individual name, whilst some meagre details are given by witnesses of the particular man's fate. 'I saw 'im, sir ... 'e were just blown to buggery... 'e were a chum of mine, sir, an' I seen 'im blown into fucking bits.' (*Her Privates We*, 21).

But that is all a soldier has—hopes of good fortune, an inner conviction that somehow he will escape death. And what perhaps strikes the modern reader most is that Bourne never questions the war or its morality. He accepts it, as the great majority did; there is only one dissenting moment when he concludes that the extreme of heroism is indistinguishable from despair (*Her Privates We*, 8). For the most part, like the men, he is anxious to remain in the middle parts of fortune—any extreme is deadly. Bourne's comrades show no zeal for the war, or take any interest in it (they talk about politics only once and that at the very end of the novel). What these men have is a 'moral power', exhibited in many forms, one of which is to treat death as one of the realities they are bound to take a chance on. Bourne, like most of them, is scathing about conscientious objectors. And although he can sympathise with the plight of a deserter, Miller, he cannot empathise with him because he has deserted his friends. In accepting the verdict of fortune, he and his friends have made a deliberate choice and asserted the freedom of their being. 'The sense of wasted effort is only true for meaner and more material natures.' (*Her Privates We*, 10).

Death, of course, admits of no degree. For the pacifist a man is dead or not dead, and that man is just as dead by one means or another, but it is the manner in which a man dies that means so much to Bourne. He has an instinctive horror of being shattered and eviscerated by a shell. He would rather be shot clean in his tracks, he reflects, than left face downwards. The fact that men accept this situation is to exert their humanity, but a dead body has lost it. It is not a pleasant sight. When Bourne himself is killed, his body provokes revulsion even from the Sgt. Major who admired him in life. But there is a quick acceptance of the fact; for him, at least, the war is over.

What many veterans found distressing after the war, after the initial pride in victory had diminished, was the intellectual charge that they had been passive victims led to the slaughter. There are always choices to be made, even in the face of ill-fortune. To claim less would be demeaning. To claim more and say they were all heroic would be wrong. To claim either is only a way of distancing ourselves from them, and we surely read novels to narrow the distance, not extend it.

Manning took the trouble to cast a private soldier as the hero of his story, though his voice suggests that Bourne is far more educated and worldly-wise, as well as much older, than most private soldiers would have been in 1916. We are never told Bourne's age, but we suspect that he is as old as Manning when he joined up—thirty-six. To be able to deal with the contradictions and ambiguities of war is a sign of maturity. He takes the same view of the war as the men did themselves, as they matured and looked back proudly on the fact that they had never broken. This fact was a matter of supreme importance to the veterans who attended the Armistice ceremonies in Britain, though inevitably the way the war came to be remembered by society at large (thanks in part to the poets) diminished their pride over time, before the last of them died in 2011. What they were celebrating was their service. As Jeffrey Thurley has pointed out in his book *The Ironic Heart*, we live in an age where savage irony can undercut any attempt to express a simple strong emotion. Many of those who joined up in the Great War came back with attitudes markedly simpler and more straightforward than our own, including pride in service, or in never mutinying like the French, or running away. For them, service and duty were the authentic tonal voice of the conflict, not the words that meant most to the poets: 'betrayal', 'waste' and 'loss'.

For us, brought up on the idea that the officers were indifferent to the fate of their men, it is striking that Bourne never questions the mechanical operation of the 'machine' or the integrity of the officers who work it. As they are about to rejoin the battle, he reminds his comrades that the officers have to think of the men as material to work with, otherwise they would not be able to carry out their own orders. They know that their original plan is no more than a map and that you cannot see the country by looking at a map anymore than you can see the fighting by looking at a plan of attack. Until they go over the top, it will be the colonel's responsibility. Once they meet the enemy it will be theirs. It is their duty to make the best of it they can.

As Bourne rediscovers when going back into action, the men too are bound together by an unbreakable tie. He passes soldiers who have been into battle and returned—some are sprawled on the ground snatching a little fitful sleep, others are weary-eyed, exchanging whispers. Whenever they were asked what it was like, they would usually reply, 'It's cushy enough.' (*Her Privates We*, 161). It is the voice of reassurance, but also something more profound—the language of work that must be done. The greater the hardship, the less they grumble. Bourne notices that at the Front the faces of men seem to become more uniform, as though the work takes on the strain of waiting. The problem which confronts them is not death so much as the affirmation of their own will in the face of it. And then Manning adds—and it is a telling sentence—'how much *confidence* they felt was the secret of their heart; they had enough courage to share with one another.' (*Her Privates We*, 188).

The story Manning tells is cut to its bare bones. Nothing much happens when they move back behind the lines. They regroup and somehow in talking of their common experience are able to master it. The move represents for them a new beginning and the scenes of army life are artfully described. There is a lot of talk of food, and even more talk of drinking. There is often nothing to do but watch the interminable train of motor lorries which pass up to the Front. They voice their petty grievances. Occasionally the war intrudes—an enemy plane drops a bomb on them as they are marching from Meaulte to Mericout. We see the men at rest, drinking too much, idling their time as best they can, chatting up girls. Behind the lines the soldiers veer from obscenity to sentimentality, from sex to love—all four seem to affirm the completeness of being. Considering his free use of Anglo-Saxon demotic words, Manning is rather coy about sex, and the scenes with the girls are not the most convincing in the novel. Even in describing them, he adopts a rare authorial voice, which betrays a certain degree of embarrassment. Or perhaps, Bourne represents his age more than we think he does. He is not judgemental, merely reticent.

What Manning shows us is a company of men who have lost touch with the existential codes of war. 'All that tempest of excitement was spent, and they were now derelicts in a wrecked and dilapidated world, with sore and edgy nerves sharpening their tempers, or shutting them up in a morose and sullen humour, from which it was difficult to move them.' (*Her Privates We*, 39). But the battalion has been thinned in the fighting and has to be pulled back to regroup. There is a tendency for individual characters to re-assert themselves, and Manning draws out the grudges and grievances. Bourne himself is largely above it all, which is why he is generally liked by the men and trusted by the NCOs, with whom he is on easy terms. Even his lamentable French is useful when chatting up local girls in the *estaminets*. In due course, he is posted to an orderly office, out of danger, in which he has to sit for the greater part of the day under the eyes of authority. The office is over-staffed and the men under-worked, and Bourne makes no attempt to ingratiate himself with the men or the officers. After ten days he is posted back to his unit.

All the time the unit is constantly on the move. Tempers fray as the men are drilled, they think, unnecessarily severely, just to kill time. When they get the news that they are to move back to the Front, they have to confront the fact that the war they are fighting is entirely indifferent to them as individuals, to all their prejudices, vanities and personal complaints. 'War', Manning writes, 'is only the ultimate problem of all human life stated barely and pressing for an immediate solution.' (*Her Privates We*, 182). And in the end, as in life, all the men have is faith in each other. 'They turned from the wreckage and misery of life to an empty heaven and from an empty heaven to the silence of their own hearts. They had been brought to the last extremity of hope and yet they put their hands on each other's shoulders and said ... that it was all right, and that they had faith in nothing, but in themselves and each other.' (*Her Privates We*, 205).

Throughout the novel Bourne himself remains something of a mystery. This may sound as though he is not a fully realised character, but this would not be true. The more we see of him, the more we warm to him, forced to respect his private world, to which we have no admission. Bourne has suppressed his thoughts the better to adjust to the external reality of the war: the great mystery of which he—and everyone else—is part. Manning tells us that each man keeps his own secret to the end (*Her Privates We*, 247). But some have more secrets than others and we never really got to the bottom of Bourne's because we know so little about him. Unlike some of the other characters in the book, Bourne does not transcend the story that gives him birth. Indeed, like the novel, he is largely unknown to the reading public; he retains still a cloak of anonymity.

There is an extraordinary veracity in war, we are told, that strips a man of every conventional covering he brings with him from the Home Front and leaves him face to face with himself. But what Bourne's conventional covering is, we are never told. There is no hint of what he himself might have done back home (neither he nor the narrator enlighten us). What we do know is that he can put no social distance between himself and the enlisted men, only an ironic detachment which is both a curse and a strength. He recognises that he is more reflective than most of them.

Bourne is clearly officer material, as the term would have been understood in those days: he is an educated man whose quiet self-confidence inspires the confidence of other men. Unlike Manning himself, one suspects, he is a natural-born leader. He is certainly more eloquent than the men in putting his thoughts into words, but he envies them the 'wanton and violent instincts' which seem to guide them. Later, his own reflective ability is clearly blunted as he goes back into battle. He is in danger of becoming too thoughtful and reflecting too much. At the end of the novel, Bourne notices in himself an increasing tendency to fall into moods, not of abstraction but of blankness. As soon as he has touched on the fringes of the mystery which is himself, he turns away from it. He prefers his mind to reflect nothing but his own immediate surroundings, just as a puddle in a road reflects whatever lees and dregs of light linger in the sky.

In the Signals Unit we see that he cannot settle down to life in an office atmosphere, or adapt to the routine of orderly rule; all he feels is a terrible emptiness. He seems to need to deny himself petty comforts, even friendships—another of the attributes that make him, in the eyes of the officers, 'a queer chap', as Sgt. Major Tozer calls him after his death. And that perhaps is why he comes to cherish the deep friendships that war offers some. There is a revealing passage when an army chaplain asks him outright whether he has any real friends in the ranks even though, but he insists he has, and adds later in conversation with his commanding officer, that he has even taken on 'their colour'. (*Her Privates We*, 90).

His attitude to officers is more complicated. He recognises their worth, and never questions the rightness of the cause for which they are fighting. Patriotism may be understated but it is clearly there, and is all the more resilient for being so muted. There are no propaganda speeches by the officers, no flag-waving episodes—even Bourne's objection to becoming an officer has no basis in the fear that it would be 'selling out'. Bourne sums it up very well. When one lives in the ranks, one lives in the world of human interest, when one becomes an officer, one becomes an inflexible and inhuman machine, 'and though he thought that the war as a moral effort was magnificent, he felt that as a mechanical operation it left a great deal to be desired.' (*Her Privates We*, 92). Bourne prefers to keep the company of the rank and file—the privates and non-commissioned officers. These are his friends, though friendship is entirely tied to the experience of the war. Bourne recognises after the death of the youngest, Mattlow, that friendships are entirely contingent, like the contingency of war itself. Mattlow and Bourne had met while recuperating behind the lines and had sat together ever since. They had nothing in common and yet there was no bond stronger than the necessity of war (*Her Privates We*, 232). If the necessity had been removed they would have parted company, keeping nothing of each other but a vague memory, grateful enough, though without substance. Good comradeship, Bourne insists, has taken the place of friendship. It has its own loyalties and affections, and it rises on occasion to an intensity of feeling which friendship in civil life never touches. It may be less in itself, but its opportunity is greater. At one moment a particular man may be nothing to you, at another you will go through hell for him. And that comradeship is entirely a product of fortune.

> No, it's not friendship. The man doesn't matter so much; it's a kind of impersonal emotion, a kind of enthusiasm in the old sense of the word. Of course, it's keyed up, a bit over-wrought, we help each other. What is one man's fate today, may be another's tomorrow. (*Her Privates We*, 80).

One cannot help feeling that the novel has been unfortunate in its history. When it came out in its expurgated version it was extraordinarily well received. Hemingway called it the greatest novel to come out of the war. But then it vanished from view, and when it surfaced again in the 1960s, Manning was misinterpreted as being critical of the war, but he simply wasn't. What he offers the reader is an attitude to war that is more common than we think. The men are certainly not unquestioning in their patriotism (they express hardly a patriotic sentiment between them), but they are not entirely horrified by the war; some of them are even excited by the experience, a mood that these days we find vaguely disturbing.

There is a passage in Book 2 of the *Iliad* (as conveyed by the poet Christopher Logue):

> See how the hairy crests fondle each other onwards as
> From hill and valley, and distant wall
> All those who answered Agamemnon's call
> Moved out, moved on and fell in love with war again. (Logue, 1991, 82).

And this is how Manning describes the men as they march to St Pol before returning to the battlefield. They are moved, so we are told, by a common impulse which gains in strength until individual anxieties are swept away, 'even those who feared made the pretence of bravery, the mere act of mimicry, open the way for the contagion ... so that ultimately they gave into it.' (*Her Privates We*, 139). Bourne admits to being swept up by it, too. When a volunteer is asked for a raid in No Man's Land Bourne puts himself forward. Only two other men volunteer. He wonders whether everything is chance. He probably would not have volunteered if he had not been invited to by Capt Marsden, but is chance the only factor? Probably, none of our actions, he reflects, are quite voluntary; if compulsion is not explicit, it is perhaps always implied. Then he begins to wonder whether his enthusiasm for the mission, which grows stronger and stronger, is not after all his real self, an enthusiasm which only needed the pressure of circumstance to be aroused and awakened. For me the strongest passage in the novel as well as the most haunting is this: 'There was no man of them unaware of the mystery which encompassed him, for he was part of it; he could neither separate himself entirely from it, nor identify himself with it completely. A man might rage against war; but war from amongst its myriad faces, could always turn towards him one which was his own.' (*Her Privates We*, 182).

Robert Jordan: I Can Do No Other

For Whom the Bell Tolls, Ernest Hemingway

Robert Jordan of *For Whom the Bell Tolls* is a man of his time, and we must judge him as such. He has hardened himself on the outside to protect whatever is left of his finer self within. Any soldier with political sense on either side of the Spanish Civil War had to do so, for it was not only the fascists who were engaged in unspeakable atrocities. The communists killed many of the Republican prisoners in Madrid— and as for the anarchists, they were dangerously idealistic. They talked of 'the propaganda of the deed' and many genuinely believed that paradise would come when 'the last king had been strangled with the guts of the last priest'; that the world could be remade with a pistol and an encyclopaedia.

The title of Hemingway's novel, *For Whom the Bell Tolls*, is particularly telling. It is a quote from John Donne's poem, 'No Man is an Island', and is used to discuss the subject of moral isolationism. Hemingway is at pains to make sure that we do not think of Jordan as an ideologue. He is not even a member of the Communist League, or a Socialist Party. He is fighting for a cause in which he believes, a cause at the core of his own identity. He is fighting because this is what he is. He is fighting for Spain and its culture, and insofar as the culture means so much to him, he is fighting for himself.

The American Marxists who joined the Abraham Lincoln Brigade were fighting for something else: a cause. They turned the war into a Marxist parable of history in which events drew their meaning from the frame of 'historical necessity'. 'All at once we found ourselves abruptly situated,' wrote Jean-Paul Sartre. Sartre went on to conclude that the Spanish Civil War was the moment that history finally forced itself into the modern consciousness. History now sought people out (Sartre, 1972, 228). Many writers really did join up for the cause, especially the Marxists. John Cornford, the youngest of the Spanish Civil War poets, reached the Front within a month of the war breaking out. He died the day after his twenty-first birthday. Christopher Cauldwell left for Spain in December 1936. Ralf Fox, the critic, and John Somerfield, the novelist, left almost simultaneously. Fox and Cauldwell were killed within a month of each other. Somerfield survived. A contemporary reviewer wrote of Somerfield's book, *Volunteer in Spain*, that the writer seemed to want to be a character in a forthcoming novel by Hemingway (a case of life imitating art) (Cunningham, 1986, 21). But Hemingway eschewed causes; the poets did so only much later, after disillusionment set in. And the poets, particularly the Marxists, were given to painting everything in broad brush strokes—Cauldwell once suggested that the eighteenth century heroic couplet was a reflection of the sorry state of bourgeois class consciousness at the time. Jordan is not given to such musings, for which the reader should be thankful.

High up in the pine forests of the Spanish Sierra, a guerrilla band prepares to blow up a vital bridge. Robert Jordan is a tall, thin American, with sun-streaked fair hair and a sunburned face. He has a predisposition for open-air life and a knowledge of Spain gleaned from almost ten years in the country. It is his facility in Spanish that establishes the partisans' trust; they do not treat him as a foreigner. If they have any misgivings about him, they are rarely voiced. When they are, it is not about his intelligence or courage, but his youth.

Jordan is in conversation with an old man, Anselmo, his guide through the mountains, who will be one of the few dependable characters in the tale, a man in whom Jordan will come to invest absolute trust. Not so Pablo, the guerrilla leader, whose nerve will be in doubt until the very end, as will his loyalty to the Republic. From the moment he sets eyes on him, Jordan has his doubts. He mistrusts the sadness that Pablo displays, the sadness a man gets before he quits or before he betrays the cause, a sadness that comes before a sell-out. Pablo has been in the field far too long. He is tired of being hunted. He has killed too many people and has had to be brave once too often. Now he is *muyflojo* (Anselmo says), he is very afraid to die (*For Whom the Bell Tolls*, 28). In the end, Pablo will come through.

Jordan and the guerrillas camp in the cave and it is there that he meets Maria, a young woman who has escaped from Franco's forces. This constitutes the love interest of the novel, which is not the most successful part. The next day Jordan comes down to reconnoitre the bridge and to note the places where explosives can be best placed. On the way back up to the mountains he enters into a brief conversation with Anselmo. The old man tells him that he must come back to hunt when the war is over. Jordan replies that he does not like to kill animals. 'With me it's the opposite', the old man replies. 'I don't like to kill men.' 'Nobody does', Jordan insists, but he feels nothing against it when it is necessary, for the cause. The irony escapes him. Anselmo is not fighting for a cause, he is fighting for a way of life that fascism will take away from him. He is fighting for himself. The killing of animals makes him proud, for he is a hunter, and proud of his skill 'but of the killing of a man, who is a man as we are, there is nothing good that remains.' (*For Whom the Bell Tolls*, 43).

What the partisans make of him also gives the reader a chance to take his measure; they see him as a boy, but a smart one 'smart and cold, very cold in the head.' (*For Whom the Bell Tolls*, 99). At times, of course, Jordan can be a bit of a prig. He takes umbrage when the older woman calls him 'Don Roberto'. He prefers to be called 'Comrade'. 'Comrade to me is what all should be called with seriousness in this war. In the joking commences a rottenness.' (*For Whom the Bell Tolls*, 69). Despite joining the side of the Republic he is fighting not for a cause, but for Spain, and yet for all his knowledge and sympathy of the culture he is offering his life not for a country so much as an idea of it. At times he tells himself he is fighting because of his love for the country, but it seems to be love of a very conditional kind. He always treats the Spanish as 'they', and he does not hold them in especially high regard. 'We' kill coldly, the Spanish with passion. 'It's their extra sacrament, their old one they had before the new religion came from the far end of the Mediterranean, the one they had never abandoned but only suppressed and hidden to bring it out again in wars and inquisitions.' (*For Whom the Bell Tolls*, 297). There are, he ruminates, no finer and no worse people in the world, no kinder people, and yet no crueller. They will turn on you often, but they will always turn on each other (*For Whom the Bell Tolls*, 368).

The reality of the Civil War is brought home to us in the story Maria tells, the story of how Pablo had captured a Civil Guard post and forced the guards to kneel with their heads against the wall, and their hands by their sides. After taking the town they put the Fascists in the City Hall and armed the peasants with flails that they used to beat out the grain. Some were taken from a store owned by a Fascist shopkeeper. They clubbed the men to death, beating them as they reached the line, beating them as they turned to walk, beating them until they fell before throwing the bodies over the cliff. By then, most of the men were drunk, and what they had done at first reluctantly as a 'duty' they now did in a frenzy. What is important about Pablo's story? It must be important, because the old woman tells it so vividly that it takes up just over thirty pages of the novel. How many times, Jordan ruminates, has he heard similar stories? How many times has he been told by a partisan about how his father had been killed in the country, and/or against some wall, or at night in the lights of a truck, beside some road? But he has never *seen* the shooting:

> She's better than Quevedo, he thought. He never wrote the death of any Don Faustino as well as she told it. I wish I could write well enough to write that story, he thought. What we did, not what the others did to us. He knew enough about that. (*For Whom the Bell Tolls*, 79).

Jordan himself has ambitions to be a writer. When he sees enemy bombers he thinks they are shaped like sharks—the wide-finned, sharp-nosed sharks of the Gulf Stream. They move like 'mechanised doom'. Amazed by his own lyricism, he tells himself that after the war he ought to become a writer (perhaps a little self-referential joke for Hemingway). Jordan sees the war itself as 'material' to draw upon. He sees it as affording him the subject matter for the big novel he wants to author (*For Whom the Bell Tolls*, 142).

The story quickens when Jordan meets the famous bandit leader, El Sordo, a short and heavy, clean-shaven, bandy-legged man of indeterminate age—a vital enough character for his novel. The bandit warns him of the increased troop movements between Villacastin and San Rafael. They would both like to blow the bridge now rather than later, but Jordan has his orders. It is to be blown up as part of a co-ordinated Republican attack. Their mutual concern is the first intimation that the situation is changing in a way the high command had not envisaged, but Jordan is determined to carry out his orders to the letter. His faith in his commanding general is never broken, any more than his belief that it is the Communists who impose the strictest discipline, and it is only through discipline that the Republic will come through.

And so the tale draws to its inexorable conclusion. In the days immediately before the Republicans are due to launch their attack, the Francoists attack El Sordo's base. The partisans want to go the bandit's aid but Jordan is adamant. It is impossible to divide the force that they have. El Sordo's band is no match for the air power that the Fascists can bring to bear, and the planes come back three times, dropping their bombs, and finally machine-gunning the hilltop. When the Francoists get to the top the bodies are impossible to identify. An order is given to take all the heads for identification. 'Que cosa mas mala as la guerra', the Fascist commander says to himself, 'What a bad thing war is.' (*For Whom the Bell Tolls*, 333). He does not want to carry out his orders, but he, like Jordan, is every bit the professional; duty is sacrosanct.

Jordan hears how they have taken the heads when Anselmo returns with the news and the episode gets him thinking. He knew Indians took scalps in the old days in the West; his grandfather had told him as much back in Missoula, Missouri. He remembers the cabinet in his father's office with the Indian arrowheads spread out on the shelf and the eagle feathers of the war bonnets that hung on the wall and his grandfather's Smith & Wesson single action, officer's model, .32 calibre with which he had killed a man, an event he would not talk about. His grandfather had also fought in another Civil War, 'the War of the Rebellion' he preferred to call it. He had fought the entire four years and Jordan realises that despite his genealogy, his genetic stain, he does not want to be a soldier. He merely wants to help the Republicans win this particular war.

By then, suspecting that the attack will prove fatal, he has tried to have the order rescinded. He sends one of his best partisans to the general's headquarters, knowing intuitively that he will not succeed. Pablo makes off with the explosives and the box of detonators, which leads Jordan into a blue funk as he curses the war, the country, the people, but never, of course, the cause. He must have known the game was up once El Sordo was attacked. He cannot base an operation on the presumption that miracles will happen and by now Jordan suspects that he is likely to get everyone killed.

The conflicting thoughts that go through his mind—his anger at himself, his disgust with the Spanish—are all a key to understanding the man. It is here that Hemingway begins to show his deepest insight into the character he has created. Jordan still wants to follow his orders because of the professional he is, but he is sadly diminished in his own eyes for betraying the trust of his followers. He grins at Maria, 'she thinks you're wonderful, he thought. I think you stink. And the Gloria and all the nonsense that you had. You had wonderful ideas didn't you? You'd all the world taped, didn't you? The hell with all that.' (*For Whom the Bell Tolls*, 402). It is at this, his lowest ebb, that his faith in the mission is unexpectedly salvaged. Pablo returns. He had betrayed Jordan, throwing the detonators down the gorge into the river, but almost immediately he had felt terribly alone. In a moment of weakness he deserted his family. He is now back with some of El

Sordo's men. At heart, he is not a coward and not quite the broken man Jordan had suspected. He had tried to abort the mission to save his friends, but found that he had failed—and having failed he could not abandon them to their fate.

With Pablo's return, Jordan's confidence comes back, breaking the pattern of tragedy into which the whole operation had seemed grooved. And with it comes the great self-revelation that he needs to see the mission through to a conclusion. It is a calm acceptance of death. It is Hemingway's creed for what makes a man a true soldier: the talent that fits him for war is the ability not to ignore but to despise whatever bad endings there can be (*For Whom the Bell Tolls*, 410–11). He knows he himself is nothing, but that fighting for others he is everything. The gift is given to him perhaps because he never asked for it. It is something that can never be taken away from him or lost.

And when the attack finally comes, those instincts do not let him down. Jordan climbs down to the bridge. As he works, wedging the explosives to the framework, he hears a rattling of firing far below on the road. He works quickly, climbing down under the bridge, a coil of wire over his arm, and a sub-machine gun slung over his back. He yells to Anselmo to blow the structure, and then there is a cracking roar and the middle of the bridge rises up in the air like a wave breaking. Anselmo is killed. At that moment Jordan feels lonely, detached and un-elated, turning despair from sorrow into the hatred a soldier must feel if he is to continue soldiering on. Shortly afterwards, however, they see the squat green, grey and brown-turret of a whippet tank coming round the bend into the bright sunlight. With Pablo's horses they manage to ride off, but the tank fires a round and Jordan is wounded. Under shell fire, he is dragged away to safety but he cannot walk and decides the best he can do is to cover the retreat of the others and help them escape by sacrificing himself. It is one of the great scenes in the literature of war. He is alone with his back against a tree. He is finally content. He has fought for what he believed in. If they win here, they will win everywhere. He reaches over for the sub-machine gun. He has half an hour at best, he thinks, before he will start firing it.

Why does Jordan choose to surrender his life for others? A clue comes halfway through the novel in one of his many reflections about war. It is the absolute belief in duty which has sustained him so far and ensured that despite all temptations to the contrary, the bridge will be blown as ordered. It is the taking part in a crusade despite all the bureaucratic politics, party strife and inefficiency of the officers. He has experienced a feeling like his first communion, a feeling of consecration to a duty to the oppressed of the world which, as an American, it would be as embarrassing for Jordan to speak about as a religious experience. It has given him a role in something larger than himself so that he can see his own death in perspective (as something unimportant except insofar as it might interfere in the performance of duty). He has learned how to endure and how to ignore suffering; in the cold wetness, and mud and heat of the summer, he has experienced 'the dry-mouthed, fear-purging ecstasy of battle.' (*For Whom the Bell Tolls*, 243).

And Jordan is lucky. On the Western Front in the First World War, or on the Italian Front where Hemingway saw action very briefly and about which he wrote in his most famous war novel, *A Farewell to Arms*, individual acts of heroism counted for very little, or went largely unobserved. In the face of mechanised slaughter, it is difficult to be oneself. In the mountains of Spain, however, Jordan's heroism will be remembered by those who make it back. His death will have personal meaning for others. In celebrating his individuality, all the talk of a planned society and a bright Socialist future mean nothing. He is giving his life for the prospects of some individuals he has come to love. He has taken to killing rather too readily and had expected to get rid of the guilt by writing about it. It is not the killing but the dying that is important, however. The big book will never be written, but his life will be consecrated with a sacrifice that makes sense of the life he has led.

I think that E. L. Doctorow has the most interesting take on the novel of any of the American novelists. One of the highlights of the book is the battle scene in El Sordo's camp, his last stand, which is as dramatically rendered as Hadji Murat's in Tolstoy's novella. But of course Jordan does not take part in that final battle. He is absent so that he can fight his own. The bell that tolls for El Sordo does not toll for him—yet. Last stands cannot be shared with others. Jordan dies heroically because he believes that his own code of honour is the only enduring value of the Spanish Civil War (and in the hope that it will inspire those he saves to fight on).

This most expatriate of American writers whose major work was to be set in Europe was, morally speaking, an isolationist. War is the means by which one's cultivated individualism can be raised to the heroic, and therefore never send to ask for whom the bell tolls; it tolls so that I can be me. (Doctorow, 2007, 92).

Jordan's whole life has been about that moment. There is another character in literature who is moved to make a similar choice in different circumstances: Mathieu Delarue, opening fire on a German unit and surprising himself in the process. Like Jordan, war allows him to break free. Delarue appears in Jean-Paul Sartre's *Age of Reason* and embodies Sartre's philosophy of life. He had 'spent [his] life reading, yawning, tinkling the bell of [his] own little problems, never managing to make a decision', watching history go by, never taking responsibility, never joining up to fight a cause. Eventually he achieves freedom by breaking free from his imprisonment, by sacrificing himself in revenge against a misspent life. Each shot he fires is for the books he never dared to write, for the journeys he never made, for everybody in general he wanted to hate, but tried to understand. 'Each one of his shots avenged some ancient scruple.' (Sartre, 2002, xiii). Sartre does not tell us whether Mathieu is killed, but hints later in the novel that he is. Jordan and Delarue are obverse sides of the same coin: one dies so that he can be himself; the other dies in order to become what he has never been, but for me Delarue never quite rings true, in part perhaps because for me Sartre is a lesser novelist, in part because his philosophy no longer has its former appeal.

Hemingway claimed to be the first American wounded in Italy. In fact he was the second, but unlike the first he survived his wounds—or did he? For his life was a mess after the war: three failed marriages, two messed up children (one self-shooting—besides the fatal one) a career that to others seemed a success but to him a failure. It is quite likely he returned from the First World War traumatised. War gets into some of his best short stories as a source of incipient panic (*The Big Two-Hearted River*), or insomnia (*Now I Lay Me*); or hysteria (*A Way You'll Never Be*). All three stories feature Nick Adams, who is sometimes understood as Hemingway's alter-ego.

A broad gulf stream of books about Hemingway flows on and on; he is probably more read about than read. He is fascinating because his writing is autobiographical. His art mirrored his life. We read 'him' into many of his characters, not least because he imagined less than most other authors. He wrote about places he had lived or visited in exotic (or what was then considered exotic) locations like Spain, Cuba and Africa. He was one of the first celebrity authors; he craved fame and fortune and had a public persona as a war correspondent, a soldier and a bullfighter *manqué*. He lived a very public life and the fact that it was tragic merely reinforced the brand. It is almost impossible not to explain Hemingway's work and his life in mutually reductive terms of each other. His was a Hobbesian world in which gentleness is only a passive-aggressive strategy, and to be selfish is simply to be human. Hemingway's message is that we must endure existence because we *are* it. This is not always heart-warming, of course. Many of Hemingway's characters are too much the authors of their own misfortune.

Hemingway's contribution to the literature of war was to spare us noble epithets by reducing adjectives to a minimum and allowing the action to speak for itself. In this he has had too few imitators until the 1960s and the appearance of Joseph Heller's *Catch-22*. But Heller's book was more subversive than anything Hemingway ever penned in providing us with a hero who Hemingway would have despised as 'unmanly'. The trouble with Hemingway, writes Paul Theroux, is his primal insecurity, which manifested itself in the bullfighting, the arm wrestling, the elephant shooting, all of which diminished him as a writer. War has always been seen as a test of manliness, ever since the Greeks told themselves that it is what men do (*andreia*—the word for 'courage'—is also the word for manliness). If Hemingway tended to take this approach to extremes he was only being consistent with the prevailing attitude in American writing, which only died out with Norman Mailer: namely that one cannot be a male writer without first proving that one is a 'man' (Theroux, 1985, 311). Hemingway thought manliness to have been the only virtue to survive the First World War and that it was best expressed in picking a fight, or killing animals. He shot a lion in Africa and a grizzly bear in the Rockies, and when he was not busy killing things, he went to see them killed—particularly bull fights in Spain. He was also in tune with his times. We are suspicious of some of his heroes like Jake Barnes and Harry Morgan, because of their anti-Semitic and racist sentiments. Jordan is for us a much more comforting hero, who rings as true as the 'true sentences' he claimed to write, ones that do not describe or communicate emotional experiences, but render the experience real.

Hemingway's characters have also been criticised for being flat, or even one-dimensional, in part because of this. They live on the page, but do not live through it. They do not evolve or become what they are. They know what they know, and know neither more nor less in the course of the action. It is the action, of course, that defines them. They make blunders and mistakes, and it is the impact of these on the lives of others that gives the novels their intrinsic interest. It has also been said that his very minimalist style compounds the problem. The flatness of the language amplifies the flatness of the characters. Critics, wrote Anthony Burgess, are not always ready to see that a style is as much a character as any of the walking creations of a novel (Burgess, 1986, 508). In many Hemingway tales they don't say enough, or Hemingway does not say enough about them, or on their behalf, to allow us to dig deeper and ask whether their actions might have been different. But none of these shortcomings appear in *For Whom the Bell Tolls*.

The fate of a man is his character, wrote Thomas Hardy. Fate decides the set of choices confronting us in life, but it is character that decides which choices are made. Circumstances make some of these choices more probable than others, but it is character which defies probabilities and leads to what Aristotle called 'unexpected decisions'. And the most important decisions are nearly always spontaneous. A soldier does not think before throwing himself on a grenade to save his friends. If he stops to calculate the odds of surviving it would be too late. We live an idealised life, an un-reflected manifestation of our own humanity. Soldiers live similarly, but often in the presence of death. And just as it is not possible for the military to prosecute a soldier for not throwing himself on a grenade (as it can for deserting a battlefield or turning his back on the enemy) so there is no 'must' in Jordan's actions. His act is entirely disinterested, in so much as it is a free choice, an expression of his freedom to act, the freedom which makes him the moral being he is.

In that sense Jordan is a distinctly modern character. Achilles is defined by what he does, by his actions. Jordan is defined by his ideas, his vision of historical forces fighting it out for the moral high ground. But his character is rooted, too, in a distinctive personal ideology, according to which he acts with unbending logic. This is what Doctorow calls his 'moral isolationism'. But is this one he chooses, or does it choose him? All we know is that Jordan learns about himself as the novel progresses. He begins with very few beliefs. 'If we were going in for judgements, he would form them afterwards.' But he acquires a belief in the value of sacrifice, and the value of love is rekindled. He dies as much for the Spanish girl Maria as he does for the partisans and their fight. And he dies for Spain, for the land to which they are anchored. He dies as himself, with infinitely more self-knowledge than before. 'I wish there were some way to pass on what I've learned, though Christ, I was learning fast there at the end.'

Is Jordan's death going to be useful? Almost certainly not. What are a few partisans in a civil war that was already turning against them? Would Jordan fight for social justice today when some of the ideas have become discredited? He would, if he is what I imagine him to be: a Rortean liberal ironist. If you were to ask a liberal ironist why he cares about others in a world in which caring is neither commanded nor justified, the answer would be that he just does. To want more is to confine oneself to the benighted rants of metaphysicians, Marxists or Fascists, those who still cling to essences and historical absolutes. It is very much the American message, Emerson's dictum: 'The only right is what is after my constitution; the only wrong what is against it.' (Bloom, 2002, 341).

Let me add a final footnote on Jordan's heroism. Heroism is rarely redeeming, and often the payoff is cruel. Most heroes commit acts of bravery that are not noticed, or go unremarked. True heroism is the measure of the man, and the only audience that matters is himself. And that is the problem with modern war. Walt Whitman sensed that there was something new about the carnage of modern war, something that resisted literary convention and ultimately language itself (Murray, 2011, 173). In the course of the century that followed, writers found it increasingly difficult to write about heroic acts in the face of mechanised slaughter. In his account of the landings at Salerno, John Steinbeck described men as 'cogs' or 'bolts' in the machine of modern warfare. 'Modern warfare is very like an automobile assembly line. If one bolt in the whole machine is out of place or not available, the line must stop and wait for it.' (Steinbeck, 2003, 283–4). At other times, he waxed natural. He compared men to ants, who 'crawled out of the ships' or crabs who 'scuttled … from bits of cover to another cover on the beach.' Anonymous, without individuality, 'they disappeared into the blackness and the silence.' (Steinbeck, 2002, 287).

Hemingway is a difficult writer because he is on the wrong side of the story we tell about war. For him true courage was to continue fighting even when one has no idea what one is fighting for. His credo is found in *A Farewell to Arms* where Lt. Henry sees Catherine dying. 'He did not know what it was all about. He never had time to learn … they killed you in the end, you could count on that.' Or, as the mayor in the story 'In Another Country', whose wife has just died, remarks, 'a man must not marry … if he is to lose everything he should not place himself in a position to lose that ... he should find things he cannot lose.' (Wilson, 1978, 46). But one does not choose to be courageous, or find oneself in love. And if you are a soldier, all you have is the courage to face up to the fact that, as Santiago says in *The Old Man and the Sea*, 'a man can be destroyed, but not defeated.' For without courage or love of others (the band of brothers) what's left? For some soldiers perhaps it will be the cause; for others it may even be themselves. Jordan, like the old man Santiago, may be destroyed but he dies undefeated and that, Hemingway tells us, is surely victory enough.

Malaparte: Bearing Witness to the Truth
Kaputt, Curzio Malaparte

Nearly everything about Curzio Malaparte, the author of *Kaputt*, was bogus, starting with his name. He was born Sukert. He was to be dubbed 'Kurt Erich', but was later called 'Curzio', a less Teutonic name. With Malaparte, no history is ever straightforward, his own no less than that of the Second World War, the subject of the novel under discussion. His life was lived and shaped by it in strange and often disturbing ways.

In both of Malaparte's novels, it is never quite clear what is truthful and what is not. In a striking instance of intertexuality, he has French officers discussing in his other novel *The Skin* whether one can believe anything in *Kaputt*. It is Malaparte who is the hero of the book, the subject of his own story, a journalist who roams across Nazi-occupied Europe, observing war from the exclusive vantage point of a facist who has fallen out of love with facism (or so he claims; his fascism is still apparent in his style and the lack of sympathy he often shows for human suffering). It is one thing to fictionalise the pogrom at Iasi (spelled Jassy in the published translation), another to claim to have witnessed it; it is one thing to describe the Warsaw ghetto, quite another to suggest to have seen it at first hand. Malaparte is something of a charlatan. He challenges us to doubt his veracity just as a con man defies us to doubt his good faith.

As a man he was politically promiscuous, given to excess, deceitful and cunning, handsome, debonair, and dead at the age of fifty-nine from lung cancer. But the essence of his personality is totally contained in his two novels. All his preoccupations are there: his love of war (largely for its aesthetics, although one is never quite sure where aesthetics end and reality begins) and his snobbery in numbering only the most famous among his friends. His books are autobiographical but often concern an imagined life. His is the most politically incorrect voice in this book. He will please very few, but he reminds us that life is not pleasant and that war is what we do because we do harm to each other all the time. He has left in *Kaputt* a warning which we would do well to heed.

I first read *Kaputt* in my late thirties when I was writing about war and twentieth-century consciousness, and was convinced that a clue to the modern age's obsession with war could be found in the fiction it gave rise to. 'They can say what they like about me', Malaparte once wrote, 'but I love war ... I love it as every well-bred man loves it, every healthy, courageous strong man, and every man who is not satisfied with humanity and its misdeeds.' (*Kaputt* 433–434). 'Well-bred' sounds a false note today; it is very snobbish. But Malaparte is a keen name-dropper, anxious to let us know that he moved in the best social circles. The word 'healthy' is also a dead giveaway. This was a time when nations talked up their own vitality and condemned others as decadent. In a letter to his erstwhile fickle patron Count Ciano, Mussolini's son-in-law and Italy's Foreign Minister, he dismissed the Greeks as a nation of half-breeds, 'bastardised' by centuries of Turkish rule. But what strikes us most is that in his 'love' of war (and especially its aesthetics), he had the temerity to bear witness to its existential appeal.

Homer set out the golden rule, writes Milan Kundera: never let the timing of a character's personal destiny coincide with that of historical events (Kundera, 2010, 54). Achilles dies before Troy falls, and Aeneas before Rome takes off. It has remained pretty much a rule of thumb ever since. Malaparte published *Kaputt*, the first of two novels, almost a year before the end of the conflict.

Kundera goes on to make two interesting observations about Malaparte's technique (he analyses *The Skin* at great length in an essay in *Encounters* (2009). The first is that Malaparte's intention was to show how war had become so omnipresent by the mid-twentieth century that it moulded men from the outside—the psychological insights into character which Dostoevsky and Tolstoy had initiated, and which were so important in the late nineteenth century novel (think particularly of Henry James), are largely absent from Malaparte's two novels. The author tells us almost nothing about himself, or his own fears; none of his characters have an inner personality. What he offers us instead is a series of set piece encounters, all of which prompt us to ask whether they actually happened.

And then there is the war itself, in all its gruesome, grotesque details—the faces of Russian partisans frozen in the ice on the edge of Lake Lagoda ('a row of glass like masks ... like the delicate and living shadow of men who had disappeared into the mystery of the lake') or the German soldiers in a Warsaw cafe with their lidless eyes (in the intense Russian cold the eyelids can drop off like a piece of dead skin), striving in vain to screen their eyes from the intense light. In such descriptions Malaparte's aesthetic intention is especially strong, and what makes it 'fictional' (whether the episodes are real or not) is that the sensitive reader automatically excludes it from the context of history (Kundera, 2009, 161). We must always remember that the novel is not written by an engaged writer so much as a poet, and the message, like the pity in First World War verse, is to be found in the poetry.

For all the ambivalent attitudes he excites, Malaparte's fame has continued to grow. Milan Kundera has written admiringly about him, as has Dominique Fernandez and Bernard-Henri Lévy, who carried *Kaputt* with him into the siege of Sarajevo. He has fewer fans in the English-speaking world, but one of them is Margaret Atwood. Malaparte could be a cynical writer, but his ability to dominate his novels and captivate his readership knows few equals and too few imitators. His characters tend to be vehicles for ideas rather than having an autonomous life of their own. But he is his own chief character in his novels, the one who always holds centre stage. Malaparte, writes Kundera (*Encounter*, 2009, 160) created a new literary form; reportage that is novelistic. The book feels, at times, like a detached work of historical fiction; at others like an eye-witness account. The novel is in fact both of these, but since Malaparte never acknowledges when switching from one genre to the other, one has the imaginative texture of fiction and the reality of reportage, and all of it framed by a man who made himself the hero of his own tale.

Many of the characters Malaparte meets in the course of the book are real, such as Axel Munthe, the popular author of *The Story of San Michele* which I read in my youth (and which, like *Kaputt*, is the autobiography of a reimagined life). Malaparte describes him in his villa in Capri: 'stiff, wooden, sulky; an old green cloak over his shoulders ... his lively, mischievous eyes hidden behind dark glasses which gave him something of that mysterious and menacing air that belongs to the blind.' (*Kaputt*, 10). There is the unforgettable sketch of Reich's Minister Frank, the Governor-General of Poland, with his wish to turn Poland into an island of civilisation 'amid a sea of Slavic barbarism' (*Kaputt*, 70). And then there is the portrait of the German boxer Max Schmeling, on a visit to Warsaw just back from the battle of Crete, to arrange a boxing match between representatives of the Wehrmacht and the SS; and perhaps the most comically sinister episode of all, Malaparte's alleged encounter with Himmler in a sauna in Lapland.

The aesthetic intention, adds Kundera (2009, 161) shows most strikingly in the originality of form. There are six parts to *Kaputt*: horses, rats, dogs, birds, reindeer, and flies. These animals are present both as material creatures, like the horses frozen in a Russian lake, and as metaphors: the rats symbolising Jews, as the Nazis thought of them, or the flies in the last part proliferating from the heat and the corpses and symbolising a war that will never end. Ultimately, the novel can be approached as a piece of wartime journalism (the book appeared even before the conflict came to an end in 1944) or as a work of fiction, but its central message is damning: war is an expression of fear, and from that fear it becomes a murderous assault on life in all its manifestations.

Malaparte gives us an unforgiving picture of the Germans (his country's erstwhile allies) naked in the sauna, with flesh like that of lobsters, pale and rosy, exuding an acrid crustacean smell. Their grim, hard faces contrast sharply with their white, flabby naked limbs. Wonderfully defenceless, they were no longer frightening. To see them naked was to grasp the secret meaning of their national identity: their strength was not in their skin or their bones, or even the blood of which they spoke so often—the real skin was their uniform. By then the winning war was over, the losing war had begun.' He saw the white stain of fear growing in the dull eyes of German soldiers as they retreated westward. 'Their cruelty became sad, their courage hopeless. This is when the Germans became wicked.' (*Kaputt*, 241).

Guy Sejer, a German soldier, writing years afterwards of the gratuitous killing of POWs, could only speculate that 'something hideous had entered our spirits', although he was never able to give it a name

(Kassimieris, 2006, 148). Where he failed, Malaparte succeeded. What the Germans carried with them most was fear—never more so when they were hanging Jews on trees in village squares or burning them alive in their homes like rats, preying on the weak, the defenceless, the sick, women and children; they were especially afraid of the aged (*Kaputt*, 12). The leitmotif of fear and of the German cruelty which resulted from that fear became for Malaparte (or so he tells us) the principal keynote of his entire war experience (*Kaputt*, 91).

It is the inhumanity of the century that we now chiefly remember. One of Malaparte's anecdotes captures this perfectly. He recounts an episode in the Ukraine near Poltava, when a German unit came under attack from partisans, mostly old men and women who had remained behind in the villages. The last partisan left was a young boy, not much more than ten years old, thin, squalid and dressed in rags. The German officer in command had a son in Berlin, a boy of about the same age. He could not bring himself to order him shot. 'Listen, I don't want to hurt you. You're a child, and I'm not waging war against children ... Lieber Gott, I'm not the one who invented war.' (*Kaputt*, 266). The officer then told the boy he had one glass eye, so perfectly made that it was difficult to tell which one was real and which was not. 'If you can tell me at once without thinking about it which of the two is the glass eye I'll let you go free.' 'The left eye', replied the boy promptly. 'How did you know?' 'Because it's the one that has something human in it.'

In Malaparte, the novel has a narrator who is acutely sensible of history and how it illuminates, often in a pitiless way, the changing character of the times. Time is the great enemy of every would-be warlord or conqueror; the days of success are strictly rationed. The losing war is never far behind the winning war. That the loser in this case ends as badly as it does should give us no comfort that we have seen the end of war, or the triumph of good. Given its protean nature, its remarkable adaptability, we can expect wars of the future to be just as bad for the principal victims—the dead.

For the true characters of *Kaputt* are the dead—the dead that are everywhere, quietly decomposing, stinking, invading conversations, memory and sleep. In obsessing about the dead, those we secretly fear and sometimes hate (those whose 'presence' is a reproach to our own humanity and a persistent reminder of our mortal condition) Malaparte perhaps said something important about war that war had been unwilling to say itself.

In Jean-Paul Sartre's screenplay *Les Jeux Sont Faits*, the dead walk as ghosts among the living. In *Kaputt*, they are all too corporeal. Malaparte recounts a day when, as a journalist attached to the German Forces, he found himself motoring in the company of a friendly German officer though the deep forest of Oranienbaum on the Leningrad Front. He recounts how they arrived at a spot where the forest was thickest and deepest. Looming out of the mist was a soldier sunk to his belly in snow, standing motionless, his right arm outstretched, pointing the way to the Front. Wasn't the poor devil likely to die of the cold if he continued to direct military traffic in such weather? Malaparte asked innocently. 'There's no danger of that', he was told. 'You can ask him whether he's cold or not.' By the time both men had descended from the car and walked up to him, it was clear he was dead. He was, Malaparte was told, one of many 'traffic police'—a Wehrmacht joke. As a Russian prisoner he had been killed with a bullet in the temple prior to being placed in the snow, a victim of war who had been put to some use so that even in death the bullet would not be wasted.

Malaparte was recording such horrors a good seventy years before historians—in the English-speaking world—began to reveal them. In one of the most recent histories of the war, an English historian introduces us to scenes that are equally disturbing, if less cruelly sardonic— an eyewitness account by an American journalist in Finland in late 1940 who saw the snowbound forests strewn with hundreds of corpses frozen as hard as petrified wood, caught in the last moment of their life, one struggling to open the collar of his coat. Almost two years later, hundreds of miles to the east, a Red Army officer came across thousands of bodies from both sides frozen solid. Some were hugging each other in a vain attempt to keep warm. Many were missing their legs, which had been chopped off by Russian soldiers desperate to get their hands on a warm pair of boots. They would take the legs back to their bunkers and pull off the boots when the ice had thawed (Beevor, 2012).

What is most striking of all is that there is not a hint of sympathy in Malaparte's account. In *The Skin*, he writes, 'I hated these corpses, they were the *foreigners*, the only real *foreigners* in the common homeland of the living.' (Kundera, 2009, 178). Malaparte clearly hated the dead—in his accounts they are a wrathful, stubborn, and stupid. They are jealous and vengeful; they fear no one and nothing; most disturbing of all, they even have no fear of death. 'They fight to the end with a stubborn cold courage, laughing and sneering, pale and dumb, those

mad eyes of theirs wide open and squinting. When finally they are vanquished, when they resign themselves to defeat and humiliation, when
they lie beaten, they exhale a sweet, greasy odour and slowly decom-
pose.' (*Kaputt*, 174).

The dead represent a multitude of human ruin, with lifeless eyes
upturned and limbs in grotesque configurations, all attitudes of pain.
We see them in freight cars at Poduloea, fleeing from the train when
the doors open, dropping in masses with a dull thud like concrete stat-
ues. All had suffocated to death in the confined space, all had swollen
heads and bluish faces. We see the dead in the Warsaw ghetto lying
abandoned in the snow, waiting for the carts to take them away, but
the death rate was high and the carts were few, and they lay for days
and days. They lay on the floors and the halls of houses, on the landings, in the corridors and on beds in the rooms thronged with pale and
silent people. They were stiff and hard just like figures in a Chagall
canvas. We see hundreds of corpses dumped in the gutters of Jassy,
heaped one upon another. 'Squads of Jews, watched over by policemen
at work moving the dead bodies to one side, clearing the middle of the
road and piling the corpses up along the walls so that they would not
block traffic.' 'Ja, es has kein kultur—yes, they have no culture', the
German Governor-General of Warsaw tells Malaparte—'these Roma-
nians at Jassy. I share and understand your horror of the massacres',
adds Frank. 'As a man, a German ... I disapprove of pogroms. The
term "pogrom" is not a German word.' (*Kaputt*, 147).

Most disturbing of all, the dead are always coming alive in Malaparte's account. We see soldiers trying to bury the dead in open graves
but not before a crowd of peasants and gypsies try to strip them of
their clothes. 'It cannot be helped', says a Rabbi. 'It is the custom ...
they'll come tomorrow to sell us the clothing stolen from the dead and
we shall have to buy it. What else can we do?' But the dead do not go
willingly. They seek to defend themselves. Sometimes they raise themselves on their elbows, bringing their white faces close to the grim,
sweating faces of those who rob them with staring eyes until finally
they fall with a dull thud naked on the ground. In Malaparte's account,
the corpses protest against one last indignity heaped on them.

> Men and women dripping with perspiration, screaming and cursing, were
> doggedly trying to raise stubborn arms, bend still elbows and knees in order
> to draw off the jackets, trousers and underclothing. The women were most
> stubborn in their relentless defence. I never would have thought it would be

so difficult to take a slip off a dead girl. Perhaps it was modesty still alive in them that gave the women the strength to defend themselves. Sometimes they raised themselves on their elbows, brought their white faces near the grim, sweaty faces of those who profaned them, and gazed at them with staring eyes. (*Kaputt*, 173–4).

An English-speaking readership, unfamiliar with war in the last 200 years as experienced in Central Eastern Europe or on the Russian Front, may think this the product of an overheated imagination. Unfortunately, this was not the case. Take an account of the exhumation of murdered Jews at the Janowska death pits in Lvov. As the Russian Army approached in the summer of 1943 the remaining Jewish prisoners were employed to remove the bodies.

The fire crackles and sizzles. Some of the bodies in the fire have their hands extended. It looks as though they are pleading to be taken out. Many bodies abound with open mouths. Could they be trying to say 'we are your own mothers, fathers who raised you and took care of you. Now you are burning us'. If they could have spoken maybe they would have said this, but they are forbidden to talk—they are guarded. (Cohn-Sherbok, 1989, 11).

Or take a similar episode the following year when the SS began burning the bodies of prisoners who had been interred in mass graves outside the Plaszaw detention camp. The surviving Jewish prisoners once again were ordered to disinter the bodies and burn them. Many were horrified to see the temporary life that the flames gave the dead. Sometimes the corpses would sit forward, throwing the burning logs aside, their limbs reaching, their mouths opening, as 'if for a last utterance.' (Keneally, 1982, 275).

War, writes Milan Kundera, brings out a truth that is both fundamental and banal, both eternal and so often disregarded. The dead outnumber us—the dead of the past and the dead of the future. 'Confident in their superiority they mock us, they mock this little island of time we live in … they force us to grasp all its insignificance, its transience.' (Kundera, 2009, 178). And towards the end of the novel, we see the flies—always the flies, proliferating in the decomposing corpses under the ruins. In Naples, where the novel abruptly ends, the locals have given up the struggle. 'We have been fighting them for the past three years.' 'Then why are there still so many flies in Naples?' 'Well, you know how it is, the flies have won!' (*Kaputt*, 428).

Malaparte invented a new form a fiction that has been copied by very few since, and none in terms of the fiction of war. And he created a new hero—himself, a man brave enough to bear witness on our behalf. Perhaps he made much of the story up as he went along. But the 'poetry of the improbable' should not blind us to the extraordinary novel he wrote. Nor should it blind us to the quite revolutionary characterisation of the dead, the true heroes of the story, so often absent from the greatest works of fiction, or decorously depicted, with a few exceptions such as *The Charterhouse of Parma*, in which Stendhal, in a departure from convention, shows them with eyes open and arms outstretched. The dead are uncomfortable characters because they are so stubbornly un-heroic, even when they are fighting back, even when others are trying to strip them of their clothes and dignity. Perhaps they are the ultimate anti-heroes, but it is their tale Malaparte ends up telling, not his own, and it has taken nearly 2,000 years of literature in the west and the most horrendous war in human history for their true role to be celebrated—posthumously, of course.

4

VILLAINS

To some extent villains in war are superfluous, for it is war itself which is supposedly villainous. But it produces villains like the five characters who appear in this book, all in their own way strikingly memorable, and each conveys the unsettling impression that they perfectly embody all of war's darkest potential. In most novels, as opposed to epic poetry or Greek tragedy, wickedness takes palpably human form in a shape that soldiers over the ages have always recognised: over-ambitious generals who do not hesitate to get men killed to advance their own careers. Tolstoy portrays Napoleon as the Devil Incarnate, a breaker of nations as well as of men, seduced by his own cover story. But then at the end of his life he thought all war to be immoral. He might well have agreed with the sentiment of Capt Willard, the hero of Francis Ford Coppola's film, *Apocalypse Now*. How many men has he killed? he asks himself. Only six he actually knows of, but does the figure really matter? 'Shit, charging a man with murder [in war] is like handing out speeding tickets at the Indy 500.'

Villainy also inheres in war itself—the people it attracts; the opportunities it presents; the corruption it produces. Human wickedness takes many forms, not all of them consciously malevolent. Ordinary people tricked by circumstance and base instincts, along with bad luck, often venture outside of the boundaries they know to be right and find themselves unable to get back. War allows small men to become particularly villainous in their confrontation with self and with the horrors they experience at first hand. Michael Herr labels this 'some heavy "Heart of Darkness" trip', a reference to Joseph Conrad's powerful novella. Can one survive such an encounter? (Herr, 1977, 8). Can one hold on to any of one's previous illusions about war, or oneself? But then the darkness a man faces is often metaphysical. It brings out a lust for power far removed from Nietzsche's understanding of the will-to-power as triumph over oneself.

Stupidity is equally villainous at times. The psychology of military incompetence is on a scale of its own because in war the stupidity of commanders claims lives, often by the thousand. But is incompetence necessarily villainous, even if it is often criminally irresponsible? To be villainous, surely truly bad men have to do bad things, sometimes knowingly, sometimes not. Even then villains can redeem themselves in battle. War may corrupt the good who prove unequal to the challenges it throws up, but bad men, as Aristotle told us, can also be courageous. Sometimes even a moment of weakness can be redeemed later in action, as Waugh's Ivor St Claire makes up for his cowardice in Crete when later posted to Burma.

Karl Marlantes recalls that back in Vietnam—'Indian Territory' for the soldiers—the badder you were as an individual, the more esteem you had among your own friends, as long, that is, as the badness did not spill over to them. There was an expression commonly scrawled on flak jackets saying, 'Yea, though I walk through the Valley of the Shadow of Death I shall fear no evil. Because I'm the meanest mother-fucker in the valley.' (Marlantes, 2011, 100). Evil can help a man survive, an evil that is not always biblical in scale or Shakespearean in intensity, as it is in Cormac McCarthy's novel, *Blood Meridian*. Often it can be so commonplace that it is not even acknowledged. This is certainly true of Sgt Cross in Norman Mailer's novel, *The Naked and the Dead*. Because it is so often unthinking, cruelty is often not only banal but pretty mundane, and when combined with being 'the meanest motherfucker in the valley' it helps some males like Cross get a spurious reputation for being *men*.

Villainy breeds and festers in the environment that war produces. And it does not have to be on a grand scale. In another Joseph Conrad novella, *The Duel*, the pettiness of military life is portrayed with an unsparing eye for detail. The concept of honour is rendered ridiculous by war itself, though the chief protagonist Colonel Feraud, a man who seeks to be avenged for an imagined slight, at one point even during the carnage of Napoleon's retreat from Moscow. There is no danger on this occasion that the reader will ever take the villain to heart. No one can question Feraud's personal courage, but the man in his single-minded pursuit of 'honour' is one of the most unappealing figures to appear in literature.

In the military, as in any other profession, there are two kinds of respect. There is appraisive respect—the value attached to achievement. Feraud is respected as a duellist, as the better swordsman, though by sheer luck his mortal enemy d'Hubert bests him more often than not. And there is recognition respect: the respect we show to someone we esteem for themselves and the qualities they are deemed to embody such as courage in a soldier. Feraud earns the first by constantly duelling, but he does not command the second because he is not very likeable and he has few friends. He lives therefore by how he is appraised, and he is especially sensitive to any slight or humiliation. And appraisive respect is even more important in a club or Freemasonry, and of these military culture is one of the best examples; it is one of the most enclosed worlds with its own fixed, immutable codes of honour. To be shamed before one's peers is even more shaming than to be humiliated in public.

Values change over time, of course; by the next century all this was history. When Guy Crouchback in *Officers and Gentlemen* is asked what he would do if someone challenged him to a duel, his answer is 'laugh', a response which is both direct and unambiguous. Guy's whole story is one of honour betrayed, but in such a world at least he can preserve his self-respect, as well as win the respect of his men. For Guy to take part in a duel would be laughable for he would be fighting for his reputation, not for his honour.

Guy's war was 'the Good War'—the war against fascism—but it also produced some distinctly ambivalent figures even on the 'good side'. It is inevitable, given that language is the currency of literature in the way killing and dying are the currency of war, that words can seduce us. In *The Naked and the Dead* General Cummings is given to fine speeches which are not quite as hollow as they seem to us now. Cummings is the price the American GIs pay for reading history, though only the most educated would have been familiar with his Hegelian and Nietzschean themes.

Mailer's novel is actually about the ambiguities of betrayal. Armies produce mutual webs of unreliability. A soldier may desert his post and betray his friends. An officer may put his men at risk for very little, or in pursuit of his own career. He may betray a code of honour and act dishonourably in the field, or behind the lines. Betrayals multiply in the world of war, and each act can have multiple meanings. One betrayal that is not there in Mailer's novel is of men fighting for a bad cause. Mailer never questions whether the Pacific War had to be fought. But however good the war, the fire Mailer's moral interrogation sparks leaves nearly everyone in the book badly singed.

General Cummings is not an ogre; he is not especially wasteful of his men's lives. What makes him truly monstrous are not his actions, but his thoughts. The twentieth century was an intensely ideological age, and Cummings is an iconic twentieth century figure. He deals with life at a level of abstraction that is now alien to us—he thinks in terms of destiny and 'the march of history' and is largely indifferent to the 'collateral damage' it brings in its wake—the death of ordinary men and women, including of course the soldiers under his command. It is *our* rejection of such ideas that has seriously compromised our attitude to war. Perhaps, even the villainous NCOs and senior officers who appear in this book have been cut down to size, too. No one can now confess to loving war; a general's job is to fight those who still do. And we are no longer given to following world historical figures to our death. In his last message to the Imperial General High Command, the Japanese commander at Iwo Jima declared, 'even as a ghost I wish to be a vanguard for future Japanese operations.' (O'Rourke, 2004, 96). If so, adds Patrick O'Rourke, he is more likely to be found haunting a Toyota factory than a battlefield for which we—and the Japanese–should be eternally thankful.

In *Dr Strangelove* we move into the nuclear age that opened when the US dropped the first atomic bomb on Japan. We also have the only non-literary character to appear in this book. There is a reason that I will explain why film characters do not lend themselves to close study. William Golding once remarked that life is a formless business and that 'literature is much amiss in forcing a form on it.' (Boyd, 2005, 121). If this is a fault of many novels it is most certainly a fault of cinema, but the difference between the two is that we can get into a literary character's mind; sometimes we can even get to know him better than he knows himself.

Strangelove's mind is curiously transparent because there is so little to know about him; he perfectly mirrors the age. D. H. Lawrence once asserted that the proper function of a critic was to save the tale from the artist who created it. But no artist could do justice to the nuclear world of the 1960s. It was absurdly monstrous, its weapons of mass destruction poised on a hair-trigger response. And, in *Dr Strangelove*, director Stanley Kubrick created a truly villainous but empty character. And he is not a villain because he is an ex-Nazi scientist who is always forgetting that he is working for what the German scientist Werner von Braun (the father of the V2 and the American space programme) famously called 'the gentle barbarians': the Americans, his new paymasters after the Second World War. His villainy is of quite a different order. It is comic.

Strangelove was modelled largely on Hermann Kahn, although Kahn was not the wheelchair-bound character who appears in the movie. On the contrary, he was a chubby, obese maestro of the lecture circuit described by one contemporary as a 'roly-poly second-strike Santa Claus' and by another as a 'thermo-nuclear Zero Mostel'. But, like Strangelove, Kahn was an eternal optimist who thought the world might well survive an atomic conflagration. He could contemplate the Armageddon to come with a cheerful heart, confident that, provided the right measures had been taken and that the survivors bred true in their nuclear shelters, the world could survive a nuclear war. Villainy doesn't need to be malevolent; often the greatest villains are those who just can't see why war is tragic. They are so alienated from their own humanity that alienation is their way of being at home with themselves.

The most villainous character of all appears last. *Blood Meridian* did not create much of a stir when it appeared in 1985. It is now considered to be its author's greatest work. The *New York Times Book Review* ranked it third in a 2006 survey of the best works of American fiction published in the last twenty-five years. A year earlier, *Time* chose it as one of the hundred best novels published since 1923.

Blood Meridian is as brutally honest a description of war as the *Iliad*, and just as bleak, if not bleaker. There are really no redemptive characters, and only one sympathetic one, a boy without a name whose flight from home sets off the story. It is, however, an epic that comes *before* the *Iliad*. It shows us our primal humanity. 'When you are philosophising you have to descend into the primeval chaos and feel at home there', wrote Wittgenstein (Steiner, 1989, 146). *Blood Meridian* offers us a philosophy of war derived from the imperatives of primal warfare, our genetic inheritance. It preaches a grim message: life is a senseless tragedy made hideously worse by the human predisposition to invest it with meaning.

The landscape of the novel is as bleak as Hobbes' state of nature, without art, crafts, or even heroic story telling. It is a hell which we have fashioned ourselves, and to which we can always revert back at a moment's notice, as we almost certainly would after a nuclear war. For what characterises the novel most is not the bleak landscape or the Indian savages, or the bounty hunters who become as savage as the 'savages' they scalp, but rather the knowledge that we are watching people like ourselves. And over it all presides Judge Holden, the most diabolic figure to appear in the American novel since Melville conceived Capt Ahab, a man whose world view is also a product of a desolate pessimism. War, as Judge Holden insists, was waiting for us from the beginning. His own consummate inhumanity is not a negation of humanity, it is an expression of it. And this is largely because we are open-ended and unfinished beings; we are a species that natural selection has made most plastic in it possibilities, for both creativity and destruction. It is that plasticity which gives us 'character'. Other animals have it as a species; all lions are brave (or so we tell ourselves; lions, of course, do not theorise about themselves). All donkeys are cowardly (a sentiment with which a donkey might take issue). Stubbornness is not cowardice. Only humans stand at a moral equinox— the blood meridian—where light and dark are equal, and our natures hang in the balance.

Colonel Feraud: Honour Betrayed

The Duel, Joseph Conrad

Does war attract particularly villainous people, or is there is something in the nature of military life that makes people irrational and often unhappy? There are some villains who are not in themselves especially villainous as we understand the term. They are empty in themselves; it is the emptiness which does the damage. Perhaps, in the literature of war, there is no emptier figure than the young Lieutenant Feraud, who we meet in the first pages of Joseph Conrad's novella, *The Duel*.

Feraud is a character who would have no personality but for the literary needs of his creator. He is a warrior whose only real skill is as a duellist, and the novella is about duels. He fights another young officer, Lieutenant d'Hubert, a Hussar like himself, though from a different regiment and a young man on the rise, who is as cool and dispassionate as Feraud is hot-tempered and who doesn't pick arguments in order to win them. Feraud pursues him across Europe in a variety of encounters as Napoleon's army marches across the continent and back. The two cavalry officers, 'like insane artists trying to gild refined gold', pursue a private vendetta through the years of universal carnage (*The Duel*, 3). Conrad shows neither the absurdity of war nor of false honour, war's necessary accessory. What he shows is far more disturbing: how war breeds a certain kind of protagonist who is blind to what honour actually means.

Conrad sets the stage in the first few lines. Napoleon's career, he tells us, had the quality of a duel against the whole of Europe, though he had little time for swashbuckling heroes and disliked duelling between officers. Nevertheless, the tale of the duel becomes a legend in the wars; Conrad's novella is actually based on a true story.

The two men first meet in Strasbourg in an agreeable imperial garrison, during a brief interval of peace. Attached to the general commanding the division, d'Hubert is despatched to arrest Feraud for fighting a duel with a civilian, against explicit orders. Failing to find the quarry in his lodging, he is forced to apprehend him, embarrassingly, in the salon of the wife of a high official. Not that d'Hubert is especially embarrassed. A uniform is a passport; his position as an *officier d'ordonnance* of the General only adds to his swagger and self-assurance; he is what we imagine a young cavalry officer of the period to be: a bit of a dandy. This, in Feraud's eyes, is the first provocation. d'Hubert finds Feraud sitting on a chair, one hand resting on his thigh, the other twirling his regulation moustache to a point. D'Hubert's second mistake is to speak to him in too animated a fashion. Feraud is a man of limited imagination who expresses no remorse for running the civilian through; he never imagined he would be brought to book. Like many such men, he feels himself to be the aggrieved party, and besides, everything should be done according to the rules, and the rules for Feraud are quite explicit: a duel is intended, if not to kill, at least to hurt one of the duellists. His imperturbable response provokes d'Hubert into speaking with unwanted vivacity. 'I am directed by the General to give you the order to go at once to your quarters and remain there under close arrest.' Feraud is not a man to be talked to in such a fashion, and like many stupid men he has a long memory for slights, real or imagined. And since, as he readily admits, he cannot punish the General for his embarrassment, he informs the astonished d'Hubert that he will call him to account instead. 'I mean', screamed suddenly Lieutenant Feraud, 'to cut off your ears, to teach you to disturb me with the general's orders when I'm talking with a lady.' (*The Duel*, 14).

I said that Feraud is entirely the creation of the author—after all, Conrad gives us little to go on in helping us understand this rather absurd little man. We know he is small in stature, like Napoleon himself, and that he is from Gascony—which, in Rostand's play *Cyrano de Bergerac* and Dumas' famous novel, produced the bravest of musketeers. No one can doubt Feraud's bravery. But in the next hundred or so pages we learn little else about the man, except the barest details of his birth (his father is a blacksmith; he is an only child; he is singularly lacking in a love interest; what he has, and cherishes most, is his hatred for d'Hubert, for whom he develops a pathological dislike).

Even at the time, Feraud's honour code would have been seen as bizarre, if not anachronistic; it might well have appealed to a new man in the Emperor's service, one not too sure of his own social standing in Napoleon's army of talents. D'Hubert is forced to fight, against his better nature. Faced with the prospect of being pursued down a street by a sword-wielding officer of the Hussars, he accepts Feraud's challenge. The duel that ensues has its comic moments. It ends when d'Hubert wounds his adversary in the arm. D'Hubert has only two objectives: first, to escape from the whole episode without ruining his reputation and inviting general ridicule; second, to secure an army surgeon to attend to Feraud's wounds. About the first fear, he is right to be concerned. He is sent back to his regiment in disgrace and shut up in close confinement.

Our first impression of Feraud is of his mock-heroic style, adopted as a way of life. He is a small man, in all respects, living a large lie; armies over the centuries tend to attract or even produce such men. What is notable about him is his excessive preoccupation with self and the unrelenting way in which he pursues his adversary across some of the bloodiest battlefields of Europe. What is truly villainous is the extent of his self-regard.

Before an inquiry into the first duel can be held, the army takes to the field. Two years later, Feraud takes up his quarrel again, when d'Hubert's regiment is stationed only a few miles away. This time it is d'Hubert who is bested, though with a non-life threatening wound. In a military culture that likes brio, both men are commended for their swordplay. D'Hubert's commanding colonel tries to get to the bottom of the affair, but fails. The young officer finds himself locked into a system which it is impossible to escape without forfeiting his reputation. 'The Colonel was well aware of the duelling courage, the single combat courage, is rightly or wrongly supposed to be courage of a special sort. And it was eminently necessary that an officer of his regiment should possess every kind of courage—and prove it, too.' (*The Duel*, 41).

In due course, d'Hubert is promoted. Now that he is an officer of superior rank, there can be no question of a duel; neither of the men can send or receive a challenge without rendering themselves susceptible to Court Martial. But the more Feraud dwells upon the fact that he has been denied satisfaction, the more he feels the injustice of his fate. And so he desires urgently to be promoted, too. After Austerlitz, he becomes a captain and clears the decks for the next challenge. The next duel is fought in Silesia, and if not fought to a finish, it is fought to a standstill. They exchange blow after blow, both wounded so seriously that they have to be dragged away by their seconds. It is the seconds who give the opinion that the next encounter will be fatal for one of the parties, such is the animosity each man now feels towards the other.

War again intervenes until after the battle of Jena they find themselves entering Lubeck together, with d'Hubert once again in a position of influence as the 3rd *aide du camp* to a Marshall. Feraud of course considers this to be another provocation. The encounter that follows takes place outside the town. This time, breaking with tradition, they fight on horseback. The suggestion is not theirs, but a fellow officer's. D'Hubert falls in with it reluctantly; Feraud with alacrity, but then the former concludes that one absurdity, more or less, does not matter after all. 'It'll certainly do away to some extent with the monotony of the thing', he reflects philosophically (*The Duel*, 49). In the event, the duel is over almost before it begins. Feraud is wounded with a cut over the forehead, which blinds him with blood and makes it impossible to go on.

From this time on there are to be no more peaceful interludes in both men's careers. D'Hubert takes to the field at Eylau and Friedland, marching and counter-marching in the snow, mud and dust of the Polish plains. Feraud is despatched to the much less glamorous battleground of Spain where he confronts a desolate warfare of ambushes and raids, which does not improve his temper. And all the time he is plagued by questions from fellow officers about the scar on his forehead and how he came by it. By now a Colonel, he has lost none of his hatred for the man who has given it him.

The Russian campaign, in which both men take part, briefly submerges all private feelings in a sea of misery. Colonels with their respective regiments, they are reduced to carrying muskets in the ranks of the so-called Second Battalion, a battalion recruited from officers of all arms who no longer have any troops to lead. As Napoleon's army retreats from Moscow, the battalion trudges along, harried by roving Cossacks, leaving behind a few lifeless bodies, tiny specks on the white immensity of the snow. In all this time Feraud and d'Hubert barely exchange a word, although they fend off an attack together. And as the retreat almost turns into a rout, the two men's careers begin to diverge. Feraud ties his colours entirely to Napoleon's mast, while d'Hubert entertains some philosophical thoughts about the uncertainty of all personal hopes when bound up entirely with the fortunes of one man, however heroic and inspiring. He is not foolish enough to voice his misgivings except in a letter to his sister, who has become a champion of the restoration of the monarchy. And his career continues to flourish even as Napoleon's begins to wane. He survives the big battles, like Leipzig, emerging unscathed with his reputation enhanced. He is promoted to the rank of General and is attached to Napoleon's personal staff, and all the time Feraud conspires against him in the only way he now can, through invective, rumouring it abroad that d'Hubert has never loved the Emperor, or truly served France.

And so the wheel of fortune turns once again. D'Hubert is wounded at Leon, and sees his enemy, now also promoted to General, replace him as the head of brigade. But his wound keeps him out mischief. Ironically Feraud's insinuations rebound to his credit; he is accepted as an anti-Bonapartiste by the restored government of the king, and kept on the active list. Feraud is kept on, too, through the patronage of the then Minister of War, Marshall Soult, who has a softness for officers who served under him in Spain. When Napoleon returns from Elba, d'Hubert is still convalescing at his sister's home. Feraud joins the Emperor readily enough but is kept in a subordinate position at a cavalry depot in Paris, despatching heavily drilled troops into the field. He misses out at Waterloo, but he owes his escape from indictment before a Special Commission to the unexpected intervention of his old adversary.

For on learning that Feraud may forfeit his life for treason, d'Hubert manages to get his old enemy's name removed from the list of officers to be arrested. By now he feels a certain perverse affection for his old rival. His own good fortune has mellowed him. He feels it is now a point of honour to save Feraud from death, persuading the authorities to order him instead into a kind of internal exile to a small town in central France. Dismissed from the army, the only world he has ever known, and informed that payment of his pension depends on the correctness of his future conduct, Feraud becomes a pathetic figure, haunting the streets of the little town, broken hearted. Once again his lack of imagination saves him. 'His mental inability to grasp the hopeless nature of his case as a whole saved him from suicide. He never even thought of it once. He thought of nothing.' (*The Duel*, 77).

And then one day in *The Gazette* he reads that d'Hubert has been called to the command of the Fifth Brigade. He comes immediately to life. He will seek satisfaction again.

> A mere fighter all his life, a cavalryman, a sabreur, he conceived war with the utmost simplicity as in the main, a massed lot of personal 'contests', a sort of gregarious duelling. And here he had in hand a war of his own. (*The Duel*, 79).

The story concludes when, months later, d'Hubert is approached by two old soldiers whilst staying with his Royalist brother-in-law. With their lean brown countenances and distinctive clothes, one with an eye patch, the other missing the tip of his nose, they look the part. Once the masters of Europe, they already have the air of antique ghosts. They seem less substantial in their faded coats than their own narrow shadows falling black across the white road—a metaphor for the tawdriness of the whole affair. They happen to be Feraud's seconds, seeking to obtain satisfaction for their friend. D'Hubert agrees after recovering from his astonishment, preparing pistols, not swords (they are now getting on in years and are much less agile). If true courage, writes Conrad, consists in going out to meet a danger from which one's heart and soul recoil, then d'Hubert shows more of it than he ever has during the war, even when charging at enemy batteries and infantry squares and riding with messages through a hail of bullets.

The final duel is different from all the others; both men know it is the last, both are engaged in a battle to the death. D'Hubert wins the engagement, more by luck than ability, and is in a position to take his adversary's life. He does not. 'He had dreaded death not as a man, but as a lover; not as a danger but as a rival; not as a foe to life but as an obstacle to marriage. And behold! There was his rival defeated!— utterly defeated, crushed, done for!' (*The Duel*, 105–106). By every rule of single combat Feraud's life belongs to him. The price he extracts for not taking it is that he fight no more duels. Feraud has hitherto forced him to mortgage his life to 'honour'; now he can regain his life by forcing his adversary to keep to his promise to give up duelling, or be eternally dishonoured if he breaks his word.

D'Hubert is generous to the end. When he judges the time right he writes a letter to his old antagonist, drawing a line under years of animosity. Feraud's reply is typical. He refuses to be reconciled. He would prefer to have been ordered to blow out his brains. As it is, he keeps a loaded pistol in his drawer. He will go to his death un-reconciled, never knowing the money he thinks is his state pension comes from his old adversary, who cannot bring himself to see him die destitute. He will end his days never suspecting that he has so fastened onto d'Hubert's feelings that he has become an intimate part of his life.

The Duel remains a classic of literature for a reason. Feraud, puzzles over the unfairness of a world in which he gives everything to war and war gives him so little in return. His friends are few, and those who latch onto him do so because of his reputation as a duellist (even though he is in every respect inferior to his rival). In later years he is given to a whispering campaign which brings into question his own integrity; there can be no greater dishonour than insinuating that d'Hubert is a self-seeker who served the Emperor but never loved him.

Feraud's extraordinary self-regard gives the novella its moments of high comedy, but Conrad subtly picks apart the honour code which underpins the whole story. Feraud thinks he is representative of a new breed of soldier who enters a career 'open to all talents'. He thinks he is Napoleon's man, but in truth he owes his promotion only to the constant thinning out of the ranks as Napoleon's ambition grows greater. Even when the Emperor returns from Elba, he is left behind in Paris, training the next generation of cannon fodder. Feraud is less representative of the new breed promoted from the ranks than he is shaped by Conrad's interest in what drives a man to defend his honour off the battlefield, though no longer fighting for his life. Even if Feraud, like the Emperor he serves, is blinkered by his own vanity and trapped by his own self-regard, he is also ensnared by war's essence: the supreme importance of recognition. In a duel two men risk death to prove to the other that, for them, absolute freedom and recognition are more important than death. And if, as Clausewitz argued, war is an act of coercion, compelling an enemy to do one's will, who can coerce a man who is willing to die? This was the question asked by Clausewitz's contemporary, Fichte.

We can be sure that the point would elude Feraud altogether. And yet this, it seems to me, is at the heart of the work. D'Hubert is never more honourable than when he finally has the opportunity to dispatch his foe. And after so many years of persecution, who could blame him? But remember what a duel—like war—is actually about. Two opponents struggle to be recognised as superior to the other, but such recognition can only come from the defeated man—the opponent must survive the struggle, otherwise the purpose of the struggle itself is defeated. The death of an opponent can even be considered dishonourable, especially in circumstances in which d'Hubert finds himself, his opponent disarmed and utterly at his mercy. Death violates the opponents' equality, the only thing that makes their recognition in any way valuable to one another.

Feraud is a thoroughly one-dimensional character because he cannot recognise this. Had he found himself in d'Hubert's position at the end he would have had no compunction in despatching his foe, and robbing him of his life. After all, he is consumed—as his opponent is not—by hatred, perhaps because he feels his social inadequacy even in Napoleon's army of all the talents; perhaps because it is impossible to be recognised as an equal by someone who is actually far more socially successful. A constant theme of Feraud's hatred is his enemy's social success, his ability to network with higher officers. He resents the fact that on first meeting, d'Hubert's is an *officier d'ordonnance* and later an *aide du camp* to a General before becoming a member of Napoleon's staff. He lives to see him marry into the restoration aristocracy. D'Hubert's insouciance infuriates him. Feraud positively screams at him when he first challenges him, 'I mean to cut off your ears.' D'Hubert's understanding of honour could not be more different.

> A duel, whether regarded as a ceremony and a cult of honour or even when reduced to its moral essence to a form of manly sport, demands a perfect singleness of intention, a homicidal austerity of mood. (*The Duel*, 19).

139

And that is precisely what Feraud lacks. What his opponent dreads most is the ridicule the duel will invite, and with it loss of promotion. What Feraud dreads most if he does not best his opponent or kill him, is loss of respect by others; what d'Hubert fears most is loss of self-esteem.

And there is another theme in the story which emerges when d'Hubert consults his wife's uncle, the Chevalier du Valmassigue, ex-brigadier of the army of the princes who, with the revolution, became a shoemaker (with a great reputation for elegance in the fit of ladies shoes). The Chevalier cannot understand why his nephew should take up the final challenge. He can imagine a world in which men will fight for honour and especially over a woman (he recalls a feud over 'little Sophia Derval' which had brought two suitors to blows three times in eighteen months). But he can only attribute Feraud's motiveless malignancy as a restored aristocrat might to 'the sanguinary madness of the revolution.' For him, the fight has become meaningless, especially with the restoration of the king. What *is* Feraud, he asks, before answering his own question: 'A *va-nu-pieds* disguised into a general by a Corsican adventurer, masquerading as an Emperor. There is no earthly reason for d'Hubert to shame himself by fighting a duel with a person of that sort.' (*The Duel*, 92).

And when we read the passage, such snobbery may draw us to Feraud's side. But it is not, even now, a side to pick. The Chevalier's distaste is not entirely a matter of snobbery. He recognises that Feraud is dangerous because he has lost control of himself. Conrad tells us that he 'screams', and 'burns' with indignation when he hears of how d'Hubert has got command of a troop. What he fears is that his niece's husband may become infected, too, and for a moment he does. But his decision to preserve Feraud's life and to keep it 'in forfeit' is his victory over himself. He abides by the rules and recognises that only mutual recognition is a lasting condition for containing war's tendency towards absolute violence. Granting recognition makes it possible to limit violence and reveal its instrumental nature. Indeed, Clausewitz's seminal concept of war as a political instrument only makes sense when linked to the requirement of mutual recognition between adversaries.

Conrad's tale is a commentary, not on the futility of war, as it is often claimed, but on the unrestrained nature of revolutionary war and of Napoleon's political ambitions in particular that lead him and his army into disaster in the Russian snows. Napoleon, after all, is a duellist at heart, and much more like Feraud than the sanguine d'Hubert. And that is why d'Hubert not only refuses to take his opponent's life, but also personally pensions him off in the twilight of that life. 'We must take care of his security to the ends of his days', he tells his wife. 'It's extraordinary how in one way or another, that man has managed to fasten himself on my deeper feelings.' (*The Duel*, 115).

What is most depressing about Conrad's tale, nonetheless, is that although both men are bound together by fate and by an absurd code of honour, they do not help each other develop. They live in cloistered worlds even when fighting on the same side. But we know with the end of the war that their circumstances change. We know that with his life now forfeit there is nothing left for Feraud but an increasingly precipitous descent into terminal bitterness. The duel, in the end, is the only thing he had left to cling onto in the wreckage of his own life.

Colonel Moredock: The Metaphysics of Indian Hating
The Confidence Man, Herman Melville

There are many types of villains in the literature of war. Some have the power of language, like General Cummings, which is reinforced by the power of ideas. Others have the power of their vanity, like Colonel Ferauld. One has the most dangerous power of all: hate, Herman Melville's 'Indian-hater', Colonel Moredock. He is one of two famous Indian haters in American literature. The other is Brigadier-General John A. B. C. Smith of Edgar Allen Poe's short story *The Man Who Was All Used Up*, an impressive 6ft tall man with flowing black hair, 'large and lustrous eyes' who so impresses the unknown narrator when they first meet that he is determined to learn more about him. Everyone thinks highly of the general, without actually revealing much about his life. They are always commenting obliquely that he is an avatar of a 'wonderfully inventive age'. When the narrator first meets him he is struck by something not quite right, by a 'primness, not to say stiffness in his carriage', and a 'degree of measured if not rectangular precision.' Smith is an 'Indian general' as the term was understood at the time—a soldier who spent his life fighting native Americans and doing so with some distinction in the swamp fights with the Bugaboo and Kickapoo tribes—and as he says, you cannot fight them and think

you'll come off without a scratch. At the climax of the story our narrator discovers to his horror that Smith has been literally taken apart
in the wars. The Indians have so hacked up his body that he is no more
than a prosthetic triumph; his legs and arms are all artificial. Every
morning he has to be reassembled before he can make a public appearance. He really is a wonderful testament to an age of invention.

Colonel Moredock appears in Melville's novel, *The Confidence Man*,
which is set aboard a steam boat on the Mississippi many years after
the date of Poe's short story (1839), and fifty years before the frontier
was officially closed and the Indians had been confined to reservations.
Moredock, we are told, is a striking figure with an eye like Lochiel, a
finger like a trigger, and nerve like a catamount's and, in case we do
not find this extraordinary enough, he has two additional little
quirks—he seldom stirs without his rifle and he hates Indians like
snakes (*The Confidence Man*, 169). All we learn of his appearance is
that he is silky-bearded and curly-headed, unlike most backwoodsman,
'and to all but Indians, juicy as a peach.'

Critics have differed over what the story is about. Of many theories,
the one I favour is that it is a novel about the consequences of hating
an enemy too much. On the first day of April, the Devil comes abroad
the boat to preach Christianity as an April Fool's joke—often, the best
haters are the best Christians. Hatred is a major theme of Melville's
work, as is his ironic attitude to Christians. In *Moby Dick*, Father
Mapel remarks, 'Woe to him who seeks to pour oil upon the waters
when God has brewed them into a gale ... Delight is to him who gives
no quarter in the truth, and kills and burns and destroys all sin.
Though he pluck it out under the robes of senators and judges.' There
are many righteous Christians on board the steam boat in *The Confidence Man* who have little love in their hearts, even for their fellow
Christians. One, a judge, relates what he calls the 'metaphysics of
Indian hating'; another tells the story of the sort of man the judge has
in mind, whose hatred was reserved exclusively for 'heathens'—by
which he means Native Americans.

Melville adapted his chapter on Indian hating from Charles Hall's
sketches of history, *Life and Manners in the West* (1839), which was
published in the same year as Poe's short story. A Missourian relates
the philosophy of Judge James Hall before recounting the life of Colonel John Moredock. Both characters are taken from Hall's book, and
as the Missourian remarks, 'Indian-hating still exists, and no doubt

VILLAINS

will continue to exist so long as Indians ....' (*The Confidence Man*, 172). And Indians—an elastic term—is one that keeps reappearing in American military history, most recently in Vietnam, when it was used to designate enemy territory. *Indian Country* is the revealing title of Philip Caputo's third novel which appeared in 1987.

The judge has developed a fully-fledged understanding of why Indians are hated so much, and takes up the point Caputo makes in a very different context, post-traumatic stress. 'Wars don't end when the shooting stops, and the treaties are signed. They go on in the wounded minds of those who did the fighting.' (Caputo, 1987). They also extend into the mind of Indian haters like Moredock long after the enemy has given up the fight. As Melville's Judge explains, hating is a mark of a particular human type—a solitary, strong but unsophisticated man who stands on his own judgement, and allows his instinct to prevail over any precepts he may have learned from reading. The Judge is quick to point out the paradox—a man who lives on the frontier may come to look like the savages he hates, but he has one advantage over them; he is in the van of progress. In a striking metaphor the Judge remarks that, 'the tide of emigration—let it roll as it will—never over-whelms the backwoodsman into itself; he rides upon its advance.' (*The Confidence Man*, 174). He is always on the frontier as it expands west-wards. He is a frontiersman; anchored to the natural life, he helps tame civilisation. What is more, he is confirmed in his opinion that Indians remain tied to nature, too, their own enduring and unchanging instinct for savagery.

If the backwoodsman inclines to knowledge, he learns from it that Indians are inclined to theft, double-dealing and murder. 'As the twig is bent, the tree inclines.' To see an Indian stepping out of his allotted role and professing Christianity or even embracing 'civilisation' is merely confirmation that he is far worse than the others—they are likely to be 'the arrantist horse-thieves and tomahawkers among them.' (*The Confidence Man*, 176). What is known as a 'friendly Indian' is a rare sort of creature, and one to be avoided; no cruelty exceeds that of a friendly Indian who turns enemy. 'A coward friend, he makes a valiant foe.' The greatest Indian haters of all, the Judge believes, are those who are resolved to seek them out and to do them as much harm as they can. They are the Indians' leather-stocking Nemesis. Colonel John More-dock is such a man, and though he appears in only four pages of the novel, his is the character we remember long after we have put it down.

143

The Colonel is born in the wilderness, and life has not treated his family well. His mother loses three husbands to the tomahawk (as Daniel Boone lost his sons). She too meets the same fate en route to the western border of Illinois. And it is the fate of his family, unsurprisingly, that leaves him in no little way unhinged. The murderers are a party of renegades from various tribes, outlaws even among the Indians. Despite this, he is in no mood to forgive or forget; he tracks them down over two winters and kills all but three who manage to escape. He is not a man, we are told, who is especially passionate; he does not rage after his mother's death; he bides his time and in his patience becomes 'a moral Manichean'—seeing all Indians the same way he wishes to be seen by them: as a hater. He is nothing if not methodical in his revenge; In the course of the next few years he tracks down and despatches the three who escaped. By this time he has developed a positive blood lust. He never 'lets pass an opportunity of quenching an Indian. Sins of commission that kind may have been his, but none of omission.' (*The Confidence Man*, 184).

By his own lights he is not an especially bad man. Indeed, he leads a comparatively virtuous social life. In an ironic note, Melville describes him as a 'moccasined gentleman' among his neighbours and friends who hold him in high regard. Indian hating, moreover, does not dominate his life to the exclusion of all else. He is a good family man, a born storyteller, and an inveterate singer of songs. And he proves to be an admirable soldier, serving in the 1812 war against the British. He is especially outraged when General Hull surrenders Detroit without much of a fight. In time he becomes a member of the Territorial Council of Illinois, and in its role helps to found the State government. But he declines to be nominated for the Governorship of the territory; he retains enough grasp of civilised life to recognise (as Melville wonderfully puts it) that it would be improper for a Governor, Indian hater or not, to steal out now and then, 'for a few days' shooting at human beings.'

And that is all we hear of the Colonel, hardly worth including in this book, perhaps, but for two factors. One is that he represents a character type, for there are plenty of Indian haters in every war; and second because there may be something of the Indian hater in all of us. With regard to the second point, Melville was careful to add that once the Indians had disappeared completely they might be replaced by white men in the eyes of other backwoodsmen. He hints at this; he doesn't spell it out but the hints are intriguing. He gives Charlie, the Mississippi man who tells us Moredock's story, Indian containers for his wine bottles and he calls the pipe of a character called 'the cosmopolitan' a calumet—or peace pipe. In doing so he seems to be making them almost 'honorary' Indians, ready to be culled in turn when there are no more Indians left. Melville has brilliantly anticipated Lewis Carroll in seeing that it is a poor sort of memory which only works backwards. Indian hating is not about the past—past injuries to be avenged, and the retribution to be exacted for past attacks. It is directed towards the future as well, one without Indians, and perhaps, one day even white Americans who have 'gone native'.

As recently as the 1920s one of the great anthropologists of the day, Franz Boas, came to the conclusion that the Americans were beginning to resemble the Indians they had displaced. Boas spent much of his life measuring the skulls of first generation Americans, comparing their cephalic index (the measure of the breadth of the human head as a percentage of its front-to-back) to the population in their countries of origin. His major claim was that the cephalic index was not stable and that it could change in the course of a single generation. His less well known research involved studying how Americans were beginning to resemble native Americans (Barkan, 1992, 84). The story would be amusing but for the fact that a few years later the Germans began conducting cephalic studies of their own in an attempt to identify the race most fitted to survive in the twentieth century. 'We human beings', wrote Nietzsche (*Daybreak*, 1881) are 'the only creatures who, if they have not turned out satisfactorily, can cross themselves out like an unsatisfactory sentence, whether we do so for the honour of mankind, or out of pity for it, or from displeasure at ourselves.'

Melville's Indian hating is pre-Darwinian, however; it is ethical, not ontological. It is not a question of the Indians' humanity or lack of it. Moredock does not kill them on sight because they are 'sub-human' as the Nazis were later to kill Jews. He does not learn his Indian hating in a classroom. He learns it the hard way, through life. It is intensely ethical and therefore far more insidious. For Moredock the essence of a human being is whatever it is that he loves—or hates—about a man and since hate is intensely personal, it is not so easy to argue him out of it. Secondly, to hate others is not to feel in a certain way about them, but to behave in a certain way towards them, and Moredock just happens to behave very badly. He likes to gun them down. Shelley once claimed that 'the great instrument of moral good is the imagination', and often it is. Soldiers today are encouraged in the ethics classes in which they enrol to imagine the plight of others, including their enemies, and therefore to behave honourably towards them, especially when their enemies have been taken prisoner and fallen into their power. It is not clear whether Moredock has an imagination to begin with. What Melville shows us is that he is not bad because he imagines the Indians fate and doesn't care. He simply does not ask the question; he lacks the intellectual resources, and is therefore a lesser character (and villain) for it.

But villainous he most certainly is, precisely because Indian hating is so elemental. It puts dislike of the out-group before any love of the in-group. Haters are instinctively shunned by their comrades when they do so because they set themselves apart from their peers. They are set against the in-group values that we celebrate, such as sacrifice. They set themselves against the moral law in which sacrifice has meaning for others. Hatred is hardly an object lesson in 'duty' because it negates the spiritual existence in which one's value as a man consists. Indian haters rarely inspire others because we instinctively distrust the bitterness that is central to their being.

None of the characters on Melville's steamboat have names. Indian hating is pretty characterless at the best of times because the object of their hate is a stereotype, too. There is very little hate in the great novels about war because in war most of the characters whose fate we care about are desperate to hang on to their own humanity, even when killing others. What is important about Moredock for this study is that he is less of a real person than an archetype. When *The Confidence Man* first appeared, critics slammed it for not being a novel at all, so much as a series of conversations. But it is actually an allegory, and allegories produce archetypal figures. There is indeed very little of Colonel Moredock to know. He is more an archetype than a personality, and a Jungian archetype at that. Perhaps we should not expect Indian haters to be very complex figures.

Moredock is a prime example of what happens when a man has dehumanised himself in his frenzy to kill (D. H. Lawrence's profound insight in his essay on Fennimore Cooper's *Last of the Mohicans*). In other words, he is in danger of becoming the very monster he is trying to eliminate. Melville was tapping into the developing science of psychology which had only recently provided a new vocabulary for describing the kind of madness at issue. The pioneer British psychiatrist James G. Pritchard had introduced the word 'monomania' into the language to replace the old word, 'melancholia', for a condition in which one broods on one idea and cannot be argued out of it.

Melville had already created the greatest monomaniac in western literature. In his masterpiece *Moby Dick*, Captain Ahab is an authentic American hero, a devotee of what Harold Bloom calls 'the American religion'. In his book *The Western Canon* he quotes Ahab's famous peroration:

> Bear me out in it, thou great democratic God ... thou who dids't pick up Andrew Jackson from the pebbles, who did'st hurl him upon a warhorse, who didst thunder him higher than a throne! Thou who, in all Thy mighty, earthy marchings, ever cullest Thy selectest champions from the kingly commons; bear me out in it, O God. (Bloom, 1994, 137).

The whale that Ahab pursues becomes the monster that the Indians are in Moredock's imagination. And if the monstrous quality of the Indians is a projection of Moredock's hatred, the whale is a projection of Ahab's. Ahab becomes a monster, too, as Ishmael who narrates the tale, discovers for himself in the course of the voyage. The whale is given a displaced voice through Ishmael's rhetorical energy and it is Ishmael who we remember at the end of the tale. 'Call me Ishmael', is one of the most famous opening lines in fiction.

What is striking, I think, is that neither Ahab nor Moredock can understand the nature of the forces that drive them on, any more than in *Moby Dick* Queequez can decipher the hieroglyphics tattooed upon his own skin. Ahab is inscrutable even to himself. But the critics have been more penetrating. D. H. Lawrence in his *Studies in Classic American Literature* saw him as possessed by a violent need to subdue nature in man. Lawrence however believed that hatred eventually rebounds on the hater. The greatest threat is not 'the other' but oneself:

> When you are actually in America, America hurts because it has a powerful disintegrative influence upon the white psyche. It is full of grinning, unopposed aboriginal demons ... America is tense with latent violence and resistance. The very common sense of white Americans has a tinge of helplessness in it and a deep fear of what might be if they were not commonsensical. (Lawrence, 1977, 56).

Moredock may not be a fully realised character, but he is certainly a disconcerting figure because we know from history that men like that exist, and always have. And if Indian hating is no longer in fashion, other prejudices like Islamaphobia can still get the better of American 'common sense'. And 'gooks', 'Tallebadies' and 'towel heads' still populate the language of military life. If Moredock is a quintessential nineteenth-century character, his psychopathology is universal. We know the type well enough: those who join up to fight the enemy so that they don't have to confront the enemy in themselves. The Indian hater will always be among us, as he will always be a figure of American literature. I recall the last line of Philip Roth's *Sabbath's Theater* (1995). 'And he couldn't do it, he could not ... die. How could he leave? Everything he hated was here.'

But there is a deeper moral in the novel. Moredock is a monomaniac bent on a single and all-consuming passion. Because he does not recognise his own humanity in the enemy he makes it impossible for his enemies to recognise their humanity in him. Melville himself would have had no truck with such men. In a review of Parkman's classic, *The Californian and Oregon Trails* written in 1846, he took note of the author's hatred of Indians. 'When in the body of the book we are informed that it is difficult for any white man, after domestication among the Indians, to hold them much better than brutes, we are told too, that to such a person the slaughter of an Indian is as indifferent as the slaughter of a buffalo with all deference we beg leave to dissent.' And what was Melville's dissent based upon? It was based on the fact we all belong to one species. 'We are all of us Anglo-Saxons, Dyaks and Indians—sprung from one head and made in one image. And if we regret this brotherhood now, we shall be forced to join hands hereafter.' Or as he put it in *The Confidence Man*, 'the grand points of human nature are the same today as they were a thousand years ago. The only variability in them is in expression, not in feature.' (*The Confidence Man*, 86).

Monomaniacs are dangerous for they bring others down with them, as Ahab does his crew. Moredock fortunately is a solitary figure. He hunts alone, but there are plenty of real-life instances in which Ahabs have commanded armies and sent men by the thousand to their death: Alexander, advancing 11,000 miles into the heart of Asia; or Napoleon on his march to Moscow. In Napoleon, the philosopher Hegel saw the World Spirit yearning for the Infinite. Kierkegaard, an altogether more modest philosopher, saw a man whose monomania destroyed him and the army he led. In invading Russia he had succumbed to vertigo.

'Frenchmen on their march across the Russian steppes where the eye seeks a point on which it can rest ... must see individuals trickle like dry sand through the fingers.' The march was, for Kierkegaard, a metaphor for what happens when young men with limitless ambition draw others to destruction (Fenves, 1993, 31). In Napoleon's case oblivion and ambition eventually met up on the vast snow-filled Russian plains. Lucky for his compatriots, perhaps, that Moredock never rises above the rank of colonel.

General Cummings: Dangerous Ideas
The Naked and the Dead, Norman Mailer

Norman Mailer went to war in 1942 determined that war would give him the experience he needed to write the great novel. It did, but not in the way he originally imagined. 'You will live with these men', George Orwell wrote of the fourteen-strong Intelligence and Reconnaissance Platoon who are the characters in Mailer's novel, *The Naked and the Dead*. In an earlier essay on the Spanish Civil War, in which he himself fought, Orwell wrote that the first thing to convey is the physical memories: the sounds, smells and surfaces of things, and this Mailer does consummately well. But not the combat. Surface is what a modern army is about. It was because he wanted to see combat that he did not use his Harvard education to get an officer's commission, but he saw virtually no action. What he observed instead was how bureaucratic the army was becoming. War was increasingly remote from the fighting and the men who were in the thick of it.

The Naked and the Dead is set in the Pacific theatre, and it is the story of a task force responsible for capturing Anopopei, an island about 150 miles long and a third as wide, with a high spine of mountains running along its axis. The Japanese have dug in for a protracted defence and constructed a powerful defence line on a front which runs from the main mountain range to the sea, named after their commanding officer, General Toyaku. The Americans make good progress in the first days of the campaign in preparation for the assault on the line and the hard war of attrition that will follow. The campaign itself begins a month later; it will take a further five months to secure the Japanese surrender.

Mailer was a young man when he wrote *The Naked and the Dead*. Years later he acknowledged that he had been carried away stylistically. Unlike Hemingway (perhaps in a conscious break with the acknowledged father of the American war novel), he overdosed on adjectives. There was hardly a noun in any sentence that was not holding hands with the nearest and most commonly available adjective, he wrote in a special preface to the fiftieth anniversary of the publication of the book. One of the examples he singled out for particular criticism was 'tremulous fear' (*The Naked and the Dead*, 5). Inevitably, in the hands of lesser authors, characters in novels are also at risk of becoming stereotypes, and some of the minor characters he portrays are caricatures from the southern redneck and Mexican-American to the Boston Irish and New York Jew; they are nothing if not predictable in their reactions to military life. Even so, the unit survives, a testament to the compelling myth of the melting pot, a myth which is often true to type, without being entirely untrue.

There are only three figures in the novel who have any real depth: Herne, a stylised version of what Mailer hated most in himself; Cross, an anti-heroic thug; and General Cummings. Of the three, General Cummings is the most complex, though less dramatically interesting than Cross, and much less sympathetic a figure than Herne. Though in part a caricature, too, he is sufficiently interesting to be worth considering. He is the most intellectual General to appear in the literature of war (the kind of general that Saul Bellow might have invented).

Cummings is a well-fleshed man of little over medium height, with a rather handsome, sun-tanned face and greyish hair. He wears a vacant expression, an ever-smiling face, and appears to be completely at ease both with himself and his own men. But he is always acting a role, and there is always a hardness in the eyes that puts most men in fear of him, even when he is at his most genial. 'The trick is to make yourself an instrument of your own policy', Cummings tells Herne in the first scene in which they are together, and that is precisely what the General does (*The Naked and the Dead*, 90). He shows the world only as much of himself as is needed to make it a tool of his own inflexible will. Herne sees from the first that he is consumed by a single-minded pursuit of power.

The General is competent enough, and admirably hard-working. Herne is impressed that on the first day of the invasion, Cummings conducts the campaign by phone for eight hours without rest, without referring once to a map or pausing for a decision after his line officers have reported back. He is a man of enormous concentration and focus, too. He has a reputation for geniality. He rarely swears and treats subordinates with kindness. Herne soon realises that he has been selected as an aide because he is the only officer to hand with the intelligence to understand his commanding officer's philosophy. This he expounds continuously in monologues which reveal much about the man, including the fact that he has spent rather too much time reading Spengler.

This was, of course, an intensely intellectual age. Saul Bellow captured it particularly well in a short story: *Mosby's Memoirs*. One of the chapter contents of his memoirs reveal him to be very much a twentieth century, a man of ideas:

> Fundamentalist family in Missouri—father a successful builder—early schooling—the State University—Rhodes Scholarship—intellectual friendships—what I learned from Professor Collingwood—Empire and the mental vigour of Britain—my unorthodox interpretation of John Locke—I work for William R.Hearst—the personality of General Franco—radical friendships in New York—wartime service with the OSS—limited vision of FDR—Comte, Proudhon and Marx revisited—De Tocqueville again.

In Bellow's story, Mosby, for all his erudition, or perhaps even because of it, makes a terrible career mistake by foolishly embracing the Burnham School of Management, 'declaring, during the war, that the Nazis were winning because they had made their managerial position first. No Allied combination could conquer with its obsolete individualism a nation which had reached a new state of history and tapped the power of the inevitable.' (Bellow, 1971,160). 'The power of the inevitable'—the authentic vernacular of an age. Characters in novels don't talk like that these days because no one expresses such sentiments in real life. But this is 1942 and the world was indeed very different. Like Mosby, Cummings has read the requisite books. Unlike Mosby, he has a more accurate grasp on the pulse of history—he knows that the United States is going to win because the American Century is about to dawn.

America is a character in his imagination, as it was in much of Mailer's writing. His ultimate confrontation was always with his own country. 'How much America becomes the character, no, the protagonist of (a) novel, no genius is large enough to write. Shakespeare would grow modest before it.' So he wrote in *Some Honorable Men*. (Wenke,

1987, vi). Americans have been the most self-regarding of twentieth century writers, preoccupied with understanding themselves more than anyone else and interrogating their past even more persistently than German authors following the Second World War. Perhaps, added Mailer, this was because America is 'the most dialectical of nations ... the best of its history is coupled with much of its worst.' (Wenke, 1987, vi).

Hitler once said that a single idea of a genius is worth more than a lifetime's conscientious work in an office. Cummings is not immune to Hitler's spell—they both believe in the inflexibility of the human will and the overriding principle of power. But Hitler was delusional, and Cummings isn't. He takes risks, but informed ones. He puts the lives of his men in danger, but he never squanders them. He is never prone to catastrophic errors of judgement, and he works with what he has. Like Hitler, however, he sees that in the twentieth century the world had become a laboratory for releasing reserves of energy and that a powerful state, provided it has the courage of its convictions, can sweep aside all the old conventions inhibiting the release of energy in the past, such as religious taboos and social conventions. And war has become the instrument by which energy moves from its promise to its realisation. 'Historically the purpose of war', he tells Herne, 'is to translate America's potential into kinetic energy.' 'Have you ever wondered why we are fighting this war?' he asks Herne halfway through the campaign:

> '...The concept of Fascism, far sounder than Communism if you consider it, for it's grounded firmly in men's actual natures, merely started in the wrong country, in a country which did not have enough intrinsic potential power to develop completely... As you put it, Robert, not too badly, there is a process of osmosis. America is going to absorb that dream, it is in the business of doing it now. When you've created power, materials, armies, they don't wither of their own accord. Our vacuum as a nation is filled with released power, and I can tell you that we are out of the backwaters of history now.'
>
> 'We have become destiny, eh?' Herne said.
>
> 'Precisely. The currents that have been released are not going to subside.'
>
> (*The Naked and the Dead*, 321).

As Herne observes ironically, the American Century has dawned. The idea (which was coined the year after Pearl Harbor by the editor of *Time-Life*, Henry Luce) is counterpointed throughout the novel with the painful moral education of the two protagonists, Herne and Cross, one diminishing as the battle develops, the other growing more confident in his own demonic power. But by far the most disturbing figure is the General, the physical embodiment of the American Century. For Cummings, history is painted in bold colours; there is no light or shade; his is a world without shadow. And yet, if he is a man of strong beliefs, he is also the instrument of the 'the good war', and by his own light (and those of the men he leads), he does the right thing. This is the strange and unsettling conundrum of the novel, and what gives *The Naked and the Dead* its power.

Within that larger vision Cummings stakes out his own ground as he tries to shape Herne to his own purposes. The only morality of the future, he tells him, is a power morality; a man who cannot find his adjustment to it is doomed. And the one thing about power is that it flows from the top down. 'When there are little surges of resistance at the middle levels, it merely calls for more power to be directed against it, to burn it out.' (*The Naked and the Dead*, 327)

Herne offers such 'surges' from time to time. He is always irritating Cummings with his ironic asides and barely disguised contempt for the general's Nietzschean musings.

> Herne was looking at his hands. 'We're not in the future yet.'
> 'You can consider the army, Robert, as a preview of the future.'
> (*The Naked and the Dead*, 329).

In the end, Cummings will break him in by sending him off to command Cross's platoon, and he and later Cross will connive at the young Lieutenant's death. But Herne, we feel, is really a victim of his own misplaced belief in liberalism.

I think our doubts about Cummings come from reading his thoughts. These allow us to read him better than he reads himself, even if he is given to moments of self-doubt. He sees himself as smaller than he would like (dwarfed by history, rather than riding the wave—'I cannot see this war ... simply and purely as a struggle between the forces of good and evil ... if I could simplify it into a phrase at all, it would seem truer to say that the forces of the past are fighting the forces of the future'). Significantly, the quotation comes from a book by Mailer's contemporary Anne Morrow Lindberg, *The Wave of the Future* (1941). It was a title that Kennedy was to borrow twenty years later when he warned the American people that unless capitalism was seen to prevail the world would conclude that Communism was the future, and the West would be swamped in its wake. This was the cruelty of history as the will to power. The subject was not the individual, but the representatives of humanity who could take many forms: a nation, a class, or even a civilisation. History was the place in which humanity became many: slaves and masters, workers and the bourgeoisie, peasants and the state. History was a discourse between them, a dialectic that could only be resolved in a final struggle between two opposing historical forces, and at the end of the novel Herne rightly suspects that he has failed to make the cut.

Cummings' villainy is to live by abstractions. He is always trying to remain in step with history as though history can be made independent of those who make it, his own countrymen. He is determined to mould his men into an effective fighting unit. He sees the army for what it is—an illiberal institution where liberal ideas have no place. 'To make an army work you have to have every man in it fitted into a fear ladder.' (*The Naked and the Dead*, 181). An army functions best when you are frightened of the man above you and contemptuous of your subordinates. The trick is to ensure that they do not turn their weapons against their own officers. Until an army is in full retreat, the officers can rest secure in the knowledge that 'the hate just banks in them, makes them fight a little better. They can't turn it on us, so they turn it outwards.' (*The Naked and the Dead*, 182).

Cummings' views on the enlisted men are not untypical of those held by many officers in the past and doubtless today (though of course this is rarely voiced openly). When the unit's discipline falters just before the attack on the Toyaku line, he ruminates that it is always dangerous to allow an army to rest and dig in. Men become dogs in their own kennel, and bark sullenly at orders. For five weeks the troops have functioned like an extension of his own body and now he finds he has lost his sensitive control. Loss of control, for a man like Cummings, is truly disastrous. The lassitude of the troops soon infects him. 'The power, the intensity of the urges within himself, inexpressibly baulked, seemed to course through his limbs, beating in senseless fury against the confines of his body.' (*The Naked and the Dead*, 307).

Hemingway never wrote the great Second World War novel, as everyone expected; by then his critical powers were already on the wane. Mailer wrote it for him, and he took a perverse pleasure from doing so because he suspected, correctly, that Hemingway was not quite the man he wanted to appear. He was not a Nietzschean. Worse still, he was a closet coward who struggled all his life with the anxiety he might be caught out (an anxiety that finally overwhelmed him in 1961 when he took his own life, which Mailer, of course, thought a cowardly act). Yet Mailer had a similar impulse to affirm manhood. It is the great problem of the American novel. Mailer's heroes are always men (never women) who take a bet upon themselves whenever they have the courage to throw themselves into a situation in which the end is unknown. War, the most unpredictable of all human endeavours, provides the greatest opportunity for such acts. In so doing, the hero enters into conflict with the world and with himself, and extends his own freedom accordingly. For freedom is the courage to be more than a product of biological and social forces. Mailer called this moral courage, but it can still be read (in Mailer's own life) as a struggle for a man to assert his own manhood when his own nerve fails. And in the case of Herne, his tragedy is to die unmanned.

Indeed, Cummings perhaps speaks for Mailer himself in despising Herne for being 'effete'—an intellectual coward, a sentimental liberal. And if our post-modern sensibilities are offended by Cummings' position we have to recognise—because Mailer forces us to—that unlike Herne, he is not a hypocrite. All of us, when it comes to war, are encouraged as liberals to condemn it. 'War: thunder against it' is one of the wisdoms in Flaubert's *Dictionary of Received Ideas*, and liberals have been thundering against war even when crusading against Fascism, or fighting to forge a New World Order, or trying to make the world 'safe for democracy' (as opposed to making democracy safe for the world). Cummings, by contrast, is quite honest in his opinions. He is one of Nietzsche's 'honest liars'. He lies, and is fully aware of it, for a purpose he knows the enlisted men would never understand, which is why he regards them not with contempt, but simply as potential collateral damage in pursuit of a larger historical end. He differs from Herne in another respect; he may betray others but he never betrays himself and betrayal is the novel's principle theme.

Herne is always betraying what he claims to value most. When at the opening of the novel he picks a fight with Colonel Conn over the latter's crass racism, he does so not because he sympathises with the minorities Conn hates, but because the Colonel reminds him of his own father's generation, and its rabid anti-intellectualism. On a per-

sonal level he is a curious combination of self-awareness and self-right-
eousness, both of which come into play whenever he is privy to one of
the General's many monologues. He can see through the General, to be
sure, but his prissiness often gets the better of him. He knows that he
is not willing to play dirty, and therefore knows he will never win.

Cummings knows the type; he has spent his whole life observing
men like Herne, even at West Point. But what he most despises is
Herne's intellectual shallowness. 'Somehow you picked it up so hard
you can't shake the idea "liberal" means "good", and "reactionary"
means "evil". That's your frame of reference. Two words.' (*The Naked
and the Dead*, 92). And Mailer hardly encourages us to take the young
man to our hearts. Several people in the course of the novel make it a
point to tell Herne to his face that he likes people only in the abstract,
an over-simplification but not without some truth. Indeed for what he
most hates about the field officers whose company he is forced to keep
is not their racial and national prejudices against Russians, 'kikes',
'niggers', or 'micks', but their human weaknesses: their tendency to
love one another but sleep with each other's wives back at home, to get
drunk together and shoot up local whorehouses on Saturday nights.

The point is that Cummings has a philosophy of life, and Herne
doesn't. He only has a set of very weak liberal ideas. Morally he is a
broken figure, too, because he cannot really empathise with anyone
under his command; they suspect, rightly, that he is not really on side.
He makes few friends, but then does not attempt to; he likes very few
people, and most of the men sense it after talking to him for a few minutes. His voice is sharp with a thin contemptuous quality, rather surprising in so physically large a man. Above all, Mailer tells us, he is the
kind of man other man like to see put in their place. Herne eventually
comes to know himself somewhat better in the course of the novel, as
essentially 'nothing but an empty shell'. (*The Naked and the Dead*,
87). So that when his death comes we do not feel we know him any
better than he knows himself.

Herne's weaknesses ironically illuminate Cummings' strengths. He
is not a particularly wicked man. He does not exult in American
power. He is merely indifferent to what it will cost the world or the
American people. At times he embodies Mailer's own personal philosophy. If Mailer was competing with Hemingway, he was also influenced by Tolstoy. And the genius of Tolstoy, Mailer wrote, is that he
teaches us that compassion is of value and enriches life only when it is

'severe'. 'Which is to say when we can perceive everything that is good and bad about a character but are still able to feel that the sum of us as human beings is probably a little more good than awful. In any case, good or bad, it reminds us that life is like a gladiator's arena for the soul, and so we can feel strengthened by those who endure, and feel awe and pity for those who do not.' (*The Naked and the Dead*, v).

The Naked and the Dead is by far the most political of the novels in this study. In part, this is because the characters of all the main actors are already formed. War does not shape them, it reveals them. What we know of Cummings as a *man* comes from one of the rather clumsy 'time machine' interludes that allow us to trace back every character to his youth. His father is a businessman from a poor background in the mid-West who has married a woman from a wealthy East Coast family, who persuades her husband to cash in his Presbyterianism for stock in the Episcopalian church, to transfer his allegiance from a Jesus who saves to one who pays a dividend on belief. He is taught by his father a hard social Darwinian lesson that life is a struggle, and the moral is drummed into him over nine years at a military school. Then, to West Point and the First World War, which is the making of him. And what he admires most is not the courage of his companions as they advance into No Man's Land so much as the courage of the officers in sending them into battle. 'There were all those men and there has been someone above them, ordering them, changing, perhaps for ever, the fibre of their lives.' (*The Naked and the Dead*, 419).

His career nevertheless does not advance as quickly as he would like, clearly because his superiors find him wanting. He is something of a martinet. When conducting inspections of men's barracks he brings a needle to probe the cracks on the floor for dust. He instructs his First Sergeant, whenever a visiting general is expected, to have the men grease the soles of their extra shoes which are placed at the foot of their beds. But all the time he reads. He is an autodidact, catching up on the education he has missed. Philosophy, psychology, history, all these transmute into a philosophy of life. Slowly he makes his way up the ladder of fear so that by the time war comes he is ready. It has been waiting for him for some time.

For me, the core of the book is Cummings' personal apotheosis, which comes towards the end of the novel after returning from a field inspection. The attack on the Toyaku line has begun again, and this

time is likely to succeed. His fears of being relieved of his command
have now passed. His men have re-discovered their old energy. But still
he is haunted by the suspicion that he has had no more to do with the
success of the attack than a man who presses a button and waits for an
elevator to arrive. When he returns to the bivouac, he writes up his
journal. What he jots down is essentially banal, and shows the coarseness of his mind. But the idiom he employs is authentic for the times:
it is the language of war in the mid-twentieth century, a language into
which he is locked as much as his creator.

The seeds of the betrayal of his men are to be found in his thoughts.
He has just returned from visiting an artillery unit where he has fired
one of the guns. The last time had been at West Point. But the most
vivid meaning of the war has been surviving a twenty-four hour artillery barrage in the Great War, an echo of which now rebounds through
his mind. The asymmetrical parabola of a shell that he has fired that
night rising in the sky before falling on the enemy below reminds him
of Spengler's theory of the life cycle of all cultures—growth, maturity
and decay. An epoch, too, seems to reach its zenith at a point past the
middle of its orbit in time, and the fall is always tragic.

> What is this curve? It is a fundamental path any projectile, of a ball, a stone,
> an arrow (Nietzsche's arrow of longing) or of an artillery shell. It is the curve
> of the death missile as well as an abstraction of the life-love impulse. It dem-
> onstrates the form of existence, and life and death are merely different points
> of observation on the same trajectory. The life viewpoint is what we see and
> feel astride the shell, it is the present, seeing, feeling, sensing. The death
> viewpoint sees the shell as a whole, knows its inexorable end, the point in
> which it has been destined by inevitable physical laws from the moment of
> its primary impulse when it was catapulted into the air.

The forces that prevent the projectile from rising are gravity and
wind resistance and the effect is proportional to the square of the
time—they feed upon themselves as time advances. If only mere gravity were working, the path would be symmetrical; it is the wind resistance that produces the tragic curve. In the larger meaning of the curve,
gravity would occupy the place of mortality (what goes up must come
down) and wind resistance would be the resistance of the medium—
the mass inertia, or inertia of the masses through which the vision, the
upward lead of a culture is blunted, slowed and brought to its early
doom (*The Naked and the Dead*, 568–569).

What Cummings sees at work is a dialectical process between his
own will to power and his men's struggle to survive. And he is willing

to betray the trust the men place in him by thrusting them out of his thoughts. He is not a monster as such. Indeed, the moment he commits his thoughts to paper he feels some distaste for what he has written, but he is not willing to give up on his thoughts any more than the men, pushed to the limits of endurance in the campaign, will give up on their dreams of surviving the war and returning home. They have no interest in their general's Spenglerian musings. They have integrated the acceptance of death into their life in different and no less heroic ways. For Cummings, their thoughtlessness—or sheer stupidity—is a betrayal of the power principle he espouses. Try though he may, he will never succeed in moulding them into avatars of his own inflexible will.

Thankfully, we have escaped the grip of the twentieth century. We are no longer given to such musings. The generals who betray the men in other theatres of war today do so in lesser ways, ones with which history is much more familiar. Men are still sent to their death for an officer's reputation, and it is the intimation of that lesser world that Cummings grasps at the very end of the novel. The campaign is won, Herne dies needlessly on a reconnaissance mission that achieves nothing. He has lost his life, Cummings reassures himself (for he does have a conscience, however residual) because he has not been big enough; he has been found wanting by history. What upsets him most, however, is that he himself was absent when the final push secured victory. And even more frustrating is that the man who claims credit for success is one of the more stupid of his high-ranking officers and he now faces the prospect of having to promote him. What disturbs him most of all, however, is his failure to read history as it happened, to penetrate the 'fog of war', the mystery of victory and defeat. His own particular success, he begins to suspect, has been accomplished merely by 'a random play of vulgar good luck loaded into a casual mess of factors, too large, too vague for him to comprehend.' (*The Naked and the Dead*, 712). We leave him with his final thoughts that the hacks will occupy history's seat after the war, the same blunderers, uncoordinated and at cross-impulses (*The Naked and the Dead*, 714). He even suspects that he will not be in the coming war with Russia, that he will be bypassed for command.

Few people would rate Mailer one of the last century's greatest novelists, but his first book is by far his best. It illuminated the big themes that came to define America's post-war role, and in Cummings' army he showed the role of betrayal in war. Enlisted men have no clear idea of why they are fighting yet they cooperate, bar the odd mutiny or the breakdown of primary group cohesion. As Jean Radford notes, the novel dramatises 'the total alienation of the enlisted men from war at any level other than their physical participation.' (Wenke, 1987, 29). This may not be true of every war, especially the 'Good War', the Second World War, but Mailer is making a point that is not necessarily untrue. Men fight for each other, rarely for a cause or country. They may join up for the latter, but soon find camaraderie is the only cause worth fighting for. It is the deeply ingrained imperative to follow orders that constitutes for many the closest thing to an actual moral code in an amoral organisation. For there is an authoritarian structure to every army that does not encourage doubt or dissent even when the official line is that soldiers should not always obey orders, but think for themselves.

The point about Cummings is that he is the archetype of the generals who really do live in a different world from the enlisted men. Cummings succeeds in exposing the lies and hypocrisies of military life by assuming their form. Men like Sergeant Cross may be unspeakable, but they are also somewhat reassuring because they can be identified, named and even vanquished. The evil of *The Naked and the Dead* is quite different. It is anonymous, and almost impossible to combat. And the sins that the novel embodies, including the abuse of authority in war, are unlikely to be so easily vanquished. We can imagine small and partial victories, but nothing like the cathartic deliverance of the kind we crave from our stories. We can hate the system, but it is more difficult to hate Cummings; after all, he is one of us.

And his betrayal raises a point that Aristotle invoked centuries ago when he said that while vice is unconscious of itself, weakness is not. Cummings knows Herne is a weak man, which is why he sends him to his death, but he is only half aware of his own wickedness. Does he know what he is doing? The problem in war is not that of generals who deliberately kill off their men, but ones who do not really think about it. Sins of omission are far more dangerous. Unlike Shakespeare's Richard III who determines, 'to prove a villain' most people we consider to be wicked would not share our opinion of themselves. In her philosophical essay, *Wickedness*, Mary Midgeley quotes Ernst Rohm, a leading Nazi. 'Since I am an immature and bad man, war appeals to me more than peace.' (Midgeley, 1984, 59). Would Cummings ever say this of himself? That he is egotistical is not in doubt; nor is the fact that he is cynical, and interested in furthering his career. But as Midgley remarks, these exceptions are so incongruous that we must find a context. Was Rohm joking, or was he displaying a rare instance of self-knowledge? No one can be expected to take a remark such as his literally, unless we know the context in which it is made.

Generals often consider they are themselves more intelligent than the enlisted men, because they see the context—'the bigger picture'. Cross knows he is a villain—another weak-willed man who needs power to make up for his own inadequacies of masculinity; the fact that his wife has cheated on him allows Mailer to highlight those inadequacies vividly. Once again, as for Hemingway, manliness is important. Mailer stresses Cummings' 'effeminacy' in the early chapters, but Cummings has the power to get thousands killed; Cross has only the power to cause the death of one man.

Cummings betrays the men for a different reason. He does not betray them, as many people in command do, out of cowardice. Cummings is an altogether more complex figure. Unlike Shakespeare's greatest warrior Coriolanus he lacks nobility and even the warrior's skill—the only fighting he does in a 280 page novel is to pull a cord and fire a gun into the jungle against an unseen enemy. But Coriolanus and he are alike in one very important respect. Both would have to betray themselves if they did not betray others. Coriolanus protests that the people are asking him to betray himself or them; he chooses to do the second by joining the enemy outside the gates. Cummings betrays the trust invested in a commander by his men when he exposes them to attack because he won't betray the ideas by which he lives. Does this make him a villain?

Like Coriolanus he is fundamentally a tragic figure. By the end of the novel he is, in his own eyes at least, something of a failure because for all his talk of the will to power, that will has not achieved very much. It has not helped him to master 'the circuits of chance'. The battle is won in his absence. The future belongs to Maj. Dalleson who wins the decisive engagement thanks to a large measure of luck.

So, let us leave Cummings with his thoughts and conclude instead with the homely realism of one of the enlisted men, Red Valsen, the most foul-mouthed of Mailer's characters, but also one of the most honest. Red is consistent in his suspicion of officers, especially the more senior they rise in rank. There isn't a good officer in the world, he insists. They're just a bunch of aristocrats who think themselves better than the men they command. Even Cummings, he adds, 'is no better than I am. His shit don't smell like ice-cream either.' (*The Naked and the Dead*, 128). In the end, there is no arguing with that.

Dr Strangelove: A Thermo-Nuclear Zero Mostel

Dr Strangelove, Stanley Kubrick

Many of the works that are discussed in this book have been the subject of films, some good, the majority indifferent. One is *Catch-22*, another *The Red Badge of Courage* and then there is Wolfgang Peterson's torrid mini-epic, *Troy*, which subverts the entire story by having Achilles enter the city in the famous wooden horse, only to die as the city falls.

Let me identify three differences between a novel and a film that are especially germane to the theme of this book—the existential core of war.

First, a film simply cannot catch the secret centre of a man's life, which is a secret even to himself. One example is the epiphany, which only a novel can evoke, the moment of transcendence or awe, for example, in Tolstoy's *War and Peace* when Pierre goes into battle at Borodino. Pierre discovers from the moment he steps out of his carriage and climbs up the hill from where the battle is visible a certain aesthetic awe. The sun shining overhead makes the field look like an amphitheatre. For a moment he is transfixed by the spectacle.

> It was the same panorama he had admired from the mound the day before, but now the whole prospect swarmed with troops, smoke clouds from the guns hung overhead and the slanting rays of the bright sun, rising slightly to the left behind Pierre, filled the clear morning sky with rosy glowing light and long dark shadows. (Tolstoy, 1982, 937).

Time stands still; reality is briefly disjointed. At this point Pierre is quite literally divorced from the battle as a spectator, unaware (as we the readers are not), of the mortal world in which soldiers are getting killed down below.

No sooner, however, has he entered the field, spurred on by an inner voice, than his perceptions change once again. For at the centre of the battle he finds what he calls a 'family animation', a family from which hitherto he has been excluded, but into which he is now inducted as the fighting unfolds. His first, unconscious delight in the sights and sounds of battle gives way to another feeling altogether. 'He was entirely absorbed in the contemplation of that fire which blazed more fiercely with every moment and which, so he felt, was flaming in his soul, too.' (Tolstoy, 1982, 945).

We find ourselves no longer observing him from the outside but from inside his mind. His external impressions are now related to his conflicting emotions. He experiences 'a joyous new feeling, the feeling of the necessity to undertake something and sacrifice something.' What that something is, he does not yet know. It is the sacrifice itself which constitutes the feeling. When the unit's ammunition runs out, it is he who volunteers unthinkingly to fetch it. Once he gives of himself in a single, reflexive act of courage, he experiences his own moral worth. Confused, frightened, but now engaged, he finds himself sharing in the lives of others.

Does Pierre throw himself into battle because he wants to be involved in something larger than himself, or is this the wrong way of looking at it? Surely what he is seeking is what he indeed finds—involvement in something more important than himself, something that makes his life meaningful for the first time. Or perhaps even this is too narrow an interpretation of his spontaneous action. What he is involving himself in is something *other* than himself, something whose value is *outside* the self. What he is trying to find is no longer meaning in life, so much as the experience of *being alive* (Kundera, 1995, 214). At one level we can explain his state of mind in bodily terms. There is no doubt that he is aroused in a physiological sense. Even terror and fear can be pleasurable at the level of initial arousal as anyone who has been on a fairground ride knows perfectly well. The presence of real danger makes arousal (for some) all the more immediate and gratifying.

Only literature can evoke such a moment. We need to be party to the protagonist's thoughts and sensations. A film can of course slowly draw us into the personal and private world of the hero, but only the novelist can give us access to the hero's innermost thoughts and subconscious desires. Take Pierre later fleeing from Borodino to 'ordinary conditions' of life, 'Feeling that only in ordinary conditions will he be able to understand himself and all he has experienced, only to discover ordinary conditions of life are nowhere to be found.' (Tolstoy, 1982, 996). Or take Prince Andrei's death in the course of the same battle, and his reluctance to part with life because of something in life he did not and cannot understand (Tolstoy, 1982, 965). As he lies mortally wounded he is suddenly filled with a sense of inner contentment, even happiness, memories of his childhood streaming through his mind. Equally telling is that no sooner does he recall his childhood than he dismisses the thoughts from his mind. As Milan Kundera adds 'a few seconds later this miraculous detail has been inadvertently forgotten by Andrei himself, just as it has probably been immediately forgotten by the majority of readers who read novels as inattentively and badly as they "read" their own lives.' (Kundera, 1995, 218).

Secondly, in a film the story is usually all-important, and it is a story that has an explicit moral. The best novels leave it to the reader to draw the moral, if there is one to be found. Most films want to get you to draw a moral by showing you 'the truth'. A novel is infinitely more complex and multi-layered; what the author may want us to read into it (implicitly or explicitly) and what the reader comes to conclude for herself may be entirely different. We can enter the consciousness of the 'other side', get into their minds, even empathise, for that reason, with a villain; in films we rarely can, though we may well find them entertaining.

For there are two kinds of empathy: cognitive and affective. The first allows us to 'understand' a character's motives, the reasons why he has acted as he has, even when on occasion he may act 'out of character'. The second allows us to feel the pain even when it may be not entirely undeserving. A film tends to direct our emotions, or channel them into certain directions. Even the music directs our thoughts (telling us when to cry or to be alarmed—it acts as a moral prompter). A novel by contrast allows us to entertain contradictory thoughts, to be swayed by opposing emotions. And these thoughts are often our own, not the author's.

Thirdly, adds the novelist Orhan Pamuk in *The Naïve and the Sentimental Novelist*, (his Norton Lectures at Harvard in 2009) the primary factor that makes a novel is the idea of a 'centre' (Pamuk, 2010, 26). Its characters may indeed be complex figures, but they owe their qualities to the idea that all their actions, habits, fantasies and dreams indicate a deeper meaning with which they are (or are not) in tune. There is an ultimate meaning behind their acts; a 'centre' which allows us to read them with a kind of hope. In real life, we are usually unable to do this. And nor can we through film. A film like *Apocalypse*

Now (a rather crude rendering of Conrad's novella, *Heart of Darkness*) does not have time to develop the levels of complexity that a novel can. It is more akin to an epic poem (where the characters are usually archetypes)

The 'centre', for Pamuk, is the author's profound insight into life—the intuition, thought or knowledge that inspires him to write. Many readers will never get beneath the surface detail, but some will. Borges once described how the readers are drawn into the centre of *Moby Dick* (Pamuk, 2010, 156). At the beginning, the reader might read the story as an exploration of the arduous life of whale hunters, and indeed in the early chapters of the book there is a wealth of detail about whaling and the lives of harpooners. But as we read on, we are compelled by the obsession of Captain Ahab, bent on hunting down and despatching the great while whale. By the middle chapters, *Moby Dick* has become a penetrating psychological study of obsessive rage.

What is the centre? It is a facsimile of life that translates into the belief that real life—the life we experience—*should* be like this. In that regard, novels structure our lives more than we acknowledge and deceive us, of course, at the same time. Reading Hemingway's *A Farewell to Arms* or Jim Jones' *The Thin Red Line* we think we know what war really *is*, only to discover, if we go on to experience it at first hand, as soldiers do, that it actually usually is not. Literature offers reference points that allow us to conceptualise war, but they are only a signpost, or a road to meaning on a journey we never complete. For the journey *is* the meaning itself.

> Ithaca has given you the marvellous journey,
> without her you wouldn't have set out.
> She has nothing left to give you now.
> And if you find her poor Ithaca won't have fooled you.
> Wise as you will have become, so full of experience,
> You'll have understood by then what Ithaca means.
> (Cavafy, 1984, 30).

In other words, there is no centre to life itself, and there is no centre to war, and the soldier in the trenches of the Western Front or on some misbegotten Pacific atoll or in street fighting in Fallujah, will always have to discover this for himself. This is why film adaptations are so deceiving. They tend to hollow out the 'centre' of a good novel, reducing the plot to a 'just-so' story, and the characters to archetypes with no real existential core.

But every so often, a film can create a character who takes on a life of his own, and one of the most successful realisations of all is the man who gives the title to Stanley Kubrick's most famous film, *Dr Strangelove, or How I Learned to Stop Worrying and Love the Bomb*. The film was nominated for fourteen awards, winning four. In the 2012 instalment of 'One hundred years in one hundred movies', a list of the top hundred US films completed by the American Film Institute, it ranks as the thirty-ninth greatest movie of all time.

When the film first came out, wrote Lewis Mumford, it was a wake-up call, 'The first break in the catatonic Cold War trance that has so long held our country in its rigid grip.' (Smith, 2007, 426). Strangelove—for him—was such a powerful figure because the fantasy of fighting and surviving a nuclear war was as horribly crippled and dehumanised as Strangelove himself. And what made Strangelove such a pivotal figure in the movie is that he became 'the central symbol of a scientifically organised nightmare of mass extermination' for an entire generation. Any story about nuclear war has no need of a person's inner thoughts for there are no battles (there will be little enough time to think once the missiles take flight). Secondly, it is impossible to see both sides of the argument if the missiles are despatched by accident (or in the film's case the psychotic delusions of one renegade commander). Finally, there is no centre to nuclear war—did not the atomic bomb, asked the poet Octavio Paz, represent the universal Accident waiting to happen, an accident that was not an exception so much as the consequence of scientific 'progress' in the conduct of war? And wasn't it essentially banal because 'in the final analysis the Accident is only an accident'? (Paz, 1982, 112).

No scene in the film is more revealing or dramatic than Dr Strangelove's emergence from the shadows in the War Room as the world begins the ineluctable count down to a full scale thermo-nuclear conflict. He does not appear in fact until two-thirds of the way into the movie, wheelchair-bound, smoking a cigarette in a black-gloved hand. He has only fifty-eight lines in the entire screenplay and yet he is the character who stays with you long after you have seen the film for the first time. Strangelove *is* the film, both its meaning and its message.

Dr Strangelove appears at the behest of the US President, who is also played by Peter Sellers, a meek, worried leader of men who is clearly out of his depth when dealing either with his own generals or his opposite number in the Soviet Union. He has just been told by the Russian Ambassador of the Doomsday Bomb which can destroy the world and with it most of humanity. Dr Strangelove, asks the President, do we have anything like this in the works? And all eyes try to locate this mysterious figure. 'A moment, please, Mr President', he replies as he stomps one foot on the floor and pushes back from the table and begins wheeling towards the discussion between the President and the Ambassador. 'It's true, Mr President.' Later, 'Mr President' will morph into 'Mein Fuhrer', as Strangelove psychologically regresses to the days in which he served the Nazis. In a world in which both sides are quite willing to blow the world to kingdom come, was there a major difference between the Superpowers and the Third Reich? It is the bomb, after all, which is important and what role is there for human agency or human will in a world in which a maverick colonel can despatch a bomber to its target and trigger World War III?

Can the Russians really have built a Doomsday device? asks the President weakly. 'Mr President, the technology required is easily within the means of even the smallest nuclear power. It requires only the will to do so.' (*Dr Strangelove*, 30). In this case the 'will' has indeed 'triumphed' and the Soviets have stolen a march on the Americans (as they had done with Sputnik in 1957). And is it really possible, the President persists with growing alarm, for such a device to be triggered automatically and at the same time be impossible to deactivate? Dr Strangelove's patience with him is admirable, less so the logic of the invention. 'Mr President, it's not only possible, it's essential.' Here, he relishes the fact that technology has a logic that cannot be denied.

That is the whole idea of the machine, you know. Deterrence is the art of producing in the mind of the enemy the fear to attack, and so, because of the automated and irrevocable decision-making process which rules out human meddling, the Doomsday machine is terrifying.

'Gee, I wish we had one of them Doomsday machines', remarks General Turgidson, a man whom, one imagines, the President's chief scientific adviser holds in no high regard. A born human meddler, like all military men. Cut them out of the loop, together with the President and the Congress, and you get a flawless nuclear world. This is the first time, of course, that Turgidson has come across the scientist. 'Strangelove, a Kraut name', he asks. 'It used to be Merkwurkdigliebe', he is told. He changed it when he became a US citizen.

Strangelove is an original, powerful character, perhaps because his appearance in the film is so brief. Indeed, Kubrick's masterpiece coined a new adjective, 'Strangelovian' to describe a person with a fatal fascination with the idea of nuclear war. In the book version which Peter George wrote after the film's release, we learn a little more about him. He had once been a scientist at Peenemunde working on the V2 rockets that were launched against Britain in the closing months of the Second World War. There he lost a right hand as a result of a British bombing raid, and can never decide as a result whether he dislikes the British more than the Russians.

But Strangelove himself is not entirely without human dimension. He is almost a cyborg, half machine and half man, trapped in a wheelchair with a prosthetic limb. But even he can be irritated by human folly, especially when the whole point of the Doomsday machine is lost (he tells the Russian Ambassador) if it is kept a secret. So why did the Russians not tell the world they had one? 'It was to be announced at the Party Congress on Monday', the Ambassador lamely responds. 'As you know, the Premier loves surprises.' (Kubrick, 2012, 31).

The film's storyline is simplicity itself. A clearly psychotic Brigadier General Jack D. Ripper, 'unmanned' by his own impotence, orders his B-52 bombers to attack the Soviet Union to force the government's hand in launching an all-out nuclear attack before the Russian High Command can retaliate. What he does not know is that they have already built a Doomsday device that will trigger a nuclear apocalypse once Soviet territory is attacked. In order to prevent the bombers from being recalled, he refuses to reveal the three-letter code. He can only send planes on his own authority in the first place because the President has devolved some command and control functions to his base commanders under 'Plan R', an emergency war plan in which a commander lower down the chain of command can authorise a nuclear strike if Washington has been taken out in a surprise attack. The President is apparently oblivious to the fact that he himself authorised the plan in a bid to beef up the deterrent when its credibility was questioned by a Senator seeking to make a name for himself. The President orders Ripper's arrest. His base is captured by an army unit after a long firefight, but before he can be interrogated he takes his own life and the three-letter code with him. Before the intrepid, if somewhat effete British Liaison Officer, Colonel Lionel Mandrake (also played by Peter Sellers) manages to crack the recall code, the Americans give the

Russians enough information to shoot down all but one of the bombers. Because of a damaged communications unit, it cannot be recalled. The stage is set for a nuclear Armageddon.

Peter George's *Red Alert* (1958), on which the film is based, was published as *Two Hours to Doom* in Britain, his homeland. In the novel, the un-recallable B-52 crashes before it reaches its target. If it had not, a Soviet bomber would have been allowed to destroy Atlantic City, as it actually does in the film version *Fail Safe*. In *Strangelove*, we get the actual apocalypse when Major T. J. 'King' Kong, the Texan commander of the B-52 which manages to get through, rides his bronco of an H-bomb down to its target. This is a superbly comic moment and one of the darkest in the movie. Apparently, there are no limits to the patriotic impulse. In the great American novel of the 1950s, *The Catcher in the Rye*, Holden Caulfield says that if he is forced to join the army, he will 'sit right the hell on top of the atomic bomb'. Major Kong—the All-American hero—gets to do just that, fulfilling Alan Ginsberg's apocalyptic wish that the US should 'go fuck itself' with the ultimate status symbol of its power.

The movie is deeply ironic from the moment we see the motto adorning Ripper's Bumpelson Air Force base, 'Peace is our Profession'. But the motto is not a fictional conceit: it was the motto of America's Strategic Air Command. It is impossible, in fact, to satirise the nuclear world of the 1960s once one enters into its folklore and learns the language. Even when the President phones Premier Kissof on the hotline (which did not exist at the time—the film inspired the two sides to install one), the two political leaders find themselves involved in an ironic competition to say who is the sorrier for the fact that the whole ludicrous episode has taken place. Only after a heated exchange of views is an 'equilibrium' of a kind finally realised.

> I'm sorry, too, Dmitri. I'm very sorry. All right! You're sorrier than I am, but I'm as sorry as well. I'm as sorry as you are, Dmitri. Don't say that you are more sorry than I am because I'm capable of being just as sorry as you are. So, we're both sorry, all right?

And even when the bombers are about to reach their targets, the spirit of competitiveness cannot be banished altogether. The Chief of Staffs are almost rooting for the last bomber to get through. Too damaged to reach its primary target, it is able to reach its secondary target, the ballistic missile complex at Kodlosk and thus trigger nuclear war. All that is left is for Strangelove to tell the President that it would be possible to preserve 'a nucleus of human specimens' at the bottom of some of the country's deeper mineshafts. Slide-rule in hand, he muses on what they would do in a hundred years in which the surviving elite would have to spend in a mineshaft before it is safe to return to the surface. A computer could be programmed, he tells the President, to find young men of sufficient sexual fertility to breed prodigiously. 'With the proper breeding techniques and a ratio of, say, ten females to each male, I would guess that they could then work their way back to the present GNP within say, twenty years.' (*Dr Strangelove*, 49).

One of the intriguing aspects of the film (in this man-dominated world of destruction) is that women are hidden in plain sight. Young secretaries warm the beds of the generals and the policymakers; 'Miss Foreign Affairs' appears in an erotic magazine adorning the cabins of the nuclear bomber pilots; and women are never far from men's thoughts. Ripper blames his own impotence on a communist plot; the crew of the B52s find their hidden desires in nylons and lipsticks of a survival kit. Shoot, declares Kong, 'a fellah could have a pretty good weekend in Vegas with all that stuff' (*Dr Strangelove*, 20). And we see Kong himself for the last time when the bomb release is jammed, releasing it manually by riding into orgasm astride a nuclear bomb.

Strangelove may be a monster, but he is not dumb, and compared with the mediocrities around the table of the War Room, he positively sparkles. He has the courage of his convictions, plus an undiminished belief in the triumph of the human will and in the necessity of eugenics, part of the cultural baggage which he brought with him from the Third Reich. In many ways he is less culpable than the generals who would launch a pre-emptive strike if they could, and whose sympathies are clearly with the benighted crew of Kong's B-52. Unlike them, he is not paranoid about Communist subversion, and has no fear of the 'Russkies'. And his calculation about the chances of survival (reached with the use of a slide rule) are no more than an exaggeration of the projections of real life figures in the nuclear arms industry were making at the time. His faults, in short, are those of his age. In the end, it is his dispassion which is truly monstrous. When the president lamely asks whether the survivors might be so grief-stricken and anguished that they would envy the dead and not want to go on living, Strangelove insists defiantly that the prevailing emotion would be one of nostalgia for those left behind 'combined with a spirit of bold curiosity for the adventure ahead.'

Dr Strangelove is an unusual film precisely because it has a 'centre' after all. Kubrick had started off with Peter George's story *Red Alert*, which offered a serious 'take' on nuclear Armageddon and how the end might begin. In the event, the film became the most grotesque comedy ever made about nuclear war, for which Kubrick had Hermann Kahn to thank. Kahn lunched with Kubrick several times during its making. He had a highly recherché sense of humour himself, once telling a distraught mother who complained that she did not want to live in a radioactive world of genetic mutations that she might come to love her two-headed children twice as much. At the Rand Corporation (or the Bland Corporation as it is called in the film), he and his colleagues used to exchange sick jokes about a thermo-nuclear conflict they were tasked to study. His humour was contagious. It certainly infected Kubrick, who later wrote that every time he sat down to write a scene for the film, 'it came up funny'. (Ghamari-Tabrizi, 2005, 276).

By the time the film came out, however, it was already dated. It had become impossible for a rogue commander to launch an air strike on the Soviet Union under the excuse that Washington and the High Command had been eliminated in a sneak attack. The Strategic Air Command still relied on bombers (and still does), but the first intercontinental missiles were already in service, including those that could be launched from submarines, and the scenario where a Chief of Staff encourages the President to launch an all-out strike out of 'military necessity' was no longer plausible as it once had been.

Strangelove himself has been identified with half a dozen possible models, including the father of the H-Bomb Edward Teller, the German rocket designer Werner von Braun, and Leo Szilard, the first man to conceive of a Doomsday bomb. But the person who has the first right to bid for the part was Kahn. In fact Kahn could have appeared as himself. He used to quip that he was one of the ten most famous 'obscure Americans'. Everyone agreed he was a man of his time, writes Sharon Ghamari-Tabrizi, although no one could agree on what he represented (Ghamani-Tabrizi, 2005, 8). It helped that the central conceit of the movie, the Doomsday machine, was also one of Kahn's ideas. Would it possible, he asked, to build a device whose only function would be to destroy all human life? If, say, five nuclear bombs erupted over the United States, 'barring coding errors' it would seem to be the ideal deterrent (Ghamani-Tabrizi, 2005, 41). Kahn, in fact, always argued that the bomb should not be built, but not for reasons his contemporaries would have found necessarily reassuring. To be effective, a deterrent had to be persuasive, non-accident prone and controllable—on these grounds a Doomsday machine might outstrip every other system. But its problem was overkill, and Kahn was always insistent that for a thermo-nuclear war to be fought successfully, its logic had to be compelling. Without the Doomsday bomb, the world might survive; with it, it would not.

Kahn has a further claim to be the prototype of Strangelove. Not only had he written about the Doomsday machine, he had also been enthusiastic about building underground shelters. An engineering firm had concluded that they would be feasible at a cost of $800 per shelter space, and that approximately 750 million square feet of available underground space of the continental United States could be made available for civil defence construction. In Kubrick's film the government prefers the cheaper option of relocating people not in concrete bomb shelters, but coal mines and quarries, and other deep rock caverns, an idea which appears in the film as the famous 'mine-shaft-gap'. Later Herbert Marcuse made fun of the whole idea in a brief footnote to his book *One-Dimensional Man*. Citing an advertisement in *The New York Times* that had offered the modern family a deluxe fall-out shelter with wall to wall carpeting, lounge chairs and TV, he wrote ironically that the consumer was afforded a chance to secure himself against nuclear war, provided he could pay the price. Here was the unique introduction of consumerism into death, an issue traditionally outside the range of consumer choice (Marcuse, 1991)

In the end, *Dr Strangelove* is a comedy but it is a very rum kind, and not one which would have met with Aristotle's approbation. Comedy, Aristotle tells us, is an imitation of men worse than the average; worse however not as regards any and every kind of fault but as regards one particular kind—the ridiculous (which is a species of the ugly). 'The ridiculous may be defined as a mistake or deformity not productive of pain or harm to others.' (Auden, 2002, 375). In his discussion of the Greeks, Auden wrote that the one comic character they did not invent was the one that we find most appealing; the comic character who is also a hero, a Don Quixote who refuses to accept the values of his neighbours or a Falstaff who refuses to pretend, as they do, to one set of values while living by another. At the same time they are heroes because they are both individuals, and not to be an individual, to think and behave in a certain way simply because everyone else does, is equally a comic madness. Kubrick is guying the 'comic madness' of a world that was ready to press the nuclear button at a moment's notice and bring the curtain down on the whole show.

But there is a deeper reason why Strangelove himself is a comic character without being in any way heroic and Marcuse offers an explanation once again in *One-Dimensional Man* in his reference to 'happy consciousness'—an understanding lifted from Hegel's lectures on aesthetics. Comedy, wrote Hegel, has as its starting point what tragedy ends with; a cheerful heart. The comic hero is the man who has an 'absolute freedom of spirit' which manifests itself in a complete complacency that everything that is real is rational, and everything that is rational is real. In the comic world there are no limits to human action.

War, by contrast, is usually tragic because people find themselves at odds with the world. They are often aware through experience of the great paradoxes, ambiguities and uncertainties powering human actions. War forces one to accept the inescapable mysteries of life, the elements of defeat in every victory, and victory in every defeat. In *Hadji Murat*, Tolstoy was at his best in showing the clash between passion and duty, the loss of opportunity in every choice, the burden of conflicting loyalties and impossible choices. Most of the characters who appear in this book find themselves tragically at odds with the world (this is the source of their enduring appeal—to be reconciled totally to war would be dangerous for the rest of us and vastly unappealing). But then there are the comic heroes, and Strangelove represents them: men for whom no obstacle is so insurmountable, no evil so unrelieved, and no loss ever so final that it is irredeemable. And that is true even when contemplating a nuclear apocalypse. For Hegel, the tragic hero encounters the world as a riddle; the comic hero knows the riddle in advance (Speight, 2001, 31).

Kahn, too, was just such a figure; his was a world in which human will could solve every problem. Even the Earth, he argued, was plastic in its engineering possibilities. Writing well before the impact of environmentalism, he once argued that 'only relatively thin margins of cost' prevented humanity from melting the ice caps and diverting the ocean currents. Everything was permitted and permissible providing it conformed to certain laws—in the case of thermo-nuclear war, the scenarios, computer models and complex mathematical codes that were produced to order in the early 1960s. In such an instrumentalised world, added Marcuse, guilt had no place. One man could give the signal that would liquidate hundreds and thousands of people, then declare himself free from all pangs of conscience and live happily ever after—in a mine shaft (Marcuse,1991, 79–80). This dread certainty was the mark of the nuclear age with its civilian analysts, think tank gurus and celebrity strategists; its sleek, computer savvy young men who thought that life could be programmed. As one of them famously remarked, rebuking a general who questioned whether a nuclear war could be fought successfully, 'General, I've fought more nuclear wars than you.'

By the 1960s war had become comic because with the invention of thermo-nuclear weapons it had escaped the limits set by political ambition, technical possibilities and even what human imagination could conceive. The H-bomb had no limits because the element of deuterium is *theoretically* capable of being designed to go onto the *nth* power. This was the promise of the Doomsday Bomb. It was also the promise of war: that we would become the weapons we built. And with no limits there is no finite end to the destruction war can unleash. War borders on the supernatural or miraculous. As Strangelove expostulates in the very last line of the film, as he rises up from his wheelchair in amazement, 'Mein Fuhrer, I can walk'.

Judge Holden: Reverting to our Primal Nature

Blood Meridian, Cormac McCarthy

Cormac McCarthy is one of the greatest contemporary American writers and in *Blood Meridian* he takes the war novel into new, uncharted territory. Based on historical events on the Texas-Mexican border in the 1850s, it is Southern Gothic at best, in the tradition of William Faulkner. Harold Bloom is often given to hyperbole, but in this case rightly so; *Blood Meridian* is the strongest book of any living American novelist. And in Judge Holden, the chief villain of the tale, we have 'a theoretician of war everlasting.' (Bloom, 2001, 255).

The book's magnificence, insists Bloom, lies in its language, its landscape, its persons, and its concepts, which transcend its unrelieved violent tone, and transform it into art. The carnage, which puts many people off, is not gratuitous. It is not even a product of the novelist's imagination. It is based on scrupulous research: much of what

McCarthy writes about actually happened. The novel is grounded in the historical record, namely the Chihuahuan scalp trade of the 1850s, and some of the characters, including Joel Glanton and Judge Holden, are mentioned in Samuel Chamberlain's narrative, *My Confession* (1840s), which only appeared in its unexpurgated version in the 1950s. Chamberlain describes the Judge as a filibustering Indian hater; at '6'6' in his moccasins, [with] a large, fleshy frame, a dull tallow coloured face, destitute of hair and all expression.' (Sepich, 1993, 125).

The fact that this is an unremembered past is partly the point of McCarthy's tale. It is buried so deep in the American psyche that it is primal, like the horrors of early Greek history which the Greeks mythologised and turned into poetry. In time, their tales were transmuted by the great tragedians: incest, blood lust, cannibalism and the murderous impulses of the main characters, all of whom, in Nietzsche's vivid turn of phrase, were 'spiritualised away' in the power of poetry. There is a distinct Nietzschean echo in McCarthy's novel, especially in the idea of the 'naturalisation of man'. The emptiness and hardness of the landscape is always compared by the Judge with the emptiness and hardness of man's true nature.

Is the Judge mortal or immortal? McCarthy hints at the latter throughout the novel, especially at the very end where we see him dancing endlessly in time. He speaks all languages, knows all arts and sciences and can perform magical tricks. Is he the Devil or a minor demon? Or is he the embodiment of a nature that is pitiless and unforgiving, and unchanging, too? For we know that he is not capable of changing, or being changed. He is an elemental figure who, unlike Achilles, is incapable of expressing remorse or showing compassion. His nature has been formed by the world itself, by the darkness that lies at its heart, as well as deep in the hearts of men. The Judge, in McCarthy's own words, is 'a vast abhorrence' (*Blood Meridian*, 243), vast from the Latin *vastus* or void; abhorrence meaning something that causes us to tremble.

And if Holden is human, is he a psychopath? Quite probably. Psychopaths have two different sets of features which the judge certainly exhibits: impulsive anti-social behaviour and emotions that can't be shared with others such as the absence of compassion or guilt. As the Judge certainly existed and McCarthy is keen on his historical research we can attempt to read him in terms of our own (in)humanity.

But once the Judge rides into the novel, taking centre stage and never really yielding it, we recognise immediately that there is something unhuman about him. He is something of an otherworldly figure in the company of men also not of this world but from an earlier era (into which they fade as the novel progresses and as they themselves regress into even greater barbarism). If Holden is the Devil they certainly sell their souls as they prey upon everyone they meet with no fixed purpose, scalping Mexicans as well as Indians when the latter become too time-consuming and costly (the scalps are similar enough that they get away with it for a long time). Whether the Judge is the Devil, or merely a minor devil, or a literary device, or a moral prompter for McCarthy's own thoughts on primal violence is something that the reader has to work out for himself.

Blood Meridian tells the tale of a teenage runaway known only as 'The Kid' who is born in Tennessee in 1833. His father is a schoolmaster, but he is also an alcoholic who teaches the child neither to read nor write, and breeds within him only a taste for mindless violence. 'All history present envisaged, the child, the father of the man.' After he runs away we see him first at a religious revival meeting in Nacejdoctnes, where he meets the Judge for the first time. It is not perhaps coincidental that the town is the 98th meridian, identified by the historian Frederick Jackson Turner as the boundary between the frontier and the wilderness, perhaps the very 'blood meridian' of the title. The novelist Michael Chabon calls *Blood Meridian* 'a bloody pasquinade on the heroic literature of westward expansion.' (Chabon, 2009, 98).

Later, after a violent encounter with a bartender which reveals how deeply entrenched violence is in the Kid's soul, he joins a party of ill-armed US Texas Irregulars on a filibustering mission led by Captain White. Shortly afterwards they are attacked by a band of Comanche warriors. They have already encountered an old Mennonite who warns that the wrath of God lies sleeping. 'It was hid a million years before men were, and only men had the power to make it ... ye carry war of a madman's making into a foreign land. Ye'll wake more than the dogs.' (*Blood Meridian*, 43). What they wake is 'a legion of horribles, hundreds in number ... death hilarious, all howling in barbarous tongues.' (*Blood Meridian*, 55). Attacked by Indians, 'a horde from a hell more horrible yet than the brimstone land of Christian reckoning', the 'unhorsed Saxons' are speared and clubbed, and scalped in turn. The Kid is lucky to escape with his life

He ends up joining a gang of scalp hunters led by Joel Glanton. His first sight of them is alarming enough, riding into town mounted on unshod Indian ponies, bearded, barbarous, clad in the skins of animals. The trappings of their horses are fashioned out of human skin, and the riders are wearing necklaces of dried and blackened human ears. Foremost among them is the Judge, outsized and childlike and with no body hair, alarmingly sexless.

Most of the tale concerns their activities and conversations, which McCarthy recounts as they travel through the desolate landscape back into humanity's primal origins.

> All night sheet lightning quacked sourceless to the west beyond the midnight thunderhead, making a bluish day of the distant desert, the mountains on the southern skyline, stark and black and livid like a land of some other order out there whose true genealogy was not stone, but fear. (*Blood Meridian*, 49).

Robert Bolasco writes that the real 'evil' in the story is the landscape: silent, paradigmatic and hideous, with a place for everything except human beings. 'It could be said that the landscape of *Blood Meridian* is a landscape out of de Sade, a thirsty and indifferent landscape ruled by strange laws involving pain and anaesthesia, the laws by which time often manifests itself.' (Bolasco, 2012, 201). But I much prefer to go with Karl Marlantes' observation about the jungle in Vietnam in which he fought as a young soldier. Soldiers hated the jungle 'It was the land that resisted us' wrote Philip Caputo '... everything rotted and corroded quickly over there: bodies, boot leather, metal, morals.' (Caputo, 1978, 27). 'When it was not raining', writes O'Brien in *Going after Cacciato*, 'a low mist moved across the paddies blending the elements into a single grey element and the war was cold and pasty and rotten.' (Herzog, 1992, 73). But Marlantes is right: a jungle isn't evil; it is indifferent; and so is the world. Evil must inhere in something man has added and then negated in himself; evil is a negation, a not caring for the humanity that we have impressed on the landscape ever since escaping the African Savannah (Marlantes, 2010).

In McCarthy's novel the inner life of the gang members, such as it is, has merged into the outer life, the harsh, unforgiving world through which they travel. Their souls become as shrivelled as the crops rotting in the empty fields; they become the wolves constantly appearing in the tale, *lupus homini hominem*. They ride on, writes McCarthy, 'like men invested with a purpose whose origins were antecedent to them, like blood legatees of an order both imperative and remote in their communal soul.' (*Blood Meridian*, 158). Everywhere they see signs of the desolation the Indians have inflicted. McCarthy's view of the West is an unfashionable one for he holds both parties, Indians and whites alike, to be equally vicious. Death is rendered by both, and death is the land's principal feature. At one point they come across an Apache encampment which Mexican soldiers had raided some years earlier, leaving bones and skulls scattered along the benchland of the Casas Grandes river, 'the tiny limbs and toothless paper skulls of the infants like the ossature of small apes at their place of murder.' (*Blood Meridian*, 95). Their own savagery is presented to us in equally unsparing terms. Scalp hunting is not for the squeamish. When the enter Chihuahana, they put eight heads on display, raised on poles opposite 128 scalps, 'their caved and pagan eyes' contemplating the dry hides of their kinsmen (McCarthy, *Blood Meridian*, 175).

In the years that stretch ahead Glanton's gang goes in for robbing settlers, from a ferry on the Colorado river. Eventually they, too, meet a thoroughly deserved end when they are ambushed and killed by a band of Yuma Indians. The Kid survives with two of his friends. Heading west they encounter the Judge who tries to negotiate for their guns and possessions and then threatens them when they refuse to part with either. Later he returns and kills one of the party. Later still, they meet up in San Diego where the Kid is briefly imprisoned until he reveals where Glanton kept the proceeds of his crime. At the very end of the novel he wanders across the American West where he becomes 'The Man'. A few pages cover most of his adult life.

Finally, in 1878 he makes his way to Fort Griffin, Texas, where he chances to meet up with Holden for the last time. The two converse in the saloon where the Judge reveals that in his eyes, the Kid has been a grave disappointment. He has shown 'too much clemency for the heathen.' And not only Indians. Several times after the Yuma attack the Kid had a chance to shoot the Judge too and declined to do so, another sign that the mindless violence in his heart that we meet with at the beginning of the novel has been tamed and brought under control. *Blood Meridian*'s end is notoriously ambiguous. The one occasion on which death is not described in vivid detail is the scene in the outhouse where two men coming out of the saloon find something that leaves them speechless. 'Good God, almighty'. It may be the Man after the Judge has finished with him; or it may not. We are not told. As for the Judge, we see him dancing and playing the fiddle back in the saloon, a dance of violence and bloodshed, a dance of the Old West, and of prehistory itself. 'His small feet lively and quick, and now in double time and bowing to the ladies, huge and pale and hairless, like an enormous infant', representative, perhaps, of the infancy of Man (McCarthy, 2010, 304).

What the novel offers the reader is a glimpse of warfare from which war emerged. Its great strength is the way in which it takes us back into a mythical past which the Glanton gang ride back into, and the Judge is their guide as Virgil is Dante's in *The Inferno*. Glanton first sets eyes on the Judge as they are fleeing for their lives from a much larger Apache group, sitting on an enormous boulder where he seemed to have been waiting for them. 'They rode past trap dykes of brown rock running down the narrow chines of the ridges and onto the plain like the ruins of old walls, such auguries everywhere of the hand of man before man was any living thing.' (*Blood Meridian*, 52). Even the Indians they encounter are degenerates from a more civilised age, such as a party of Chiicahuas, 'jackal warriors', 'Stone Age savages' sitting half-naked, 'daubed with clay paints in obscure charges, greasy, stinking.' (*Blood Meridian*, 238). One of the key scenes in the novel is when the Judge tells his comrades of the Azanzi, 'the old ones', who quit the cities, defeated by drought and disease, and had become mere 'rumours and ghosts in this land.' (*Blood Meridian*, 152). The Azanzi have practically passed without leaving any trace, only the human detritus, the leftovers of a once flourishing culture. Their descendants now crouch in their huts and 'listen to the fear seeping out of the rocks.' The tools, the art, the buildings of the 'old ones' all stand judgement on them. McCarthy prompts us to think that civilisation itself is a mirage, occurring once and only briefly, only to be soon rubbed out. 'All progress is from a higher to a lower order are marked by ruins and mystery and a residue of nameless rage.' Holden certainly has a way with words, that much we know about him. We are all, he warns us, destined to subside into the 'primal mud, with scarcely a cry.' Those who build in stone are challenging the order of the universe and will defy it only for a time. 'The way of the world is to bloom and to flower and die, but in the affairs of men there is no waning, and the noon of his expression signals the onset of night.'

And as they journey back further into the 'Heart of Darkness', one of the moments of high symbolism arises when they encounter a band of Indian hunters coming towards them, a reflection of themselves, a party of riders pieced out of darkness by the intermittent flare of the day, lighting the north. They are creatures from the past, dressed in skins, sewn with the ligaments of beasts, and sitting on their animals in the way of men who are seldom off them. They parley while dismounting, and so the parties divide, 'each passing back the way the other had come, pursuing, as all travellers must, inversions without end upon other men's journeys.' (*Blood Meridian*, 127). They are all journeying back into the Indian past which is also the white man's, of course, and all the time the Judge expostulates upon the common theme—the link between the two worlds, and man's susceptibility to violence. It makes no difference what men think of themselves. War endures. 'War was always there, before man was, war waited for him. The ultimate trade awaiting its ultimate practitioner.'

This, for me, is the most significant moment in the novel, fixing the Judge in our minds if not our affections. He is not a psychologically complex figure, and he is not meant to be. What he has is the gift of language; he is entirely persuasive and forces us to see that all human achievement as transitory. We will never fully escape the state of nature. All we have is culture—the buildings of stone—which is the distance we put between ourselves and the state of nature which we can never put behind us; we can escape history, but never our past which can reclaim us at any time. Only the Judge is intelligent enough to entertain let alone express such thoughts, and we can be sure the other gang members will be quite unable to fix his message in their minds for long.

His erudition is never in question. We see him discoursing about the Children of Ham, the lost tribes of Israelites, quoting passages from the Greek poets and engaging in anthropological speculation as to the propagation of the different races and their racial traits. Among his gifts, he is a good draftsman, and when not drawing he is always taking notes of the pieces of flint or pot shard or tools of bone he finds on the journey. When asked what he intends to do with these notes and sketches, he announces his intention to expunge all trace of these early human origins from the memory of Man (McCarthy, 2010, 147). He adopts much the same attitude to the Indians, playing god with their lives. He is a great believer in Darwinism before Darwin. He is a great exponent of the 'fitness' school of life and he is not unwilling to help more degenerate specimens of humanity depart the scene a little sooner than natural selection had intended.

McCarthy paints a frontier world in which people do not do much talking. Eloquence is largely absent, which is why the novel has such a narrative drive, but in the Judge he has created one of the most frightening characters of American fiction, and a man who is thoughtful enough to produce monologues that have almost perfect pitch. In *Blood Meridian* eloquence is evil, it is almost out of place in the barren, bitter landscape of warfare which the author implants in our mind. The Judge is clearly larger than the lives of those he intersects with. But he is also a very old figure, as old as the land through which they travel. The Judge is the warfare we left when we turned our violent impulses into violent desires, when we first translated warfare into war. We should not expect any psychological realisation in this figure. He is mythical, almost on a par with Achilles, though Achilles is a warrior with whom soldiers can identify in a way that they would never be able to identify with the Judge. He has looked into the souls of men and has found what he expects to find there. Only two people in the entire novel stand up to him. One does so lamely and meets his end at the end of hangman's noose in Los Angeles. The other, the Kid, ultimately rejects his message. 'You ain't nothing', he tells him at the end of the book. He is reclaimed by civilisation as the novel concludes, but it is not enough to save him.

The Judge's vision of man is not necessarily false, but it is despairing, and it is entirely misanthropic. The journey we are taken on is not of the human race's moral education, violent, grim and destructive by turn; it is only part of the story, and it is grotesquely exaggerated at that. There is a passage in G. K. Chesterton's essay 'Orthodoxy' (1908) that captures what is truly evil in the Judge's heart, if he has one. 'The evil of the pessimist is ... not that he chastises gods and men, but that he does not love what he chastises.' (Chesterton, 1996, 97). The Judge loves warfare and his love is heroic because it is unconditional; everyone who loves war must love conditionally if they are not to be claimed by the dark. Unlike warfare, war, after all, is not what the Judge claims. It is not all there is, and it is not life, and it is not a phenomenon which includes all other trades. 'Is that why war endures?' asks one of the most vicious of the young gang members, David Brown. 'It endures', Holden tells him, 'because young men love it and old men love it in them.' For him violence is 'a forming of the unity of existence.' (*Blood Meridian*, 261). All that matters is that men test their will, that they forego any further argument over beliefs or ideas; let force decide the issue. In the world of warfare there is no moral law. And yet a few gang members, and not only the Kid, refuse to embrace this message. One of them, Tobin, a former novitiate to the priesthood who has taken up instead a life of crime, rejects Holden's claim that 'journeymen priest or apprentice priest ... men of God and men of war have strange affinities.' 'I'll not second say you in your notion', said Tobin. 'Don't ask it.' 'Ah, Priest', said the Judge. 'What could I ask of you that you have not already given?' (*Blood Meridian*, 262).

And it is in this unforgiving philosophy that Holden apostrophises at the end of the novel in the saloon surrounded by every kind of herder and bullwhacker, peddler and gambler, drifter and whore. 'The dregs of the earth in beggary a thousand years.' There he sits alone as if some other breed entirely, little changed over the intervening years. 'Do you believe it's all over?' the Judge asks the Man—the dance, the way of warfare, not war. Even at the time in which the action takes place, in the 1850s, the kind of filibustering that Glanton's gang engages in was coming to an end as the frontier moved ever westwards and the wilderness was tamed. As Glanton himself remarks when negotiating the price of the scalps they are promising to bring in, his men are 'contracted for the war. You'll not see their like again.' (*Blood Meridian*, 87).

The Judge laments that as war becomes dishonoured and its nobility called into question, the true warriors, the men seeking only their destiny and discovering their own fate, will be excluded from the dance, which is the warrior's right.

> Only that man who has offered himself up entire to the blood of war, who has been on the floor of the pit and has seen horror in the round, and learned at last that it speaks to his innermost heart, only that man can dance. (*Blood Meridian*, 345).

Perhaps, the Judge is already anticipating a future in which the warfare of the frontier will be turned into war. The novel concludes with an epilogue in which we see a nameless man walking over the plain, digging holes in the ground, striking fire in them to make fences. He is literally fencing in the frontier. The novel ends in 1878. Twelve years later the frontier was officially closed, by which time the Indians were all penned into reservations. With the closing of the frontier warfare is translated into war, and with it history begins, one in which the Indian haters will be discredited and we will forget that Indians were not always the victims and white men the villains. McCarthy has no patience with the re-writing of what happened. For him all men are unremittingly bloodthirsty, poised at a peak of violence, the meridian from which civilisation sooner or later will eventually decline.

In an interview with the *New York Times*, McCarthy insisted that there is no such thing as a life without bloodshed. He was especially dismissive of the idea that the species could be improved in some way. 'Those who are afflicted with this notion are the first ones to give up their souls, their freedoms. Your desire that it be that way will enslave you and make your life vacuous.' (Evans, 2011).

It was said of Sidney Keyes that he went further than any of the First World War poets in 'the realisation that mankind was at war because it was not yet ready for peace, because men were proud and greedy and destructive at heart.' (Blythe, 1982, 14). Literature does not define human nature so much as exemplify it which is why, perhaps, there is so little great literature on war; war is so central to our humanity that it hardly seems worthwhile dwelling on it. From the perspective of evolutionary theory, one can see the biological imperatives in war as a return to a primal darkness. The Judge we suspect probably would not be particularly scandalised by Darwin's *The Descent of Man* because he is interested in much the same question: what are we? The Judge speaks from the perspective of the evolutionary biologist who tells us that we will never eliminate violence, individual or collective, and that we will never disavow war because there are limits to how much we can change. Our skulls are still lumbered with Stone Age brains that are maladapted to modern life; we still disregard long term threats because we are hard-wired to take more urgent note of short term concerns. Humanity is said to have emerged from the Pleistocene socially adapted for the transformation to come; but it has still not done so in terms of moral progress. It is our animal nature that we cannot escape; any more than we can emancipate ourselves from our evolved biology (Gottschal, 2008, 160). Evolutionary psychologists are pessimistic about the human condition for that reason—they recognise that we are what we are and there may be limits to how much we can change. There may be a limit, in other words, to what we might yet 'become'.

And so we are left to ponder our eventual fate. Nietzsche always insisted that the Greeks were right in telling us, almost from the beginning, that in escaping warfare (the state of nature) into a world at war with its protocols and conventions, and even rules on killing, we had not escaped the meaninglessness of life. The Greeks overcame the lack of meaning by inventing in the *Iliad* a spectacle in which destruction and ruin acquired a life-affirming beauty—they spiritualised away the cruelty in verse. But did they succeed or did they suspect that man remains at heart irredeemable? In the final book of the *Iliad*, Achilles and Priam sit down and dine together. It is the most inspiring passage of the poem and it shows our humanity at its best. We are capable of both empathy and compassion; we can even identify with our enemies in *their* grief; we instinctively recognise that we are human only to the extent that others (including our enemies) can recognise their own humanity in us. But the passage is often read in a truncated version. Even when Achilles has proved that he is the true warrior by embracing the old man and releasing Hector's body to his care, he is capable of reverting back to type at a moment's notice. At one point he is so angered by Priam's interminable lamentations that he threatens to murder the old man where he stands. He only restrains himself with difficulty, bounding out of his hut 'like a lion.' (*Iliad* 24.572). These days we don't tend to compare our animal nature to lions so much as killer apes, or in McCarthy's vision, to wolves and we do so with scant respect to the true nature of either animal. If there is a good deal of the wolf in man, fortunately there is little of the 'man' in the wolf, whose nature is far less vicious and more predictable. Achilles remains a killer to the end—an incomplete man, our forefathers might have said, except they would have been wrong. We are all 'incomplete' in the journey to become human. For us, our humanity is a 'work in progress' and it is as well we understand the experience of war and how it infects the interior self if we are to continue with the work.

Holden speaks for the low intensity, irregular wars of the present that disfigure the political and social landscape of so many societies today as they dissolve into darkness. The romance, glory and glamour of war in the West has long been renounced or commodified in video games; for others violence is a common enough fact of life, unadulterated and unvarnished. The main characters in this book, especially the warriors and heroes (even men like Jordan fighting in a civil war) try their best to keep to the 'rules'. The Judge argues that the rules are more fictional than real and that we adopt them in a vain attempt to attach meaning to a meaningless existence, and an even vainer attempt to put some distance between ourselves and our true nature. What in the end is most villainous about him—that he is an Indian hater, a murderer and a child molester (he is undoubtedly all three); or that he is so intent on robbing us of the hope that we can ever put out past behind us? In McCarthy's version of nihilism there is no life-affirming vision, only a despairingly honest depiction of humanity—that is, of course, if we are willing to buy into it. But if we are, then it surely follows that we must give Judge Holden the benefit of the doubt.

5

SURVIVORS

Survival is more than merely a matter of returning from war in one piece, mentally or physically. It is about a soldier's inner life remaining intact, and his refusal to allow war to mould him in its own image, or grind him down, still less get the better of him. More than any other personality types in this book, the survivor is the most modern. Other than the 'victim' he is most in tune with the times.

Today's survivors tend to be distinctly un-heroic (to be a hero is the shortest career there is, remarked Will Rogers). They survive because their vocation is failure (they fail to live up to what others want them to be). But survivors are not always un-heroic even by their own lights, and in the twentieth century, survival itself came to take on a heroic patina. It is only through access to a survivor's inner life that the novel gives us that we can really appreciate what makes survival so very different from, say, desertion, or cowardice in the field, or betrayal (the man who chooses to betray his friends rather than risk his own life, a stock trope in popular fiction).

What makes the survivor so fascinating is the strength of character that it takes to survive, especially in the bureaucratic machine that the military became in the modern age. To survive is to rise above it all; the pettiness of rank, the mindless conformity; the psychology of military incompetence; the pig-headed generals and brutal master-sergeants, and above all, the mind-numbing boredom. But there is more to it than that. Survival is often more demanding still. It is the willingness to stand out without at the same time betraying one's friends. We all mind what other people think of us, anyone that is who has a sense of honour, as most of us do. Most of us see ourselves through the eyes of others, and have need of them for our existence because the image we have of ourselves is indistinguishable from that presented by other people.

Survivors are to be found in every war, even the Trojan. Thersites is one of the first, a man who is always grumbling about the war in Homer's tale and who frequently gets kicked for his pains by Odysseus, in one of his less well known roles as Agamemnon's enforcer. Another is Falstaff who, like the odious Thersites (and there the comparison ends), lives in the company of heroes and has to appear to live up to the heroic ideal at best he can by doing what comes naturally to him: telling tall tales. He acts as a foil for two of the greatest heroes in Shakespeare's canon: Hotspur, the young, headstrong Harry Percy, and Hal, the future Henry V. Falstaff is an altogether more attractive character but his life instinct is no less developed; he wants to live and so he does but at a price, for there is always a price to be paid for survival. Critics have noted a darker mood in the second of the Henry IV plays. There is less vivacity in Falstaff as the end of his stage life as his hopes of advancement fade. There is a darkening of mood, and that is the point. Falstaff, the soldier, cannot escape war's instrumental nature. The existential dimension is never enough. There is no absolute freedom, even for Falstaff—to pursue absolute freedom is to invite disappointment.

Falstaff makes it through the civil broils but dies a disappointed man. Gustav Hašek's hero Švejk is much luckier but then he demands much less from life. We know Švejk survives the war (even though the novel was never completed) because Hašek tells us in a preface that we might meet him in the streets of Prague—a shabbily dressed man who is not even himself aware of his own significance in the history of the great new era, the era of the common man. The twentieth century was the era of a new kind of hero. Hašek tells us that great times call for great men, but that the century has no need of an Alexander or a Napoleon. Its heroes are those who go on their way, bothering no one. 'Unlike the stupid fellow Herostrates, Švejk did not set fire to the Temple of the Goddess in Ephesus just to get in the newspapers and school books.' And that is enough, Hašek adds. Herostrates is what we would call today a celebrity-terrorist, and terrorism is the art of being noticed.

Švejk is a new kind of hero who does not want to be noticed at all, much less to stick out.

Throughout the novel some think of him as a scoundrel, and others as a half-wit. It is not always clear whether he is either or both. The moral lines are often obscured. What he is particularly good at is playing cards, getting drunk and making himself a nuisance, and of course the reader loves him for it. In Švejk's world, sanity exists only outside society, and the army and its craven officers, and the police and their informers, and the clergy and its drunken priests who have long since lost their faith. Švejk is not against society, unlike his creator Hašek, who was an anarchist. He actually believes in law and order, as peasants usually do. And he is not unpatriotic, though whether he is a Czech nationalist is not entirely clear. But he chooses to survive a society that is always conspiring against him. He is a little man caught up in a big power war, and he is heroic because he survives.

In Yossarian, Joseph Heller created a more contemporaneous survivor, a member of the fictional 256th Squadron based on the island of Pianosa in the Mediterranean. In later life he was often asked why he had never written another book as great as *Catch-22*, to which he would reply, 'Who has?' *Catch-22* is by far the best of his books, though it owed a lot to the editorial finesse of the former editor of *The New Yorker* who licked it into shape (Manguel, 2007, 133). Perhaps, because it is based on Heller's own experience as a bombardier, it speaks truth to the power of war and captures its bureaucratic absurdities. Structurally it works at all levels: as a story, as a dialogue between its diverse and humorous characters, and as a morality tale. And behind it all is Yossarian's understanding that the chief enemy is not over the horizon manning the anti-aircraft batteries; it is behind the lines, in plain view. It is the system itself which is off-side.

Yossarian is assailed not so much by the fear of death, as by what war had made the US Air Corps: an unrelenting totalitarian machine. The most significant moment in fixing the young man in our minds and in our affections comes at the end of the novel when he chooses to escape the war by setting out to sea. The conflicting claims of loyalty to himself and loyalty to his friends pull him this way and that on almost every page, and at the end, in choosing to be loyal to himself, he stays loyal to his friends.

Yossarian discovers almost too late that war has become the master not the servant of policy. Perhaps it is always in danger of becoming so, as Clausewitz warns, but this danger is often obscured by the old words in which no one now believes—such as glory and honour. In Hemingway's novel *A Farewell to Arms* Lieutenant Henry chooses to survive too. He too views abstract words such as 'glory', 'honour', 'courage' as obscene, next to the names of actual villages, roads and rivers where real people have died. He flees to Switzerland, as Yossarian will later flee to Sweden, and his sentiments might be Yossarian's too, 'I've been fighting ... to save my country. Now I'm going to fight a little to save myself.' Both men in a sense elect to sign a separate peace but Heller's hero is actually the more heroic in maintaining his covenant with his friends.

Survivors take many forms—one of the most poignant appears in a novel by the only non-western author in this study. Bao Ninh's book is not without its faults but it is totally realistic nonetheless, and raw in its depiction of its chief character, Kien, who is emotionally and psychologically damaged. Unlike most American soldiers in the Vietnam War he has to fight much longer, in far worse conditions, often without food, with little rest and recuperation or the long furloughs back in the cities of the South which his enemies enjoyed when they were not in the field. He loses his one and only love together with any faith that he might have had in Communism.

But his real tragedy is the fact that he has survived. It is called survivor's guilt and involves a feeling of shame made up of many different elements. One is the reacquired consciousness of having been diminished—not because of cowardice but the terms on which one had to survive with all their petty compromises that can usually be avoided in civilian life. More important, perhaps, is an irrational feeling of being alive in place of another, of taking someone else's place, someone who has not returned home, someone much more worthy than oneself. It is not the 'best' who survive (they are the ones who get killed first); war involves the survival of the worst—the fittest. Primo Levi (a survivor of Auschwitz) put it best: 'It is the impression that the others died in your place; that you are alive *gratis*, thanks to a privilege you have not earned, a trick you played on the dead.' (Todorov, 264–265). 'We, the survivors are not the true witnesses' he added in another work; those best placed to bear witness died, not despite their valour but because of it. Those even better placed can't bear witness; they return home mute because they have touched bottom. The survivors who can write or talk about their experiences are the ones who have survived because of their prevarications, or abilities, or simply good luck—those are the soldiers who have not looked the Gorgon in the face (Levi, 1988, 64). All of which also reminds us why many soldiers choose not to survive; that those who go to their certain death running headlong into machine gun fire do so because that is what the men to the left and the right of them are doing. Over the centuries, writes Sebastian Junger, men have chosen to die in battle with their friends rather than flee on their own and perhaps, survive (Junger, 2010, 242). Survival is often a choice, one that men have to live with for the rest of their lives.

Survival has a privileged place in the literature of war—it has produced the most comic characters which can mislead us into ignoring the guilt, or the shame that often accompanies it—for survivors are also often the collateral damage of conflict. But comic writers like to satirise war to be better placed to condemn it, or they employ irony to put us at some distance from the experience, so that we are less estranged from ourselves. In the figure of George Macdonald Fraser's Flashman we encounter one of life's born survivors, and the most scandalously uplifting one of all. Like O'Brian's Jack Aubrey, Fraser created a real figure for the times in which his adventures are set, the Victorian era. He does the scene-setting very well, like his description of the siege of Cawnpore (which is up there with *The Siege of Krishnapur* by J. G. Farrell). He is representative of a breed of soldier well known through-out history—the adventurer who dons a uniform to make a profit, and you can't turn a profit if you get your head blown off. Flashman doesn't join any colours but his own; notoriously, he serves on both sides in the American Civil War and thus sets a very high standard for self-interest. With *Flashman and the Great Game* the action becomes more serious, the farce less marked. There are even elements of pathos. What McDonald Fraser found most 'pathetic' of all was that Flash-man's final adventures were written at a time when the British army once again fighting in the old imperial theatres such as Afghanistan, and fighting for a lost cause, this time not to maintain 'national hon-our', but what honour had become in the modern age—'credibility', on another larger canvas, the War on Terror. No wonder the character of Flashman, rogue though he is, appeals to so many soldiers who still struggle to survive the incompetence of their own generals, and the delusions of the politicians who despatch them off to fight. In that respect, not much has changed over the centuries.

The survivors who appear in these pages, even Flashman at his basest, have a high sense of self-esteem because they retain their honour to the end. We tend to dismiss survivors as 'lesser' people, but they are really not. Of all the character types that appear in this book, the warrior and the survivor are most popular with serving men and women. They know an authentic man when they encounter one. They have an insight into the circumstances against which men like Yossarian are revolting, or simply 'sitting out' in a way that the more traditional heroes may not. Often they have a keener sense of what is fitting to ask of a soldier, or for that matter a man. Survival after all, to quote Geoffrey Grigson, is one of 'the recipes for being human.'

Falstaff: The Reluctant 'Man of Action'
Henry IV, Parts I and II, William Shakespeare

Falstaff is the first person to use a now rather dated, but once popular term: 'man of action'. When in the second part of *Henry IV* a dozen captains assemble outside a bawdy house to summon him to war, he tells the girls, 'you see, my good wenches, how men of merit are sought after; the under-server may sleep when the man of action is called on.' (*Henry IV, Part II*, 4.1, 406). He is being deeply and lovingly ironical. Falstaff is an educated man gone to seed, but with high intelligence (he is, as Nuttall suggests, the very first man in Shakespeare to 'philosophise'). And yet he has very little sense of self-importance. He relishes being discovered for what he is: a coward. And he represents a particular kind of soldier, one who is determined to survive, come what may, and who resolutely refuses to be taken in by all the great speeches and sentiments that the phenomenon tends to evoke. In Falstaff we find a magnificent zest for life, as well as a supreme contempt for the high command who sacrifice men without thinking.

In any production of *Henry IV*, Falstaff usually steals the show. He is a larger than life figure who bursts the bounds of the play and ultimately lives independent of his own author. Coleridge, one of the most perceptive of Shakespeare's critics, admired the fact that his characters, 'like those in real life are to be *inferred* by the reader.' We will never know them inside out because they do not know themselves. Lear has 'ever but slenderly known himself', complains one of his daughters;

Iago does not really know why he hates Othello (Coleridge talks of his 'motiveless malevolence' which Hannah Arendt took to be a sign of 'radical evil'), and even Hal, the young Prince who will one day become king, is often at sea in the play named after him (a play which Shakespeare promised would portray Falstaff as well, but which killed him off, and offstage at that).

In the two plays that we have, *Henry IV* Parts 1 and 2 however, we come to know more about Falstaff than we do about his creator. No-one has ever accused Falstaff of not writing his own lines. He is a great wencher, past his prime, who still manages to ensnare older women who should know better, such as Mistress Quickly. Hotspur, the young Harry Percy, the young Hal's bitter enemy, has no character outside the play. Falstaff is larger than the plays in which he appears. We cannot imagine a novelist like Robert Nye writing a novel about Hotspur, as he did Falstaff in 1976.

Falstaff is both endearing and reprehensible because he never allows his private life to be defined by his public service. Rather he straddles both worlds, and although a soldier, he is happier living in the second, in the days before soldiers began to think of themselves as public servants. When he describes himself, he lists courage (largely bogus, but not entirely absent) last by way of identifying himself:

> Sweet Jack Falstaff, kind
> Jack Falstaff, true Jack Falstaff, valiant Jack Falstaff
> and therefore more valiant being as he is old.
> (*Henry IV, Part I*, 2.4, 463–4).

For a medieval knight, Falstaff has lived a comparatively long life, and he has not survived to old age by taking unnecessary risks on the battlefield. The true warrior in the play is young Hotspur, who gets killed for his courage. The problem is that Hotspur is largely a cipher, an abstraction of honour, as we shall see. Bloom argues that he is merely a fiction, whereas Falstaff is a person (Bloom, 1999, 282). And that is true up to a point. He is larger than life because he loves life so much. Hotspur would follow Hal's philosophy—we all owe God a death, and the sooner we discharge the debt, the better. Most of us, like Falstaff, would prefer to prolong our lives, not hazard them in battle, and civilians warm to Falstaff for that reason. What we love about him most, perhaps, is that he is so determined not to act his age, to remain in touch with his youth, to deny death its sting. When the Lord Chief

Justice reproaches him for not acting his age, and condemns him for his devilish pranks and general bawdiness that un-becomes an old man: 'is not your voice broken, your mind short, your chin double, your wit single and every part about you blasted with antiquity?', Falstaff replies magnificently that he was born with a white beard and something of a belly. The truth is, he lost his voice with the singing of anthems. He is old only in judgement (*Henry IV, Part II*, 1.2 181–192). 'I would t'were bed-time, Hal, and all well', he says in a childlike way to the Prince towards the end of *Henry IV, Part I*. (*Henry IV, Part I*, 5.1, 125). He dies eventually, sucking on his finger's end like a baby, and looks on his death bed as he did when he came into the world, if we are to believe his account of his birth.

To us, he appears as he would insist, not as a 'counterfeit' but as a 'true and perfect image of life'—'a good, portly man … of a cheerful look, a pleasing eye.' (*Henry IV, Part I*, 5.4, 118). He would prefer to be fifty, but is in reality he is much older. And he follows up this description with the kernel of his philosophy: 'to die is to be a counterfeit, for his is but the counterfeit of a man who hath not the life of a man.' And to leave us in no doubt that the lives the philosophy he teaches, he adds, 'the better part of valour is discretion.' We can be sure he practices what he preaches, which is why he has lived for so long.

Like most survivors, he always has his eye on the main chance after the war is over. When he tells Hal that 'Worcester is stolen away tonight', and that the rebellion against the King has begun, he knows he will have to go to the wars with the young Prince. But he always has an eye on the world he will come back to, and what war will bring: falling property prices and property to snap up. 'Your father's beard has turned white with the news. You may buy land now as cheap as stinking mackerel.' (*Henry IV, Part I*, 2.4, 349–51). To which Hal replies, punning on the word 'maiden' (the common name for a fish), 'Why then, if there come a hot June and this civil buffeting holds, we shall buy maidenhood as they buy hobnails, by the hundreds.'

Hal, of course, has his eye on the throne, and the day that he will succeed his father. 'Civil buffeting' is not an opportunity to be exploited but a danger to be contained. Falstaff hopes to profit greatly from Hal's succession. In the preface to the Arden edition of *Henry IV, Part I*, David Scott-Kastan presents us with two versions of Falstaff— the vitalist truth teller who exposes the life-denying lies of power, and the disruptive force of misrule, who fragments the hope for order and coherence. The same might be said of the medieval era which Falstaff represents; feudal knights alone curbed the powers of the monarchy and held the monarch to account while at the same time treating the kingdom as a private fiefdom to be exploited either with the king or in defiance of the king's wishes. The age was an anarchical one in which misrule was never far away. Take the scene in which Falstaff, flush from his false heroics on the battlefield, mocks and insults the Lord Chief Justice, the representative of order. We love him for it, but we cannot admire him. We love false heroics, but we cannot approve of them, even though some of us may suspect that the 'order' that the Chief Justice embodies is not everything we might want it to be, and that Hal is not as virtuous as he appears, or Hotspur quite as headstrong as he is represented.

Is Falstaff a coward? After being 'outed' as a coward and rogue in the Gad's Hill prank (in which Flastaff is tricked into waylaying some travellers, including the young Prince in disguise, and runs away when he thinks his life is in danger), he tells Hal, 'why thou knowest I am as valiant as Hercules, but beware instinct [where beware means paying heed to] Lives not a coward on instinct.' When he ran away he did so because, like a lion, he recognised the Prince as one of the attackers, and he fled because a lion (according to Elizabethan folklore) would not hurt a Prince. But Falstaff has many other instincts apart from the ability to recognise, intuitively, a Prince in disguise. He knows when to run away. We warm to Falstaff because he is not a hypocrite; he knows himself too well. What we like most about the man is his mockery of pretentiousness—Hotspur's excessive love of honour; the patriot's willingness to sacrifice everything for a cause at whatever cost to himself or others He is definitely not the *miles gloriosus*, the braggart warrior, of which there are many in Shakespeare (one thinks of Timon of Athens in one of his most misanthropic moods, entertaining the hope that the 'unscarred braggarts of war' will derive some pain, if not from their wounds, at least from the syphilis they will contract from whoring (*Timon of Athens*, 4.3, 153–68). Falstaff exaggerates his success on the battlefield, half knowing he will not be believed. It is a joke against himself, as well as against an unforgiving world.

The problem we have with him today is not his cowardice, real or exaggerated, but his callousness. Falstaff has no qualms about despatching his retainers to their deaths. He is not a soldier with a twenty-

first-century sensibility; he has the medieval attitudes to the poor that
were to persist well into the modern era. When the Lord Chief Justice,
his sworn enemy, sends a page to ask him to come over for a chat,
Falstaff deliberately mistakes him for a beggar and reproaches him for
not going to the wars:

> A young knave, and begging? Is
> There not war? Is there not employment?
> Doth now the King lack subjects?
> Do not the rebels need soldiers?
> Though it be a shame to be on any
> Side but one, it is worse
> Shame to beg than to be on the
> Worst side....
> (*Henry IV, Part II*, 1.2, 71–75).

'Food for powder, food for powder', he later jokes when Hal claims
that he never 'did see such pitiful rascals' as those Falstaff has recruited
for the war. They are indeed a miserable lot, 'discarded unjust serving
men, younger sons to younger brothers, revolted tapsters and ostlers
trade-fatters—the cankers of a calm world and a long peace.' No eye
had seen such 'scarecrows', many of them recently out of prison. But
as Falstaff reminds Hal, this is not the point. 'They'll fill a pit as well
as better.' (*Henry IV, Part I*, 4.2, 63–6). At the end of the battle of
Shrewsbury, Falstaff boasts, 'I have led my ragamuffins where they are
peppered; there's not 3 of my 150 left alive, and they are for the town's
end to beg during life.' (*Henry IV, Part I*, 5.3, 35–8).

Falstaff is thoroughly in tune with his times. When Justice Shallow
his old friend at the Inns of Court, questions his selection of men to
fight another battle in the second of the two plays, Falstaff reproaches
him as he did the Prince. 'Will you tell me, Master Shallow, how to
choose a man?' and then in true Falstaffian fashion proceeds to com-
mend each chosen man's physical infirmities:

> ... care I for the limb, the thews, the stature
> bulk, and big assemblance of a man? Give me
> the spirit, Master Shallow. Here's Wart; you see what
> a ragged appearance it is—a shall charge you, and
> discharge you, with the motion of a pewterer's
> hammer, come off and on swifter than he that gib-
> bets on the brewer's bucket. And this same half-
> faced fellow Shadow: give me this man, he presents

no mark to the enemy—the foeman may with as
great aim level at the edge of a penknife. And for a
retreat, how swiftly will this Feeble, the woman's
tailor, run off! O, give me the spare men, and spare
me the great ones...
(*Henry IV Part II*, 3.2, 252–265).

Here, Shakespeare is quite literally parodying the military art of the times. In the Auden edition of the play, the editor quotes Matthew Sutcliffe's *The Practice, Proceedings and Laws of Armies* (1593) which counselled that men of mean situation were for the most part more vigorous and courageous 'and commonly excel great bodied men in swiftness and running.' (*Henry IV, Part II*, 109). In the case of these particular recruits, their luck will hold since Falstaff arrives too late on the battlefield for any harm to come to them.

All that one can say in Falstaff's defence is that his retainers are victims of war, as he would be if he did not have a philosophy to sustain him in addition to his well-entrenched instinct for survival. 'I like not such grinning honour ... Give me life, which if I can save, so... if not, honour comes unlooked for", he remarks.' (*Henry IV, Part II*, 5.3, 60–1). Grinning means the death rictus, the honour that survives a man's death in the field. Falstaff prefers not to seek out either honour, or an early death. And he can secure his own life if his luck holds because he is a gentleman; the medieval grunts cannot. But Falstaff would never seek a war, and indeed he is merciless in his criticism of those who would. When Worcester tells the King that he had not wanted to rebel; he had not sought 'this day of this dislike', and the King replies sharply, 'How come it, then?' our hero goes in for the kill. 'Rebellion lay in his way, and he found it.' (*Henry IV Part I*, 5.1, 26–8). He remains suspicious of any values that put life at risk such as patriotism, which as Susan Sontag once remarked, is the cruellest form of unrequited love.

The centrepiece of Falstaff's philosophy is celebrated in the heat of battle at Shrewsbury where Hotspur meets his death. Harold Bloom writes that the battle scene is much livelier than that of Agincourt, and it is livelier because of Falstaff's determination to survive it (Bloom, 1999, 303). Everything revolves around one word: 'honour'. Hotspur's honour is never in doubt. There are frequent references to it throughout the play and at the very beginning the King regrets that he himself has not been blessed like Northumberland with 'a son who is the theme of honour's tongue.' (*Henry IV, Part I*, 1.1, 80–82). Hotspur himself positively embraces the word; he is always first to attack the 'dishonourable' natures of others. He is unwilling to share his honour with anyone, and therefore all the more inclined to throw himself into battle before he should. Worcester notes that Hotspur is as much a danger to himself as others. 'He apprehends [conceives of] a world of figures but not the form [the actual substance] of what he should attend [think about].' (*Henry IV, Part I*, 1.1, 80–82). Falstaff by contrast does apprehend the form; he knows its substance well enough. His philosophy has no room for the honour with which young Hotspur is so in love, and he would blanch to hear Hotspur's credo:

> ...this is no world
> to play with mamarets and to tilt with lips.

he tells his wife on the eve of going into battle. 'We must have bloody noses and crack'd crowns, and pass their current, too.' (*Henry IV, Part II*, 2.3, 87–89). This is no world, in other words, for fondling breasts and kissing women; it is a world in which a man's vocation is to break heads and do so with such panache that he will inspire his sons to do the same.

In an earlier conversation with Falstaff, Hal had bluntly told the old man to say his prayers in case he did not survive the next day's battle. Henry is his usual self: cold, dispassionate and entirely in awe of his own sense of honour which is different again from Hotspur's, but it is no less deadly for those who follow him into combat. We all owe God a death, he tells his friend. Falstaff's reply is thoroughly Falstaffian: 'Tis not due yet. I would be loath to pay him before his day.' It comes from the most famous passage in the play, when Falstaff goes on to soliloquise about honour in terms that we probably find more sympathetic than did his contemporaries.

> ... Well, 'tis no matter; honour pricks me
> on't. Yea, but how if honour prick me off when I come
> on? How then? Can honour set to a leg? No, or an arm?
> No, or take away the grief of a wound? No. honour
> hath no skill in surgery, then? No. What is honour? A
> word. What is in that word 'honour'? What is that
> 'honour'? Air. A trim reckoning. Who hath it? He that
> died o' Wednesday. Doth he feel it? No. Doth he hear it?

No. 'tis insensible then? Yea, to the dead. But will it
not live with the living? No. Why? Detraction will not suffer it.
Therefore I'll none of it. Honour is a mere
scutcheon. And so ends my catechism.
(*Henry IV, Part I*, 5.1. 123–140).

And Falstaff is as true to that catechism as he is to his love of sack
and gluttony. When he sees the dead Sir William Blunt, he remarks,
'there's honour for you.' To escape being killed by Douglas, he feigns
his own death. To ensure that Hotspur has been killed by Hal, he stabs
his dead body—as dishonourable an act as there could be for a medieval knight. And then, to add insult to injury, he claims the credit for
Hotspur's death so that he can claim a reward, perhaps an Earldom, or
even a Dukedom. If he is certain that honour is nothing worth dying
for, he is no less certain that it is something that will help him live a
more prosperous life. As indeed it does, in the next play. His reputation as Hotspur's killer goes before him. Coleville of the Dale surrenders immediately after he catches sight of him. 'I think you are Sir John
Falstaff/and in that thought yield me.' (*Henry IV, Part II*, 4.3, 16–17).
Lest we be misled by the comedy of it all, we should not forget that
Coleville is executed after he surrenders, a disturbing switch from his-
trionic farce to historical fact. Honour may be a word, but it is a very
useful one, and in the Hobbesian state of nature which was the mediaeval world, reputation is everything.

And Falstaff does indeed win renown after Shrewsbury, at least for
a while. The Lord Chief Justice admits that 'it hath a little gilded over
his Gad's Head exploit', and when Falstaff first appears in the second
part of the play, he enters with his sword and buckler borne by a page-
boy. After the battle, as he prepared for the next, he makes the most of
his reputation, ill-gotten though it is, by bragging and complaining that
there is not a battle in prospect but he is 'thrust into it'. It is a failing
of the English to make too much of a good thing, he complains. 'I
would to God', he tells the Chief Justice, 'my name were not so terrible to the enemy as it is. I would better to be eaten to death with a rust
than to be scoured to nothing with perpetual motion.' (*Henry IV Part
II*, 2.11, 2–21).

In other words, Falstaff survives not because he is a coward (no soldier who survived the medieval battlefield could ever claim to be that)
but because he recognises that there is a great difference between existential courage and instrumental discretion. Hotspur's single-minded

pursuit of it is as much a danger to everyone else as Patroclus' single-minded wish to be heroic. To die honourably in the end means more to him than success. At a significant moment at Shrewsbury, Hal stands between what he takes to be the body of Falstaff and that of Hotspur who he has just killed. Hal embodies the uniting of the existential and instrumental. For his honour he will sacrifice much, but never success. Yeats called him an 'amiable monster' for that reason. And though Hal loves Falstaff, he does not love him enough to mourn his death for long. While pretending to be dead, Falstaff overhears the Prince say: 'What, old acquaintance, could not all this flesh keep in a little life? Poor Jack, farewell.' Here is 'authority', the death of a soldier, no sooner witnessed than forgotten. Hal is indeed 'monstrous', as Yeats claimed, because he is ready to sacrifice his own life for the pleasure of destroying the lives of others. And he is amiable because he is such a vivid personality, and has a charisma of almost Weberian proportions. He is cold-hearted and pragmatic, and will soon banish Falstaff from his presence, in the process breaking his heart.

Many commentators have read into the play a dialectical tension between Hotspur's sense of existential honour and Falstaff's dishon-our: two ends of a spectrum resolved in Hal's self-image as honoura-ble and pragmatic at the same time. But Falstaff gets up after playing dead; Hotspur does not. And he lives to serve the young Prince again. The survivor triumphs, at least for a time, by refusing to subscribe either to Hotspur's conception of honour or Hal's, the latter of which has inspired a generation of patriotic young Englishmen. As David Kasten adds, he is always a survivor, suspicious of any value that might put that survival at risk, and holding up the values of others in the light of common sense, allowing us to see them for what they truly are (*Henry IV, Part I*, 51).

What Shakespeare achieved was radical in terms of literary history. He freed the hero from being a one-dimensional representative of a sin-gle virtue or vice. Falstaff is no 'pious Aeneas, or even Chaucer's 'per-fect knight'. Shakespeare transformed him into a character with conflicting emotions and desires which are revealed in his thoughts (especially the soliloquies). What is so heroic about Falstaff is his love of life. It was a radical departure to juxtapose him to one of the great-est English warriors of all and his triumph is that he comes out all the better for the comparison. W. H. Auden was the first writer to note how in his soliloquies Henry can sound as devious as Iago (Nuttall,

2007, 151). Falstaff by comparison is more than just a buffoon; he is intensely human. The point is that he has a humanity that the young Prince notably lacks. Henry too, is a troubled soul who on the eve of the battle of Agincourt finds himself torn between his impulse for glory and a less than clear conscience about sending men to their death for a questionable cause (his own claim to the throne of France). But he dares all to win the throne and is willing to pay the price in men's lives, including of course his own.

We read Shakespeare to understand human nature as much if not more than life itself, writes Harold Bloom. Bloom provokes controversy, of course, and one of his most persuasive critics takes issue with him for making too much of the characters, and too little of the plays. (Rosenbaum, 2008, 400). And there are even times when Bloom is guilty of misreading the play, and never more so than when he claims that Falstaff is critical of war. He is not. He is merely a lover of life (as most soldiers are; few have a morbid obsession with death).

To be sure, Falstaff ridicules honour but he does so not because he is fallen out of love with war; he has simply lived long enough to become cynical. What makes Falstaff so heroic a figure is his defence not of cowardice but forbearance which is a form of courage in itself. He reasserts his own right to survive Henry's political needs; he is unwilling to become merely an asset or resource to serve larger ends. Falstaff offers a modern audience a voice because of his scepticism. And his scepticism has its own profound roots. In his book *A New Mimesis*, A.D. Nuttall claimed that Falstaff is the first person we meet in Shakespeare to have a philosophy, and we find it in his famous speech on honour. It is a faithful reflection of medieval Nominalism, the belief that universals were mere words; and that truth lies in particulars. The idea that universal concepts like 'beauty' or 'honour' are empty (mere air, as Falstaff suggests) can be found in Duke Theseus' speech that love or joy can only inhere in the particular, or the person, though the poetic imagination can realise them in more abstract or universalist terms. Imagination, he remarks, 'gives to aery nothing/a local habitation and a name.' (Nuttall, 2007, 157).

The importance of Nominalism is that it was the seed bed of modern scientific materialism, especially in its contention that there is no humanity, only human beings. If honour exists in war, it exists in the people who fight it. The survivor's philosophy is that honour—as an abstraction—will get you killed. What matters most is other people.

When translated into practical advice this would mean going to war for something specific, not for an illusion. If we take Falstaff to be a Nominalist in all but name we can even claim that he has an honour code of sorts. If Henry is to fight for his own honour, let old men die, not young ones. Fast forward to the famous scene where Falstaff turns down two robust young men, Mouldy and Bullcalf because they bribe their way out of service. Pocketing the money Falstaff then signs up three decrepit retainers, Wart, Feeble and Shadow. His justification? We have heard it before. 'They'll fit a pit as well as better.' 'Tush man, mortal men, mortal men.' (*Henry IV, Part I*, 5.2, 66–67).

It may sound cynical to our ears and deeply inhumane to our modern sensibilities, but is it not better to send the old or the ill to their death rather than the young? Nuttall adds that the words 'mortal men' are suddenly resonant. The standard syllogism of the school, 'all men are mortal; Socrates is a man; therefore Socrates is mortal' collapses into an intuition of the undifferentiating character of the death that awaits us all (Nuttall, 2007, 161). In the play Falstaff will have nothing either of the young Hotspur's absurdly romantic notions of honour (a man who despises poetry and loves only fighting) ('methinks it were an easy leap/to pluck English honour from the pale faced moon'); and Hal, who is always going on about the honour of princes, but does not quite believe what he overhears himself saying. 'If it be a sin to covet honour/I am the most offending soul alive.' (*Henry V*, 4.3, 28–29). Henry may endear himself to the audience by the recognition of his own faults (compared with Hotspur who is quite incapable of recognising his own), but today's soldiers would recognise the type. These men can spin words. 'We few, we happy few, we band of brothers.' But they are the ones that get you killed. You follow them at your own risk.

There is an old Jewish proverb that man thinks, and God laughs. Man thinks all the time. In the soliloquy, Shakespeare gives us the quintessentially modern means to overhear another's thoughts, as we do Hal's (now King) on the eve of Agincourt when he mixes with his men and offers them 'a touch of Harry in the night'. God will be laughing that evening. We think we know what is right or wrong, and when a war is just or unjust. But the truth will often escape us, and historians will spend their time arguing the toss, as historians always do. The more a man thinks, the more someone else will come to the opposite conclusion. And as we so often find, we are never really the people we think we are (which is why war is such a challenge—it finds this out faster than any other activity).

God laughs, too, because we take ourselves so seriously. Falstaff is someone he would find not un-wanting when the Judgement Day comes. He is cowardly and venal, and promiscuous, and disloyal (to everyone except the young Prince, his meal ticket for the future), but he never takes himself seriously. He never claims to know the truth. He despises humourless Puritans and fundamentalists. He is an enemy of cant, and positively scorns commanders who would be happy enough to condemn to their death not a few old crippled men, but thousands of young men to prove a point. In such a world there is something to be said for the old hands like Falstaff, who have seen it all before, and more important *heard* it. There is something to be said for the survivor who insists on retaining his own humanity, and who in laughing at himself is merely echoing God's own laughter.

There is only one reason why Falstaff appears in this book: he is a soldier. His is not a dissenting voice. He is not against the corrupt state of the world, he is determined to make the best of it, especially war which is his stock in trade. It is just that he has few illusions left about it. He is intelligent enough to make out a case against war if he wished, but he never does and we should respect his reticence. Whether Shakespeare himself was opposed to war is another point. We are all prisoners of the age, and pacifism as we understand the term today is very much a late modern phenomenon. One of the principal themes of Shakespeare's plays is war, and some of his most inspired characters are warriors but we see them in unfamiliar contexts, compressed in the case of *Henry V* in the wooden 'O', the Globe theatre; satirised and even mocked in a problem play like *Troilus and Cressida*; and exposed in all their vulnerability in *Coriolanus*. Henry V is an 'amiable monster'; Achilles is represented as a pantomime buffoon, an incarnation which contemporary drama tends to hype up; and Coriolanus is cut down to size by a woman, the mother from Hell. Behind the patriotic sound bites of *Henry V* there is an intelligent mind at work that sees war for what it is, and not what some would like it to be, and there is no doubt in my mind that Shakespeare saw warrior-princes as disturbingly dangerous figures.

His heroes may be soldiers but he is far more interested in their thoughts than actions, and he did not always get the balance right. Dr

Johnson complained that *Coriolanus* was a flawed play—there was 'too much bustle in the first act, and too little in the last.' Although war is a theme of many of his plays, we don't really know what Shakespeare thought about it; he rarely takes sides. In the end, it is probably best if disquieting to agree with William Empson's critique of T. S. Eliot's anti-Semitism: 'a writer had better rise above the ideas of his time, but one should not take offence if he doesn't.'

Falstaff's determination to survive, come what may, is *not* a protest against war, but against its follies, which explains why we warm to the old rascal despite his heartlessness in sending his retainers to their death. He backs the right side politically (the King's cause at Shrewsbury) but it avails him very little. Falstaff is as expendable as the men he recruits for the wars; friendship counts for little in politics. He finds out to his cost that the distinction between the personal and the political is not the same as that between the moral and the political. Soldiers are not necessarily moral for putting their own cause first any more than states are immoral for being 'political'—for sacrificing men for a greater end such as the King's claim to the throne or in the case of the young Henry V his claim to someone else's. The personal and the political are interlinked; both reinforce each other. Falstaff is foolish to think that Hal will put his personal pleasure first, though he is right to think the worst of him for betraying friendship. Nominalism comes closest to understanding that moral questions are never distinct from political ones. We may all owe God a death but the God we worship is reflected back in humanity, in the individual human form which is why we should never treat each other as abstractions—so much cannon fodder, or 'collateral damage', as if individuals have no value in themselves but only as a means to a larger political end.

Ultimately, Falstaff is undone by his own naivety. We hope at the end of *Henry IV, Part II* that he will leave the wars and settle down to a life of less than domestic bliss with Mistress Quickly. But we learn, of course, in the play that followed, *Henry V*, that he dies still un-reconciled to his fate, still mourning the world of possibilities that has slipped from his grasp. Doubtless, if he had not died of a broken heart he would have died of a broken head. His luck would not have held had he lived to see another battle. He would have been dragged down by the undertow of history. He might have joined the King's expedition to France and not lived to return, like Bardolph, his old carousing friend who gets hanged for theft. He might have died in the breach at Harfleur or on the field of Agincourt. It is actually appropriate that he should have died in bed rather than lived to see the victory won on St Crispin's day. In the heat of battle Henry rallies his men in one of the greatest patriotic perorations of English literature, declaiming that 'gentlemen in England now abed/shall think themselves accursed they were not here.' (*Henry V*, 4.3, 64–55). Not Falstaff. To die in bed, given his survivalist creed is a signal victory; it is his own very personal act of defiance.

Švejk: 'I am an official idiot'

The Good Soldier Švejk, Jaroslav Hašek

The first thing to say about *The Good Soldier Švejk* is that it is unusual in that its hero is an enlisted man. Up to then all the great novels about war, with the exception of Stephen Crane's, had officers as the main characters. Tolstoy, despite his sympathy for the peasants, would never have cast an ordinary soldier in a leading role (though one is a minor character in his novella *Hadji Murat*). He was too much of an aristocrat for that, and you do not get more aristocratic than Prince Andrei in *War and Peace*.

The second point about *The Good Soldier Švejk* is that he is not Henry Fleming. Fleming volunteers to go to war out of youthful romanticism. We see Švejk setting off for the recruiting office in very different circumstances. In one of the most amusing episodes of the entire book, Švejk is called up for a routine medical examination and sets off to the Ministry of War (they did not call them Ministries of Defence in those days) in a bath chair borrowed from the confectioner's stall around the corner from his lodgings. The citizens of Prague are treated to a rare sight—his charwoman, Mrs Muller, pushing a uniformed man through the streets, waving his crutches in the air, and shouting out in patriotic enthusiasm, 'To Belgrade, to Belgrade!' (Belgrade was the capital of Serbia, the country with which the Austro-Hungarian Empire was then at war.) (*The Good Soldier Švejk*, 59).

His misfortune is to encounter a German Chief Army doctor who sees in everything a criminal attempt to evade military service and who holds the Czech people in particular contempt as a nation of malingers. No reference to Švejk's rheumatism or his crippled state has any effect on the doctor's heart. Stripped naked for examination, Švejk chastely hides his nudity behind his crutches. 'That's really a remarkable fig leaf', he is told. 'There are no fig leaves like this in paradise.' The next moment he is accused of trying to evade military service and escorted to gaol under armed guard. And thus his adventures proper begin.

Jaroslav Hašek portrays a common feature of war, but one that had largely been missing from its fictional representation: the fact that many soldiers who fight, and not only conscripts, would rather not be there. The press-ganged foot soldier; the enlisted but reluctant peasant and the unhappy conscript have all been stock figures of war from the beginning. Only Hašek, however, really brought them into the light, and he did so using their own chief weapon: humour, the adamant refusal of soldiers across the centuries to allow military life to get them down. Not that Švejk necessarily speaks for them. He is a born coward, and not a coward by conviction. He frequently lies and cheats and steals his way through the story, and as a result he has outlived it just as he survived the war.

The Good Soldier Švejk was modelled to a certain extent on Hašek's own life. Like Švejk, the novelist got himself committed to an asylum to avoid conscription (after feigning a suicide attempt off the Charles Bridge). After that, he took it into his head to form his own cynological institute (a pretentious name for a dog shop). Like Švejk he was eventually drafted into the 91st Infantry Regiment where he was able to observe war at close hand. Many of the characters who appear in the book are named after those he met with in real life—Cpt Sagner, the Company Commander, Luv Lukas, the Lieutenant to whom he was personally devoted, as well as Lukas' batman, a Private called Straslipka.

But Švejk differs from Hašek in many respects too, and one above all. He appears to be a consummate idiot. 'And so they have killed off Ferdinand', is the comment with which the book begins. The words are addressed to him by Mrs Muller, who has been looking after him ever since he was discharged from the army for being a certified imbecile. She has just informed him of the assassination of the Archduke Franz Ferdinand in Sarajevo, the spark that ignites the Great War. 'I know two Ferdinands', Švejk tells her. 'One a messenger at Prusa's, the chemist's, who once drank a bottle of hair oil by mistake; the other Ferdinand Kokoska, who collects dog manure—neither of them would be any loss.' (*The Good Soldier Švejk*, 4). There are many scenes when

Hašek is forcing himself to make Švejk more stupid than he naturally is, and this perhaps is one of them. But the conversation sets the tone of the whole novel. Later, we will feel we know Švejk better than Hašek does himself (we see through his idiocies and find the ironies in his conversations with officers). But here we must take the story at face value. 'Take that idiotic expression off your face', demands a Police officer. 'I can't help it', he replies. 'I was discharged from the Army for idiocy, and officially certified by a Special Commission as an idiot. I'm an official idiot', he says, not exactly defiantly but not without pride (*The Good Soldier Švejk*, 120).

He is always reducing officers to tears with his homely analogies, and his habit of simplifying all life to the narrow social circle in which he moves. But Švejk is not as stupid as he looks. His idiocy is protection against an insane world that is fighting an insane war. Švejk falls foul of a Kafkaesque world that is forever locking him up—on one occasion for being a spy and on another for being a Russian soldier because he happens to don an abandoned Russian uniform to see his own reflection in the water. When asked to explain why he has not immediately owned up to the deception he replies that no one had asked him the question directly. All the questions have been:

> Do you admit that you voluntarily and without any pressure put on an enemy uniform? Since this was true, how could the answer be anything else but 'yes'—

> 'The fellow's a complete imbecile', said the General to the Major. 'Only a bloody idiot would put on a Russian uniform left on the dam of a lake by goodness knows whom and then get himself drafted into a party of Russian prisoners.'

> 'Humbly report, sir!' Švejk said. 'You're right, sir. I do sometimes notice myself that I'm feeble minded.' (*The Good Soldier Švejk*, 716).

We suspect before long it is all an elaborate ploy. For every time Švejk drags out his own existence by getting the authorities—Judge-Advocates, sergeants, police inspectors, all officers of state, to run senseless and time-consuming investigations into his conduct so his arrival at the Front is forever delayed.

And he is not quite the idiot he likes to be seen as. His brother is a school master and he himself has an encyclopaedic knowledge, if of a rather restricted scope. He can converse about St Augustine and has a ready wit when it comes to all things religious, calling a catechism, 'a

Baedecker for spiritual pastors.' (*The Good Soldier Švejk*, 141). He can quote Czech poets like Vrchlický as well as snippets from Shakespeare, ending a ghost story about a station master with the reflection, 'you see, there are more things in heaven and earth than are dreamt of in our philosophy.' (*The Good Soldier Švejk*, 227). And he can be witty when he wants to be. 'How long do you think the war will go on, Švejk?' he is asked. 'Fifteen years', he answers. 'That's obvious, because once there was a Thirty Years' War and now we're twice as clever as they were before, so it follows that thirty divided by two is fifteen.' (*The Good Soldier Švejk*, 739). The German Field Marshall von Moltke, when asked by the Kaiser what the next European war would look like, prophetically responded. 'The Thirty Years' War compressed into four.'

But then again, Švejk is not a particularly admirable figure. He believes in nothing in particular, and even his subversive humour can be interpreted as a lack of moral courage to stand up for what he believes, perhaps because he really does believe in nothing at all. He is not a man who makes sacrifices. He has the typical peasant's cunning that would have come in useful in every war in which peasants were conscripted or press-ganged or forced to join up by their masters, but the war in which he serves is an industrialised one, and soldiers from the cities had a class consciousness as well a rudimentary education (many could read and write and even those who couldn't could think for themselves).

If Švejk has no apparent political or moral convictions, he makes up for it (in the eyes of his admirers) by his undoubted zest for life and kindness towards most of the men he encounters. His human feelings come through time and again, for instance in spending all his money on giving a fellow soldier a drink or two, which leads him to a series of misdemeanours after missing his train and being forced to walk to Budjevoic on foot. He cries during a sermon in which a military chaplain has told the enlisted men that God is supremely merciful but only to decent people and not to scum like them. Švejk confesses that he cried only because he suspected the chaplain needed to discover at least one reformed sinner, and there were none in the congregation that day. 'Humbly report, sir ... my intentions are always the best ... just like the martyr there in the picture' (a sly reference to an unknown saint gazing open mouthed while Roman soldiers are sawing through his buttocks) (*The Good Soldier Švejk*, 89). He also has the useful capacity of getting others to like him, though the long-suffering Lieutenant Lukas has a love-hate relationship with Švejk. At one point he admits to himself that he may speak drivel, but he himself just happens to serve it up in a different form. (*The Good Soldier Švejk*, 170). Later, Lukas' superior, Colonel Schroeder, also takes a liking to our hero, and to Lukas' dismay makes him a company orderly.

The only person who does not warm to him is the incompetent and truly idiotic Lieutenant Dub, in civil life a schoolmaster (one imagines not dissimilar from the one who encourages Paul Baümer and his friends to join up in Remarque's *All Quiet on the Western Front*). Schoolmaster or not, he is none too bright. Dub, after Lukas, is the most finely drawn character of the supporting cast. He is always provoked by Švejk's look of serene complacency to shout, 'Do you know me? You don't know me yet', invariably adding: 'You may perhaps know me for the good side, but wait till you know me for the bad side … do you know me? … but I tell you, you don't know me … but wait till you get to know me.' (*The Good Soldier Švejk*, 526). Such is his credo, and any soldier reading the book will recognise the type at once.

Švejk's treatment of him borders on insolence, but he can never be quite caught out. 'Breathe on me', roars Dub, who suspects him of being drunk.

> Švejk breathed out on him the whole storehouse of his lungs, like a hot wind carrying to the field the fragrance of the distillery.
>
> 'And what do you smell of, you bastard?'
>
> 'Humbly report, I smell of rum.'
>
> 'And so you see, you bloody scoundrel', Lieutenant Dub called out triumphantly. 'I've got you at last!'
>
> 'Yes, sir', said Švejk without any sign of disturbance. 'We've just drawn our rations of rum for the coffee, and I had drunk the rum first. If, sir, there's a new order that the coffee should be drunk first and the rum afterwards, then please excuse me, it won't happen again.' (*The Good Soldier Švejk*, 587).

At one point Dub even threatens him with a gun, so moved is he to anger. He dreams of bringing him before a wartime Court Martial, but we know he will always fail in his ambition.

Hašek is always careful to remind us that Švejk is clever enough to have recognised from the beginning that, for the military high command, enlisted men are merely cannon fodder. An army doctor at the

beginning of the tale tries to send them off to battle with a few patriotic injunctions—urging inspiration in the example of Radetsky and
Prince Eugene so that their blood will help 'fertilise the vast fields of
glory of the monarchy and victoriously accomplish the task to which
history had pre-destined them.' (*The Good Soldier Švejk*, 77–78). Later
the young doctor is told by a more seasoned officer that even Radest-
sky or Eugene would have been unable to make soldiers out of 'bastards like them.' At one point Švejk attempts to console some men by
reminding them what Lieutenant Zimmen had told him, that if they
are killed their bones will not rot in vain; they will be able to make a
kilo of bone charcoal from each of them. 'You pack of swine', Zimmen
had told Švejk's comrades, '…you haven't an inkling of how useful
you're going to be to your descendants after your death.' When Švejk
asks whether the bone charcoal made out of officers will be worth
more than that made out of the other ranks, he gets three days' solitary
confinement for his insolence.

The Good Soldier Švejk, for all its comic elements, captures the experience of war as a relentless force that drives everyone to destruction.
In the *Iliad*, at least everyone knows the cause of the war—the need to
restore Menelaus' honour and that of his kin, and to punish those who
had dishonoured both. But by the twentieth century honour had
become credibility—stripped of its existential core, it became instrumentalised; out went glory and reputation, in came respect very nar-
rowly conceived as the power to get another to acknowledge its right
to exist. And the state's credibility is an abstract force quite detached
from the real world in which Švejk and his conscripted companions live
their ordinary lives. They go to the Front like most others without
knowing why, and what is more shocking, without wanting to know.
In *The Three Soldiers*, John Dos Passos also looked at the effect of a
bureaucratic war machine on the lives of three American soldiers. Each
of the chapter titles describes a machine designed to condition them
and strip them of their individuality. 'Making the Mould' (the first
chapter) describes basic training; the last, 'Under the Wheels', relates to
their court martial for desertion. As one of the three soldiers remarks
ironically, 'I would love war much more if it wasn't for the army.'

But Hasek's novel is quite different; it is more political and central
European. It is at one with the nightmare world of Kafka's novels and
it is no coincidence that both Kafka and Hašek were Czech. In Kafka
the victims never find out why they are punished. K goes to his death

for a reason he cannot fathom: the land surveyor is persecuted by the Castle for reasons beyond his ken. 'Why am I here?' asked the Italian chemist Primo Levi when he arrived in Auschwitz, only to be told by a prison guard, 'There is no "why" here.' The millions who were sent to the Gulag by Stalin, the Jews sent to the death camps by the Nazis, or the men dispatched to the Front in both world wars, were often uncomprehending victims.

In the course of the century, writes Milan Kundera, war became indivisible, ambulant and everlasting ... 'the long desired unity of mankind'. The unity of mankind means, no escape from anyone, anywhere'. (Kundera, 2007, 11). Ordinary men have always been caught up in collective violence; they have always been the main victims of war, rarely uncaring but often unknowing. Švejk just happens to also be a citizen-soldier, and to be born a citizen in the twentieth century was to be born in uniform, and if you were particularly unlucky, to be monitored and supervised by an impersonal bureaucracy.

At one point Švejk is locked up for being a spy; all the local police stations are on the lookout for suspicious people. They have been given orders to ascertain the attitude of the local population. They have directives on how to converse with the local inhabitants and are required to complete a questionnaire about how they react to the war loans which have been issued, and another on the morale of the members of the local government. There are instructions on how to recruit paid denouncers and informers, and to obtain information on the contacts of people suspected of disloyalty to the regime. The Ministry of the Interior has even invented a complex series of grades for 'assessing political loyalty'; *ia, ib, ic, iia, iib, iic; iiia, iiib, iiic; iva, ivb, ivc*. The last *iv* meant in conjunction with *a* 'treason and the gallows'; with *b* 'internment'; with *c* 'keep under observation and behind bars'. The interrogator nevertheless meets his match in Švejk who sits through his interrogation quite impassively and even compliments the interrogator on the warmth of the prison. 'That's very cunning of him', remarks the Sergeant. 'He acts as though it didn't concern him and yet he knows that he is to be shot. That's character ... For that you need iron nerves, self-denial, firmness and enthusiasm.' (*The Good Soldier Švejk*, 259). All Švejk is trying to do (or so he claims) is to be reunited with his regiment at Budejovica.

Švejk adapts to the world around him by feigning idiocy, because he sees that the world is senseless. He survives by turning it into a joke, a pretty bleak joke of course, but one that is also peculiarly life-affirm-ing. Hašek's army is a giant bureaucracy and like all bureaucracies it has no soul. It is as alien to the old military virtues such as courage as Kafka's bureaucratic world of *The Castle* and *The Trial* is to the old political virtues such as integrity. Both deny those caught up in its embrace any dignity, and both are ultimately stupid because they have no rationale for their actions except the power of 'force'. The differ-ence between the two authors is that Kafka's characters embrace their fate (K shields his executioners from the eyes of the municipal police who might have saved him); Švejk refuses to embrace his. We must count him a survivor for that reason.

What is remarkable about Švejk is that he is the only character in this book who has no intellectual life. The novel is a triumph for Hašek's writing, but less perhaps for Švejk's character. He can be criticised either for having no moral convictions or for having no real backbone; he is not prey to any inner struggles, and he shows no moral growth in the course of the work. Indeed, he is as uncomplicated as Kafka's char-acters are complex; his world is as black and white as Kafka's is grey. Of course all this can be explained away by reference to Kafka's genius as a writer, and his psychological insight, but I think that there is another explanation. Kafka had a creed; Hašek did not.

> Man cannot live without a permanent trust in something indestructible in himself, though both the indestructible element and the trust may remain permanently hidden from him. (Bloom, 1996, 455).

Švejk has no real core persona for that reason. There is nothing really that the authorities can destroy, as they can in Kafka's charac-ters, and the humour that he shows is that of the prankster and prac-tical joker, an entertainer of the rank and file. Perhaps in the end it is the hollowness of his core that allows him to survive—he is actually only a comic version of Conrad's hollow men. But then perhaps we should also give him the benefit of the doubt. The world of the Austro-Hungarian army was authoritarian, not totalitarian. It was bureau-cratic, to be sure, but it was more unimaginative and unaccountable than wicked. It was not even particularly ill-meaning, unlike the differ-ent bureaucratic world that Joseph Heller's anti-hero Yossarian has to survive, as best he can. Švejk, because he is so uncomplicated, is more likeable than any of Kafka's characters and therefore deserves his reprieve. And he remains by far the most striking incarnation of the humorous sensibility that helps so many soldiers to struggle on when fate takes a turn for the worst. It is humour that no regime or army, however totalitarian or bureaucratic, can destroy. It is humour, at least for those fortunate enough to be spared death or maiming or war's psychological horrors, that constitutes the very centre of a soldier's indestructible self.

Yossarian: Defying the System
Catch-22, Joseph Heller

Catch-22 is often voted one of the greatest American novels of the twentieth century. It is the author's only real success as a novelist and probably will be the only one of his novels that will still be widely read in fifty years time. And Joseph Heller's limitations as a novelist are a feature of the story. It is a satire of war, though it has its moments of pathos. Some characters get killed; indeed most of those to whom we are introduced. But their fate often seems as inconsequential as their lives. They have no real interior life. Yossarian is an exception, though even he is inadequately rendered at times. He remains a bit of an enigma, even to himself. He is not a man we can warm to but we can respect him, especially when he deserts at the end—it is his most moral act.

There have been many attempts to ape Heller's work, to apply his dyspeptic irony to other wars (one thinks of James Blinn's not entirely successful take on the First Gulf War, *The Aardvark is Ready for War*). But all, however entertaining, merely underline Heller's originality. None of them achieve sufficient sharpness of focus, and none create a character quite like Yossarian. Kurt Vonnegut once claimed that he, Heller, James Jones and Irwin Shaw, who returned from the Second World War to tell their stories, wrote about war better than anyone else in the English-speaking world because 'we were on the edge of it.' The claim reminds me of Finnery's credo from Vonnegut's first novel, *Player Piano*: 'out on the edge you can see all kinds of things you can't see from the centre.' (Sumner, 2011, 284). And it is true that some of the great American writers have had very little experience of combat including Hemingway, most famously, and Norman Mailer who spent his months in the Pacific theatre as a filing clerk. Heller's experience was quite different. He enlisted in the US Army Corps in 1942 at the age of nineteen, and flew sixty combat missions as a B-25 bombardier. And this may well account for the success of the novel.

Heller tumbles one joke after another as the story descends downwards through betrayals, unnecessary deaths and a Rome that is not unlike Dante's Inferno. The comedy, if not quite as dark as this summary makes it sound, is sharp enough to be searing, and it is searing because it is based on his first hand experience. The turning point of the novel comes when Kid Samson, fooling around on a raft, is cut in two by a plane propeller. Here, Heller was recalling the daredevil flying stunts the pilots used to get into in Corsica, the island of Pianosa in the novel. Major Major is based on Dr John Campbell, who served as a real life major in the army. Heller's brush with death in August 1944 in the nose cone of a B-25 gave him a revelation that 'man was matter' (Daugherty, 2010). In other words, episodes in real life crowded his consciousness, and later conscience.

Yossarian's world is therefore real, but of course it is conveyed through satire, and satire works most effectively when it tries to transcend its own time. The novel was soon taken to be a critique of Vietnam though it appeared in 1961. It helped that there are anachronistic moments in the book—references to helicopters (already invented, but not in general use in the Second World War), and IBM computers (also invented in 1944, but not used until later). There is something to be said for the claim that the novel works best as a critique of the bureaucratic imagination that has been a feature of war since the early twentieth century, and which became much more so in Vietnam with its 'body counts' and computer modelling. But the air war in Europe twenty years earlier had its performance related targets too and its non-character specific judgements on the value of command. Major Major, after all, has been selected by an IBM computer with a sense of humour simply because of his first name.

At the heart of the novel is a proposition that was radical at the time: war is, frankly, absurd. It is not a comforting idea because not every war seems absurd; some are well worth fighting, though we find them more and more difficult to justify either to ourselves or others. We may have no intention of going out of the war business yet, but it is definitely becoming more difficult to keep the faith. Oscar Wilde once remarked that as long as war was considered wicked it would retain its appeal; once it was considered vulgar, its appeal would rapidly diminish. There are many acts of wickedness in war but the real wickedness is not to be attributed to pantomime villains or callous acts; these, being extreme, tell us little. The relationship is more complex and deeply rooted. What Heller suggests is that the wickedness of war is to be found in its logic, and in the case of the air campaign over Europe in the Second World War, that logic was deeply inimical to the lives of pilots and crew. It was a vehicle whose wheels were about to come off, and one should think of the characters who appear in *Catch-22* as some of the looser screws.

We first meet Yossarian in a hospital ward where he retreats whenever he feels in danger, complaining of an 'undiagnosed liver complaint'. He is a captain in the 256th Squadron based in Italy and, like Heller, a bombardier. He is a very frightened man. Outside the hospital there is a war going on and he has a passionate conviction that everyone is out to kill him. 'No one is trying to kill you', he is told. 'Then why are they shooting at me?' he asks. 'They're shooting at *everyone*... they're trying to kill everyone.' 'And what difference does that make', Yossarian responds bleakly.

It is one of the joys of the book that Heller spins the illogical absurdity of war which logic itself is unable to resolve. Yossarian is a child in an adult world, and like a child can see the Emperor's nakedness all too clearly. The passages in which he questions the madness around him are crucial to the novel. After all, he reasons, why does he have to die? History does not demand his premature demise; the justice of the cause will be satisfied without it. Men will die, of course, as a matter of necessity; *which* men will die is a matter of circumstance, and Yossarian is willing to be the victim of everything but circumstance.

In another of his many attempts to be sent home he confronts Major Major. 'I'm afraid', he tells him. 'We're all afraid', Major responds. 'Besides, would we want to see America lose the war?' 'We won't lose', Yossarian rejoins. Ten million men in uniform could replace him. 'Let somebody else get killed.' 'But suppose everybody on our side felt that way?' 'Then I'd certainly be a damned fool to feel any other way, wouldn't I?' (*Catch-22*, 135). The much less sympathetic Major Sanderson reprimands him for being immature and for entertaining a deep-seated survival anxiety, He has an unhealthy aversion to dying; an irrational dislike of bigots and bullies; a perverse objection to the idea of being exploited, degraded or deceived. 'It wouldn't surprise me if you were a manic depressive!' (*Catch-22*, 384–385). Yossarian is not a manic depressive, of course, and he is not crazy. It is just that he has recognised, rather late in the day, that he is surrounded by crazy, and sometimes very bad people, and he is not prepared to allow his 'self-hood' to be extinguished simply because they have surrendered theirs. Heller is not saying that every war is absurd. He is merely telling us that Yossarian has found himself trapped in an absurd situation.

There are plenty of examples of the greatest fear of all soldiers; that war may become absolute the longer it goes on, and that its only rationale may become its own perpetuation. Bomber crews are asked to put themselves at risk in bombing villages to delay German rein-forcements at a time when the allies are not even planning an offensive. Worse still they are put at risk so that they can produce General Peck-em's bomb patterns, a term he has dreamed up, but which soon takes on a life of its own. It means nothing, Peckem is the first to admit, but it shows that the war is still generating new thinking. 'You'd be sur-prised at how rapidly it's caught on. Why, I've got all sorts of people convinced I think it's important for the bombs to explode in neat aer-ial photographs.' (*Catch-22*, 411). And always in the foreground is what made the novel famous from the beginning: Catch-22. A doctor can ground pilots if they are crazy but they have to ask him first. If they ask him they are clearly not crazy since it is no mark of madness to avoid death. That *is* the Catch. What is the punishment for coward-ice? Court martial. What is cowardice? The fear of death. Wherever he turns Yossarian is confronted by the absurd logic of modern warfare. 'That's some Catch, that Catch-22', he observed. '"It's the best there is", Don Daneeka agreed.' (*Catch-22*, 62–63). It doesn't actually exist, of course, but that hardly matters; everyone thinks it does, and that is worse for there is no text to refute, criticise, amend, rip to shreds or burn. And as the number of missions continues to be raised, so Yossar-ian's crew becomes more listless, drifting around like useless men in a depression, 'moving sideways like crabs, waiting for orders to return from the 27th Air Force, knowing from bitter experience that the num-ber of missions might be raised at any time ...'

Flying bomber missions was the most dangerous job in the Allied Forces, on a par with serving in a U-Boat for German submariners. Yossarian cares enough for himself and his fellow crew members to insist on flying in an unorthodox fashion. He is not the best bombar-dier (he is not the best at anything, except complaining). The best bombardiers fly straight and level all the way to their targets, giving the German gunners below time enough 'to set their sights and take their aim and pull their triggers or lanyards, or switches, or whatever the hell they did pull when they wanted to kill people they didn't know.' (*Catch-22*, 42). Yossarian's crewmates love him because whenever they go on a bombing mission he makes sure that their plane comes barrelling in over a target from all directions and at every height, climbing and diving and twisting and turning so steeply and sharply that the pilots of the accompanying planes have difficulty staying in formation. Yossarian has decided to live forever, or die in the attempt. But he is a problem for the high command because for them living forever is not an option, any more than living very long.

Our response to the novel depends to an extent on whether it is more than just a satire, whether it conveys a real truth. It is certainly unsparing in its depiction of the air war; pilots get killed and emotions frayed. And Heller does not spare the reader some of the sights he witnessed himself, such as planes 'threading their swift way through the swollen masses of new and old bursts of flak like rats racing in a pack through their own droppings', or in falling out of the sky in flames, 'spiralling down slowly in wide, tremulous, narrowing circles ... billowing gigantically like a monstrous blood-red star.' (*Catch-22*, 194). And he does not spare the sight of the survivors who do make it back, so badly burned that they are often unrecognisable. Like the airman in the next hospital bed to Yossarian who we encounter early on, a man without a name, constructed entirely of gauze, plaster and a thermometer: 'like an unrolled bandage with a hole in it, or like a broken block of stone in a harbour with a crooked zinc pipe gutting out.' (*Catch-22*, 214–15).

At one point in the novel the Air Force decides to conduct educational sessions two nights a week, which the men subvert by asking questions like, 'who is Spain?', 'why is Hitler?', and 'when is right?'. But Yossarian asks the most subversive question of all, 'where are the Snowdons of yesteryear?', a reference to a colleague who has been killed in a raid over Avignon, and it is Snowdon's death which is recounted almost at the very end of the novel in the most poignant passage of all, in horrifying detail.

> Yossarian was cold ... and shivering uncontrollably. He felt goose pimples clacking all over him as he gazed down despondently at the grim secret that Snowdon had spilled all over the messy floor. It was easy to read the mes-

sage in his entrails. Man was matter, that was Snowdon's secret. Drop him out of a window and he will fall. Set fire to him and he will burn. Bury him and he will rot, like other kinds of garbage. The spirit gone, man is garbage. That was Snowdon's secret. Ripeness was all. (*Catch-22*, 554).

If *Catch-22* is framed by anything in particular it is Snowdon's death. It haunts the novel from the moment Yossarian asks his question—'where are the Snowdons of yesteryear?'—and it ends the novel, as we learn the ghastly secret which Yossarian has discovered, that the human body is merely a fragile shell.

The problem with war in the third dimension was that the pilots died anonymous deaths. It is the plane's death, not the crew's, that is usually witnessed by their comrades. It is precisely because you cannot see the death of your friends that victimisation seems so vivid. What distinguishes the *Iliad* is the way in which Homer details the death of heroes with almost clinical rigour, like an autopsy report. In the space of just eighty-two lines we are told how eight soldiers meet their death at each other's hands, and we are told in exquisite detail; nothing is left to the imagination. Homer's reports from the front are graphic and at times tedious, and they lent themselves to parody even in the ancient world (particularly in Ovid's *Metamorphoses*, by which time the classical world had become more cynical). But the air war over Europe was a battle of machines. It is their fate which is chronicled (Tatum, 2003, 123).

Whenever they are ordered to fly another mission Yossarian as a bombardier finds himself trapped in a Plexiglas nose cone in an aircraft with twin rudders and engines and wide wings. The single fault of design is the tight crawl-way separating the bombardier from the nearest escape hatch. Yossarian longs to sit at the top of the escape hatch, his parachute already hooked to his harness, one fist clenching the red-handled ripcord, the other gripping the emergency hatch release that will spill him earthward into the air at the first sign that his plane is about to go down.

Like a film, a novel is both made and broken by its casting. If it is believable only because of the vividness of its characters, it would be difficult to believe. And Heller's figures are almost Dickensian in their grotesqueness: Doc Daneeka (one of Yossarian's few friends, who is terrified of grounding the men and releasing them from the 'Catch' for fear of being sent to the Pacific theatre); Major Major, who is not an unsympathetic man but is never in his office because of his fear of personal confrontation; and the odious Colonel Cathcart, whose first act after his predecessor is killed in a raid on Arezzo, is to raise the number of missions from twenty-five to thirty. They, too, are what war has made them, and they ring true enough. Yossarian is defined by his responses and reactions to these other characters. They may all be absurd, but they serve to remind Yossarian that war produces a madness of its own. Heller's eccentrics are a vivid reminder of the enemy aircrews fear the most: not the enemy over the bomb line, shooting away at you as your plane passes overheard, but the rear echelon officers who have put you in the plane to get shot at.

Take Major Major, an ineffectual, if well-meaning, officer born too late for the physical well-being of his mother and who is too mediocre for the well-being of his men. His father had christened him 'Major'— rejecting the other excellent substitutes, Drum Major, or Major Minor, or Sergeant Major, or C Sharp Major. He is a docile man, easily put upon by others, as he is put upon by life. In the base on Pianosa, he is ignored by his equals and bullied by his superiors. All he wishes to do is to conform, to be absorbed into the unit, and every time he stands out as a squadron commander for not being what others want him to be, his predecessor, Maj. Duluth. It is precisely because he retires into his own cocoon that he is never available to see his men. And when he is not in his office, he cannot be asked to consider sending any of them home. Yossarian really does have no other recourse than to report sick from time to time and seek sanctuary in the hospital.

And then there is Milo Minderbinder, perhaps the greatest comic creation of all, who runs an export-import business syndicate called 'M & M Enterprises', the letters standing for Milo and Minderbinder to nullify any impression that the syndicate is a one-man operation. Minderbinder wants to put war on a businesslike basis. He flies surplus army supplies and in the spirit of modern capitalism gives his fellow soldiers nominal shares in his ever-expanding empire. Unlike Lehman Brothers, M&M Enterprises is too big to fail. When he finally over-extends himself the US government has to step in and rescue him from financial ruin. But Minderbender is a dangerous man. He removes the parachutes from planes to sell them on, as well as the morphine from First Aid kits. Milo almost gets Yossarian's friend, Orr, killed when his plane crashes in the sea and his life jackets fail to inflate because he has removed the twin carbon-dioxide cylinders from the inflating chambers to make the strawberry and crushed-pineapple ice-cream sodas he serves in the officers' mess.

Other characters are much truer to life, like Lieutenant Sclhiesskopf, an ROTC graduate, an ambitious and humourless man with poor eyesight and a chronic sinus problem which keeps him out of combat. He loves military life, especially the parades with their yellow and red pennants awarded to the best cadet. To Yossarian, the idea of pennants as prizes is, of course, absurd. What is the point of an award if it comes with no money or pass privileges? And Yossarian, as to be expected, hates parades; he hates hearing them, seeing them, being trapped in traffic by them, and most of all, he hates having to take part.

And finally there is Colonel Cathcart, Yossarian's nemesis, a slick, slipshod, unhappy man of thirty-six, who wants to be a general and never makes the cut. Heller describes him as a swashbuckling, beefy, conceited man, proud that he was a full colonel at such an early age but also disappointed that he is already thirty-six and still only a full colonel. He lives by his wits, oscillating hourly between anguish and exhilaration. Cathcart is the enemy not because he believes what he says, that the men of his outfit are ten missions better than any other, but precisely because he does not. And it is both the posturing and the war that is to blame in equal measure. As a commander, Cathcart can succeed only by outperforming other commanders and it is Cathcart, of course, who in the end will turn out to be the most deadly enemy of all.

For when Yossarian learns that his friend Nately has been killed in a crash over Spezia, he refuses to fly any more missions. In an attempt to silence him, Cathcart dispatches him to Rome for a few days of rest and recuperation. Yossarian is later arrested by MPs for not having a pass, and returned to base, where he is told he can go home, although—inevitably—there is another 'catch'. He cannot be sent home for refusing to fly, leaving the rest of the men behind. Instead, he will be promoted to Major, given a medal for his 'deep and abiding loyalty to the outfit', and then recalled to work as a Public Relations Officer. The catch is that he will have to praise Cathcart as the inspiring officer he is not. If he refuses to do so, he will be court-martialled.

And it is at this point that Yossarian finally comes though for his comrades. He knows they will be easy enough for Cathcart to discipline and control once he has gone. Instead, he determines to desert rather than fall in with the Colonel's plan. He has often dreamed of deserting—to sanctuaries such as Majorca, or Spain, or Switzerland where American flyers could be interned for the duration of the war. He had become in time the squadron's leading authority on internment and now only awaits the piece of flak that would knock out the engine of his plane and provide him with the excuse for heading over the Italian Alps to a long, extended Swiss vacation. He dreams most of all, however, of escaping to Sweden where he can swim nude with beautiful girls, with low, demurring voices, and sire happy, undisciplined tribes of illegitimate Yossarians that the state will assist and launch into life without stigma (*Catch-22*, 392–3). But Sweden is out of reach, or so he had thought. For he is finally told by the chaplain that his friend, Orr, who everyone had thought was dead, had managed to actually make it to Sweden by rowing there in a dinghy, paddling through the Straits of Gibraltar at night. Yossarian chooses to follow him. If he insists on being reprimanded for refusing to fly more than fifty missions he will be court-martialled. But he will give those who fled an excuse to refuse to fly any more. The Air Force could never find so many inexperienced replacement crews without an investigation. Cathcart will be caught in his own trap.

In fact, he is offered no real choice. For an official report has already been drawn up, claiming that he was involved in an extensive black market operation, involving the sale of military assets to the enemy. Yossarian chooses to desert rather than be tried on a fake charge, or return to the US and act the role Cathcart demands of him. In the preface Heller wrote to the 1994 edition of the novel he added that because of the movie version, even close readers of the novel had a lasting image of him paddling towards freedom in a yellow inflated lifeboat. In the novel we never see him make it that far. At the end of *Closing Time*, the disappointing sequel Heller wrote a few years before his death, we find him still alive forty years later, still wishing to live forever. 'Everyone has to go', his physician friend reminds him in the novel. 'Everyone!' So Yossarian does escape the war in one piece. It seems to me that Heller was right to leave the novel so open-ended. Sweden may indeed by an impossible dream, a country too far, almost a Utopia but I think Heller is right to cut him some slack. It is not necessarily a happy ending, either. War has such survivors. We meet them time and again in literature, as in real life. Yossarian is positively Falstaffian in his wish to live. Neither are willing, if they can help it, to let their various enemies extinguish the flame of life. And both are larger than life figures because of it. We cheer on both not because they get the better of their enemies (Prince Hal wins, and so in a way does Cathcart), but because they get the better of war. Falstaff ends up a broken man, of course, but not because of war, rather because of the fickleness and hypocrisy of kings. Yossarian lives on into an old age which is not especially heroic. Neither story ends up happily for either character, but Yossarian is a different hero from a different age, and so we must take it on its terms, not ours.

My favourite minor character in the novel is the wicked old man (as Heller calls him) who Yossarian finds in conversation with Nately when he visits a Roman brothel. Wicked and depraved he may be, sitting on a musty blue armchair 'like some Satanic and hedonistic deity on a throne, a stolen US army blanket wrapped around his spindly legs, aged 107 (or so he claims)', but he does have the best lines in the novel. America will lose the war and Italy win it, he opines. The Germans are being driven out and the Americans, too, will leave eventually. Italian soldiers (probably 'second to all') are no longer dying, while German and American soldiers are dying on their behalf. The problem, he goes on to opine, is that America puts so much stock in winning wars; the real trick lies in losing them, and knowing which wars to lose. Victory gives countries an insane delusion of grandeur. 'Now, we are losing again, everything has taken a turn for the better. And besides, with so many countries fighting in the war, they can't all be worth dying for, can they?' 'Anything worth living for', replies Nately, 'is worth dying for'. 'And anything worth dying for', rejoins the sacrilegious old man, 'is certainly worth living for.' (*Catch-22*, 314).

This kind of cynicism became fashionable in the Vietnam era and it is still in fashion in some circles today. But it was not Heller's philosophy. Towards the end of his life he confessed that he had actually enjoyed the war, and he certainly saw the Second World War, as did most of his contemporaries, as a 'good' war. It is not Yossarian's philosophy either. He has flown the missions the Air Force expects of its pilots. It is Cathcart, not the high command, who arbitrarily raises the number of missions the men have to fly before being relieved from combat—from forty-five to seventy to eighty in the course of the novel. Yossarian also keeps faith with his friends. When he learns of Nately's death he is inconsolable with grief—'like Achilles', Colonel Corn sneers, so pleased with the simile that he files a mental reminder to repeat it the next time he finds himself in General Peckham's presence

(*Catch-22*, 495). The old man speaks for a different generation than the young men fighting the war. He may know more than they do, but he understands less. Cynicism, in fact, is no part of Yossarian's character.

Catch-22 is about much more than the question of Yossarian's personal survival. It is about the nature of survival itself, and the point Heller is making is germane to all wars, and provides an insight into the traumas, psychological and emotional, that it produces. If one is put constantly at risk there can only be two responses, or two ways of alleviating anxiety: death or psychotic breakdown. Many of Yossarian's colleagues escape into death in the course of the novel. Others come up with their own survival strategies, all of them crazy or psychotic, all of them far more selfish than Yossarian's, and more dangerous for those around them. Doc Danneka appears to be a sympathetic figure until we discover that he has made a private pact. What he fears most is being sent off to the war in the Pacific; to avoid it, he will not allow any airman to return home before his quota of missions has been met for fear of alienating Cathcart and being punished. Cathcart, too, has only his own survival in mind. He appears to be a career officer, anxious to make his name in the *Saturday Evening Post*, but his craving for publicity is a survival strategy as well. It would buy him recognition and thus make it difficult for him to be replaced. And he is deeply anxious about annoying the officers higher up in the chain of command. His own survival is purchased at the expense of those he commands. As with every other senior officer in the novel, survival means aspiring to reach the top, the safest place to be. As Lieutenant-Colonel Corn, Cathcart's own nemesis, puts it, 'everyone teaches us to aspire to higher things. A general is higher than a colonel, and a colonel is higher than a lieutenant-colonel. So we are both aspiring.'

And the principal message of the novel is that, in order to survive, nearly everyone has to sell their soul. Cathcart and Corn both do, and so does Daaneka. Yossarian doesn't. He saves his soul by choosing to desert. Sidney Hook put it best: 'The man who declares that survival at all costs is the end of existence is morally dead because he is prepared to sacrifice all other values which give life meaning.' The critic Robert Brustein quoted this passage in his famous 1961 review of the novel, which is still considered by many to be definitive. What we admire and soldiers today often envy about characters such as Achilles and Falstaff, he wrote, are their sheer irresponsibility. They owe allegiance only to themselves, and their own sense of what is right. They are not on contract to anyone, not the army, or the state or even a military unit. But since the rise of the nation-state the military has grown hostile to 'Falstaffian irresponsibility'. It is not a bad description, I feel, of Yossarian's own personal act of defiance. (Brustein, 2001). For his obsessive concern for survival makes him one of the most morally vibrant figures in modern literature.

Ultimately, Yossarian asserts 'the freedom to *be*' in a world dominated by cruelty, carnage, and inhumanity. Heller, in short, came up with a new morally based idea—the morality of refusal. It is that refusal which goes back to the beginning, to the Ur text, to the *Iliad* and Achilles' refusal to betray his own code of honour. Achilles refuses for a time to re-join the fight (though when Patroclus dons his armour the reader often misses an important Homeric touch: Achilles urges him to hurry. He too is not a moral isolationist). Yossarian, on the other hand, leaves on his own terms. Neither is desertion as the term has been traditionally understood. Both men from very different historical eras refuse to accept defeat but neither, of course, is victorious. The military always wins in the end.

Kien: Survivor Guilt

The Sorrow of War, Bao Ninh

On the banks of Ya Co Crong Pocco River in the Central Highlands of Vietnam, the Missing in Action (MIA) body-collecting team awaits the dry season of 1976. The mountain and jungles are water-soaked day and all night. The water steams produce a sea of greenish vapour over the jungle's carpet of rolling leaves. 'They are forgotten by peace, damaged or impassable; all the tracks disappearing bit by bit, day by day, into the embrace of the coarse undergrowth and wild grasses' (*The Sorrow of War*, 1). So begins Bao Ninh's *The Sorrow of War* which first appeared in 1991 and was translated into English three years later. The author served with the Glorious 27th Youth Brigade. Of the 500 men who went to war with him in 1969, only ten survived. *The Sorrow of War* was his first novel. Because of censorship it was not published in Vietnamese until ten years after its publication in English, a telling commentary on how even a 'victorious' nation can find little solace in a surviving soldier's uncompromising memories of war.

Vietnam produced a rare kind of story, half-memoir, half-fiction. The most famous example is Tim O'Brien's *The Things They Carried*. One of its characters, Mitchell Sanders, likes to tell stories, to pin down the final and definitive truth, though he is always failing. He likes to find the moral of the stories he tells, or the stories told by other people, and never succeeds in finding them—perhaps, adds O'Brien, because there is no moral to find. If there is a moral, it will not be good. What does he mean by this? Many things, but one is that even heroes are not untouched by evil and are grimly aware of its depth. And rarely are enemies beyond the reach of compassion. It is the knowledge, perhaps, that war is rooted in the bitter and inarguable experience of being human. For the common soldier, at least, there is no clarity in war— the old rules are no longer binding, the old truths no longer true. The only certainty is overwhelming ambiguity. 'In war, you love your sense of the definite, hence your sense of truth itself, and so it's safe to say that in a true war story, nothing is ever absolutely true.' (*The Sorrow of War*, 78).

Bao Ninh's novel has often been compared to O'Brien's but the differences are more interesting than the similarities, the same point that Tolstoy makes for unhappy families in *Anna Karenina*. O'Brien's characters make it back to the US, albeit it sometimes as damaged individuals. The hero of Bao Ninh's tale is very different. For Kien, to have survived when so many friends did not is one of the sorrows of war. Survival itself is a kind of defeat. In Kien, we have one of the most striking characters of any Vietnam War novel, so different from the more familiar characters who appear in the American frictional representations of the war. Kien's suffering is distinctive both to the man and his society, and there are at least three differences from the American representation of the Vietnam war which are worth dwelling on.

In the first place, there is the response to the war itself. Paul Fussell calls the style of the Vietnam War itself half-ironic, half-subversive. With Tolstoy and the modern sensibility irony became a feature of war writing but in Vietnam, irony became even more subversive. The sarcastic tendency, he adds, made the war more than a modern one; in its style, at least, it was history's first 'post-modern' conflict. It was imbued with a self-consciousness bordering on a contempt for the very medium, war itself. And that, it seems to me, is a distinctive feature of many Vietnam War novels, and their chief characters who are defeated as much by the times as by the violence (the cynical misleading of the press by officers at press briefings; the business techniques and management style—when soldiers desecrated bodies they would often leave behind their 'business cards'. One American vehicle was neatly painted 'Vietnam: Love It or Leave It') (Fussell, 1991, 655).

Even the terms of engagement differed significantly. The average age of the American soldier in Vietnam was nineteen; Kien's comrades in arms were often younger (Kien joins up at seventeen), and the length of service was quite different. Usually it was twelve months for an American soldier (only part of which was spent in a combat zone); if you were Vietnamese, you could find yourself at war for the duration. And unlike many American soldiers who could find no sense in the war—their lives were, in the common parlance of the time, quite literally 'wasted'—the young Vietnamese tended to soldier on inspired at least to begin with by a mixture of *dukkha* (Buddhist suffering) and Marxist zeal. It is the absence of politics in the typical Vietnam war book (at least in conversation between men) and its presence in Bao Ninh's novel that is so striking. 'Politics continuously; politics in the morning, politics in the afternoon, politics again in the evening.' (*The Sorrow of War*, 5). The Vietnamese lived and breathed politics, at least in the early years of the 'struggle'. 'But you and I, we went off to fight for an ideal', reminds one of the characters in Duong Thu Huong's *Novel Without a Name* (1995), but another cuts him short: 'Words are like everything else in life. They are born, they live, they age, they die.' (Huong, 1995, 161). Kien's generation soon lost their faith but not their courage.

The Sorrow of War is not only an indictment of war, it is even more an indictment of Marxism not so much as a philosophy than as a political religion. Indeed, Marxism owed a large debt to Christianity in secularising the doctrine of Providence, converting the belief in salvation into a metaphysical historicism, a substitute religion, if you will, that became the faith of those whose scepticism was not vigorous enough to dispense with religion altogether. Communism was also definitively Christian in its themes (in its opposition between Free Will [liberty] and Pre-destination [history]). Not even God was absent from the text; history assumed his functions, if not his face, with one critical difference. Unlike the Christian God, history did not assume a human form. And it is their betrayal by History (in the form of the Marxist dialectic) that informs Bao Ninh's novel. For neither he nor his friends find any personal redemption through their personal experiences. They have fought for a new society, and started out with many hopes only to become disillusioned:

> Our history-making efforts for the great generations have been to no avail … from the horizon of the distant past an immense sad wind gusts and blows through the cities, through the villages, and through my life. (*The Sorrow of War*, 89).

Of course, this experience of disillusionment is present in most wars. Most wars are 'ironic' in the sense that they are much worse than the soldiers have been led to expect. And frequently they are disappointing in their outcome. Victory, after all, is rarely conclusive. But the truly ironic note in Kien's reminiscence is that despite eventual victory the socialist order had not been forged and humanity was not redeemed; indeed, for the North Vietnamese, the glorious socialist future had not lasted very long. At one point, Kien thinks of his life as a sampan drifting upstream towards the past. 'The future lied to us, there long ago in the past. There is no new life, no new era …'

> He discovered he was happier when looking into the past; his path to life which he had once assumed would be towards a beautiful future had done a U-turn and taken him backwards into the murky darkness of the hard times his homeland had experienced. Happiness seemed to lie in the past. The older he grew, the rosier the past looked to him. (*The Sorrow of War*, 42).

In short, Kien has a much more complex inner life than most of the characters in American fiction because he comes from a more complex (if brutal) world. Or, to put it differently, his inner and outer life are fused (war is peace, and peace is war) as they were not for most Americans. But something more is involved. For Kien this is not an expeditionary war, but a total one. Most Americans could return home and pick up what was left of their lives. Frequently they returned to a society that dishonoured them as 'baby killers'; but the draft dodgers and flag burners were often unconsciously envious of an older generation which had lived to serve something which had been worthy of service. The Second World War had been the 'good' war; Vietnam simply wasn't. George McGovern's message 'Come home, America' was a call for salvation to save the soul of the nation. Frances Fitzgerald, whose Pulitzer Prize work *Fire in the Lake* (1971) became *the* text of the anti-war generation was followed by another called *America Revisited*.

For Kien there was a Home Front, too, but the situation could not have been more different. Whenever he returns home on leave he finds a city under siege. The windows of the buildings are boarded up; notes are left pinned on doors informing returning soldiers where their families can be found. And always there is the constant threat of being bombed if they travel by rail. Some of the most graphic scenes of the novel are not set in the war zone at all, but in the North Vietnamese countryside, and its cities. 'The bodies lay scattered all around ... Kien began stepping through the bodies as though it were an everyday event for him ... This was his new-found strength, to stay cool under fire.' (*The Sorrow of War*, 196). Tellingly, of course, he comes under fire at home, and under fire from the air (something which American soldiers never experienced).

At the end of the conflict Kien and the surviving members of his brigade return home, too, but for them there are also no trumpets, no drums, no music. The general population is as indifferent to the veterans as the American public was often hostile to its own. The authorities, far from congratulating the soldiers, cynically searched them for loot. And the country they returned to was devastated—pock-marked by American bombs from the day- and night-time visitations of the B52s. Post-war Hanoi was the scene of 'unbroken monotonous suffering'. The citizens were united in the shared loneliness of poverty. There were some joys, but 'those images blinked on and off like cheap flashing lights in a shop window.' (*The Sorrow of War*, 138).

In a strange way it is easier to identify today with Kien's world than with that of many American novelists which now seem somewhat 'dated'. There are (and will be) no more draftees sent off to fight expeditionary wars. But the enemies in the battle-zones into which we send our own professional soldiers—in the streets of Tikrit and Fallujah, and in provinces like Helmand in Afghanistan—are often young men like Kien, ordinary men (and women) who find themselves in extraordinary circumstances. For them, the Home Front is the only front; they are fighting for the duration, too.

My final observation is that Bao Ninh's novel differs from most comparable American works and is all the stronger because its subject matter is not confined to war. 'Is it too much to predict that (it) will become the *All Quiet on the Western Front*?' asked a critic in *The New Statesman*. This entirely misses the point. Where Remarque's novel is about war, pure and simple, Bao Ninh's tale is a love story, a book about more than lost youth and lost illusions. It is a book about lost love. The original title was *The Destiny of Love*. It was its Australian transcriber who gave it the title by which it is now known. Tolstoy's *War and Peace*, too, is a novel about love as well as war. Who can forget Natasha's anguished question on hearing of Prince Andrei's death. 'Where is he, and who is he now?' (I quote John Bayley's suggested literal translation, which brings the anguish home more poignantly than most English translations).

Kien's love interest is a girl called Phuong whom he first meets at school. They survive the disapproval of the Communist state and their teachers; they dare to defy the 'three Don'ts' which forbade sex, love or marriage among young people. Love affairs for 10th formers were regarded as disgracefully unpatriotic (*The Sorrow of War*, 121). Much of the novel is a haunting story of a love that can never be recaptured. And what makes the war so terrible for Kien is the discovery that war pays for all the suffering and loss with more suffering and loss.

Many American soldiers suffered emotionally, too. They also returned to find their girlfriends had married, or moved on. Married men returned too shattered to make a go of their own marriages. O'Brien paints a picture that will be familiar to many returning soldiers, the inability to tell stories to the folks back home. 'The war was over and there was no place in particular to go' is how the story *Speaking of Courage* opens in *The Things they Carried* (O'Brien, 2009, 131). One of the characters returns to the town in which he had been born and spent much of his youth. But his friends had moved on and were living in Des Moines, or Sioux City, or going to school somewhere else, or holding down jobs. The high school girls were either gone or married, and the lake had drowned his best friend, Max, at least keeping him out of the war. But Kien's plight is different again. For on the home 'front' Phuong has had to survive first a rape, and then the material deprivations that war brought, and then the American bombing, unrelenting in its ferocity. And she has done so by turning to prostitution and taking up with any man who would keep her. Their love is rekindled briefly when Kien returns from the war, but it does not last long. As Phuong tells him, she is a dark chapter in his life, and with that, she passes out of it forever.

The book is above all about the ghosts of comrades long dead and departed, and Kien lives among them all the time, the ghosts of the dead floating alongside the sides of incinerated animals, in a slipstream whose surface water is rust-coloured from their blood. Kien is more superstitious than the average American soldier—the North Vietnamese have their ancestors, the Americans do not. And in Vietnamese society, the dead are not truly dead. The area in which Kien has to recover the dead bodies is called 'the Jungle of Screaming Souls' after the dead of the Lost 27th Battalion, which is almost totally wiped out in an American strike. He is posted to an MIA team charged with gathering the remains of the dead from the worst battlefields in the Central Highlands, uncovering fallen soldiers buried under a mantle of jungle, some who have been vaporised, or blasted into small pieces and liquidised into mud. They too, drag the sorrow of war into his life, giving him terrible nightmares.

Kien decides the only way he can survive is by writing a novel. It is his personal act of atonement; it is the last duty of a soldier, to expose the realities of war he has witnessed and unfairly survived; it is his own personal gift to the dead. It is a sacred undertaking and it is also his own separate peace, his spiritual act of defiance against an unforgiving regime for the spirits of those killed in the war still remain with him, 'beyond all the war's political consequences.' (*The Sorrow of War*, 57). In this act of expiation he constantly relives the war—cutting a lone and lonely figure in an untidy, cramped apartment with his hands numbed by cold and his lungs suffocating with cigarette smoke. It is the deaths he recalls most vividly—the deaths that provide the rhythm of his writing; those who had died in fire fights or in ambushes, or had been blown apart by helicopter gunships; those who were killed one at a time, or all together; those who were killed instantly or slowly bled to death. 'Kien's deaths had more shapes, colours and reality of atmosphere than anyone else's war stories. Kien's soldiers' stories came from beyond the grave and told of their lives beyond death.' (*The Sorrow of War*, 82). This too, is one of the sorrows of war, in some way similar to the sorrow of love—it is a kind of nostalgia.

And what gives Kien his peculiar authenticity is that his character is deliberately understated; he is, in part, also a ghost, an incomplete figure. The comrades he remembers as he writes his novel are all the more real for that; like his Scout, Phan, or his first commander, Kuang; they are believable because we learn so little about them. They are not anonymous, but they do not live off the page because they live so briefly on it.

In Kien's atonement for surviving there is a vital psychological insight which we can derive from Freud's writing on melancholia. The ghosts that haunt the pages of the novel are very real. They are a projection of Kien's survival guilt. And they haunt him relentlessly, draining him of the will to live, hollowing out any residual faith in humanity, his own or other people's. Literature, Freud tells us, is the way by which we can often recall the lost in a different incarnation, thus allowing us to exorcise the ghosts of our past. Poe caught this too in his story *The Cruel Portrait* in which the painting is complete only when the sitter dies, her vital force absorbed into the artefact. In writing a novel and transforming the dead into characters in the tale, Kien can complete his own ritual exorcism.

In his reflections on the First World War, Freud explained ghosts as inventions of our primitive ancestors who accepted the reality of death while simultaneously disavowing its permanence; for the dead can always return. He explained that melancholia in the modern age is our own subconscious wish to remember the dead in the same way that our early ancestors thought of themselves as possessed by demons. Writing, he explained, could be a form of ghost-busting (Freud, 2005, xxii-xxiii). Recalling his own horrified response to the conflict, Freud admitted that he had previously thought Europe had been living 'psychologically beyond (its) means.' (Freud, 2005, 21). Men had become too studious in denying death, in banishing it from the family home to the hospital, in sanitising life by never referring to it, except obliquely. In war at least, he supposed, it would be better to let the ghosts back in. He concluded—with the innocence of the age into which he was born—that once the Great War was over, soldiers would return to their former way of life, largely untouched by the deaths they had witnessed. Now, we know that memories are not so easily banished. The ghosts did indeed come back into the picture, and in some cases required exorcism. One way, as Kien realises, is through literature—remembering the dead as characters in another person's story.

Kien himself is eventually reborn, probably (though not certainly) into Bao Ninh (which is itself a pseudonym for the author's true name, Hong Au Phung). The novel, indeed, has three authorial voices: a nameless narrator's, then Kien's and finally the author's own—and the last is the most heart-warming. Towards the end of the novel Kien tries to burn his manuscript just as his father had burned all his paintings. His father had been criticised throughout his life for not painting pictures that the masses could understand. Instead, he depicted human beings with dismal expressions, their bodies stretched, coloured in a variety of tones but principally yellow (an ambiguous colour for the Vietnamese, evoking autumn and impending winter). In the pictures the characters wander aimlessly across unreal landscapes like withered puppets; the tail-end in these processions made up of the artist, who cast himself as a tragic figure. His father had burned his paintings on the day he expected to die, in the Spring of 1965, on the morning Hanoi heard its first air raid siren.

Kien disappears as well, joining the ghosts whose lives he tried to capture, the lost and un-remarked. But unlike them, he leaves behind a manuscript that he has tried but failed to burn. Later, the author of the novel tells us that he obtained the remains of the manuscript and read the pages out of curiosity, rearranging them first in chronological order, only to find there was no order that he could readily discern. Instead there was only a description of plot, a disconnection, a loss of perspective. There were also no heroes, only deadbeat characters, some of whom had been turned into ghosts, who made known their presence in dreams or night-time visitations. And so the *Sorrow of War* came to be written, copied from the pages the author had acquired. But as he edited the text he found that inside Kien's story there were ideas and feelings of his own. By some coincidence of plot, Kien's life and his had become intermixed. Slowly it dawned on him that they had met during the war. They had shared one fate; they had both been crushed by the war in different ways. And thanks to their mutual sorrow, they had been able to walk their respective roads again.

Flashman: Winning Through Despite It All

'The Flashman Papers', George McDonald Fraser

> Bullying underlings and whipping trollops always excepted, I'm a gentle fellow, which means I'll never do harm to anyone if there's a chance he may harm me in return. (*Flash for Freedom*, 273).

Accordingly to one (doubtful source) this is how the Charge of the Light Brigade may have begun. Many of us may think we know the story. An imprecise order led the Light Brigade at Balaclava to charge the Russian guns against all the conventions and practices of war. The whole question, writes Flashman's editor, McDonald Fraser, hinges dramatically on when Captain Nolan, conveying the order to charge from the British Commander, Lord Raglan, pointed to the target— down the valley towards the Russian guns, or towards the redoubts where the British guns were being removed by Russian soldiers. How great was the angle of difference anyway? Did Nolan say 'our guns', or 'your guns' (or what)? And if it was his fault, he certainly paid a high price for it: with his life (*Flashman at the Charge*, 323).

But the account we have from one of the survivors is very different, and it is enlightening, if not particularly edifying. The survivor was Colonel Harry Flashman. He had been sent by Lord Cardigan to instruct the Light Brigade to stop the British guns from being taken away. Against his better inclination he had been forced to convey the message, his bowels none too secure from Russian champagne he had consumed the night before. Flashman was a natural coward who never sought a fight if he could avoid one, which only added to his intestinal distress. To his horror, Lord Lucan, in charge of the cavalry, had appointed him Lord Cardigan's 'galloper' (or messenger), because neither man, though related by marriage, ever communicated with the other if he could avoid it. Assigned his post in the charge, suddenly without the slightest volition on his part, there was the most crashing discharge of wind, like the report of a mortar. 'Christ, as if the Russian artillery wasn't bad enough', someone giggled, and another voice said, 'we've 'ad whistlin' Dick—now we get Trumping Harry an' all.' A few seconds later there was another thunderous discharge from Harry Flashman's bowels, at which point the charge began, with our hero soon abreast of Lord Cardigan, first in a canter and then a gallop. Galloping into an inferno of bursting shells and whistling fragments, of orange flames and choking smoke, he rode like a madman. *The Times* correspondent who witnessed the charge wrote that he had even overtaken Lord Cardigan, 'his eye flashing terribly as he swung the sabre that had stemmed the hoards at Jalalabad' (where he had seen action in the First Afghan War in 1839). All Flashman could do in reality was to try to rein in his horse, only to be thrown out of the saddle. At that moment his innards were seized with a fresh spasm, and had he been a fanciful man, so he tells us, he would have sworn that he had blown himself back astride the beast (*Flashman at the Charge*, 122).

Flashman is heroically honest; it is the only thing that is heroic about him. He leaves nothing out of the account, even the grimmest details about the state of his bowels. We learn for example in another tale that the Sioux Indians called him by the Indian name for 'Wind Breaker'. Flashy's motto in life is that if you had the press on your side, you were halfway there, which is why he never bothered to correct the glowing tributes that came his way and thought it a shame to do it, at last, in those imperishable memoirs that have made his name so famous. As he himself remarks, his career had seen 'ten men's share of service through no fault of my own.'

I first read the *Flashman* novels in my teens. I had also read *Tom Brown's Schooldays*, though never made it to *Tom Brown at Oxford*. The 1960s were the era of youth rebellion and although I hated the chic radicalism of 1968, even then, I caught enough of the infection to spurn doing team sports at school whenever I could and found especially distasteful the 'improving books' which even then a young boy of my generation were still given on birthdays or Christmas. So the *Flashman* series, which began life in 1969 when I was sixteen, came as a remarkable antidote. Flashman is an authentic villain, even though he is not really villainous; he does not get other people killed. He is more of one of life's supreme survivors, and in a great jest against history he rises to the very top of Victorian society. He triumphs over the lot of them, including the unspeakable Tom Brown.

I sat down to read the entire *Flashman* canon again in order to write this book. Some of the books I had read already, some I had not, but I enjoyed them all as much as I had at sixteen. Flashman is a wonderful hero for our times, with a single overwhelming desire to succeed through excess. Sure, he can be a bastard, but he is one of 'our' bastards (as the Americans used to call the Third World dictators they supported in the Cold War). We do not have to like him to love him, and we do not have to love him to like him or to see why today's soldiers often serving in the same theatres of operations as he did (such as Afghanistan), embrace him almost as a human mascot. After all, he is luckier than they. He usually gets the better of everyone, including Her Majesty's enemies on the Frontier, which is a good deal more than our soldiers do today. The villains Flashman meets usually come in pantomime dress, and were treated as such by the British public (though they were often far less villainous, in our eyes, than the tribal thugs, ethnonationalists, jihadists, and drug cartel members our soldiers are expected to fight). Our villains are not only more villainous, they are more one-dimensional. They are without the human interest which marked the Ashanti, the Zulu, or even Afghans of old. To be frank, they are simply not as interesting.

When the first book came out the American critics were taken in by it. Fraser claimed that he had stumbled upon a cache of memoirs and personal papers in 1965. In other volumes he carried on the deception with end notes that tried to either 'confirm' or 'correct' Flashman's own account of his life. This scholarly apparatus misled many of the first reviewers into believing the documents were real. Almost a third of the original American reviewers thought the book semi-autobiographical, which prompted the editor of the *New York Times* to publish a selection of the best and most embarrassing reviews four years later.

Flashman's military career spans forty years from his first tight spot in Afghanistan to his last appearance in the Zulu War. Fraser died in 2008, before he could write the volume he had intended, and we do not know what would have been its theme. We must assume, however, that there is not much to relate after he reached the age of fifty-seven. Flashman died in 1915, having taken a reluctant part in the great campaigns and battles that distinguish British military history, including the episodes the British army would prefer to forget such as the battle of Isandalwana (a rare defeat). And he comes through them all. Even in the Charge of the Light Brigade he made it all the way to the Russian guns, only to flee in panic straight into an entire Russian regiment, which only added to his heroic stature in the eyes of his contemporaries.

War tends to attract men like Flashman—adventurers, schemers, charlatans, men with an eye to the main chance. The Homeric heroes were no different. They came to plunder what they could. The Trojan War was, amongst many other things, a business venture. War attracts other types as well, those who cannot fit in anywhere else, the human flotsam and jetsam, the bankrupt, the out of work, the internal exiles from life, the adrenaline junkies, the terminally bored. War has its entrepreneurs, and always has done. Today they take many forms: private security contractors, pilots subcontracted to fly military flights (like those who appear in the Vietnam war movie *Air America*), the middle-men who 'facilitate' NATO's operations in Afghanistan today. These and others all play their part; they have their separate exits and entrances. Flashman is a much larger character than any of them. He sees the whole world as a theatre for his own energies, and for his personal enrichment, whether it is taking part in the Atlantic slave trade

(*Flash for Freedom!*); making a profit out of the Civil War in China (*Flashman and the Dragon*); or aiming for the famous Ko-i-Noor diamond (*Flashman and the Mountain of Light*). He is acting on a much larger stage and aiming high, and if he is perpetually in danger of overshooting the mark, he always falls on other people's feet.

War is often like that. It creates opportunities for some, while ruining the lives of others. Reputations are won and lost equally quickly, and once lost a reputation is difficult to win back. And reputations are won undeservedly all the time. Mark Twain wrote a short story in which a British general blunders his way to promotion and honours, as generals often do. Doctors bury their mistakes; generals file them away in their despatches.

And Flashman is, we should always remember, not really a Victorian figure at all. He is a leftover from the eighteenth century. He represents a world that Dickens captured in his early novels, and rarely left behind, which is why the 'Dickensian' as a term really refers to the characters from his early, not late novels. Unlike Dickens, of course, Flashman has no sympathy with Victorian morality, and especially the good causes such as the anti-slave trade or the civilising mission which Dickens and many of his contemporaries took to heart. He is an historical throwback to the men who won India in the eighteenth century, and ran the slave trade in the Caribbean (men like his grandfather). And, though we can hardly call him moral, this adds to his integrity, too. Like Achilles he admits to owing loyalty to no one but himself. He obeys no other commands than his own self-advancement. He is also, in his own words, 'a toady'. He flatters and turns on the charm whenever he is in danger. In eschewing the Victorian pieties he is being true only to himself. And that is what today's soldiers probably find most sympathetic about him as they navigate their own way, a hundred years later, through a world of humanitarian aid workers, NGO representatives and 'human factor analysts' (academic anthropologists operating with the military), as well as politically savvy generals and nation-builders, all of whom Flashman would have despised, as much as he despised the Empire builders of his own day.

So we must cherish the memory of Sir Henry Paget Flashman, VC, KCB, KCCE, Chevalier de la Légion d'honneur, the US Medal of Honor, and the San Serafino Order of Purity and Truth, Fourth Class. He is a man of almost Falstaffian energy (and charm) who awaits his own Harold Bloom to do justice to his career. He is also a great yarnspinner, like Falstaff, and Flashman is given some wonderful lines and a style that is entirely his own. If most of the characters in this book are fully realised people, very few, Falstaff aside, have such a distinctive emotional register, especially the one-liners that would melt any humanitarian's heart. 'If you have to run slaves ... the way to do so is by steamboat.' One of the valued features of the novels for today's military is not only that Flashman is so politically incorrect (even for his own day), but that he is not into the humanitarian agenda that they have to apply.

What are the essential features of Flashman's character? The first is his cowardice. There is a great line in *Flashman and the Dragon*: 'for a well-decorated hero, I've done a deal of surrendering in my time—which is doubtless why I remain a well-decorated hero.' (*Flashman and the Dragon*, 102). He sums up his personal creed thus: 'the ideal time to be a hero is when the battle is over and the other fellows are dead, God rest 'em, and you take the credit' (McDonald Fraser, 2010, ix). What soldiers also love about him is that frequently his is the only sane voice in a world gone to ruin, for the senior officers are often far more reprehensible and bloodthirsty than our hero. They are fanatical when he is refreshingly cynical; pompous and overbearing when he is charm itself.

His cowardice is real and entirely self-serving but he is not without principles—very strong principles at times. One is that it is no duty of a soldier to get himself killed because of the stupidity of his generals. On the day war is declared with Russia, marking the outbreak of the Crimean conflict, Flashman finds a scene of chaos in Lord Raglan's office at the Horse Guards: 'all work and fury and chatter, and no proper direction whatever, and a great consulting of maps: where the devil *is* Turkey, someone was saying.' (*Flashman at the Charge*, 46). Military blunders cost lives. On the retreat from Kabul we glimpse a woman who has lost her child; an officer who is snow-blind, walking about in circles until someone leads him away; a British trooper reeling drunk on an Afghan pony, falling off and dozing in the snow, only to be found dead the next morning. The genius of Fraser's conception was to make Flashman's world as vivid as Flashman himself. His is a world so different from our own, one that is far more colourful, and much more brutal, in which life is cheap for both officers and enlisted men alike, and of course, for the 'natives' most of all. And as the Victorian era progresses from the heroic folly of the first Anglo-Afghan War to the squalid frenzy of the partition of Africa (a 'scramble' for the British, a 'steeplechase' for the French, and most revealingly of all, perhaps, a *Torshlusspanik* for the Germans—a race to get through the door before it is closed), so Flashman becomes more endearing, and less of the mean little rotter who bullied Tom Brown at school.

The second essential feature of Flashman's character is his enormous good luck. He survives as many near-death experiences as James Bond, and although he has his share of misfortune, Fraser is keen to set these right in the footnotes at the end of each volume. He is not, however, as lucky as first appears. Fraser has inserted Flashman into the chaos of history—if left to his own devices, we suspect that Flashman would prefer to lead a much less eventful life. As the series progresses, Flashman feels the burden of his humanity but prefers to lighten it by reflecting that cruelty is the way of the world. That is why we should not wish to be him, and why we cannot admire him—but then, after all, he does not admire himself. His honesty about his own cowardice is what endears him most to his readers. He survives nevertheless; it is his *métier*, as the French would say. Moreover, his actions make him an accomplice to what he witnesses—the horror of war. In that sense he can be numbered among war's victims since he is always in the wrong place at the wrong time and suffers for his bad judgement. He may escape being killed or badly wounded, but he spends a lot of time in prison (and some of the vilest hell-holes, at that).

He expects no better—that is the point: it is the saving of him. He never takes himself or war seriously but then he is not given to introspection or reflection on the mindlessness of others. There is a kind of integrity, too, in the way he remains true to his own creed, rather than the creed of others. Though he is of course not entirely outside his society with his talk of 'niggers', and his bullying of natives, both of which mark him out as a Victorian, like the Victorians he is more complex than we often imagine. Flashman has many talents, too many perhaps for his own good. He has a facility for language and can disguise himself as a Danish prince or Texas slave-driver, an Arab Sheikh or Yankee naval lieutenant, and even a Pushtun (an 'Asian-Afghan nigger') (*Flash for Freedom*, 459). None of these disguises are as hard to sustain, of course, as his lifetime impersonation of a British officer and gentleman.

But then the Victorians spent years on the Frontier, often respected by the 'natives'. They lived closer to them than any NATO task force member in Afghanistan does today. They did not need to win hearts and minds because the Empire was based on power and brute force; these 'sahibs' could live *in* the hearts of sepoy soldiers in a way today's soldiers can only envy, and win their affection in a way we no longer can. Not for the Victorians putting anthropologists in the field—those 'human terrain' teams, always ready to remind us that war is a human endeavour (the Victorians knew it without having to be told)—nor drones overhead with their hours of video-streaming. We may have more information than the Victorians ever had, but we understand our enemies much less. What the soldiers most like about Flashman, I suspect, is that here too he was nearer to what they themselves would like to be.

The last essential facet of Flashman's character is fornication. 'Sex and death—the front door and the back door of the world' writes William Faulkner in *Soldiers' Pay*. 'Where are sexual compulsions more readily answered than in war?' (Faulkner, 2007, 146). As Flashman observes, this is hardly surprising; only women prefer to see soldiers as Greek heroes instead of the 'drunken whore-mongering clowns' they actually are—the Greeks themselves were probably no better. Eros and Thanatos are the Siamese twins to whom the Greeks first introduced us. And sex in war is so central because the omnipresence of death underlines life's fleetingness.

'Men love war' and women (or so men tell us) love warriors (they certainly love Flashman, however politically incorrect the sentiment may be). At 6'2" he cuts a striking figure. His somewhat dark colouring suggests perhaps a case of miscegenation in the family; this is not unsurprising as the family fortune (such as it is) was made in the slave trade, and we can imagine the liaison between his rather rum grandfather and one of his slaves. It is the dark look that allows him to pass as a Pashtun in the first tale in the series. Flashman is guilty of one rape but he is generally far too charming and handsome to need to resort to violence. Women fall for him all the time. His sexual conquests include a Maharani, at least two Queens and the Imperial Chinese concubine, Ci Xi, who later becomes the Dowager Empress. 'I dare say I am just a snob', he remarks, with disarming candour. Today's soldiers like him because he is so brazen and unsentimental about his sexual conquests. Women, anyway, men like to tell themselves, fall for cads all the time (which says little about their paternal concern, so much as their perennial envy of the Alpha male's success).

E. M. Forster observes in *Aspects of the Novel* that there are two kinds of characters created by novelists: 'flat' characters and 'round' ones. Dickens, Forster goes on to tell us, is the master of flat characterisation. All his personalities are entirely themselves (they are incapable of acting out of character). Thus Pickwick is always Pickwickian, and Macawber is also Macawberish. Flashman is a flat character, too (most heroes of popular fiction are; James Bond is always Bond; Rumpole is always Rumpole of the Bailey). John Sutherland, however, adds a useful rider that Dickens' characters can be said to be analogies to what Picasso does when he shows two sides of the same face on the same plane. There is something artfully duplicitous about Dickens' best characters, and Sutherland goes on to note that the villains are often in strange relationship with the heroes: Copperfield and Steerforth; Pip and Orlik; Carlton and Darney (Sutherland, 2012, 156). In Flashman's case this is true of the villainesses of the tales; it is the women (not the men) who are the most interesting protagonists. He comes nearest to death at their hands—like the prostitute he sells into slavery, not to mention the evil Queen Ranavalone of Madagascar. We can imagine why he finds sleeping with natives (only the highest caste, of course) much more rewarding than with the 'civilised' women whose company he has to endure at home. His most ardent lovers are on the other side of the imperial bed sheets, except for Elspeth, his wife, to whom he remains fiercely loyal in his own fashion, despite the fact that she is socially beneath him (and worse still, a Scot!).

In a letter from Helmand Province in Afghanistan, a British lieutenant-colonel informed the readers of *The Times Literary Supplement* that young officers still read the *Iliad*, but the 'perennial favourite' were the Flashman novels of George Macdonald Fraser (*Times Literary Supplement*, 25 Nov. 2011, 32). There is a remarkable pathos to this, I think, which cannot be grasped at the time the series was first conceived when the British were pulling out east of Suez—1968 was the first, and so far only, year which has not seen the loss of a single British soldier. Rather, in Fraser's last years the British military were back on the Frontier, engaging a new cast list of villains; Jihadists, war lords and militias, and of course Pashtun tribesmen, checking in their Kalashnikovs with their prayer mats. Had we learned so little, Fraser asked, from the past? Flashman's past is always threatening to catch up with him, but the same could be said for the country he served so faithlessly. And like the Victorians and the Indian Mutiny—which was neither a mutiny nor what Indians now like to call it, the First War of Independence—you can escape history, but never the past. It either catches up with you or catches you out.

The Victorians did things differently. They had what we do not: self-belief. For them the 'civilising mission' was real, and in their heyday they did it supremely well (if ruthlessly). Today, we don't. Flashman himself, of course, has no time for the *mission civilisatrice* anymore than were he alive today he would go along with the nonsense of nation building, the earnest liberal internationalist mission to terra-form countries like Afghanistan. He goes along with the empire build-ing because it suits him, but he is not is a hypocrite. He has a peculiar kind of integrity which lends an aura of decency to his actions, despite his better self. And that integrity is a measure of war itself. Every age defines and redefines its heroes in its own fashion. Flashman is an authentic figure for our cynical times. A hero he is not: he defies clas-sification, but if we are to categorise him at all, it would be as a survi-vor, a triumphant one, representing the irrepressible will to treat war as he did Tom Brown at Rugby—he refuses to be impressed by the code of muscular Christianity, and would have been equally aghast at the 'muscular liberalism' that took NATO to war in Libya. Flashman would have had no time for Tony Blair's 'liberal vigilantism'. War is a murderous trade, he knows all too well, because he has seen it. 'It ain't conducted by missionaries, or chaps in liberal clubs, snug and secure.' He has absolutely no time for the liberals who go to war with mission-ary zeal, or talk themselves into it in liberal debating societies. 'There is nothing crueller than a justified Christian.' (McDonald Fraser, 2010, 785).

Flashman is full of human emotions which are significantly reshaped and heightened for the purposes of the novel. His redeeming friendship with Lincoln, the only true 'great man' he meets in life, is a case in point. 'Just why I liked him I can't say; I suppose in his way he had the makings of as big a scoundrel as I am myself, but his appetites were different, and his talents were infinitely greater.' Even Flashman can recognise a great man when he encounters one just as when he was a boy he could recognise a pious little creep like Tom Brown. He even has a moral centre of a kind. In India he sees only the power of the white man over the black 'and power is a fine thing to have', he adds, 'only as long as the moral authority holds.' (*Flash for Freedom*, 62).

When authority breaks down as it does with the Mutiny, is the candle really worth holding to the devil? It leads to a shocking response and usually great cruelty and Flashman is stunned by the burning of the Summer Palace in Peking. He can imagine himself smashing up the place when drunk, but not doing so methodically, smashing the doors with axes, and putting every building to the flame. 'Next to the wreck of the human body nothing looks so foul as a pretty house in its setting when the smoke eddies from the roof and the air shakes with the heat.' (*Flashman and the Dragon*, 295).

I suspect what our soldiers like most, though, is his contempt for the generals who have led us into many a disaster in recent years. Flashy waxes angry about the incompetence of the men he serves under like Cardigan, Custer and Raglan, and worst of all, Elphy Bey, in Afghanistan. Fictional characters are not always under-determined—we know only a few of their properties, but often we know more about them than they do themselves, and every time we re-read a good novel, we discover something else. Some novelists even come to like their characters much more in the course of writing about them. In the preface to *Major Barbara* (1905) Shaw wrote that when Cervantes relented in his originally critical portrait of Don Quixote and Dickens in his portrait of Pickwick they did not become more impartial; 'they simply changed sides and became friends and apologists where they had formerly been mockers.' A few novelists come to hate their own characters, think of Conan Doyle and Sherlock Holmes, or Flaubert and Madame Bovary. Doyle tried to kill off his hero—and failed. On his own deathbed, Flaubert remarked that his protracted end was made more miserable by the knowledge that 'that whore, Emma Bovary, would outlive him.' McDonald Fraser clearly came to love Flashy more over time. We love him too because without such characters there would be less life in literature, and less literature in life.

6

VICTIMS

Of all the archetypes that feature in this study victimhood is one that passes into literature least mediated from life. And victimhood has a special place in war. Simply to experience war is enough for many of us to be victimised. Pacifists (though not all) will claim that even warriors are victims of their own beliefs and passions. Victimhood is one of the *leitmotifs* of the war literature of the previous century, just as war was once the accredited theme of modern life.

Victimhood comes in many forms, and has many faces, and the important thing in its fictional representation is that we should believe in it. Does it illuminate a dimension of war which some of the greatest writers have preferred to air brush out of the account? Does it diminish the characters concerned, or enhance them by extending their moral education and ours? Less often asked is whether a 'victim' may be counted lucky (Henry Fleming, after all, envies the walking wounded their 'red badge of courage'). Some of the victims in this section tend to be larger than life, especially the first, Philoctetes. In the real world many are so crippled or maimed either in mind or body, that they appear to have no interior life at all, like the 'white-soldier' in *Catch-22*, all gauze and bandages lying inert in his bed waiting to die, or the young peasant soldier in *Hadji Murat* who is very much alive when we meet him but who is condemned to die a meaningless death on the 'frontier of progress', serving the Tsar.

All these are minor casualties, or what we would call today with a lack of sensitivity unique to our age, 'collateral damage', and their fate is not especially illuminating. The victims of fiction in that sense have to be archetypal and inevitably their suffering has to have meaning for the reader. We are, in that sense, voyeurs—complicit in their misery. But that is the price we pay for reading fiction, just as it is the price that they often find themselves paying for reading history, for fighting for King and Country, for taking the national myths so much to heart.

We may feel that the victims we read about on the page are not 'authentic', but they are authentic enough if we learn something from their fate, if we are the better informed about our own humanity as a result. And we do not have to make the mistake of reading into the intensity with which their suffering is rendered, any particular message, including the usual post-1918 received idea: to be any good a war book must be anti-war.

Even the Greeks never lost sight of the cost of war. For every poem in the *Greek Anthology* celebrating the martial virtues, there are three that regret the loss of life and livelihood. Even in the classical world the poets were free to explore the darkness, as well as light. Euripides, in particular, writing at the time of the most destructive of all wars in the Greek world, positively parades the victims for us in plays such as *The Trojan Women*. But Sophocles is the only one of the great tragedians to portray the 'walking wounded', a soldier who returns to battle unwillingly to confront his own demons, a warrior—as well as a hero—who quite possibility is suffering from post-traumatic stress, one of the chief challenges that today's soldiers have to confront.

It may be chronologically anomalous perhaps to start with Post-Traumatic Stress Disorder (PTSD) as only in the last two hundred years has it been officially recognised as a medical condition (though not by that name). But it is almost certainly as old as war itself. Both Herodotus and Thucydides described classic symptoms in their respective histories, a rare case of where the professional historian's powers of imagination ran ahead of the poet's. Or perhaps prose writing is a licence to report back what poetry does not confront because of its traditionally higher status and social role. Until the appearance of the novel in the eighteenth century, poetry's principal duty was to reflect the idealised face of war.

In Sophocles' play, the Homeric hero Philoctetes is bitten by a serpent and left in terrible pain; though one of the great heroes, he is transfigured by his wound and becomes a victim. His moaning is an affront to everything the heroes hold dear about war and themselves. To avoid confronting their own private demons—for his screams of pain echo the screams they would have heard every day on the battle-field—they banish him, at Odysseus' instigation, to the remote island of Lemnos to eke out a subsistence living. In addition to his very real pain Philoctetes also has to endure the stigma of estrangement. He is stripped of his status as a hero and ultimately of his humanity for in the Greek world to be cast out from the community was to be out-lawed and divested of everything that made one a man. The hero's fate is a warning of the nothingness into which any human may descend if fate is against him.

From the moment that Philoctetes is 'wounded', the play is an account of how he drags himself—just about—through the days and nights that follow. It does not make us admire him, nor are we meant to. He wallows in his solipsistic misery and yet somehow remains above it. He still retains our sympathy. He has imagination and a large heart. But he has become asocial. He has become 'the whole catastro-phe', to borrow a striking phrase from *Zorba the Greek*. He has lost his trust in the world, as well as his faith in humanity. And it is this loss of trust that is one of the most tragic manifestations of traumatic ill-ness. 'Clearly there is no pharmacological panacea' writes one contem-porary psychologist 'for the spectrum of psychological, biological, spiritual and existential injuries that can be sustained from combat or operational stress. No magic pill can erase the image of a best friend's shattered body or assuage the guilt from having traded duty with him that day.' Medication cannot re-establish a person's trust in his mas-tery of the world, or restore his lost innocence. (Clayton, 2007, 219).

We tend to take most note of those who return in one piece mentally or physically only to find that they are no longer recognisable as the men who left for war. They often leave a little of themselves behind, often the best part. The characters in an early story by William Faulkner find themselves lost in peace when Armistice Day arrives on 11 November 1918. Thirteen years later we see that they actually died on 11 November, 'they are thick men now—a little thick about the waist just sitting behind desks, and maybe not so good at it, with wives and children in suburban homes almost paid out, with gardens in which they putter in the long evening after the 5.15 is in, and perhaps not so good at that, either. The men, the hard, lean men who swag-

gered hard and drank hard because they had found that being dead
was not as quiet as they heard it would be.'

In Colonel Chabert, Balzac created another returning soldier who is
dead to the world, a man who survives his wounds only to find himself lost in the world to which he returns. His wife had married him
out of convenience, to escape the gutter, and then immediately resented
it. Their life together, one imagines, though the colonel does not actually say so, was one of sourness and subterfuge; that was before he
went off to fight in another of Napoleon's campaigns and this time did
not return. It didn't take his wife long to have him declared dead, keep
his fortune and remarry. In his novella Balzac captured the tribulations
of an old soldier who finds himself dishonoured and unacknowledged
by his own countrymen, and worse still, his own wife. At the end of
the tale he disappears back into the shadows once again leaving behind
nothing at all, not even an absence.

The victims we tend to think of most, of course, are those who don't
return from the field of battle. In Paul Baümer, we see a man deceived
by his nation, his teachers and ultimately by life itself. Remarque's
book was on the bestseller list from the moment it first appeared, and
sold even more copies after it was filmed. The author had to flee Nazi
Germany which also claimed that young soldiers (the 'Fallen' as the
euphemism went) had been betrayed, not deceived by their elders, however, but 'stabbed in the back' by Bolsheviks and socialist politicians.

The novel is passionately anti-war (indeed, it is the only avowedly
anti-war book to figure in this study), and few of us these days feel like
celebrating war. We endure it with grim determination in the conviction that some wars are worth fighting and that evil people still need to
be confronted, even on ground of their own choosing. Remarque's generation hoped the First World War would be the 'war to end wars'; if
it had been, we would doubtless honour their 'sacrifice' more than we
do. Knowing what we do, we tend to find it instead a terrible 'waste'.
A historical perspective often works from the top down, attempting to
get us to see the big picture; literature usually attempts the opposite. In
using a 'from the bottom up' perspective Remarque illustrated a 'truth'
about war: soldiers are rapidly disillusioned and often the experience
is without meaning, or without a meaning they can readily discern.
'The' truth about a war may be very different. Even the First World
War had to be fought (we do not need to be told this about the Second), but 'a truth' and 'the truth' are just different sides of the same

coin, and all truth is elusive. What Remarque did was to shape our view of the First World War; his novel is now the lens through which it always likely to be 'remembered'. The actor Dirk Bogarde chose *All Quiet on the Western Front* as his 'Book of the Century', concluding that 'no one has better explained the fate of the ordinary men engaged uncomprehendingly in the viciousness, uselessness and utter waste of war.' (Bond, 2002, 113). Most wars are vicious, of course, but only a few are 'useless' and even the waste of life in the Great War, though obscene was not without historical significance. Remarque simply was wrong. The war in which he himself fought shaped the twentieth century world. As one historian concludes, 'it was emphatically not a war without meaning or purpose.' (Strachan, 2006, 331).

Finally, there is another kind of victim: the soldier who like Billy Pilgrim returns from war to be haunted by memories of what he has seen. This is the theme of the last novel to appear in this section, Kurt Vonnegut's *Slaughterhouse-Five*, which is often treated as a companion piece to the other successful war book of the 1960s, *Catch-22*. Indeed, there were some odd synergies between the lives of Vonnegut and Heller. The two met on stage at a literary festival in 1968, and became great friends and eventually neighbours. Heller's war was up in the air, as a bombardier in the nose cone of a B-25. Vonnegut's was at ground level, as an infantryman in the battle of the Bulge, and then beneath ground level in the basement of Slaughterhouse-Five. Heller's book appeared in 1961 and became an 'existential field manual' for the anti-war movement, a 'must-read' for the grunts and soldiers doing the fighting. Vonnegut's novel came out in March 1969 by which time the anti-war movement had hit its stride (*New York Times*, 25 November 2011).

But while Heller's hero is a survivor, Vonnegut's is a victim and Vonnegut himself was as fragile in his own way as Billy Pilgrim. He spent twenty-three years searching for the right form, tone and voice, meanwhile displacing the theme into other stories. He wrote another Second World War book, *Mother Night*, in which a central character, Howard Campbell, delivers propaganda for both sides and so serves 'good too secretly and evil too openly.' The novel, like *Slaughterhouse-Five*, seeks to chronicle the absurdity of human endeavour. For Vonnegut, only the fantastic (in his case science fiction) could make sense of the senseless and he could only make sense of the bombing of Dresden as a form of displacement. Billy Pilgrim is kidnapped by an alien race, introduced as a result to an alternative process of history in which life is experienced in vivid and often horrifying instances (like the bombing of Dresden); in which time is reversed, and there is no beginning and end, and therefore no meaning that can be attached to events. One has to roll with the punches, as best one can ('So it goes', Vonnegut insists).

Philoctetes: The Traumatised Hero
Philoctetes, Sophocles

There are many Sophocleses. The playwright unconcerned with ideas; the artist obsessed with character; the pious man who respects fate and the gods; the first psychologist whose famous irony puts the characters at some remove both from the gods and themselves. Only seven of his tragedies have survived, of which the two most famous are *Oedipus* and *Antigone* (made more famous still by the importance attached to them by Freud). I shall be discussing a neglected play, *Philoctetes*, which is now popular with the US military for the light it is deemed to throw on trauma, the greatest medical problem that the armed forces now face.

Sophocles was a writer whose primary interest was states of mind, those that the main characters acknowledge and which are subject of debate and judgement by others. In *Philoctetes*, Sophocles gave himself a challenge that no Greek writer had tackled: to show an Homeric hero in a very un-heroic light. In so doing, he presents us with a figure not entirely unlike ourselves.

The story is about the attempt by Odysseus and the young Neoptolemus (the son of the great Achilles, no less) to obtain a bow from one of the Homeric heroes, Philoctetes. They are sent by the Greek high command to the island of Lemnos where Philoctetes had been marooned ten years earlier on the advice of Odysseus himself. Philoctetes was a brave warrior, but he had been bitten by a serpent and infected with a suppurating wound that not only wouldn't heal but had left him in perpetual agony. His cries of pain had so distressed his fellow Greeks that Odysseus and the senior commanders decided to expel him from the camp.

Philoctetes' wound elicits disgust, and the problem with disgust is that it is contagious. Disgust has evolutionary origins. It translates readily enough into distaste based on sensory overload, such as decaying corpses, or human faeces. It also, and often simultaneously, translates into danger. We instantly know what it is safe to eat and what we should avoid. Disgust can also be an affront, a social taboo which has been broken. Neither distaste nor fear require that we put the offending object out of sight, still less out of mind. We have to live among many dangerous objects all the time; we just have to avoid them and what some find distasteful, others may not. Distaste is a cultural construct, as our ancestors found out when encountering other cultures. Sheep's eyes used to be a standard example in Hollywood's 'orientalising' of Arab culture; but fastidious Arabs would find it equally disgusting to be served a roasted pig with its head intact and an apple in its mouth. Disgust is far more pointed than distaste. It is fear of the object being ingested or incorporated into our own body, metaphorically or literally. It is an ultimate form of contamination. It is precisely to avoid being contaminated that we tend to project our fear outward so that it is not to be found within. One could say without exaggeration that the root of disgust is primitive shame, the unwillingness to be a needy animal (Nussbaum, 2008, 221). Philoctetes is expelled from the Greek camp precisely because of his needs; he has become an invalid and he represents the man that any hero could, in certain circumstances, become.

As Odysseus tells Neoptolemus when they first land on the island to which he has been exiled:

> .... I am the one
> That dumped him, him and his cankered foot
> Or what had been a foot before it rotted
> And ate itself with ulcers.
> It was awful.
> We couldn't even get peace at the altar
> Without him breaking out in these howling fits,
> And slabbering and cursing.
> He was putting us on edge,
> He couldn't be stopped
> Everybody's nerves were getting raw.
> (*Philoctetes*, 3–4).

But they have returned with a purpose. A recent prophecy has revealed that they will only take Troy if they succeed in securing Philoctetes' bow, the one given to him by Heracles himself. What the prophecy does not make clear is how the bow is to be secured, whether by force or persuasion, or whether Philoctetes himself should also be brought back if they are successful.

Of the play's three leading characters, Sophocles is especially damning about Odysseus, who appears in a much more heroic light in an earlier play, *Ajax*. The Odysseus he portrays is a political soldier, every bit the hero of course, but one more renowned for his cunning than his bravery in battle. He is the man who will eventually help the Greeks take Troy where Achilles has failed, by stealth and deceit, rather than courage on the battlefield. He is not a 'political' general as we understand the term today—an office-seeker, still less a self-serving career officer. But he sees himself as an agent of a cause, an impersonal actor who is willing to set aside feelings for the greater good. He is a realist, a man who cuts corners and gets things done, a soldier who knows that sometimes one has to be unscrupulous to achieve an end goal, and admits to no shame in taking short cuts, or cutting one's losses when possible. What is interesting about the play is that both Philoctetes and Neoptolemus come to know themselves much better in the course of the drama; Odysseus doesn't. In his last scene, hovering on the outskirts of the action where he belongs, he remains every bit the character we saw in the Prologue (Winnington-Ingram, 1980, 282). The great triumph for Philoctetes is that he moves centre-stage at last. Being spoken about, even admiringly, is never as liberating as being able to speak for oneself.

As for Neoptolemus, he is an impressionable young man who still lives in the shadow of a famous father, weighed down by all the expectations that others have of him and which he can never hope to realise. At one stage, Odysseus reminds him, 'as long as you're alive/your father is never going to be dead' which has a double-edged meaning. He is trying to persuade Neoptolemus that he must not bring shame upon himself because to do so would be to shame the great Achilles. But that, of course, is the point. He has to live perpetually in the shadow of his father, and from the beginning he is in awe of Philoctetes, who is after all, an authentic hero who his father had known in person. And because he is in awe of his reputation, he is ashamed of the role that is allotted to him, which requires him to betray one of his father's former friends. Members of the Achilles family, after all, do not lie; they do not weave webs of deceit around other people. What they want, they take by force.

Odysseus has promised him, however, that the prophecy has revealed that it is he who will have the honour of taking Troy where his father failed, as indeed is the case, but that the city can only be taken if they obtain Philoctetes' bow. In that regard, the play has a sub-theme; how an impressionable young man is caught on the horns of a dilemma, and how at the very end his honour wins out. He defies orders and returns the bow to Philoctetes, allowing him to decide whether he will surrender it or not, or whether he will return with the two men back to Troy, to confront his own past.

The play begins in earnest with Philoctetes' first appearance. The Chorus expresses disgust and pity at the same time. They are disgusted that he has been reduced to living the life of a savage, 'dragging himself through bushes after/game, festering inside and out', but they also ask why if it is the lot of human beings to suffer, a hero of the war should have to suffer so much. Philoctetes, for his part, is overjoyed to meet a fellow Greek and catch up on the news about the war. All that he has been left, however, is life, or what passes for it. 'My whole life has been just one long cruel parody', he remarks. 'Every day has been a weeping wound.' (*Philoctetes*, 18). He has become what today we would call one of the 'walking wounded'.

Indeed, he now begs to be taken back to Troy. He offers to hide away from view of the crew in the hold or the stern, or even under the prow, for he knows that he is the last thing that they will want on board. And he reminds the young man that no one should consider himself blessed, even at the height of good fortune. There but for the grace of God, go I, which is why we should always be ready to pity other people. The Chorus, surprisingly, agrees, and urges Neoptolemus to show compassion—unlike the gods, who have no pity for humanity. 'Do justice and upset them all at once', they counsel. Neoptolemus replies that they should be careful what they wish for. Will they feel so compassionate 'when he is stinking up the boat, and your stomach is turning.' (*Philoctetes*, 28). But he is willing to maintain the charade. He warns Philoctetes that Odysseus has set sail to secure him and his bow by force; they must leave while they still have time. And so they set out but not before Achilles' son has been allowed to touch the famous bow (and the arrows that never miss their target), the bow that Heracles gave him for his courage in setting fire to his funeral pyre and granting him the gift of death. At this point Philoctetes stumbles in pain, and for the first time Neoptolemus is moved to genuine compassion. Hitherto he has lacked the imagination to realise the hero's plight. Now, he feels ashamed that he has shown only what Seamus Heaney, in a felicitous phrase, calls 'an economy of kindness.' (*Philoctetes*, 37).

But it is important to remember that his compassion extends only so far. He is still loyal to the cause, it is just that he has decided to reinterpret his 'orders'. The bow without Philoctetes is not enough. They need the bowman as well as the bow, and there is nothing for it now but to confess the deception and try to persuade the older man to return to Troy of his own free will. And so the truth comes out and an outraged Philoctetes reacts in an equally complex manner. First, as the truth hits home he accuses Neoptolemus of bringing disgrace to his family name. This is followed by an argument that he himself is not the man who left Troy, and therefore that the young man should not even seek to persuade him to leave the island.

> ...the man you tricked
> Was never the man you came to snatch away.
> You'll be showing off a phantom to the Greeks.
>
> ...you overpowered a cripple without weapons
> And even then, you did it underhand.
>
> (*Philoctetes*, 52).

It is this moment that Odysseus returns and the play draws to its conclusion. The confrontation between two bitter enemies is certainly dramatic. Odysseus warns him that he will return to the war, herded like a wild animal, if necessary. 'What do the gods care? It's what they say that matters/and they say you'll march.' (*Philoctetes*, 55).

Philoctetes is undoubtedly the most physically repellent of the characters to appear in Greek tragedy. The Greek word for sickness (*nosos*) resonates throughout the play. He stinks, quite literally; his sores discharge pus and blood; he freely admits that people find him disgusting. But his physical corruption only serves to highlight Odysseus' moral cynicism. Philoctetes may be damaged but he has retained his humanity enough for Neoptolemus to admire, and even embrace him. In this—the only all-male play to have survived from the ancient world, there is not a trace of homo-eroticism, but there is a powerful affirmation of the military ideal of the young recruit looking up to the older man as part of his own initiation into manhood. Trauma, we can read from this, does not necessarily rob a man of his identity. Indeed, the 'cure of Troy' will allow him to rediscover it.

But the Chorus can also see what Philoctetes in his grief cannot; suffering can make one more compassionate. We are only now beginning to recognise that war can produce post-traumatic growth as well as stress. A soldier can become more caring, wiser or more mature. His priorities may change (he may even give up soldiering). Philoctetes has not grown as a person. He no longer values relationships as he once did. He is consumed by his own misery. His refusal to return is based in part on the fact that he is devoted to his own plight. As the Chorus reminds him, 'Your wound is what you feed on, Philoctotes/stop eating yourself up with hate and come with us.' (*Philoctetes*, 61). And Sophocles captures that solipsism by showing us how Philoctetes has peopled his island with personifications, including his disease, the 'sickness in whose company' he has been abandoned, and which like a greedy animal he has to feed. Closest of all to him is his hatred of his fellow Greeks. And it becomes a question whether this companionship, which makes it psychologically possible for him to survive, is something he can relinquish or renounce.

It is at this point that Neoptolemus repents. Where words have failed, deeds may re-establish trust, which makes the healing possible. He hands back the bow, much to Odysseus' indignation. It is an action that elicited Aristotle's praise and it is not unproblematic, of course, for the greater the gulf between Neoptolemus and Odysseus, the greater the gulf between Odysseus and the young man's father, Achilles (Hobbs, 2000, 197).

The young man now tries to persuade Philoctetes that the Chorus is right. He really must return with them. In this, he fails, and Philoctetes, after all, has every reason to be distrustful. But what is involved is more than just a question of distrust. He rejects Neoptolemus' offer of friendship. He rejects the human bond which is his only chance of healing. As Neoptolemus reminds him:

> You're a sick man
> The snake bite at the shrine was from a god
> But the gods send remedies, and they expect
> Obedience then as well.
>
> (*Philoctetes*, 72).

And Philoctetes' reply—the most famous speech in the play—is frightening for that reason. He dares to blaspheme against the gods. In our eyes, he goes much further. His real crime is to blaspheme against friendship which was at the very heart of the heroic code. Years of loneliness have intensified and rendered more intractable a heroic resentment of injury.

In the end, the gods themselves have to intervene in the person of Heracles, though it is significant that until recently he was a mortal, and when he speaks it is at a very human level.

> History says, don't hope
> On this side of the grave
> But then, once in a lifetime
> The longed-for tidal wave
> Of justice can rise up
> And hope and history rhyme.
>
> (*Philoctetes*, 77).

This is to say the least an unsatisfactory conclusion. More satisfactory is what Heracles does *not* say. He says nothing about the fall of Troy as an end in itself. He says nothing about whether Odysseus was right to banish Philoctetes in the first place. And he says nothing about whether Philoctetes was right to be resentful of this 'betrayal'. What he does speak about is toil and tribulation. He has endured his twelve labours and so must Philoctetes endure his hardship. And it is finally to this injunction that Philoctetes responds, one hero to another. For the cure of Troy is ambivalent. We understand only part of it: confronting one's fears is at the heart of all psychic healing. But the trauma of war is not so easily resolved. It is, in the end, friendship that is the great healer, as it is the consoling factor of war. The Chorus leaves us with this final reflection: 'I leave/half ready to believe/that a crippled trust might walk/and the half-true rhyme is love.' (*Philoctetes*, 81).

But love is conditional and war is a harsh taskmaster. In his speech, Heracles addresses the young Neoptolemus and tells him to conclude 'the sore and cruel stalemate of our war', but to do so by fair combat. Reprisal killings are out. 'Show the gods respect/reverence for the gods survives our individual mortal lives.' (*Philoctetes*, 79). The last line may seem somewhat gratuitous, but Sophocles does not deal in gratuitous sentiments. The lines are there for a reason, to remind us that lessons we learn in war don't always 'take'. Pity can be fleeting, especially when a blood lust is up. Nothing can be taken for granted. Young men kill. Like his father, Neoptolemus is a 'lion' (the animal Homer compares heroes to most often), but we must always remember that lions are predators, and the force of the simile 'like a lion' owes everything to its nature, its ferocity.

We don't know what happened to Philoctetes subsequently. None of the extant myths relate his fate, but they do tell us what happened to Neoptolemus. Ignoring Heracles' injunction, he is destined to kill Paris, the great archer, with his arrows: a fitting end. But he is also destined to slay Priam at the altar, the old man who his father had revered, and whose life he had spared when he came to the camp to ask for the return of Hector's body.

Philoctetes is being re-discovered. We are still pretty far removed from understanding the etiological roots of major psychological disorders; we are not even sure whether all cases of PTSD belong in the medical arena in the first place. Should we rely simply on symptoms and behaviour to construct an illness, and on pharmacological means to alleviate suffering? It is with this in mind that the US Military employed 'Warrior Theater' as a therapeutic device before abandoning the programme because of cost, using two plays by Sophocles as aids to psychic healing. One is *Ajax*, the other *Philoctetes*. And the endeavour is not without its critics. Did Sophocles write about trauma at all?

The inclusion of *Ajax* is, for me, the most problematic aspect of the project. Ajax was second only to Achilles. He may even have been superior in some of his fighting skills. Homer tells us he was only slower; 'fast-paced Achilles' could outrun him. In Sophocles' play Ajax is driven mad through frustration when he fails to secure Achilles' armour after the latter's death. As 'second only to Achilles', he is shamed by the insult. Odysseus wins the honour instead. In his distress, Ajax slaughters a herd of cattle which he mistakes for his fellow Greeks. The slaughter of cattle, argues Barry Strauss, was no unimportant matter. Cattle represented all the effort that had gone into the many raids, often led by Achilles; they represented wealth to be brought back from Troy when it finally fell, as well as the sacrifices that would be made to the gods for victory. This final act is indeed shaming. Not even Achilles in his rage turned on his own men; he merely turned away from them. Including *Ajax*, it seems to me, is a mistake—a category error, one might say in philosophy, for I see little sign of trauma in all of this, so much as wounded pride.

But *Philoctetes* is a different matter. Here is a truly damaged soldier, and I think, with a little more justification, that we can read PTSD into his symptoms. In every respect he is an unusual hero, very much the odd man out. The life he had imagined ahead of him had ended at Troy. Ultimately it is not the war but the refusal of his friends to acknowledge the trauma of his experience that takes him to the edge of insanity.

Classical scholars will probably continue to blanch at the claim that the Homeric heroes, too, could suffer trauma, but whenever we read any text from a different era we have to interpret it in the light of our own concerns. All interpretation has three meanings: an interpreter is first a decipherer and communicator of meanings, then a translator between languages and cultures, and lastly, above all, he is one who 'acts out' the material before him so as to give it intelligible life (Steiner, 1989, 7). Provided then that the interpreter has the seriousness of purpose and more than average intelligence there can be no 'misreading' of a text. Indeed, it is the interpretation that can give life to a text.

Whether Sophocles might have explicitly conceived of these hints of trauma is irrelevant. The point is not that he may have chosen to tell so little, but that he knew too much and lacked the science to explain what he knew. The knowledge may be beyond the reach of the characters in the play and the audience watching it, as well as the playwright, but it is not surely beyond ours. Cynthia Ozick writes of what Henry James called 'the sacred terror', the 'withheld glimpse' of what is truly horrible. A glimpse can be withheld; to be permitted more than a glimpse would be to know, perhaps, too much. The sacred terror is, in fact, the sensation—not simply fright, but a kind of revulsion—that comes when glimpse perilously lengthens into gaze (Ozick, 1995, 111).

As to whether Sophocles' play is true to life, I think this question also misses the point. Tragedy is meant to be untrue, to show human suffering in grandiose terms that define something about the human condition. The appalling reality of Auschwitz or Kolyma cannot be rendered tragic, although there are plenty of moving stories both about the Holocaust and the Gulag, including the incomparable *Kolyma Tales*. Staged tragedy is precisely that—staged. It either propagates a lie, such as the claim that suffering ennobles, or else tacitly confesses to one—'it's only play acting' after all. But it is much more than either of these. For Aristotle what was important was not the state of mind of the audience at the time of the play, but their state of mind when they were leaving the theatre. The point, he insisted, is that tragedy should be cathartic. We must accept what we have seen on the stage as unreal. Dr Johnson was never more Aristotelian than when he wrote, 'the reflection that may strike the heart is not, but the evils before us are real evils, they are evils to which we ourselves may be exposed ... the delight of tragedy precedes from our consciousness of fiction.' (Nuttall, 2001, 16–17). It is the fictionalised version that allows us to open up our minds to the things that in real life we would rather ignore or forget.

Philoctetes is a strange hero, one of a kind in Western literature up to that date, and well beyond it. He is defeated by war itself, his stock in trade, his vocation. He is a victim of war, and possibly of life; for the Greeks the two were the same. What men call 'peace', wrote Plato, is only an interlude between wars (though to be fair he wrote this in the last of his works, *The Laws*, the product of his dyspeptic old age). Philoctetes we know will return to Troy, but the triumph will not be his; Neoptolemus will have the honour of killing Paris when Troy finally falls. Philoctetes' heroism lies in daring to return to face again his fellow men-at-arms, to brave their sneers, and their ill-meaning looks. Whether it leads to a cure we are never told by the sources. One must assume it does. For the gods do not deceive, do they? Homer tells us otherwise, of course, which is why Plato thought we should be left with our illusions and that Homer's works should be banned.

Colonel Chabert: Coming Home
Colonel Chabert, Honoré de Balzac

In his introduction to *The Oxford Book of Short Stories* (1981), Victor Pritchett, one of the great short story writers of the last century, described the form in a vivid way: 'The novel tends to tell us everything, whereas the short story tells us only one thing, and that, intensely.' Balzac wrote only two works on war to my knowledge, though he wrote more books than any other major author. One is *Colonel Chabert*, the other is *The Black Sheep*, which treats the military way of life quite differently. The former was published separately and it is not technically a short story, so much as a novella. It is included in his series of novels known as *The Human Comedy* which savagely parodies French society in the period of the Restoration (1815–30) and the July Monarchy (1830–48) that followed it.

The Human Comedy, in which Chabert appears, is a great mosaic of an epoch with many scenes and no overall plot, which is why it was destined never to be completed (like Robert Musil's *Man Without Qualities*, an altogether less enjoyable read). What it attempts to show, in his own words, is the *what* of life and the *why* of sentiment. Balzac is famous for many sayings. One is that the modern novel should have no heroes and no monsters, which is a difficult prescription when life, especially in wartime, produces both. He is also famous for calling the novelist a 'historian of manners', and insisting that he is obliged to obey harsher laws than the professional historian. 'He must make everything seem plausible, even the truth, whereas, in the dominion of history, properly so-called, the impossible is justified by the fact that it occurred.' (Boorstin, 1993, 361).

Whatever humanity is to be found in *Colonel Chabert* is located in its eponymous lead. It is the tale of an old soldier—believed long-dead—who returns home to discover he has lost his wife, his fortune and even his name. His widow has remarried and liquidated his belongings. Seeking redress, Chabert hires an attorney to win back his home and his honour, and it is clear that he values the second more than the first. In the end he walks away empty handed after one last honourable deed, and spends the rest of his days quite destitute in a paupers' hostel, mourning his absence from his own life.

Balzac's story is not the first on the theme. Homer's *Odyssey* suggests that it is as old as war itself, though Odysseus is more fortunate in finding that his wife has kept faith in his own faithfulness to her. In Balzac's story, writes Andrew Brown, Penelope re-weaves the web of her life story to edit out her missing husband so that she can marry again. As Pritchett would argue, this is not only its principal theme, it is also its exclusive focus. *Colonel Chabert* is less a novella than an enlarged short story, and one famous for the way it begins, not at the beginning, but in mid-action, so to speak, with a lawyer's clerk (a 'gutter-jumper' or messenger) looking out of the office window and mocking an old man in the street. Lawyers' clerks were commonly young adolescents who carried writs to the bailiffs and petitions to the court. To the clerk's surprise the old man comes up to the office in a shabby box coat which is almost as frayed as his old body. He demands to see the attorney, Monsieur Derville. The young clerks have guessed that he may be an old soldier. The attorney is shocked to be told that he is

actually Colonel Chabert, a soldier famous in Napoleon's day for his
bravery in the field, and who was killed—or so everyone thought—at
the battle of Eylau (1807). Legend had it that he had fallen in one of
the several furious French cavalry charges against the Russian lines
that allowed Napoleon to avoid what would otherwise have been a
disastrous defeat.

Chabert is asked to return to the office, which he does later that
evening, when he recounts a remarkable story. We know that the
Colonel is a shadow of the man he once was, and Balzac is artful in
conveying his reduced circumstances in appropriate imagery: to the
attorney his new client looks like a waxwork; his eyes seem shrouded
in transparent film, his face is pale and thin as a knife. The lawyer's
clerk earlier in the day had seen only his surface features—the absence
of all fire in the eye and the first symptoms, perhaps, of senility. The
attorney reads in this stricken man signs of deeper sorrows. As Balzac
adds, a judge, like an author, might have noted Chabert's resemblance
to one of the grotesques which artists amuse themselves by sketching
in conversation with their friends.

After the initial shock has subsided, the attorney invites the old man
to tell his tale, which he proceeds to relate, no doubt embellishing
details here and there, as old men are wont to do. He had indeed been
felled at Eylau but not killed. Napoleon himself had enquired whether
he had survived and despatched two surgeons to see whether he was
still alive. Doubtless, they could not be bothered to feel his pulse;
instead they reported back that he had died. A certificate of death had
probably been issued and he was duly buried. When he came to, he
found that he had been buried alive. By raising his hands he had discovered a vacant space formed by two bodies that had fallen crosswise
over him so as to form an angle like that of two cards leant against one
another by a child building a castle (Balzac as ever had an eye for the
telling detail). The fresh air he was able to breathe had given him the
strength to dig himself out, at which point he was spotted by an old
woman and her husband who promptly conveyed him to the hospital
at Heidelberg.

Unfortunately, the Colonel has not emerged unscathed. He may be
physically free of the grave but he is now dependent on others, and it
is this paradox that is at the heart of the plot. He has won his freedom
only to be tied to a past in which no-one believes. 'You will understand, Monsieur, that I had emerged from the belly of the common

grave as naked as the day I emerged from my mother's womb.' (*Colonel Chabert*, 22). It takes him six months to remember who he is, and when he does so, the other patients and nurses think him deranged. Only one of the surgeons is willing to sign a deposition vouching for his true identity.

But from that day forth he wanders constantly like a vagabond, not fully recovered but liable to frequent lapses in health. We might, but Balzac does not, call it delayed shock (or trauma), a condition that was not to be identified until after Balzac's death. The novelist hints at this, if somewhat obliquely when he writes he was suffering from a malady for which medicine had no name, 'a disease which we can only call the 'spleen' of unhappiness.' (Ibid., 44). Eventually he finds his way back to Paris, where he wants his life back. It is the knowledge of his former life that makes the story so melancholic, for he has returned quite literally to a different world, one that has turned its back on honour. The world of Louis XVIII was a shallow one in which status was guaranteed by wealth, and no one enquired too closely how it was come by.

Worse still, he has discovered that his former wife, now officially a widow, has remarried. She is now a Countess whose husband Monsieur Derville represents. And the Count has married her in large part because of her fortune—30,000 francs a year which by rights belong to Chabert. Chabert has been deceived in love as well as life. His two letters to her have gone unanswered. Once forlorn, he has at last a fixed purpose. He is in the mood for revenge. In the end he won't be successful. In reality he cannot face the prospect of returning home for he has no home to return to. All he will finally seek to obtain is his money, and this he will renounce to preserve the honour which was buried with him on the field of battle but which he has brought back with him from the grave. It is the one thing that gives shape and momentum to what is left of his life.

We do not really get to know Derville in the course of the story. He is one of those characters largely shaped by the needs of the tale. What we see is a man not devoid of imagination and certainly not without compassion, but he is also a lawyer whose profession allows for few illusions. All he can do for the old man is to minimise the damage and exploit whatever opportunity presents itself. In that sense, he is not a man of honour, as Chabert would understand the term, but then the Colonel is outflanked by the world he has entered. Derville may be without 'honour' but by his own lights—and ours—he is not a dishonourable man.

Anxious to help his new client, the lawyer advises him that to begin a law suit against his wife would be a complicated business. There will be many preliminary enquiries, and every question will be submitted to the Supreme Court and give rise to costly suits. He proposes a financial settlement which will be the best solution in the circumstances, both for the Colonel and his former wife. 'That would be to sell my wife', expostulates Chabert. 'With an income of twenty-four thousand francs', the attorney rejoins, 'you will have in the position you find yourself in plenty of women who will suit you better than your wife, and will make you happier.' (*Colonel Chabert*, 43). Chabert is visibly distressed, for he is being asked to renounce the one thing they have not taken away from him: his honour. He is still a Grand Officer of the Legion of Honour. 'I'll go to the foot of the column on the Place Vendome', he exclaims, 'and there I'll cry out: "I am Colonel Chabert, the one who broke through the great Russian square at Eylau!" At least, the bronze statue will recognise me.' (Balzac, 2003, 45).

At this point the old man is close to collapse. The only justice he knows is military justice, which is simple and swift. He is appalled to see himself chained to a lawsuit. It seems a thousand times simpler to live as an indigent or even enlist as a common trooper, if any regiment will have him in his current state. Though an old man, he still can dream, and for him, honour, though devalued and debased in the France of the Restoration, is not only a last resort, it is his only resort, and his eventual triumph will be to retain it to the very end.

The second half of the tale features two dramatic scenes, one between the Comtesse Ferrault and Derville, in which she proves herself to have forfeited any honour she ever had. She is, as the French would say, *sans pudeur*. A former prostitute who Chabert had rescued from the streets, she is unwilling to part with anything. Derville is unmoved. He tells her plainly that Chabert can prove his claim. She will only keep her present husband, the Count, if she agrees to a settlement, and keeps the matter out of the courts.

The second scene brings Chabert and his wife together for the first time. With the money Derville has advanced him, the Colonel now looks more like his old self. He even wears the band and ribbon of the higher grade of the Legion of Honour. More to the point he has recovered his soldierly pride. Seeing him, writes Balzac, 'passers-by would easily have recognised one of those fine pieces of debris left over from our bygone army, one of those heroic men who reflect our national glory in the same way that a sliver of ice lit up by the sun seems to reflect all its rays.' (*Colonel Chabert*, 59). He is no longer the Chabert who had gone around in an old greatcoat, any more than an old sou resembles a newly minted forty franc coin. But it is a chilling reunion. There is no sentiment, nor even passionate vindictiveness on the part of the Comtesse who exhibits no remorse for what she has done and no concern for his present plight. She is willing to sell herself once again but the price she wants is a high one. To the attorney's suggestion that she assign 24,000 francs to her husband for joint stock held in his name to revert to her at his death in return for annulling the former marriage together with his certificate of death, she explains that it is much too dear, a remark which drives the Colonel to distraction. Knowing how he might react to the bargaining Derville had begged him not to attend the meeting. His presence has confirmed his identity in the lawyer's mind when the Comtesse flees the office when Chabert reminds her of her sordid past. But the fact that she still maintains her pretence of not recognising him means that he is indeed unrecognisable, and that no court of law is likely to challenge her testimony on that score.

And so the story continues to its inevitable denouement. For as the Colonel leaves the lawyer's office apparently defeated, the Comtesse, who has been waiting for him at the bottom of the staircase invites him to share her carriage where she proves as devious as she is still beautiful. 'Monsieur', she remarks in a soft and deeply ambiguous tone:

> The old soldier shuddered on hearing this single word ... it was at one and the same time a reproach, a prayer, a pardon, a hope, a despair, a question, an answer—this one word said it all. (*Colonel Chabert*, 64).

Truth, Balzac adds, is less complete in its utterance; it does not put everything on the outside; it allows us to see what is within. 'Monsieur', she repeats, 'I *did* recognise you.' And so she spins a web of deceit, well versed as she is in guile from her time as a streetwalker. She has indeed received his letters, she tells him, but she has not recognised the handwriting. To avoid disturbing her new husband's peace of mind, she has been obliged to be ever on the lookout for any swindler passing himself off as her former spouse. She will now trust to his kindness and his compassion, for she loves Ferraud as she had once loved him.

The Comtesse sweeps the old man off to her country estate. She may not be a strategist, but she is a consummate tactician, moving her charms into play and waiting for the enemy to make the first false move. And the Colonel stumbles when he admits that if he could separate her from her husband, he could never separate her from her children. Perhaps, writes A. N. Wilson, we should not be too unsympathetic to Chabert's wife. Wives, as James Michener wrote in the most famous novel to come out of the Korean War, *The Bridges at Toko-Ri* (1953) are the first casualty of war. Balzac does not take sides and perhaps we are not supposed to, either, but we cannot help noticing that Chabert treats her in the same mercenary fashion as she does his money. 'I picked you up in the Palais Royale (Je vous ai prise au Palais-Royal)', he reminds her—the verb *prendre* is loaded with as many meanings as the English, 'to take'. It is a possessive word, and he still treats her as a possession, one that he has unaccountably lost (*Colonel Chabert*, ix). She, too, is making her escape from the old world to the new, to a husband who knows nothing of her past, and she is determined to keep it that way, for the sake of her children—or so she tells the Colonel, seizing on the fact that he may be prepared to dishonour her, but he will never dishonour them. And so in the end he leaves defeated but not dishonoured; he departs the field relinquishing any claim to her wealth.

On a summer's day twenty years later, Derville and his former second clerk, now an attorney, travelling together on a case, recognise an old man sitting under an elm tree, living out what is left of his days in a hospice for the aged. Two days later they visit him but he is in his own mind no longer the Colonel, but No. 164, Room 7. He gratefully receives the twenty-five franc piece they give him, but he then retreats into silence (the only retreat that as a soldier he has ever executed). Derville is moved to wax lyrical as he looks at the senile old man before him who has lived there some twenty years. What a destiny— to start life in a foundlings' hospital and end it in a pauper's hostel, having in the interval helped Napoleon to conquer most of Europe. There are three men in the modern world, he remarks, who can never think well of the world—a priest, a doctor and a man of law. And all three wear black robes, perhaps because they are in mourning for every virtue and every illusion that humanity foolishly entertains. The most hapless of the three by far is the lawyer. For when a man comes in search of a priest, he is at least prompted to confess his sins; his faith may even redeem him. When he consults a doctor, he may hold on to some residual hope of being cured. But lawyers see the same evils repeated again and again which nothing can correct.

Chabert is a striking instance of the absence of a man from his own life. The question remains: even if he had regained his fortune, would he have kept his honour? And what is honour in a post-Napoleonic world? Part of him really did die at Eylau. He returns to a society that wants to forget the Napoleonic epic and to move on, one that has no time for returning heroes. He symbolises all that the new France refuses to acknowledge; Napoleon, heroism, and especially 'glory'. France has changed by accepting the monarchy, just as his wife has changed by remarrying a count. French history in the nineteenth century was a series of return acts, of restorations and revisitations, or what the French call *revenants*, a beautiful word for what is often an unedifying story.

Chabert cannot be welcomed back because he is dead in the hearts of his countrymen, and in a more uncaring, cruel world than that of today he cannot even be welcomed back as a scapegoat or a victim. He reminds me of the young man in *Indian Country* who returns from Vietnam to a father who has been bitterly opposed to the war and who cannot, or will not, accept him as his son: 'My son left a long time ago ... he never came back.' (Caputo, 1988, 105). The father is not making any money out of his son's repudiation, of course, unlike Chabert's wife; he is incurring a personal, emotional loss. But the young man is as lost to his father as the Colonel is to his wife. Neither of them are the men they were when they left for battle. Whether this is the worst fate of all is not entirely clear. Current war fiction does not engage in the big theme—war itself. It rarely explores it; instead it explores personal emotions. The best of the war novels, like *War and Peace*, help us to understand the phenomenon; today's works don't—but then perhaps the problem is war itself. The conflicts in Afghanistan and Iraq don't seem important enough to bear the weight of literary re-imagination. Our soldiers, writes Bryan Appleyard, quoting one contemporary novelist who has written about Afghanistan, tend to disappear once they are sent out. The public watches the news and moves on; it remains largely unmoved by their fate. At least, complained one soldier in Vietnam, they came home and were hated. Now they are ignored. (*The Sunday Times*, 8 July 2012).

Chabert's experience is much more akin to that of the American veterans who returned from Korea to a country that had 'no interest whatsoever in their experience', as Max Hastings writes (Herzog, 1992, 47). And this is no less challenging for some than the frayed marriages, the struggle to adjust to civilian life (which often seems much smaller in scale in the range of emotional experience). Chabert's real tragedy is that he has outlived himself. One of the underlying questions of the novella is whether it is possible to resurrect a life that no longer exists. Just because Chabert presents himself in person does not mean that the hero has come home. Unable to come to terms with the world, does he ever come to terms with what he too has become?

Paul Baümer: Youth Betrayed

All Quiet on the Western Front, Erich Maria Remarque

All Quiet on the Western Front is probably the best-known novel about the First World War, not only in Germany but also the English-speaking world. Within a year it was translated into twenty-eight languages, sold nearly 4 million copies and became an academy-award winning film. Remarque served in the war and saw battle in the Ypres sector before being invalided out a few months later. The success of the novel made his reputation in America and Britain at the same time as it ruined it in Germany once the Nazis emerged as the leading political movement. He unwisely wrote a sequel, *The Road Back* (1931) which brought Paul Baümer back to life and related the story through his own words. It was not a great success any more than Joseph Heller's decision to bring Yossarian back to life. Shakespeare wisely chose not to allow Falstaff even a walk-on part in *Henry V* even though that meant breaking his promise to the public.

The title, as we know it, is not strictly an accurate translation. The book appeared in Germany for the first time as *Im Westen Nicht Neues*. There is a different kind of irony here. Nothing new on the Western Front. But the translation by A. W. Wheen in 1929—the year of the novel's publication—struck a chord with a generation that had difficulty re-integrating itself into post-war life. Almost as famous is the epigraph Remarque gave the novel. 'This book is intended neither as an accusation nor a confession, but simply as an attempt to give an account of a generation that was destroyed, even those of it who survived the shelling.'

Remarque's book became one of the best selling books of all time. It is now seen as a cry against the madness of war, but it sold so many copies because it was understood by many readers at the time to be an adventure story about a band of young men, just out of school, experiencing life more dramatically than those born too late to be conscripted. Remarque's work has worn well because it broke with much of the German war literature of the 1920s—the cult of heroism of the young, the forging of a new man, as Josef Wehner had it in his novel *Seven Before Verdun* (1930) which is also the story of a group of young men experiencing war together. 'We went over the top into timelessness.' One contemporary reviewer found Wehner's characters 'truer than all truth'. But the fact is that these books have not worn well, and are no longer in print (Mosse, 1990, 200).

Most important of all, Remarque's novel came to define the Great War experience. The first novels to emerge in the 1920s had often cast the conflict in a positive light; after 1929 the war began to be remembered quite differently, not as an Allied victory or a German defeat but as a human catastrophe. *All Quiet on the Western Front*—in the words of one historian—made it impossible for those who came after to see the war from any other perspective. But the book is less about war (we are given few details of dates, places or units) than about the effects of war on the narrator. The characters are merely victims—a portrayal that one might expect of an author who was conscripted in the penultimate year of the conflict, thrown into the hell of the Ypres sector where food was scarce, living conditions appalling and defeat impending. The novel is first and foremost not about the truth of the war but its truth for one man, Erich Remarque (Eksteins, 1980, 21).

Much of today's First World War literature remains wedded to this 'truth', cataloguing a life of undiluted misery in which the soldiers are little more than vectors through which misery can be relayed to the reader. In the case of many novels there is no attempt to define or develop character; the personalities on the page are normally blank because of the author's need for the war to define them. Often they seem to be more interested in depicting the landscape of war than the mental landscapes of the protagonists. What is remarkable about Remarque is that he does both. The achievement of the novel is to portray a horrific landscape of war with a minutely detailed portrait of the inner life of a man thoroughly lost in it.

Most of the fictional characters I have chosen to discuss offer us an insight into the nature of war. Remarque's hero doesn't. He isn't unobservant; his acute observations give the book its power, and he leaves nothing to the imagination, which is why the Nazis so disliked the novel and later forced its author to flee the country. What the English liked most was its portrayal of a generation that was 'lost' from the very beginning; that was too young, or too naïve, to reach any real conclusions about the appalling experience they endured. As Brian Murdoch maintains, the characters' very inability to articulate a firm view of war is the point of the book. The reader is left to draw his own conclusions (*All Quiet on the Western Front*, 207) and this in part explains why Paul is so difficult to pin down. Paul is simply overawed by the experience of war, which makes him almost as elusive as Philip Jenkins, the narrator of Anthony Powell's novel, *The Dance to the Music of Time*. His failure to tell us much about himself and Remarque's refusal to get us to see him through the eyes of others is indicative of the novel's other central theme: the young men who join up with Paul are overwhelmed by death: its constant presence; its relentlessness; its indiscriminate nature. Living under the criss-cross of shell trajectories, the soldiers exist in a perpetual state of anxiety. One can be squashed flat in a bomb-proof dug out and survive without a scratch for hours in the open under the heaviest barrage. In an attempt to stay one step ahead of death, Paul deliberately loses himself in the crowd; only after the ranks have been thinned does he return to narrating again in the first person.

First person narratives can be difficult frameworks within which to explore deep themes, but Baumer's narrative voice changes from time to time. Sometimes he uses the first person singular; at others the first person plural, and when he uses the word 'we' it is often ambiguous. The reader does not always know whether he is referring to the group of school friends with whom he has joined up, or to the members of his company, or to the 'lost generation' (a misleading term which Remarque helped popularise in the English-speaking world). At the end of the novel, the death of his friends leaves him alone with his thoughts. He is forced to return to the first person singular as he struggles to come to terms with the war as it draws to an end. In the last paragraph a new narrator appears who is never named, to report Paul's death. He is now presented in the third person as another anonymous victim of the fighting

The few personal details Paul tells us about his childhood are revealing for that reason. He used to play, he tells us, in the meadows behind his home town which featured a row of old poplar trees that rose up the side of a stream. He used to spend hours listening to their gentle rustling. It was the quietness (for the Western Front is never quiet—even in the depots way behind the lines, the buzz and muted thundering of the guns is never far away) that is the most striking thing about them. Paul recognises this is not reality (as he recalls his childhood days in the thick of war), but for him they still have that quality. All his memories have the same theme:

> … They are soundless apparitions which speak to me by looks and gestures, wordless and silent—and that silence is precisely what disturbs me, forces me to hold onto my sleeve or my rifle so that I don't abandon myself to this seductive dissolution, in which my body would like to disperse itself and flow away towards the silent powers that lie behind all things. (*All Quiet on the Western Front*, 83–4).

At the Front he is always seeking to escape into the silence, or in this case the primal earth. When a soldier presses himself into the earth during a bombardment, he urges himself deeper into the earth all the time, with the fear of death upon him. Remarque associates this with a return to the womb, to primal existence (*All Quiet on the Western Front*, 39). Other writers were much less lyrical. In Barbusse's novel *Under Fire* one of the characters is described as 'an ape man, decked out with rags and lurking in the bowels of the earth (the trenches),' (Adas, 1989). It is the animal instinct reawakened, Paul concludes, that alone allows a man to survive death, if he is lucky, the instinct that turns a soldier into a 'human animal'. The earth becomes especially important when Paul, returning from home leave, volunteers to join a patrol in No Man's Land. He finds refuge in a hollow. The voices of his friends in the trench behind him afford him another opportunity to survive by losing himself in a crowd. 'I'm no longer a shivering scrap of humanity alone in the dark—I belong to them and they to me, we share the same fear and the same life … I want to press my face into them, those voices … which will be my support.' (*All Quiet on the Western Front*, 145).

Eventually, Paul will dissolve into the silence himself—into death. When his body is finally found, his face appears to wear an expression, we are told, so composed that it looks as if he were almost happy that it had turned out this way. The passage still divides commentators and puzzles readers, but one interpretation is that he is claimed by the 'quietness' which is the only refuge from the horror of the moment; another is that he has suspected for some time that even were he to survive there would be nothing to return to. He would no longer have any real links with the way he used to be; he would no longer feel a kinship with the world of family, friends and home. He might be present in that world, but no longer alive in it.

It is this attitude that illustrates the predicament of men too young to make any sense of the war, or their experiences. The fact that Paul is given to thinking about war more than his comrades merely throws this into especially stark relief. Each chapter ends with an observation about the war, but though these illuminate the darkness, they do not lead to any general conclusions. Paul is an intelligent young man, but he is only nineteen when he volunteers, too young perhaps to make much sense of the experience.

The youth of the soldiers is highlighted from the very beginning. Paul introduces us to his schoolmates as they are sent up to the line as relief troops. Little Albert Korp, who is the cleverest of the friends and the first to make it to acting Lance-Corporal; Muller, who lugs his school textbooks about with him and still dreams of taking his school leaving diploma; and then Leer, old enough to grow a beard, who is obsessed with the girls who serve the officer-only brothels, and who he thinks are obliged by army regulations to wear silk slips and take a bath before having sex. All are the same age as Paul, as are the other soldiers who are from the same school, the skinny former locksmith, Tjaden; Hie Westhus, a peat-digger who is not very bright, and Dettering, a farmer who thinks about nothing but going home to his wife and his farm.

The overwhelming theme is betrayal. The sense of betrayal comes out most from the absence of the enemy, for the real enemy is behind the lines. We hardly ever see the British, and the very word 'enemy' hardly ever appears in the text. Paul always refers to 'the others', or 'to those over there.' Instead we hear much more of the Germans, especially the schoolmaster who urged them to join up to serve the Fatherland; he represents the older generation who should have guided the young men into adult life, into the future. Their first experience of artillery fire shatters that illusion, as well as their trust in life. From that moment they know they are on their own. They soon lose their youthful innocence and ambition to make more of their abilities; they grow old before their time. All they know in some strange and melancholy way is that they have become hardened.

Another betrayal involves their self-belief. They have been told that the future was theirs to make of using their individual talents. Once they join up they find themselves swallowed up into a collective which demands they surrender their individual personalities more completely than they could ever have imagined possible. The brutality of army life, especially in training, is vividly portrayed, as is the shock of being bullied by men that they would have despised in civilian life (it is Paul's bad luck to fall foul of Cpl Himmelstross, 'the stickiest bastard' in the whole barracks).

The third betrayal involves history. As they leave for the Front, an older officer is moved to refer to the company as 'young heroes'. History, they have been told, is made by its heroes, but the war they are asked to fight in is hardly heroic, and it is epic, if at all, only because of the scale of the carnage. Albert puts it best: 'The war has ruined us for everything.' He is right. 'We're no longer young men, we've lost any desire to conquer the world. We're refugees. We're fleeing from ourselves. From our own lives. We were eighteen years old and we had just begun to love the world and to love being in it; but we had to shoot at it. The first shell to land went straight to our hearts.' (*All Quiet on the Western Front*, 61). Later Paul adds, 'We're dead men with no feelings who are able by some trick, some dangerous magic, to keep on running and keep on killing.' (*All Quiet on the Western Front*, 80). This, surely, is not how history is supposed to be made?

This is an avowedly anti-war book. If we are given few details of battles, we are given death in all its hideous and varied forms. A sharpened spade, we are told, is a more effective weapon than a bayonet. With it, you can split a man diagonally between the neck and shoulder, as far down as the chest. We see what happens when a gas attack takes place. We are shown men with blue faces and blackened lips, their lungs burnt to pieces, coughing up blood and slowly suffocating to death. We see men still alive with the top of their skulls missing; and soldiers who continue running when both their feet have been shot away, stumbling on their splintered stumps to the next shell hole and back behind the lines. When Paul is sent to a field hospital he sees every way a soldier can be wounded or killed: in the stomach and spinal cord, in the arms or legs, in the jaw or in the throat, in the lungs or pelvis, in the kidneys or testicles. War is another cause of death, like cancer or TB or influenza or dysentery. The fatalities are just more numerous and more horrible. The very matter of fact style makes the horror even more palpable.

Paul grows in the course of the novel in the company of death. In many ways his growing disenchantment, his dispassionate recording of the horrors he is forced to observe, his emotionally null life (which we witness when he is on home leave and visits his mother who is dying of cancer) stems from the fact that those back home—on the so-called 'home front'—cannot grasp the reality of Paul's world. He is sustained increasingly only by a crude will to survive. Life on the very edge of death restricts itself to what is absolutely necessary. Every activity is geared exclusively to survival and is automatically directed to that end. And the survival instinct grows all the stronger, as one by one all Paul's old school friends are killed. Muller by a Verey light in the stomach; Bentik, the company commander, by a shot in the chest before a piece of shrapnel smashes away the lower part of his face. The same piece of shrapnel rips open Leer's side and causes him to bleed to death before anyone can come to his rescue. And then there is finally Paul himself, the last of the seven friends from the same class to die, though we are never told how. In the last days he had mused that the worst fate of all is that he and the others can make no sense of the war. Had they come back in 1918 they could have unleashed a storm out of the pain and intensity they have experienced. Now they are just too burned out, rootless and weary to cope:

> We are superfluous, even to ourselves; we shall grow older, a few will adapt, others will make adjustments, and many of us will not know what to do—the years will trickle away, and eventually we shall perish. (*All Quiet on the Western Front*, 199).

These are the last thoughts of a young man undone not by life but by war, a war that has become his life. No Man's Land, he observes at one point, is not only outside, but inside our hearts. Remarque's despairing conclusion is that even had Paul survived there would be no progress in his understanding; he would merely have taken his incomprehension into the peace that follows.

Paul is not representative of a 'lost generation', he is not even representative of a very large number of soldiers who were ruined by war. He represents, instead, those who lost their illusions. Nationalism is an embodied idea, and all ideas can be dangerous for that reason. Wittgenstein said it for us: the best image of the soul is the body in pain. We must be careful in what we believe precisely for that reason. But Remarque's book makes its central point with conviction. Old men still send the young to their death with brave words and even braver visions; countries still squander the lives of the young often for spurious purposes of their own. The First World War was an obscene waste of life, even it had to be fought. The world was a better place for the Allies' victory, but writers like Barbusse were right also to find the very word victory 'nauseous'. Remarque clearly wants us to identify with Paul but he does not compel us to. We can witness his fate, recognising it represents 'a' truth about war, though not necessarily 'the' truth about this or any other conflict. If it did, the novel would be so time-locked in its concerns that it would not transcend its historical moment. Many more soldiers, even those who were conscripted (unlike Paul and his friends who join up) retained their faith in the cause for which they were fighting right up until the end. Paul does not survive and the experience is no less true for him than it is for others. And Remarque had one card up his sleeve, of course, that invests his novel with authority. His anti-war stance in no way invalidates Paul's 'testimony'. In the horror Paul draws for us he strikes at a truth we would often rather not contemplate. The novel's main theme is human suffering and its two most extreme aspects; abnegation and heroism. The novel portrays in the rawest form not the suffering the gods inflict on man in the *Iliad*, but the pain we inflict on each other, a theme which unfortunately is as old as history itself.

Guy Crouchback: The Disillusioned Soldier
Sword of Honour, Evelyn Waugh

Evelyn Waugh had a disastrous war. He took part in the debacle of Dakar (when the British ran away and Waugh never left the ship), as well as a farcical scuffle at Bardia, which saw only one casualty, a commando shot by his own men. Later he saw action in Crete though he reached the island just in time to take part in the evacuation. And then there were the long months in Yugoslavia watching the British government sell itself out to Tito and the Communists. When he was not on 'active service', he was at home, partying, complaining, bitching, making himself a complete nuisance to everyone he met. 'We keep company in this world with a hoard of abstractions and reflections and counterfeits of ourselves', he wrote in *Brideshead Revisited*, these days his most famous work. 'Captain Waugh' was a counterfeit of himself that he finally tired of as the war drew to an end. His thorough disillusion-ment at his role-playing as a Royal Marine Commando and then one of the Blues is reflected in Guy Crouchback's progress through a world at war, one which has no place in its heart for the old verities that are so central to his life, above all honour.

Waugh began his career as a comic novelist, and it as such that he is read today. His characters are in a tradition that goes back to Sterne and Dickens, who both had a vitality of invention that few have sur-passed. But as his mood deepened (as did that of Dickens in later life) the novels take on a more serious and sombre tone, none more so than his war trilogy. It is made up of three works—*Officers and Gentlemen* (1952), *Men at Arms* (1955) and *Unconditional Surrender* (1961). They all capture a deep and despairing view of the world which plagued Waugh's last years. If in *Brideshead Revisited* he consciously set out to write the obituary of the doomed English upper class, the *Sword of Honour* series was an obituary of England, and the military tradition that had underpinned the Empire at its height. Indeed the tril-ogy ends with a brief chapter in 1951 set against the Festival of Britain, a pale echo of the Great Exhibition a century earlier when British power had been unchallenged and seemed unchallengeable. There was little popular exuberance on the part of a public that had little money to spend and was still on rationing.

It is no coincidence that as the US took to its new role as a Super-power, so the literature of war in the English-speaking world began to be dominated by American writers such as Mailer, Vonnegut and Heller (all of whom served in the war, like Waugh himself). Waugh's novel in the revised form in which the author himself wished the three books to be read (and the one I have employed here) is the last major work of English war fiction. Beginning with Korea and extending most recently to Iraq and Afghanistan, the British Army has shad-owed its American ally, not always with great success. In 1940 it was fighting for itself, and also for what the Americans came to call the 'Free World'.

In the figure of Guy Crouchback we have a very English 'victim'. He sees too much, or rather sees too little in which he can take pride, espe-cially after the US enters the war and the honour of standing alone goes with it. This mood and attitude still dominate much of the literature such as Robert Harris' *Enigma*, the story of the decoding of military German codes at Bletchley Park, one of the great success stories of the

British war effort. But Harris paints a picture of a country that is finding it difficult to sustain the illusion of being on an equal footing with the US or USSR. Waugh had little time for the first and abominated the second. His take on US society comes out in one of his funniest books, *The Loved Ones*, which preceded *Men at Arms* by a few years. But by then the best of the comic books had been published—they all came out in the 1930s (*Black Mischief, A Handful of Dust* and *Scoop!*). There is much humour in the war trilogy and marvellously realised comic characters such as Ritchie-Hook, but then these were dark days for Waugh personally and the mood is reflected in the trilogy itself.

In Crouchback, by contrast, Waugh created a character who finds it increasingly difficult to navigate the ever widening gap between his world and that of the People; between a historically rich past and a bleak future; between a world of principle and one of purely utilitarian calculation. Guy is a fully realised character but he is also rather a bland one, in part because he joins the war under false pretences and finds out that he has been duped fairly early on. He enters the war to fight for what he cherishes—tradition and honour, only to discover he has been suborned into fighting the People's War instead. He enters the fight to save England only to find that the future belongs to its allies, America and Soviet Russia. At the end of each novel, Guy suffers a personal defeat which can be read as indicative of one of war's principal features. We fight and lose the battle, wrote William Morris, and the things we fight for come in spite of our defeat. But when they come they turn out not to be what we understood and other men have to fight for what we meant under another name.

There are many parallels between Guy's career and Waugh's. Like Guy, Waugh was rather old for active service; he was almost thirty-six in 1939. Like Guy, Waugh's Royal Marines (the Halberdiers of the novel) were transferred to an abandoned private school where he later met Brigadier Albert Sinclair-Moreford, who was the model for Ritchie-Hook in the novel. Like Guy, Waugh served in Crete, arriving too late to see much action. Waugh got back to England via Egypt on a troop ship which voyaged around the Cape across to the West Indies and then back to Britain. Finally, like Guy, Waugh served in the Balkans as a member of the Second Special Air Service Regiment (SAS), but he suffered injury in a parachute jump and was retired from active service. He was fortunate since he still wanted to take part in the war as it came to an end, to be invited to join Fitzroy McLean's mission to Tito's partisans in Croatia, and the last novel in the trilogy is largely about the political manoeuvrings as the West began to adjust to the post-war world.

It is equally important to acknowledge, however, that Guy and Waugh lived separate lives. Guy is popular and protective of his men in a way Waugh was not. He is not witty like his creator. Indeed, he is pretty bland, but he has sufficient interest to be a personality. And he comes from the kind of ancient family to which Waugh aspired to belong. After marrying he takes his younger son's share of the patrimony and a diminished family fortune and moves to the white highlands of Kenya where he lives for a time in unruffled good humour. Later he moves to Italy where he has a fondness for fascism and even admiration for Mussolini but he has no truck with appeasement because he knows fascism too well. The signing of the Nazi-Soviet pact allows him to go to war with a good conscience. It gives him a place in an unfolding historical struggle. In the most famous passage in the work, we learn that everything had now become clear. The enemy had at last thrown off all disguise—the collusion of Fascism and Communism represented *The Modern Age in Arms*. 'Whatever the outcome there was a place for him in that battle.' (*Sword of Honour*, 4). Guy's last act before leaving for England so that he can join up is to visit the tomb of an English knight who had died before ever reaching the Holy Land, to fight in the Second Crusade. He feels a special affinity for '*Il Santo Inglese*' and asks Sir Roger to pray for his endangered kingdom. Sir Roger's fate, of course, will eventually be Guy's for he too will fail in his own personal crusade against the modern age, just as Sir Roger failed to reach Jerusalem.

This is another kind of victimhood in war—wanting to play a role and yet finding no part. It is this interaction between public and private that defines the trilogy. 'I don't ask anything of you', he tells God after returning from his father's funeral, but he is willing to do his duty, if asked. That is the deadly core of his apathy, and it leaves a terrible emptiness even at moments of enthusiasm and activity he finds in the army:

> In the recesses of Guy's conscience there lay the belief that somewhere, somehow, something would be required of him that he must attend to the summons when it came. (*Sword of Honour*, 500).

He sees himself as one of the labourers in the biblical parable who sat in the marketplace waiting to be hired and was not called into the vineyard until late in the day. He does not expect an heroic destiny—all that matters is to seize the chance when it is offered. For one moment he finds it in Croatia where he tries to save some Jews from destruction, and equally quickly he loses it again. For Guy there are no heroic moments in war, only quiet moments of desperation in a largely empty life. He finds that he is fighting for a lost cause, not even a losing one, which means that as the war draws to a conclusion, he is not elated or relieved, but increasingly disillusioned. Inevitably he finds himself fighting against history; consequently he becomes an empty vehicle for all kinds of experiences, both comic and tragic.

Guy joins up in a fashionable regiment, the Halberdiers, where he meets the main character of the first novel, Althorpe. Both had arrived from his past life in Africa (we are never told where or why). Althorpe, in a sense, is more fortunate than Guy. Both men embrace the tradition of the Halberdiers unreservedly; for Guy, of course, they are part of the tradition he is defending. But Althorpe at least goes to his death still believing in them (he is buried to 'the faultless balance of the Halberdiers' slow march'). For Guy, the reality of modern war has already begun to intrude. His first awakening is a misguided operation against the French stronghold of Dakar, a town in West Africa which he imagines to be a typical French outpost, 'all boulevards and brothels'. He takes part in a foolish night raid independently organised by Ritchie-Hook, who is keen to go 'boffing' (killing). The mission is a disaster, more comic than tragic, or rather tragi-comic, in that inadvertently it leads to Althorpe's death, for which Guy must take much of the blame.

The first intimation of Althorpe's illness is a message from up country by telephone from the native telephonist. 'Capt Althorpe, "im very sorry off colour requests extension leaves."' When the unit next catches sight of the captain he is slung in a sheeted hammock between two bearers, 'looking like a Victorian wood cut from a book of exploration.' When Guy visits him in hospital, he unwillingly shares a glass or two of whiskey, even more unwisely leaving the bottle behind. Althorpe overdoses on alcohol and goes into a coma from which he does not awake. At thirty-six Guy has killed his first man. The army chooses to let Guy go unpunished, letting the suspicion fall on the hospital orderlies and native porters who are in and out of the hospital and might have sold Althorpe the stuff. It is not the first deception in which he is involved; it is merely one of several moral 'compromises' in which the characters of the novel engage in a war which is about to be totally compromised by the alliance Britain will soon enter into with Stalin's Russia.

It is worth putting in a word here for Ritchie-Hook, the great Halberdier *enfant terrible* of the Great War, the youngest commander in the history of the Corps, yet the slowest to be promoted. Twice court martialled for disobedience to orders in the field, twice acquitted in recognition of his bravery; where lesser men collect enemy helmets, Ritchie-Hook once came back with the head of a German sentry in either hand (no doubt decapitated, though we are not told, by the entrenching tool for which he has a special affection). In the inter-war years he pitches up anywhere where there is a conflict, from County Cork to the Holy Land. We see him at Dakar coming back from the ill-fated raid where he has landed against orders, with a negro head. We see him last in Croatia single-handedly attacking a fortified position, 'attended' (according to later German reports to HQ) by a small boy, in another by a midget. This was an attack which had 'no precedent in Clausewitz'. (*Sword of Honour*, 646). The 'midget' is in fact a cameraman (a figure first seen in the Spanish Civil War) who, like a 'pet dwarf privileged to tumble about the heels of a prince of the Renaissance, was gambolling around him with his camera, crouching and skipping, so small and agile as to elude the snipers on the wall.' Ritchie-Hook meets a typical death, leading the partisans who do not owe him any allegiance, and think the attack as mad and misguided as it undoubtedly is. And the death is subtly relayed by Waugh who manipulates *us* the readers.

Waugh should have known that most of his readers even in the 1950s would have had a tough time identifying with Ritchie-Hook's schoolboy antics. They had no place even in the Second World War. They were an echo of an era that had died in the Great War, in battles like Loos and Ypres and Gallipoli—all names of the dormitories in the school where the Halberdier unit is billeted, Kut-el-Amara House, Southend on Sea. This is another comic touch, for it is the name of a town in Iraq where British soldiers had surrendered to the Turks ignominiously in 1916. Guy's character throughout the trilogy is deliberately understated, and we don't learn whether he is saddened by Ritchie-Hook's death, but Waugh leads us to deduce it. And through the inference we too may be sympathetic to Ritchie-Hook's plight, that of an honourable but ludicrous old man whose career, like his strides, have grown shorter and shorter, faltered and almost come to a stop (*Sword of Honour*, 635).

In his death, Ritchie-Hook commits what Shelley called 'the generous error', the error of those who try to live life by their own vision of it, thus transforming the world about them and impressing upon it their own character. His vision of life takes over whenever he takes centre stage. Unfortunately it is a vision that betrays him, as we know it must. The Dakar expedition is a sufficient throwback to an imperial past for the vision to hold, just ('we are not here to conquer Africa', Richie Hook reassures his followers). By 1944 that world had long since vanished and the semi-Falstaffian figure pays the price for being, like Guy, out of step with the times. In *Put Out More Flags* (1942) most of the characters belong to an old world that died with the war, and Waugh knew it. He calls them 'a race of ghosts ... no longer contemporary in sympathy.' It is the new men and the Communists who will own the future.

Ritchie-Hook's death brings Guy back to reality and robs him of his remaining illusions. When he first learns to parachute in *Unconditional Surrender*, he experiences a rapture. He finds himself floating free, 'he was a free spirit in an element as fresh as on the day of its creation' but the reality in the form of gravity forces him out of his reverie. He finds he is falling fast to the ground. It is a lesson that every soldier has to take to heart. It is rare for a soldier to find himself fighting 'a good war', and even rarer to find his faith in life or the future confirmed. The universe, in the end, is indifferent to our fate. Fortune, wrote Waugh, 'is the least capricious of deities and arranges things on the just and rigid system that no one should be very happy for very long.' (Boyd, 2005, 197).

Guy's disillusionment is amplified even more in Crete, the centrepiece of the second volume of the trilogy, and it comes in the form of personal betrayal by a man whom he holds in high regard. By now he has joined the Commandos, the 'flower of the nation', and Guy thinks the description not entirely unmerited. Ivor Claire is one of them. 'Ivor Claire, Guy thought, was the finest flower of them all. He was quintessential England, the man Hitler had not taken into account.' (*Sword of Honour*, 318). The Commando is initially posted to Egypt in February 1941. It is when Guy visits Ivor in a private nursing home where he has absented himself after a minor accident in the desert pursuing Arab marauders that he hears of Julia Stitch, who will figure prominently in the events that follow.

For the war is going badly. The British are driven out of Greece, and soon Crete is under threat. By the time the Commandos arrive, the Germans have landed by parachute and the island is almost in their hands. Guy and his unit find themselves taking part in a belated and dangerous rear-guard action. In the end, they are the last to be left to cover the final withdrawal by sea. Guy comes into his own when the chips are down. Unlike his commanding officer who suffers a breakdown, he remains in good heart for much of the fighting. Cut off from his unit, he finds himself 'eased at last from the dead weight of human company' but when he meets up with a battalion of his old regiment, the Halberdiers, his sense of desolation returns (*Sword of Honour*, 404). He feels like Philoctetes, set apart from his fellows by an old festering wound; Philoctetes without his bow (Sir Roger without his sword) (*Sword of Honour*, 410).

Guy Crouchback is told that if he meets up with his unit they are to wait for the Halberdiers to catch up. He takes note of the time and lines of march in which they will meet up with X Commando. When they do meet up, he enters into a long conversation with Ivor Claire who is aghast to hear that the Halberdiers will embark before them, 'leaving the fighting troops behind and taking off the rabble.' (*Sword of Honour*, 420). Ordered to surrender after the Halberdiers have sailed off Claire is reluctant to comply. He asks what he thinks of honour. Is it not a concept that is always changing? Was duelling not *de rigeur* once and is now laughed at? Guy Crouchback adds that it was not moral objections that ended the practice, it was democracy.

> 'And in the next war', Ivor replies, 'When we are completely democratic, I expect it will be quite honourable for officers to leave their men behind. It'll be laid down in King's Regulations as their duty—to keep a cadre going to train new men to take the place of prisoners.' (*Sword of Honour*, 421).

Guy is sticking by the old rules. A captain should never abandon his ship, and certainly not leave before the rest of the crew. Claire speaks for the Modern Age in arms, for democratic common sense. 'Don't you think in a really *modern* army they would respect them the more .... I reckon our trouble is that we are at the awkward stage—like a man challenged to a duel a hundred years ago.' And Claire proves true to these new principles. He chooses to desert. Guy chooses to stay behind and surrender with the men, but in the event they unexpectedly find a boat which though barely seaworthy, allows them at some risk to escape.

Throughout the novel Waugh presents Guy's undoubted courage as being an argument with his principles. True to form, he had remarked that there are soldiers who might prefer to try their luck in the mountains with local Cretans, but that were they to be captured they would only be taken prisoner; the partisans would be shot. Claire believes that in a future age it would be perfectly honourable for officers (not enlisted men, of course) to desert so that they can train the next batch of recruits. Guy observes coldly that perhaps 'men wouldn't take kindly to being trained by deserters.' He is being true here to his social code, and it is precisely the code and his belief in it that allows him to master his fear when others cannot master their own. The plight of his unit is grave but he rises to the occasion as he feels he *must*. Even at this stage of the war, he still remains convinced that the old values are still worth preserving, and more important can still be saved which is why Claire's desertion comes as such a shock.

Guy survives their escape at sea, waking up in a hospital with Mrs Stitch as his first visitor. At first he is overjoyed to hear that Ivor has made it, too. 'It's the best thing that's happened.' There is no irony intended. 'Well of course *I* think so', said Mrs Stitch 'I'm on Ivor's side, always.' (*Sword of Honour*, 433). Guy does not immediately recognise the qualification in her tone. She is not on his side, the side of tradition and honour. She has made a choice. Aware that Guy can destroy Ivor's reputation she tries to persuade him not to report his desertion. Everything was chaotic, after all. Nothing made much sense. No one had any reason to be proud of themselves. 'Obviously by the end there *weren't* any orders.' Ivor has already been sent to India at Julia's instigation to escape the damaging gossip about his behaviour, and we later learn he distinguishes himself after joining the Chindits in Burma, winning a DSO and an honourable incapacitating wound. In the last pages of the trilogy he is to be found propping up the bar at Guy's club, now fully rehabilitated, thanks to the fact that Guy agrees to go along with the story.

War offers many opportunities for betrayal, perhaps more than any other activity. Personal betrayals, such as the betrayal of friends who are let down, or find that others will not go the extra distance, and those larger betrayals when we change sides and go over to the enemy. Ivor Claire does not betray his country; he is not a traitor, but for Waugh he has a traitor's heart. He betrays his friends, and the social code that unites them. We can figure him much more than we figure

Julia Stitch. He has acted as any of us might under fire. She is much more manipulative.

'I hope I would rather have the guts to betray my country than my friends', E. M. Forster famously averred after the treachery of his Cambridge colleagues became known in the early 1960s. Julia is reading Forster's book on Alexandria when Guy first meets her, the connection is purely accidental but serendipitous. Julia is very much of Forster's persuasion. She will never betray a friend; Guy, betrayed by Ivor, loses all affection for him. They will never again be friends, though as Englishmen of their generation they will be polite enough when they meet up at the club. There is a logic, of course, in going along with the deception. No one has died as a result of Claire's desertion. He had not endangered any position. His desertion made no difference at all to the outcome of the war. But it makes a terrible difference to Guy. It matters that the friends he left behind in Crete have become Prisoners of War. It matters even more that the man he had thought a friend had betrayed him. Above all, he is beginning to lose belief in the war with its petty betrayals and moral compromises.

Guy is a much more admirable figure than those of his own class like Claire. He sides with those he does not know personally—the anonymous men in the ranks whose lives count for him as a fellow Englishman. Forster felt as remote from them (the men Guy Burgess betrayed in the Cold War) as Guy feels from the people (the other ranks) in this, the People's War. But he finds himself in the same situation, and that makes the crucial difference. Julia is the worst offender of all. She is remarkably shallow. She holds to no political ideals or opinions, and owns up to no loyalty to country, either. She is fiercely loyal, however, to her friends, shorn of any of the political or patriotic identities that define them, which is why she ultimately betrays herself, because her friends are only an extension of herself. Aristotle tells us that perfect friendship is a form of self-love, not unlike that of a mother for her children: what is done by one's friends is done to oneself which is why Guy, of course, feels so implicated in his country's betrayal of the old values. Ivor St Claire's betrayal of his men is merely a microcosm of Britain's betrayal of Guy. Soldiers live with real betrayal and it costs lives (if not their own, then those they are fighting for), and they have no redress, which is why betrayal is so absolute. And with few exceptions, it does not work the other way round—they do not have a chance to betray their country for their friends. If they do, they usually pay the ultimate price.

Unconditional Surrender opens in August 1943 and ends a few months
before the end of the war. The central scene is set in Croatia, part of
German-occupied Yugoslavia, where Tito's partisans are fighting the
Germans. Guy is attached to them as a Military Liaison Officer. Guy's
job as a superannuated officer past his prime is not to take part in the
fighting, but merely to report back home one the military situation. He
becomes personally involved one day when he meets up with a group
of Jews, or 'displaced persons'. He finds them somewhat grotesque in
their remnants of bourgeois civility. There were Semites among them,
but the majority were fair, snub-nosed, high cheek-boned, the descendants of Slav tribes Judaisised long after the Dispersal. One of the leaders with whom he can converse in Italian is Mme Kanyi, who tells him
that they are all survivors from Italian concentration camps, rounded
up by the Italians to save them from the murderous Ustachi. Their
wish now is to get to Bari and out of the hands of the Yugoslavs,
including the partisans.

In the course of the tale Guy visits their quarter in a school near a
ruined Orthodox church. He finds them living in miserable conditions,
sleeping huddled in little nests of straw on the floor. Mme Kanyi lives
apart from the rest in a potting shed in an electrical plant where her
husband continues to work. 'She was younger and better fed, and
therefore more hopeless than the others.' She knows the risks in even
talking to him but agrees to provide a list of the people in Bari who
might help them. Guy is later ticked off by a partisan commander who
reminds him that the fate of Yugoslavs is an internal matter. Guy has
to apologise, but it rankles with him. '… in a world of hate and waste,
he was being offered the chance of doing a single small act to redeem
the times.' (*Sword of Honour*, 617). He still feels it possible to play a
historical role however minimal. It is therefore a joy that he receives an
unexpected order to despatch two of the Jews to Bari by plane. Since
the Communists will not release the Kanyis, he chooses two other leaders of the group, offering them 'a little kindling of human hope.' The
plane arrives with Guy's old Halberdier commander De Souza, a new
man, a fellow traveller, a Communist in all but name whose loyalty is
not to Britain but Communism. And even though he is a Jew, he takes
no interest in the fate of his fellow Jews. They must accept the verdict
of history. In times like these you must forget you are a Jew and simply remember you are an anti-Fascist. Individual identity must give
way to historical abstraction.

And so to the final act of the drama. On his forty-first birthday, Guy receives a despatch telling him that he can put some of the Jews on four Dakotas arriving the next day. Once again Waugh stresses this historic window of opportunity made more historic still by an analogy that Guy draws. 'It seemed to Guy in the fanciful mood that his lonely state engendered that he was playing an ancient, historic role as he went ... to inform the Jews of their approaching exodus. He was Moses leading a people out of captivity.' But fog bears down, preventing the Dakotas from landing. Over the next three weeks the refugees are marched out twice to the airfield and marched back to the internment camp. And after the fog comes the snow making any further landing impossible until the Spring. Crossing the Strait to Bari is obviously more difficult than crossing the Red Sea.

Guy's final encounter with Mme Kanyi is perhaps the most controversial passage in the trilogy and it doesn't make for easy reading even now. Mme Kanyi asks Guy bluntly:

> Is there any place that is free from evil? It is too simple to say that only the Nazis wanted war. These communists wanted it too. It was the only way in which they could come to power. Many of my people wanted it to be revenged on the Germans, to hasten the creation of the national state. It seems to me there was a will to war, a death wish everywhere. Even good men thought their private honour would be satisfied by war. They could assert their manhood by killing and being killed.............I knew Italians—not very many perhaps—who felt this. Were there none in England?
> 'God forgive me', said Guy. 'I was one of them'.
> (*Sword of Honour*, 655–656).

It is a conversation that casts Guy in a particularly unfavourable light. Are we being asked to confront a proposition that is historically unsustainable, namely that everyone wanted war in 1939, or that there was a collective death wish that seized hold of humanity, or that every man wanted to assert or re-assert his own manhood? And did Mme Kanyi's own people, the Jews, really want war in order to get a Zionist state? Is the Holocaust the cost of their own dreams and desires? Or is Guy's apparent assent to the assertion merely indicative of the fact that he has completely lost heart and is now prone to self-despair? If so, he has one other shock in store for him, when he is air-lifted out of Yugoslavia to Bari because the Communists have found him irritating (and the British embarrassing). He is appalled to find that even the Jewish office in Bari has no interest in him either once they understand that he has not come to sell them illicit arms, or even in the fate of the Kanyis, once they learn that they had intended to emigrate not to Palestine but Australia. On the day before he is due to leave Italy for England, he learns that the Kanyis have been tried for treason by a People's Court. Mme Kanyi stands accused of being the mistress of a British Liaison Officer, Guy, and because of the American magazines which Guy had given her, she is also accused of being a counter-revolutionary. Once again, he has inadvertently caused another person's death.

And it is not only the fate of the Kanyis that casts Guy in a particularly unfavourable light. It is also his shallow understanding of history which allows him to conclude that Churchill 'betrayed' the Yugoslav people by backing Tito and the communists. It is true that Churchill received reports from Fitzroy Maclean based largely on partisan sources, and that a British Communist at Special Operations Executive HQ called James Klugmann, attempted through underhand means to halt all British support for Tito's rival, the Royalist guerrilla leader, Mikhalovic. But Waugh and Guy were no more party to the larger picture than was Maclean. Churchill and his senior commanders received many other intelligence sources that revealed how increasingly compromised and ineffective Mikhailovich's forces were. They were also predisposed to support the Communists for another reason—with the Allies planning the Second Front there was a perfectly pragmatic interest in short-term gain, one which went a long way to overriding any concerns about the long-term consequences of backing the Communists. What Guy cannot admit to himself is the fundamental inability of the old order to engage in serious resistance with the occupying forces. He is always intent on ignoring the fact that the Yugoslavs look on the British as allies, but the Russians as friends, and that they have no reason to feel especially grateful for British support; after all, it is they who are doing most of the fighting.

In Thomas Keneally's *Season in Purgatory*, a novel also set in wartime Yugoslavia, Waugh finally appears as himself, a man who Fitzroy Maclean recalls as being the only officer who served under him who was loathed unconditionally by his men (Boyd, 2005, 233). A new arrival describes his original departure from Bari for Croatia. 'They have a quite famous officer there, waiting to be parachuted into Yugoslavia. Famous novelist. Evelyn Waugh. Very snooty. Hard man to deal with. Quick wit. Couldn't understand half his allusions.' Guy is none of these things. He has intelligence but little wit. He is not unimaginative but he is not in touch with the times. He enters the war in optimistic innocence but reads the signs of betrayal too late.

And so Waugh sets us up for the biggest betrayal of all, the betrayal not of his country, but by it, which implicates the man that most of his countrymen had expected would save England: Churchill himself. For Guy, the pact with Russia undoes everything that made him join up. After such a sordid arrangement it is impossible to be honourable any longer. Before he wrote *Unconditional Surrender*, Waugh told a friend that it would concern 'Crouchback's realisation that no good comes from public causes; only private causes of the soul.' (Rutherford 1978, 130). And as his father writes to him at the very end of his life saving one's soul is much more important than saving face. In defence of the Catholic Church for compromising with Mussolini in the 1920s he adds, 'if only one soul was saved, that is full compensation for any amount of loss of face.' Perhaps the same could be said of Britain. The values for which Guy thinks he is fighting, 'to defend the old against the new—the modern age' may have been abandoned, but the values concerned may already have been hollowed out. All surface and no substance. Waugh's world was already passing, as he was astute enough to recognise privately long before the outbreak of war. For Guy none of this matters. He will to be faced with the same dilemma: the public life of compromise or the private life of virtue. And in the end he will choose to make his own little peace, by choosing the latter.

Guy's personal philosophy—that there can be no good in public causes, only in private ones, is not one that the English as a nation embraced, even after recognising how the war had cost them their own position in the world. The moral of the war surely is that in an imperfect world, imperfect people are still capable of compassion, or fighting for the right cause, and that history is not made by great impersonal forces, but by people. Waugh, as ever the consummate artist, tries to lead us by the nose in sharing his own views by getting Guy, not himself, to articulate them. There are never times when the authorial voice sounds leadingly flat on the page. We are asked to make up our own mind, and so most of us do. Things, we are told through the voice of his brother-in-law Box-Bender, have turned out rather well for Guy in private life. And given the situation Britain faced in 1940 we may conclude that historically things turned out much better for the British people than they or anyone else at the time had reason to expect.

Billy Pilgrim: Memory Disjointed
Slaughterhouse-Five, Kurt Vonnegut

In the spring of 1945, three weeks after VE Day, Private First Class Kurt Vonnegut wrote a letter home to his family to tell them that he was still alive. He had survived much, including the bombing of Dresden, which had been incinerated by British and American bombers a few months earlier. 'Their combined labours killed 250,000 people in twenty-four hours and destroyed all of Dresden—possibly the world's most beautiful city', Vonnegut wrote. 'But not me'. (Shields, 2012). Already we see the hallmark features of Vonnegut's style. The ironic detachment of the 'combined labours'; the exaggeration—only 35,000 people were killed in Dresden, not that Vonnegut would have known this at the time, and the word 'only' in this context grates. There is also the sense of the absurd—'but not me'. It is a phrase which keeps cropping up in the letter, and which would be transmogrified years later into the author's signature tune, 'And So It Goes'. What is this refrain if not that of a damaged mind trying to resist the passing of time with its subtle erasures?

And Vonnegut spent years attempting to write his novel. It was not only a question of confronting the horrors of his past or exorcising the demons he brought back home with him; the very subject matter seemed to defy language. 'There is nothing intelligent to say about a massacre', he cautions the reader on the first page of his novel, *Slaughterhouse-Five*. Writing as he was in the late 1960s, twenty-five years after his own wartime experiences, he chose to het around the problem using a unique narrative device. Billy Pilgrim gets unstuck in time, finding himself one moment in the future, another in the past. One of the main effects of war, Vonnegut writes, is that people are discouraged from being characters but Billy remains one because of his time travelling (*Slaughterhouse-Five*, 134). No sooner is he at Dresden than he zooms via a time warp back into the 1950s, and then further back to his early youth. Burdened by none of the physical constraints of the theatre and allowed the time-shifting properties of film, Vonnegut was able to break the bounds of physics, to split and re-forge the molecular structures of Billy's life.

'Listen, Billy Pilgrim had got unstuck in time'. It is where the tale begins in earnest and the sentence, stripped to its bare bones, says it all. *Slaughterhouse-Five* was the expression of a deeply held need to bear witness. It also offers an insight into the way war overwhelms the memory and makes it so difficult to do so. How can someone who was there tell others what it was like, especially if they cannot find a moral in the story they wish to convey?

The principle theme that I take Pilgrim to represent is that many soldiers return home from war with parts of the past missing, and they spend the rest of their lives trying to put the past back together again. Vonnegut employed the technique of time travel as a heuristic device. Billy can walk through a door in 1955 and come out of another in 1941. He witnesses his birth and death many times, and pays random visits to the events in between. He is in a constant state of stage fright because he never knows what part of his life he is going to visit next. But this is not only a narrative device, a medium with a message. It *is* the message. Throughout the book, Billy not only wanders back and forth through time, he also visits an alien planet and learns the philosophy of their inhabitants: all moments, past, present and future, have always existed and always will. The Tralfamadorians can look at all the different moments at once just as we look at the Rocky Mountains. 'It's just an illusion we have here on Earth, that one moment follows another one, like beads on a string, and that once a moment is gone, it's gone forever.' (*Slaughterhouse-Five*, 64).

Billy is based on the young man that Vonnegut himself was when he was drafted. He is as young as the author was in 1944, and for Vonnegut the war is what its subtitle says, 'the Children's Crusade.' Many of the young recruits, in fact, were in their early twenties (older, of course, than the average age in Vietnam, which was nineteen). But Vonnegut's disjointed style lends itself to the youthfulness of the theme. In the boxcar taking them into captivity, Billy finds himself sharing space with young boys 'at the end of childhood.' (*Slaughterhouse-Five*, 56). In the Prisoner of War camp in which he ends up, the British prisoners are surprised by the youthfulness of their American allies—they have been captured early on and imagined war being fought by ageing men like themselves. Vonnegut is eager to tell us that this is a young man's war, and for the young men of his age, war is always difficult to make sense of.

Billy, from the beginning, is clearly out of his depth. He is a funny-looking child who becomes a funny-looking youth. He is unusually tall and yet also frail and shaped like a bottle of Coca-Cola. He is equally at a loss when he finds himself posted to an Infantry Regiment fighting in Luxembourg in December 1944, just in time for the battle of the Bulge, the last great German offensive of the war. He survives the attack but finds himself cut off behind German lines with a ragbag group of other soldiers without food, or maps, marching Indian-file and delivering themselves into a silence ever more profound. Last in line comes Pilgrim himself, empty-handed, 'bleakly ready for death'. (*Slaughterhouse-Five*, 26). 'Get off the road, you dumb motherfucker!' The last word was still a novelty in the speech of white people in 1944, Vonnegut tells us. 'It was fresh and astonishing to Billy who had never fucked anybody—and it did its job. It woke him up and got him off the road', and so into the story which Vonnegut is about to tell.

In the 1970s, Vonnegut, who had been so reticent about his war experience, began to open up a little. He confessed he had been as scared as Billy because he too had not been prepared for battle. He had been trained to operate a 240mm Howitzer rather than act as a point man in the infantry, so that when he found himself with fifty or more GIs trying to survive off the land, he felt displaced, just as Billy gets displaced in time. For no sooner is he lost in the confusion of battle then he experiences a time-shift and finds himself visiting an old people's home where his mother twenty years in the future is barely alive, hardly able to speak, except in the thinnest of registers, finally managing to whisper a complete sentence, 'How did I get so *old*?' (*Slaughterhouse-Five*, 36). Billy drifts through time, as he drifts through the snow-covered landscape on his feet, without army boots, which they have not had time to issue, but low-cut civilian shoes which he bought for his father's funeral. Everything about the spare, unforgiving landscape tells us what to expect next. His readers know we are going to be drawn into an even more desolate interior landscape when Billy and his friends are taken prisoner, though nothing warns us what they will witness in Dresden where they finally end up.

They are eventually captured by five German soldiers and a police dog on a leash engaged in the 'divinely listless love-play that follows the orgasm of victory called mopping up.' (Ibid., 43). Two of his captors are boys even younger than himself; two are old men 'droolers, as toothless as carp.' Their commander is a middle-aged corporal, wounded four times, patched up and sent back to battle, a very good soldier about to quit, desperate to find somebody to surrender to. Billy and the group are force-marched to their eventual incarceration. On the way they are joined by more American POWs with their hands on top of their haloed-like heads. 'They were moving like water, downhill all the time, and they flowed at last to a main highway on a valley's floor. Through the valley flowed a Mississippi of humiliated Americans.' (*Slaughterhouse-Five*, 47). In the reduction of things to their constituent elements, Vonnegut echoes Primo Levi in recounting his experience in Auschwitz. Levi used the Periodic Table to tell his tale, to sketch episodes far worse than anything that the POWs meet up with in their internment camp, far worse even than the bombing of Dresden by the Allied Forces, the culmination of the novel. Both authors use scientific detachment to tell the story as objectively as they can. In Vonnegut's novel, the retreating soldiers become a river, and a city is transformed into minerals: 'Dresden was like the morine now, nothing but minerals.' (*Slaughterhouse-Five*, 146). And another scene awaits Billy when they enter a railroad yard where rows and rows of boxcars are waiting to convey them into captivity. Later they will 'ooze' their human cargo as if they are liquids out of these wooden cages, just as individuals will turn to inert objects or steam.

Billy moves forward in time again, this time to his daughter's wedding. He finds himself in a room with a TV showing a Second World War movie. It is one of the most powerful and lyrical passages in the novel as he rewinds the scene backwards in his head. A formation of bombers flies backward over a German city in flames; the bombers open their bomb bays, exerting a miraculous magnetic attraction which shrinks the fires, gathering them into cylindrical steel containers and lifting the containers into the bellies of the planes. Back on base, the steel cylinders are taken from the bomb racks and shipped back to America where factories operating night and day dismantle them, separating the dangerous contents into minerals, which are then shipped to remote areas where they are hidden in the ground so that they will never hurt anybody ever again.

The American flyers turned in their uniforms, became high school kids. And Hitler turned into a baby, Billy Pilgrim supposed. That wasn't in the movie. Billy was extrapolating. Everybody turned into a baby and all humanity, without exception, conspired biologically to produce two perfect people named Adam and Eve, he supposed. (*Slaughterhouse-Five*, 61).

A similar game, though this time spatial rather than temporal, had been played a decade earlier by the German novelist, Gert Ledig, whose novel *Payback* (1956) details seventy minutes of an Allied bombing raid at different altitudes, the American bomber crews in the skies above, the German anti-aircraft gunmen on the rooftops, the workers in the streets and the families cowering inside buildings, or basement shelters. Ledig closed his novel by noting, 'an hour was all it took for terror to triumph ... It was unstoppable. It just wasn't the Day of Judgement, and so the bombing resumed another day.' (Ledig, 2003).

The theme of *Slaughterhouse-Five*, writes John Sutherland, is T. S. Eliot's observation that mankind cannot bear too much reality. Life is so horrible that only fiction can deal with it, and crucially, the more horrible the war experience, the more fantastic fiction becomes (Sutherland, 2012, 588). The problem for some readers is the novel's style—its profundity is belied by the lightness of tone; others find the science-fiction passages annoying, and a distraction from the main theme. Vonnegut once explained that they were like the clowns in Shakespeare—they were there to release the tension (Sumner, 2011, 133). But the comic moments have a purpose. When we are confronted with horror, we take refuge in the past, especially in childhood memories or child-like dreams. When Billy is taken aboard the spaceship he asks 'why me?', only to be told that it is a very 'Earthling' question. (63). The question 'why' is also one that Andrei asks at Austerlitz and Fabrice at Waterloo (Tolstoy and Stendhal both show them taking part in history, but becoming unstuck in time, unable to grasp its meaning).

Whenever we look back to the past, we always try to find a meaning. Billy cannot succeed because he is sucked into the vortex, but at least Vonnegut can. On Trafalmodia, the Earthling figure that the inhabitants find most engaging is Charles Darwin 'who taught that those who die are meant to die, the corpses are an improvement. So it goes.' (*Slaughterhouse-Five*, 173). And is that philosophy any better than our own? The Tralfamadorians tell Billy that there is no such thing as Free Will, that we—and they—are all simply 'trapped in the amber of the moment.' Indeed, there is no 'why' there, either. It is an horrific philosophy for a prisoner in a death camp, but is it so bad for a child of the Depression with its insecurities and anxieties (which

Vonnegut escaped only because of Pearl Harbor), and is it so depressing for a soldier finding himself, like Tolstoy's heroes, tossed about by the random fortunes of war? The senselessness of war erupted into Vonnegut's life earlier than it did for most. In later life he liked telling the tale of how he broke the news of Pearl Harbor to his college fraternity brother at Cornell while he was showering (he promptly slipped on the floor, and died).

The real problem comes in piecing together the fragments after the hostilities have been concluded and the soldiers sent home. The French essayist Leon Bloy, full of Catholic angst, penned an epigram that sums up Vonnegut's position much more succinctly and savagely than he managed to do himself: 'Man has places in his heart which do not yet exist, and into them enter suffering in order that they may have existed.' The young Vonnegut really did have to make a place in his heart for the memory of Dresden so that he could bear witness not only to what war does (*Slaughterhouse-Five* is not an anti-war novel as is so often claimed), but what it does to those who feel that they have survived in order to bear witness. People are not supposed to look back. Look what happens to those who do. Lot's wife turns into a pillar of salt. Vonnegut tells us he loves her for that, because it was such a human gesture, and that is surely the point (*Slaughterhouse-Five*, 18). Billy is human, after all.

After his brief sojourn on the alien planet, Billy is sent back to Earth, back to the boxcar. The train arrives at its destination. They are issued army greatcoats, once worn by Russian soldiers who are now dead. A bunch of Russian POWs are in camp as the Americans are marched into it. Billy sees his first one, 'a ragbag with a round, flat face that glowed like a radium dial.' (*Slaughterhouse-Five*, 67). They are led to the showers where they are de-loused. It is not the only humiliation visited upon them. In their emaciated state, they look particularly grotesque in their greatcoats, like an organ-grinder's monkey. After a few days in the camp Billy collapses and has to be hospitalised and given a shot of morphine. Life there is a series of episodes, some comic, some grotesque. In his morphine-induced coma he returns to the alien planet where he is dead to the world, but not actually dead. How nice, says one of the doctors, to feel nothing and still get full credit for being alive (*Slaughterhouse-Five*, 86). But the days in the camp are brief. For Billy and a group of other prisoners are told they are going to be marched to Dresden, one of the great baroque cities of Europe which so far has escaped the bombing. 'You'll be out where the life is', they are told by one of the English prisoners. Shipped into the camp in only two box-cars, they are shipped out in four. When the boxcar doors are opened the doorways frame the loveliest city the Americans have ever seen— to Billy it looks like a Sunday school picture of Heaven (*Slaughter-house-Five*, 122). They are marched to where they will stay, the fifth building of a Dresden slaughterhouse, a one-storey cement block cube with sliding doors in front and back. Built as a shelter for pigs who were about to be butchered, it becomes the home of a hundred Prison-ers of War. They are told to memorise the address—*Schlachthof-Funf*— 'Schlachthof' means 'Slaughterhouse'; 'Funf' was 'good old five'. (*Slaughterhouse-Five*, 126).

Their time in Dresden is punctuated by a series of different incidents that define the war. One day Billy sees a Pole, a farm labourer, who has been hanged in public for sleeping with a German woman, a racial crime in Nazi Germany. He meets an American Nazi, Howard Camp-bell (who had first appeared in an earlier novel, *Mother Night*) who addresses the POWs, urging them to join the war effort against the Russians' '"You're gonna have to fight the Communists sooner or later", said Campbell. "Why not get it over with now?"' (*Slaughter-house-Five*, 134). His peroration provokes the oldest prisoner, a school-teacher, Edgar Derby, 'mournfully pregnant with patriotism and middle age and imaginary wisdom' to lumber to his feet and explain why Nazism is worth defeating. (*Slaughterhouse-Five*, 123). 'One of the main effects of war', writes Vonnegut, 'is that people are discouraged from being characters.' But old Derby was a character now. And so was Vonnegut, who became a spokesman for a small group of prisoners in 1945. The little German he possessed allowed him to communicate with the guards, and he got beaten up quite often for telling them what was going to happen to them when the Russians eventually arrived.

But the first people to arrive are not the Russians, but British and American pilots in their bombers. On one particular March night, they hear sounds like giant footsteps. Occasionally a guard would go to the head of the stairway to see what it was like outside. By the end, the whole city was one big flame which ate everything organic, everything that would burn. Billy emerges from his shelter the next morning to see little logs lying around, charred remains of people who had been caught in the firestorm. The buildings that still stand are ghosts of themselves, their windows and roofs gone, and nothing inside but ashes and dollops of melted glass (*Slaughterhouse-Five*, 147).

At this point Vonnegut is so overwhelmed by the meaning of the event that he loses faith in his own powers of narration. He quotes a history book and reminisces about two of the Allied Air Force Marshals and generals who he held to be especially culpable for the raids. It is a rather lame device. Malaparte would have relished describing the scene (his account of the British bombing of Hamburg in *The Skin* is the most graphic and grotesque ever penned). But there is a clue as to why he flunked the final test, and refused to fictionalise his account. At one point Billy is told that everything there is to know about life is in Dostoevsky's novel, *The Brothers Karamazov*. 'But that isn't enough anymore.' (*Slaughterhouse-Five*, 83). Even Dostoevsky could not have done justice to the horror visited on Dresden that night, even though he had anticipated some of the forces that unleashed it.

But then there is very little more to add. Vonnegut had borne witness to what happened that night in February 1945, and there is not much he can tell us. The American prisoners are marched into the ruins to help dispose of the bodies without the benefit of the rum rations that were issued to German soldiers. They are given picks and shovels and wheelbarrows from their neighbours. Billy finds himself paired as a digger with a Maori who had been captured at Tobruk. As they dig deeper they find thousands of 'corpse-mines', meaning dozens of bodies buried, some sitting on benches, some still in bed, like exhibits from a waxwork museum. The illusion soon vanishes as the bodies begin to rot and liquefy in the heat. The Maori soldier soon dies of the dry heaves after being ordered to go underground into the stink. He tears himself to pieces throwing up. 'So it goes'. And the poor high school teacher Edgar Derby is arrested for plundering the ruins and stealing a tea box. It is a mistake, but that does not help. He is tried and shot. 'And so it goes'. (*Slaughterhouse-Five*, 177). And so it does, for it brings little solace in the retelling.

'So it goes' is the most famous phrase in the book: it is Vonnegut's signature tune. Dresden is destroyed and one man is shot for a crime he never committed, and another dies a squalid death, but life goes on. What Vonnegut doesn't tell us, however, is as revealing as what he does—at least one group survived the bombing in two senses of the word. The remaining Jews of the city had been awaiting their imminent deportation and were perfectly aware of what that meant. In the chaos that followed they were able to remove their yellow stars, join the homeless 'Aryan' masses and so avoid deportation to their deaths. (Kershaw, 2011, 237).

What do we remember in the end? The absurd injustice of war; the moments of personal loss; the biblical wrath unleashed by the bombers? 'Ignore the awful times and concentrate on the good ones', the Tralfamadorians tell Billy, but Earthlings are not aliens, and of all the different inhabitants of many planets, they alone, Billy is told, have an absurd belief in Free Will (*Slaughterhouse-Five*, 96). Well, whether we are free or not, we tell ourselves that we are. We are free to remember what we want, or to bury a memory as Vonnegut did his own for almost twenty years. Soldiers remember in their own way and in their own fashion. Like Billy, many are condemned to come unstuck in time. Others remember the horrors they have witnessed at times not of their own choosing. But in reality the Tralfamadorian idea of history is the experience of war for many.

Memory is something like a movie; it ends at different times for different people. Some watch the last minutes of credits until the final image fades out of the screen; or when the last title has rolled. Others head towards the exit as soon as the main action concludes, and others are still in their seats craning to watch every last credit. Films seem to meander on and on, never managing to draw to a genuine and satisfying conclusion. And so too does life. For the Tralfamadorians there is no beginning, no middle, no end, no moral, no causes, no effects. 'What we love in our books are the depths of many marvellous moments seen at one time.' (*Slaughterhouse-Five*, 72). As Earthlings ourselves we cannot be expected, I think, to sympathise with this point of view, but it is clever storytelling nonetheless. We are programmed to find some episodes in our lives more meaningful than others; we live according to linear time but nightmares are not linear, and bad memories cascade. They are as disjointed or as spastic as Billy's life. War is frequently so different from the civilian world in both the scale and the intensity of its incidents that memories are difficult to integrate into a coherent pattern. Vonnegut's principal theme is the subjectivity of time. Our memories follow us back from the battlefield, catching us out. A memory can steal into the mind unbidden, or stay stubbornly filed away. Memories are always making *us* unstuck in time.

Vonnegut began his odyssey visiting his old friend O'Hare with whom he later travels to Dresden. At first, he was unenthusiastic in helping his old buddy recall the bad times. I think the climax of the book, remarks Vonnegut, should be the killing of Edgar Derby, the irony is so great. A city gets burned down and thousands killed, and one American soldier is tried and shot for stealing a tea pot.

Don't you think that's really where the climax should come? 'I don't know anything about it', (O'Hare) said. 'That's your trade, not mine.' (*Slaughter-house-Five*, 4).

7

WAR IS KIND

A FINAL SUMMING UP

> Do not weep, maiden, for war is kind
> Because your lover threw wild hands towards
> The sky
> And the affrighted steed ran on alone,
> Do not weep.
> (Stephen Crane, *War is Kind*).

War offers few consistent morals. What it does tell us about the men who fight it is that they are violent but never fully in control of their emotions; that they are heroic but often only in the last resort; that they are weak, fallible beings but capable of moments of great strength of will. War as a mystery will continue to escape full understanding and the characters who play their parts are deeply ambiguous for that reason. Our heroes are not always as heroic as we would like them to be; our villains are not always villainous in the pantomime terms by which we like to judge bad men. The great writers show us heroes with feet of clay and bad men who can be brave in battle but the inescapable message of this work is that it is largely fought by men. All but 99 per cent of combat soldiers today are men even if there are more women in uniform than ever. Yet the chief victims of war continue to be women.

War is Kind is Stephen Crane's most famous poem. Novelists often end up writing poetry as Thomas Hardy did with *The Dynasts*, his epic

297

of the Napoleonic Wars, and Herman Melville, who spent his last years trying to grasp the American Civil War through a poetic vision, and did so far less successfully than Walt Whitman, who was the first to suspect that the poets would have to treat war on entirely new terms.

Crane's poem is the first of a series, 'War is Kind and Other Lines', published at the very end of the nineteenth century. It is a stark piece in twenty-six lines and five stanzas, focusing on the emotional lives of three women, whose lover, father and son respectively die in battle. Crane's poem highlights the loss, fear and pain that every war tends to bring. Crane writes how war claims the lives of 'the little souls who thirst for fight', rather like Owen's young men who went to their death 'for some desperate glory'. These men, writes Crane, were born to dwell and die by the thousand for the 'battle god', by which presumably he means the god of war, Ares, whom Homer loathed the most. After the lover, the daughter whose 'father tumbles in the yellow trenches' under some 'blazing flag of regiment', dead to all but the 'virtual slaughter', drilled only in 'the excellence of killing'; and finally the mother whose son is clothed in a 'bright, splendid shroud'. 'Do not weep/war is kind', Crane tells her, too.

The lines 'the virtue of slaughter' and the 'excellence of killing' add their own ironic patina to the text. And other ironies abound, such as 'a bright, splendid shroud'. But we are ironic for a reason—to get us to take note of an anomaly or ambiguity. The 'excellence' of killing is something the Greeks would have applauded, and we no longer do. Over time sensibilities change. To admit to liking war today, still less to enjoying the killing, is almost a ticket out of military service.

Every war is unkind, isn't it? We immediately think of the victims, including the five character types that I have discussed. Sjvek may survive, but he is representative of an entire class of people who have been victimised over the centuries—the conscripted, the oppressed, the cannon fodder which Falstaff recruits with complete indifference to their fate. War is equally unkind, however, to the warriors for whom it is a vocation. It is unkind to Achilles—it takes his life, and denies Aeneas the un-heroic life he craved. It is unkind to Robert Jordan, who, if asked, would probably have preferred to return to the United States even without his illusions. It is even unkind to the villains who it finds out in its own subtle ways. 'Indian hating' is not a recipe for happiness. General Cummings knows himself to be less than the man he would like to be. It is unkind to the survivors who never return the men they were, or have wanted to become. Falstaff dies embittered; Kien vanishes into his own story. If war strips warriors of their hopes of 'desperate glory' it robs many others of their faith in humanity, their own and other people's.

But the greatest irony is that war is also kind and that is something we must acknowledge if we are to grasp its enduring appeal. Tim O'Brien relates the story of a soldier who went AWOL in Vietnam, and lived for a time in Da Nang. For him, the war was over but later he rejoined his unit 'all that peace, man, it felt so good it hurt. I want to hurt it back.' (O'Brien, 2009, 34). Of course, O'Brien knows the story is largely fictional, but he adds tellingly that it is all relative; you find yourself pinned down in a hellhole in Indo-China, and then for a brief second you see the sun and the clouds, and an intense sense of serenity flashes through your whole being. The whole world gets re-arranged, even though you find yourself pinned down by a war, you never feel more at peace. In other words, for some soldiers, peace is found in the midst of the carnage. This passage always puts me in mind of Wordsworth's wonderful words in 'Tintern Abbey' as he contemplates nature, 'For I have learned/to look on nature, not as in the hour/of thoughtless youth, but learning oftentimes/the still, sad music of humanity.' War too is part of that 'still sad music' and it is never more 'musical' than when relayed through fiction.

In the account of his own war experience, Sebastian Junger writes that war is so obviously evil the idea that there is anything good in it seems almost profane. And yet for many combat veterans, the civilian world to which they return seems frivolous, with very little at stake, and all the wrong people in power. One of the chief characters to appear in his book, O'Byrne, insists that when soldiers drink themselves into oblivion, it is not to forget the bad stuff; 'we drink because we miss the good stuff'. They miss the world in which trust is at a premium—the trust you invest other people with your life. They miss a world in which everything is important and nothing is taken for granted. He writes that in war, combat is the kindest experience of all. It offers 'that profound and mysterious gratification in protecting another person with your life.' (Junger, 2010, 232–34). All that matters is the dedication to a group, and that is impossible to fake. Months after returning from Afghanistan, Junger received a note from O'Byrne explaining why he wanted to go back into the Army. 'It's as if I'm self-destructive, trying to find the hardest thing possible to make me feel accomplished ... a lot of people tell me I could be anything I want to be. That's true. Why [not]... lead a normal life? Probably, because I don't want to.' As Junger adds, 'maybe the ultimate wound is the one that makes you miss the war you got it in.' (Junger, 2010, 268).

War is kind because it allows Henry Fleming to discover that estrangement from oneself means estrangement from others, too: it allows Robert Jordan a moment that sums up his entire life—his death is a gift, as well as a sacrifice. It allows Aeneas to keep faith with his ancestors, and Hadji Murat to die as he wished to live: nobly. It allows Bourne to band with men with whom in civilian life he would share nothing in common, and to enjoy an intensity of friendship that can never be replicated back at home. The Napoleonic trio—Chabert, Ferualt and Gerard—would almost certainly not trade places with the lesser figures who they encounter in the course of their military careers. War is not only their profession, it is their *métier*. Even Flashman knows it (as does Falstaff)—without it neither would be the men they are. Such men are not deluded or naïve, or particularly wicked. The only truly demonic figure in this book is largely inhuman: McCarthy's Judge Holden.

I have written this book to explain why war provides such an existential return: why it makes some men happy, even in death, particularly if it is freely chosen. But the irony is that it makes men like O'Byrne deeply unhappy, too. None of the characters in this book are especially happy except Vollmer, precisely because happiness is no longer one of his mission parameters. He is robbed of every one of war's existential returns. He is left a cipher. War is unkind to the patriots and the profiteers, the victims as well as the villains. Even those who it does not find out or break, or maim, or traumatise, or destroy in other more inventive ways, will always be in danger of discovering its unkindness the longer they ply their trade. Even Jack Aubrey's 'luck' will one day run out. Unhappiness itself seems to be part of the package.

But Crane's poem is not about the men who fight but about the women they leave behind to mourn their loss. And it is the women who are the missing voices in this particular book, as well as war's chief victims, victims of a social practice that though unique to our species, is practiced by only one half of it: men. There is a striking passage in *The Odyssey* about the fall of Troy:

> At the sight of the men panting and dying there
> She slips down to enfold him, crying out

Then feels the spears, prodding her back and shoulders
And goes bound into slavery and grief.
(Heaney, 2007, 166).

Even today, almost 3,000 years later, the callousness of the spear shafts on the woman's back and shoulders, writes Seamus Heaney, survives time and translation. The Greeks knew well enough that women were the chief casualties of war: the lovers, wives and mothers of men were all part of the collateral damage.

Alessandro Baricco writes that there is a feminine side to the *Iliad* hidden in plain view. It is the women who express the desire for peace that men dream of but find impossible to attain. In Book 6, in 'a small piece of sentimental geometry', Hector returns to Troy and speaks with three women: his mother who asks him to pray; Helen who invites him to rest; and Andromache who urges him to remember that he is a father and husband as well as a warrior. 'Two possible worlds stand facing each other and each has its arguments.' (Baricco, 2008, 153). And those of women are only just being heard. But Baricco is an uncompromising writer and he is under no illusions why the first voices have dominated history so far. To say that war is only hell and nothing more is a damaging lie (Baricco, 2008, 157). It is hell but it is also much more. It may be unkind but is also kind to some, and the great many who read the novels that feature in this book, and number men like Jordan and Aubrey, Yossarian and Achilles among their acquaintances. Life is larger because they exist. If we truly want peace we must remember that war is 'beautiful' too, and that 'men have always thrown themselves into it like moths to the fatal light of the flame.' Only by constructing another kind of beauty can we turn our back on it, and that work of construction has only just begun.

BIBLIOGRAPHY

'At their meeting he was struck for the first time by the endless variety of men's minds which, prevents truth from ever penetrating itself identically to two persons.' (Tolstoy, *War and Peace*, 507).

The critic Frank Kermode contends in his book *The Sense of An Ending* that it is not expected of critics, as it is of poets, that they should help us to make sense of our lives; they are bound only to attempt the lesser feat of investigating the ways in which we try to make sense of our lives (Kermode, 1967, 3). And this is what I have attempted in this book by examining writers engaged through the portrayal of their characters in acts of imaginative exploration. Through their characters they help us to understand the existential reality of war, and in the case of soldiers who have first hand experience, re-imagine it in the different dimension of fiction. As a critic (or rather, a social scientist), all I have tried to do in this book is to explain how this is done. My interest, after all, is not fiction, but war, and I would hope that some of my readers would be soldiers who, unlike me, (and many of the writers I discuss) know war for what it is.

Of course, a soldier or sailor might well ask why they should expect to learn anything about their trade from reading fiction when reality is so much more immediate. But many do read books, and they read for a reason, like the rest of us—story telling is hard-wired into us. We all love stories. Narrative is stitched intrinsically into the fabric of human psychology—we spend a good part of our lives locked in fictional worlds: in daydreaming, reading novels or constructing the life narratives we like to weave about ourselves. 'Neverland is our evolutionary niche, our spiritual habitat', wrote the evolutionary psychologist Jonathan Gottschall (who has also written a groundbreaking analysis of the *Iliad* from the perspective of evolutionary psychology (Gottschall, 2012). Most of us spend far more time in the imagined than the real world, both awake and asleep.

The adaptive value of stories is fairly self-evident: they allow us to experience life before we encounter it for real; they allow us to plan ahead and prepare ourselves for what life has in store, and so not be entirely at a loss when we find ourselves sucked into its undertow. They tell us the likely consequences of our actions and teach us basic social values so that we know how to behave; stories tend to encourage pro-social behaviour. The five archetypal characters in this book illustrate five important features of the existential dimension of war. Warriors inspire us to fight on, as Darwin insisted in *The Descent of Man*—they inspire emulation, and self sacrifice which benefits the tribe. The heroic, as William James wrote, is the struggle with our own mortality and helps us to understand that no loss is ever final; our death can have meaning for others. Stories of survival allow us to escape feelings of hopelessness and despair, and so encourage us to face the worst with the strength of will to carry on. And stories of victimhood warn us of the cost of taking part in other peoples' stories, and the need to be careful about the stories we tell. Villains usually come to a sticky end or end up disappointed—villainy is rarely rewarded in fiction, as opposed to real life. Most stories are moralistic and encourage moral behaviour—but then again we live in more cynical times. Melville killed off Ahab; Cormac McCarthy allows Judge Holden to continue to wreak havoc, a symptom perhaps of the extent to which we have fallen out of love with war itself, and one day may even prefer to contract it out to machines. Humanity and war are joined at the hip and it is most unlikely as a species that we have done with war yet.

In the course of writing this book I have discovered how much writers influence each other. Joseph Heller would never have written *Catch-22* had he not first read *The Good Soldier Švejk*. Stephen Crane was influenced especially by Tolstoy's *Sevastopol Sketches*, and of course Homer, always, and Tolstoy, more often than not, cast a long shadow. And fictional characters also refer to one another all the time. *The Red Badge of Courage* is the novel that the 'old man' Edgar Derby reads in a prisoner of war camp in *Slaughterhouse-Five*. In *Flash for Freedom*, Captain Spring, the captain of a slaving ship, reads aloud to his crew from the *Aeneid*. Guy Crouchback with the benefit of a classical education thinks of himself as a 'Philoctetes without his bow'.

Each of these characters has been grouped into five 'archetypes', and all the works discussed in this book are in print. I derived both the idea for this book and its format from the magnificent work *Faulks On Fiction* in which the author discusses the history of the novel through twenty-six fictional figures grouped into four archetypes: heroes, lovers, snobs and villains. Finally, let me be the first to acknowledge that my reading of these very different characters is not going to be the same as every reader. What Hemingway called the 'absolute truth' can only be discovered by the reader. Some of the 'heroes' I have chosen may, in your eyes, be less than heroic, and some of the villains not especially villainous. All readers are co-authors of the works they read, so how can I expect anything less of my own readings?

BIBLIOGRAPHY

Warriors

Homer, *The Iliad*, trans. Robert Fagles (London: Penguin, 1991).
Virgil, *The Aeneid*, trans. Robert Fagles (London: Penguin, 2006).
O'Brian, Patrick, *Master and Commander* (London: Harper Collins, 1993) *HMS Surprise* (London: Harper Collins, 1993); *The Letter of Marque* (London: Harper Collins, 1994); *The Far Side of the World* (London: Harper Collins, 1994).
Tolstoy, Leo, *Hadji Murat* in *The Cossacks and Other Stories* (London: Penguin, 2006).
DeLillo, Don, *Human Moments in World War III* in *The Angel Esmeralda: Nine Stories* (London: Picador, 2011).

Heroes

Crane, Stephen, *The Red Badge of Courage*, ed. Donald Pfizer (New York: Norton, 1994).
Conan Doyle, Arthur, *The Complete Brigadier Gerard* (Edinburgh: Canongate, 2010).
Manning, Frederic, *Her Privates We* (London: Serpent's Tail, 1999).
Hemingway, Ernest, *For Whom the Bell Tolls* (London: Arrow, 2004).
Malaparte, Curzio, *Kaputt* (New York: New York Review Books, 2005).

Villains

Conrad, Joseph, *The Duel* (London: Melville House, 2001).
Melville, Herman, *The Confidence Man* (London: Penguin, 1990).
Mailer, Norman, *The Naked and the Dead* (London: Flamingo, 1992).
Kubrick, Stanley, *The Dr Strangelove Continuity Script*, http://www.visual-memory.co.uk/amk/doc/0055.html, (accessed 30 January 2012).
McCarthy, Cormac, *Blood Meridian* (London: Picador, 2010).

Survivors

Shakespeare, William, *Henry IV, Part I* (Arden Shakespeare; London: Methuen, 2002).
———— *Henry IV, Part II* (Arden; London: Methuen, 1981).
Hašek, Jaroslav, *The Good Soldier Švejk* (London: Penguin, 1974).
Heller, Joseph, *Catch-22* (London: Vintage, 1994).
Ninh, Bao, *The Sorrow of War* (London: Minerva, 1994).
McDonald Fraser, George, *Flashman; Flash for Freedom; Flashman in the Great Game* (London: Everyman, 2010); *Flashman at the Charge* (London: Harper Collins, 2006); *Flashman and the Dragon* (London: Harper Collins, 2006).

Victims

Sophocles, *Philoctetes* (see Seamus Heaney, *The Cure at Troy: A Version of Sophocles' Philoctetes* (New York: Farrar, Strauss & Giroux, 1991).

BIBLIOGRAPHY

Balzac, Honoré de, *Colonel Chabert*, trans. Andrew Brown (London: Hesperus, 2003).

Remarque, Erich Maria, *All Quiet on the Western Front* (London: Vintage, 1996).

Waugh, Evelyn, *The Sword of Honour Trilogy* (London: Penguin, 1999).

Vonnegut, Kurt, *Slaughterhouse-Five* (London: Vintage, 2000).

Secondary Bibliography

Adas, Michael, *Machines as the Measure of Men: Science, Technology and Ideologies of Western Dominance* (Ithaca: Cornell University Press, 1989).

American Film Institute (AFI), *AFI's 100 Years ... 100 Movies 10th Anniversary Edition* (2007), http://www.afi.com/100years/movies10aspx (accessed 30 January 2012).

Anderson, William, *The Art of the Aeneid* (London: Duckworth, 2004).

Armstrong, Karen, *Myth: A Short History* (Edinburgh: Canongate, 2005).

———*The Great Transformation* (London: Atlantic Books, 2006).

Auden, W. H., *The Complete works of W. H. Auden Volume 2 1939–48*, ed. Edward Mendelson (Princeton, NJ: Princeton University Press, 2002).

Baldick, Chris, *In Frankenstein's Shadow: Myth, Monstrosity and 19th Century Writing* (Oxford: Clarendon, 1990).

Barkan, Elazar *The Retreat of Scientific Racism: changing concepts of race in Britain and the United States between the two world wars* (Cambridge: Cambridge University Press, 1992).

Baricco, Alessandro, *An Iliad: a story of war* (Edinburgh: Canongate, 2008).

Beevor, Anthony, *The Second World War* (London: Weidenfeld 2012).

Bellow, Saul, *Mosby's Memoirs and Other Stories* (London: Penguin, 1971).

Bendiner, Elmer, *The Fall of Fortresses* (New York: Putnam, 1980).

Bergonzi, Bernard, *Heroes' Twilight; a Study of the Literature of the Great War* (London: Macmillan, 1980).

Bettelheim, Bruno, *Freud and Man's Soul* (London: Penguin, 1982).

Bloom, Harold, *Ruin the Sacred Truth* (Cambridge: Harvard University Press, 1989).

——— *The Western Canon* (London: Papermac, 1996).

——— *Shakespeare: The Invention of the Human* (London: Fourth Estate, 1999).

——— *Genius* (London: Fourth Estate, 2002).

——— *Where Shall Wisdom Be Found?* (New York: Riverhead Books, 2004).

Bolano, Roberto, *Between Parentheses: Essays, Articles and Speeches 1998—2003* (London: Picador, 2011).

Blythe, Ronald (ed.), *Writing in War* (London: Penguin, 1982).

Bond, Brian, *The Unquiet Western Front* (Cambridge: Cambridge University Press, 2002).

Boorstin, Daniel, *The Creators: A History of Heroes of the Imagination* (New York: Vintage, 1993).

Boyd, William, *Bamboo* (London: Bloomsbury, 2005).

Brustein, 'The Logic of Survival in a Lunatic World,' *The New Republic* (2001).

Burgess, Anthony, *Homage to Qwert Yuiop: Selected Journalism 1978—85* (London: Abacus, 1986).

Campbell, James, *Myths to Live By* (New York: Bantam, 1978).

Caputo, Philip, *A Rumour of War* (London: Macmillan, 1978).

Cavafy, C. P., *Collected Poems*, trans. Edmund Keeley/Philip Sherrard (London: Hogarth Press, 1984).

Chabon, Michael, *Reading and Writing Along the Borderlands* (New York: Harper Collins, 2009).

Chesterton, G. K., *Orthodoxy* (London: Hodder and Stoughton, 1996).

Cohn-Sherbok, Dan, *Holocaust Theology* (London: Lamp Press, 1989).

Coker, Christopher, *Warrior Geeks: How 21st Century Technology is Changing the Way We Fight and Think About War* (London: Hurst, 2012).

Crane, Stephen 'War is kind' in *The Red Badge of Courage and Other Stories* (London: Penguin, 2005).

Cunningham, Valentine (ed.), *Spanish Front* (Oxford: Oxford University Press, 1986).

Danto, Arthur, *The Analytical Philosophy of History* (Cambridge: Cambridge University Press, 1965).

Daugherty, Tracy, *Just One Catch: The Passionate Life of Joseph Heller* (New York: Robson, 2010).

Doctorow, E. L., *Creationists: Selected Essays 1993—2006* (New York: Random House, 2007).

Dostoevsky, Fyodor, *Crime & Punishment* (London: Penguin, 1951).

Eagleton, Terry, *The Event of Literature* (New Haven: Yale University Press, 2012).

Eksteins, Modris, '"All Quiet on the Western Front" and the fate of a war', *Journal of Contemporary History*, 15 (1980).

Euben, Peter, *Platonic Noise* (Princeton, NJ: Princeton University Press, 2003).

Evans, Michael, 'American Irregular: Frontier Conflict and the Ferocity of War in Cormac McCarthy's "Blood Meridian"', *Small Wars and Insurgencies*, September 2011.

Faulks, Sebastian, *The Fatal Englishman: Three Short Lives* (London: Vintage, 1997).

—— *Faulks On Fiction: A Story of the Novel in 28 Characters* (London: BBC Books, 2011).

Faulkner, William, *Soldier's Pay* (New York: Vintage, 2000).

Fenves, Peter, *Chatter: Laughter and History in Kierkegaard* (Stanford: Stanford University Press, 1993).

Fleming, Chris, *Rene Girard: Violence and Mimesis* (Cambridge: Polity, 2004).

Finch, Shannon, 'The code of the warrior' in R. Parkin (ed.), *Warfighting and Ethics* (Canberra: Land Warfare Studies Centre, 2005).

Ford, Dennis, *The Search For Meaning: A Short History* (Berkeley: University of California Press, 2007).

Forster, E. M., *Aspects of the Novel* (London: Penguin, 2005).

Freud, Sigmund, *On Murder, Mourning and Melancholia* (London: Penguin, 2005).

Fussell, Paul, *The Bloody Game: an anthology of modern war* (New York: Scribners, 1991).

Gallie, W. B., *Philosophers of War: Kant, Clausewitz, Marx, Engels and Tolstoy* (Cambridge: Cambridge University Press, 1979).

Genevoix, Maurice, 'Conversations on the War: some meanings', in George A. Panichas (ed.), *Promise of Greatness: The 1914–1918 War.*

Ghamari-Tabrizi, Sharon, *The Worlds of Hermann Kahn* (Cambridge: Harvard University Press, 2005).

Glover, Jon and Silkin, Jon, *First World War Prose* (London: Viking, 1989).

Gottschall, Jonathan, *The Storytelling Animal: How Stories Made Us Human* (New York: Houghton Mifflin Harcourt, 2012).

Gray, Glenn, *Warriors: Reflections of Men in Battle* (New York: Harper & Rowe, 1970).

Greenfield, Susan, *You and Me: The Neuroscience of Identity* (London: Notting Hill Editions, 2011).

Greenwell, Graham, *An infant in Arms: Letters of a Company Officer* (London: Lovat, Dixon and Thompson, 1935).

Griffin, Jasper, *Homer on Life and Death* (Oxford: Clarendon Press, 1983).

Haidt, Jonathan, *The Righteous Mind: Why Good People Are Divided by Politics and Religion* (London: Allen Lane 2012).

Haythornthwaite, Philip, *Die Hard* (London: Cassell, 1996).

Heaney, Seamus, 'Crediting Poetry' in *Nobel Lectures for the Literature Laureates, 1986–2006* (New York: New Press, 2007).

Hemingway, Sean (ed.) *Hemingway on War* (New York: Scribner, 2003).

Herr, Michael, *Dispatches* (London: Picador, 1977).

Herzog, Tobey, *Vietnam War Stories: Innocence Lost* (London: Routledge, 1992).

Hillsman, James, *A Terrible Love of War* (London: Penguin, 2004).

Hobbs, Angela, *Plato and the Hero: Courage, Manliness and the Impersonal Good* (Cambridge: Cambridge University Press, 2000).

Huong, Thu Duong, *A Novel Without a Name* (London: Picador, 1995).

Hume, David, 'A Treatise of Human Nature' in *The Philosophy of David Hume* (New York: Modern Library, 1963).

Hynes, Samuel, *The Soldier's Tale: Bearing Witness to Modern War* (London: Pimlico, 1998).

James, William, *Varieties of Religious Experience*, Essential Writings (ed. Bruce Wilshire) (Albany: Suny, 1984).

Johnston, *English Poetry of the First World War: A Study of Evolution of Lyric and Narrative Form* (Princeton, NJ: Princeton University Press, 1964).

Jones, James, *The Thin Red Line* (New York: Dell, 1998).

Kassimeris, George, *The Barbarisation of Warfare* (London: Hurst, 2006).

Keneally, Thomas, *Schindler's Ark* (London: Sceptre, 1982).

Kermode, Frank, *The Sense of an Ending: Studies in the Theory of Fiction* (Oxford: Oxford University Press, 1968).

Kundera, Milan, *The Art of the Novel* (London: Faber & Faber, 1988).

—— *Testaments Betrayed* (London: Faber and Faber, 1995).

—— *The Curtain: An Essay in Seven Parts* (London: Faber & Faber, 2007).

—— *Encounter: Essays* (London: Faber & Faber, 2009).

Lawrence, D. H., *Studies in Classic American Literature* (London: Penguin, 1977).

Ledig, Gert, *Payback* (New York: New York Review Books, 2003).

Levi, Primo, *The Drowned and the Saved* (London: Michael Joseph, 1988).

Lewis, C. S., *Lost Aeneid: Arms and the Exile*, ed. A. T. Reyes (New Haven: Yale University Press, 2011).

Logue, Christopher, *Kings* (London: Faber & Faber, 1991).

Marcuse, Herbert, *One Dimensional Man* (Boston: Beacon Press, 1991).

Marlantes, Karl, *Matterhorn* (London: Corvus, 2010).

—— *What It's Like to Go To War* (London: Corvus, 2011).

Manguel, Alberto, *The City of Words* (London: Continuum, 2007).

Meir, Christian, *A Culture of Freedom* (Oxford: Oxford University Press, 2011).

Midgley, Mary, *Wickedness: A Philosophical Essay* (London: Ark, 1984).

Morwood, James, *The Tragedies of Sophocles* (Bristol: Phoenix, 2008).

Mosse, Georg, *Fallen Soldiers; Reshaping the Memory of Two World Wars* (Oxford: Oxford University Press, 1991).

Munton, Alan, *English Fiction of the Second World War* (London: Faber & Faber, 1989).

Murray, Sylvie, *A Student's Guide to Writing World War 2* (New York: Hill and Wang, 2011).

Nietzsche, Friedrich, *The Gay Science* (ed. Bernard Williams) (Cambridge: Cambridge University Press, 2001).

Nussbaum, Martha, *Upheavals of Thought* (Cambridge: Cambridge University Press, 2008).

Nuttall, A. D., *Why Does Tragedy Give Us Pleasure?* (Oxford: Clarendon, 2001).

—— *Shakespeare: Thinker* (New Haven: Yale University Press, 2007).

Oatley, Keith, *The Passionate Muse: The Exploration of Emotion in Stories* (Oxford: Oxford University Press, 2012).

O'Brien, Tim, *If I Die in a Combat Zone* (London: Flamingo, 2003).

—— *The Things They Carried* (New York: Mariner Books, 2009).

O'Rourke, Patrick, *Peace Kills* (London: Picador, 2004).

Orwell, George, *The Penguin Essays of George Orwell* (London: Penguin, 1994).

Ozick, Cynthia, *What Henry James Knew and Other Essays on Writers* (London: Jonathan Cape, 1993).

Pamuk, Orhan, *The Naïve and Sentimental Novelist* (Cambridge: Harvard University Press, 2010).

Paz, Octavio, *Conjectures and Refutations* (New York: RK Publishers, 1982).

Piette, Adam, *Imagination at War: British Fiction and Poetry 1939–45* (London: Papermac, 1995).

Pinker, Steven, *The Better Angels of Our Nature* (London: Viking, 2011).

Powell, Anthony, *The Valley of Bones* (London: Fontana, 1973).

Rorty, Richard, *Contingency, Irony and Solidarity* (Cambridge: Cambridge University Press, 1989).

Rosenbaum, Ron, *The Shakespeare Wars* (New York: Random House, 2008).

Rutherford, Andrew, *The Literature of War: Five Studies in Heroic Virtue* (London: Macmillan, 1978).

de Saint-Exupéry, Antoine, *Wartime Writings 1939–1944* (London: Picador 1996).

Sartre, Jean-Paul, *What is Literature?* (Paris: Gallimard, 1972).

——— *Iron in the Soul* (London: Penguin, 1985).

Selwyn, Victor (ed.), *The Voice of War: Poems of the Second World War* (London: Penguin, 1996).

Sepich, John, *Notes on Blood Meridian* (Austin: University of Texas Press, 2008).

Shields, Charles, *And So It Goes: Kurt Vonnegut, a Life* (London: Henry Holt, 2012).

Simpson, Keith, 'The British soldier on the Western Front' in Peter Liddel (ed.) *Home Fires and Foreign Fields: British social and military experience in the First World War* (London: Brasseys, 1985).

Smith, P. D., *Doomsday Men: The Real Dr Strangelove and the Dream of the Super Weapon* (London: Allen Lane, 2007).

Sontag, Susan, *At the Same Time* (London: Penguin, 2007).

Speight, Allen, *Hegel, Literature and the Problem of Agency* (Cambridge: Cambridge University Press, 2001).

Strachan, Hew, *The First World War* (London: Pocket, 2006).

Strauss, Barry, *The Trojan War: A New History* (London: Hutchinson, 2007).

Steinbeck, John, *America and Americans, and selected non-fiction* (London: Penguin, 2003).

Steiner, George, *Tolstoy or Dostoevsky: An Essay in Contrast* (London: Faber & Faber, 1960).

——— *Real Presences* (London: Faber & Faber, 1989).

——— *No Passion Spent* (London: Faber & Faber, 1996).

Sumner, Gregory, *Unstuck in Time: A Journey Through Kurt Vonnegut's Life and Novels* (New York: Seven Stories Press, 2011).

Sutherland, John, *The Lives of the Novelists* (London: Profile Books, 2011).

——— *A Dickens Dictionary* (London: Icon Books, 2012).

Tatum, James, *The Mourner's Song* (Chicago: Chicago University Press, 2003).

Temes, Peter, *The Just War* (Chicago: Ivan Dee Press, 2003).

Theroux, Paul, *Sunrise with Monsters* (London: Penguin, 1985).

Todorov, Tzvetan, *Facing the Extreme: Moral Life in the Concentration Camps* (London: Phoenix, 1996).

Tolstoy, Leo, *War and Peace* (London: Penguin 1982).

—————— *The Cossacks and Other Stories* (London: Penguin, 2006).

Watson, Peter, *The Great Divide: history and human nature in the Old World and the New* (London: Weidenfeld and Nicholson, 2011).

Wenke, Joseph, *Mailer's America* (University of New England Press, 1987).

Wilson, Colin, *The Outsider* (London: Picador, 1978).

Winnington-Ingram, R. P., *Sophocles* (Cambridge: Cambridge University Press, 1980).

Woolf, Susan, *Meaning in Life and Why It Matters* (Princeton, NJ: Princeton University Press, 2010).

Wood, James, *The Broken Estate: Essays on Literature and Belief* (London: Picador, 2010).

INDEX

Achilles (character): 9, 16–17, 25–7, 29, 32–3, 184, 222–3, 250, 255, 298, 301; characterisation of, 34–5, 43–4, 54, 116; criticisms of, 23–4; death of, 24, 36, 119, 162; development of character of, 27–8, 30; family of, 248, 250–1, 253; fight with Apollo, 30–1; heroic image of, 11, 15, 17–20, 23–4, 35–6, 181; relationship with Patroclus, 26–7, 32, 34, 43

Adams, Nick (character): as alter-ego of Ernest Hemmingway, 114

Adler, Irene (character); 89

Aeschylus: 41

Afghanistan: 241–2, 299; Helmand Province, 228, 240; Korangor Valley, 77; NATO presence in, 235, 238; Operation Enduring Freedom (2001–), 35–6, 73, 77, 264, 273

Agamemnon (character): 24–5, 188; characterisation of, 34

Aeneas (character): 15, 44, 46, 298, 300; characterisation of, 17–18, 37–40, 43, 45–6; death of, 119; family of, 40–3; killing of Turnus, 44–5; leading of Trojans into exile, 37, 41; lover of Dido, 18, 43

Ahab, Captain (character): 132, 147; obsession of, 147, 165

Ajax (character): 16, 23, 35

Alexander the Great: 188

Althorpe (character): death of, 276

American Century: origin of concept, 152–3

American Civil War (1861–5): 7, 78, 80–1, 298; Battle of Antietam (1863), 72; belligerents of, 78–9, 191

American Film Institute: Top 100 US Films, 166

Anchises: death of, 39; family of, 39–40

Ancient Greek Underworld: 42; characters condemned to, 41; Judgment of Minos, 40; ventures of characters into, 32, 34, 40–1

Anglo-Zulu War (1879): 235

Anselmo (character): 111; death of, 112; motivation of, 108–9

Apollo (deity): 25–6, 28; fight with Achilles, 30–1

Appleyard, Bryan: 264

Archer, Isobel (character): family of, 85

Arendt, Hannah: 193

Aristotle: 56, 116, 128, 172, 253, 256–7

Arjuna (deity): 30; dialogue with Krishna, 31
artificial intelligence (AI): depictions of, 22
Ascanius: family of, 41–2
Asimov, Isaac: *Caves of Steel, The*, 21
Atwood, Margaret: 120
Aubrey, Jack (character): 55, 58, 191, 300–1; characterisation of, 57, 59–61; influences upon creation of, 20–1; naval career of, 57; relationship with Stephen Maturin, 55–7, 61–2, 90
Auden, W.H.: 200–1; *Auden*, 26
Australia: 284
Austro-Hungarian Empire: 205; military of, 212

de Balzac, Honore: 261–3; *Black Sheep, The*, 257; *Colonel Chabert*, 13, 246, 257–9; death of, 260; *Human Comedy, The*, 257–8
Barbusse, Henri: 272; *Under Fire*, 268
Baricco, Alessandro: 301
Barker, Pat: *Regeneration*, 7
Barnes, Jake: (character): bigotry of, 115
Battle of Dakar (1940): depictions of, 272, 278
Bäumer, Paul (character): 209, 246, 269–70; death of, 268–9, 271; 'resurrection' of, 265; shifts in narrative voice of, 267–8; visit to field hospital, 270–1
Bayley, John: 228–9
Berlin, Isaiah: 43
Bhagavad Gita: 30–1
Bellow, Saul: *Mosby's Memoirs*, 151
Bentik (character): death of, 271
Beowulf (character): heroic image of, 18–19
betrayal: 9, 85, 101, 129–30, 155, 158–60, 187, 214, 226, 254,

269–70; of country, 281, 285; personal, 278, 280–1; self-, 37
Bey, Elphy: 242
Bezukhov, Pierre (character): 162–4; motivation of, 163
Blair, Tony: foreign policy of, 241
Blinn, James: *Aardvark is Ready for War, The*, 213
Bloch, Marc: military service of, 80
Bloom, Harold: 2, 174–5, 197, 201, 236; *Western Canon, The*, 11, 147
Bloy, Leon: 291
Boas, Franz: 145
Bogarde, Dick: 247
Bogdanovich (character): 49
Bolasco, Robert: 177
Bolonsky, Prince Andrei (character): 69–70, 72, 93, 205; death of, 164, 228
Bonaparte, Napoleon: 13, 55, 87, 89–92, 94, 133, 138, 140–1, 148, 188, 263–4; death of (1821), 87; depictions of, 127, 258–9; Hundred Days (1815), 136; Invasion of Russian Empire (1812), 70, 72, 129, 136, 140, 148–9; personal staff of, 136, 139
Bosnia and Herzegovina: Sarajevo, 206
Bosnian War (1992–5): Siege of Sarajevo (1992–6), 120
Bourne (character): 96, 99, 102–5; as modern hero, 73–4; background of, 101; characterisation of, 99–101, 103–4; death of, 101, 104; development of, 103–4
von Braun, Werner: 131; as model for Dr Strangelove, 171
Briseis: 25
Brustein, Robert: 223
Buddhism: *dukkha*, 226
Burgess, Anthony: 116
Burgess, Guy: member of Cambridge Five, 281

INDEX

Burma: 128, 280

Calchas (character): 25
Cameron, James: *Terminator, The* (1984), 23
Campbell, Dr John: as basis for Major Major, 214
Campbell, Howard (character): 247, 292
Caputo, Philip: 85, 177; *Indian Country*, 143
Cardigan, Lord: 233, 242
Caroll, Lewis: 145
Cathcart, Colonel (character): 219, 221; characterisation of, 220; survival aims of, 223
Cauldwell, Christopher: death of, 107; service in International Brigades, 107
Caulfield, Holden (character): 169
de Cervantes, Miguel: 242
Chabert, Colonel (character): 246, 258, 300; family of, 258, 260, 263–4; return of, 258–60, 264
Chabon, Michael: 89, 176
Chamberlain, Samuel: *My Confession*, 175
Chechnya: 20, 46
Chesterton, G.K.: 'Orthodoxy' (1908), 181
China: Civil War (1927–36/1946–50), 235; Peking, 241
Christianity: 142–3, 226, 241
Chryses (character): 25
Churchill, Winston: 284–5
Ciano, Count Gian: family of, 119; Italian Foreign Minister, 119
Claire, Ivor (character): 278; betrayal of, 281; desertion of, 279–80
von Clausewitz, Carl: 1–2, 4; concept of war, 139–40, 189–90
Cochrin, Jim (character): 81; death of, 83
Cold War: 166, 234, 281; nuclear deterrence in, 169–71

communism: 153, 190, 226
Conan Doyle, Arthur: 72–3, 87–9, 91, 93–5, 242; *Adventures of Gerard, The* (1903), 87; *Exploits of Brigadier Gerard, The* (1896), 87; *Greek Interpreter, The*, 87–8; 'How the Brigadier Rode to Minsk', 89; *Strand, The*, 87
Conrad, Joseph: 79, 91, 212; *Duel, The*, 128, 132–3, 137–8, 141; *Heart of Darkness*, 128, 165
Cooper, Fennimore: *Last of the Mohicans*, 146
Coppola, Francis Ford: *Apocalypse Now*, 127, 164–5
Corn, Colonel (character): 222–3
Cornwell, Bernard: *Sharpe* (series), 55
Cossacks: 47, 51–2, 88, 136
Crane, Stephen: 300; *Red Badge of Courage, The*, 6–7, 72, 77–9, 81, 85–7, 162; *Veteran, The*, 79; *War is Kind*, 297
Crete: 128, 274, 278–9
Creusa (character): family of, 43
Crimean War (1853–6): 46; belligerents of, 92–3; Charge of the Light Brigade (1854), 232–3, 235; Siege of Sevastopol (1854–5), 69–70
Croatia: 275–7, 284
Cross, Sgt (character): 128, 150, 152–3; villainy of, 160
Crouchback, Guy (character): 129, 275–6, 279–83; as victim, 273–4; disillusionment of, 278; military career of, 274; role in death of Althorpe, 276
Cuba: 114
Cummings, General (character): 150–2, 157–62, 298; as tragic figure, 161; background of, 157; dislike of Herne, 155–6; physical description of, 150; self-image of, 153; speeches of, 129, 152–3; villainy of, 130, 141, 154–5, 161

Leer (character): 269; death of, 271

Levi, Primo: 190; imprisonment in Auschwitz, 211, 289

Lévy, Bernard-Henri: 120

Libya: Civil War (2011), 241; Tobruk, 293

Liger (character): family of, 43

Lincoln (character): relationship with Colonel Harry Flashman, 241

Lindberg, Anne Morrow: *Wave of the Future, The* (1941), 153

literary criticism: 13, 56, 115–16; criticisms of, 116

Loud Man (character): 81

Louis XVIII of France: 260

Lucheus (character): death of, 43; family of, 43

Lukacs, Georg: 20

Lukas, Luv (character): 206; relationship with Švejk, 209

Luttwak, Edward: 33

Luxembourg: 288

Lycaon (character): family of, 34

Mailer, Norman: 9, 99, 115, 154–6, 159–60; focus on masculinity, 155; military service of, 149, 213; *Naked and the Dead, The*, 98, 128–30, 149–50, 153, 157; *Some Honorable Men*, 151–2

Major, Major (character): 214–15, 218–19; background of, 219

Malparte, Curzio: background of, 118–19; depiction of dead, 122–6; influence of, 125–6; *Kaputt*, 75–6, 118–19, 121–3; *Skin, The*, 118, 123, 293; writing style of, 119–24

Malraux, André: *Man's Hope*, 74

Mandrake, Colonel Lionel (character): 168–9

Manning, Frederic: 73, 95, 97, 99–100, 102; *Her Privates We*, 13, 95–6, 98, 106; writing style of, 102–4, 106

Marcuse, Herbert: 174; *One-Dimensional Man*, 172–3

Maria (character): 108, 111, 116

Marlantes, Karl: 128, 177

Martlow (character): 74

Marxism: 107, 226

Mason, Zachary: 87

Maturin, Stephen (character): relationship with Jack Aubrey, 55–7, 61–2, 90

McCarthy, Cormac: 300; *Blood Meridian*, 131–2, 174–7, 181–5

McGovern, George: 227

McLean, Fitzroy: 275, 284

Melville, Herman: 298; *Confidence Man, The*, 13, 142, 144–8; *Moby Dick*, 132, 142, 147, 165

Menaleus (character): 34, 41

Michener, James: *Bridges at Toko-Ri, The* (1953), 263

Midgeley, Mary: *Wickedness*, 160–1

Mikhailov, Lt. (character): focus on duty, 70–1

Millefleurs, Marshall/Captain Alexis Morgan (character): 88

Miller, Arthur: *Tragedy and the Common Man*, 86

Minderbinder, Milo (character): 219

Mistress Quickly (character): relationship with Falstaff, 193, 204

von Moltke, Field Marshall Helmuth: 208

de Montalvo, Garci Rodriguez: *Amadis de Gaula*, 19

Moredock, Colonel (character): 141–3; background of, 144; hatred of Native Americans (Indians), 141, 143–8

Morgan, Harry (character): bigotry of, 115

Moriarty, Prof James: 88

Morris, William: 274

Muller (character): 269; death of, 271